ESSENTIAL

Bible
Study
Tools

FOR MINISTRY

ESSENTIAL

Bible Study Tools

FOR MINISTRY

DAVID R. BAUER

Abingdon Press

Nashville

ESSENTIAL BIBLE STUDY TOOLS FOR MINISTRY
Copyright © 2014 by Abingdon Press

This book is printed on acid-free paper.

ISBN 978-1-4267-5517-0

14 15 16 17 18 19 20 21 22 23—10 9 8 7 6 5 4 3 2 1

MANUFACTURED IN THE UNITED STATES OF AMERICA

To my students, who give me joy in teaching

Contents

Contents

Introduction

The interpretation of the Bible is a central concern to all Christian ministers, for integrity demands that all ministers, in whatever capacity they serve, be professionally informed and personally shaped by the message of the Scriptures. The interpretation of the Bible involves, first of all, direct, firsthand study of the text. But it must also include, at the proper time, the use of various kinds of secondary sources. These resources are the indispensable tools of the biblical interpreter. I have compiled the following bibliography with these considerations in mind.

Although this book includes approximately twenty-two hundred titles by thirteen hundred scholars, it is still a highly selective bibliography, containing only a fraction of works that could have been included. Inclusion of individual items was based on one or more of the following considerations: (1) usefulness for the theological interpretation of the Bible within the context of the faith of the church; (2) significance in the history of interpretation; and (3) representation of evangelical and especially evangelical Wesleyan scholarship. I have annotated those items deemed most helpful, approximately seven hundred in number.

I readily concede that any attempt to develop a bibliography and to identify within that bibliography works deserving special attention is a matter of individual judgment; no two scholars would agree on the selection. Thus, I present this bibliography as a suggestion, a place to start, inviting students to test the worth of these items in the process of the interpretive task.

I have prepared this volume for use primarily by seminary students and ministers. For that reason, almost everything included is in English. But I also hope that scholars will find help here in identifying major works in areas outside of their specialization. This bibliography is intended, first of all, to acquaint students with major works, significant publishers, and prominent scholars in biblical studies. Its second purpose is to help students develop their personal libraries. The inclusion of many titles that are presently out of print should alert the student to the importance of stores, distribution houses, and online vendors that trade in theological used books, and in some cases to electronic access to these older works. The ultimate purpose of the bibliography, however, is to direct students to those works that will be most helpful in interpreting the Bible for preaching and teaching in the church and for personal formation in Christian discipleship. I emphasize interpretation, since all of these works assist in the *exegetical* process. I have not included essentially homiletical or devotional volumes, not because they lack value as such, but because they stand outside the exegetical focus of this bibliography.

I have operated throughout on the basis of a number of assumptions. The first assumption is that biblical interpretation is foundational for both ministry and personal discipleship and is therefore to be pursued with all seriousness. I also assume that although the direct study of the text should be given priority in the interpretive process, this process necessarily involves the employment of secondary sources, in order (1) to aid in the direct study of the text itself (e.g., the use of concordances); (2) to provide knowledge of background (both semantic and historical) that will lead to a "competent" reading, i.e., a reading that makes use of the kind of knowledge the original biblical writers assumed their readers possessed; and (3) to enter into dialogue with the community of interpreters, recognizing that, in the final analysis, interpretation is a task that God has given to the church as a whole and must be done within the context of the church's struggle to understand these texts. This final point, however, must not lead to the conclusion that we should consult only those authors who write from the perspective of faith, for all serious and accurate study of the Bible illumines the meaning of the text and is thus helpful for the use of the Bible within the community of faith.

Finally, I assume that real value exists in encountering interpreters from various periods and theological traditions. While affirming the necessity of understanding the Bible according to contemporary issues and the importance of teaching and preaching the Bible to our own age, we should recognize that the parameters of our specific historical existence limit our ability to understand dimensions of the text that were perhaps much clearer to persons who lived in a different age. And while celebrating our participation in our own theological traditions, we should recognize that the meaning of biblical passages is often larger than the construals of individual theological communities, so that our interpretations can be enhanced by insights from those whose theological commitments differ from our own. Hence, I have included authors from a variety of theological traditions, while giving some special consideration at points to evangelical Wesleyan scholarship. And I have incorporated items that represent or discuss interpretive work from different periods, though of necessity giving primary attention to current scholarship, which builds on the interpretation of the past and carries it forward. I have also attempted to include works representing different cultures; the number is not as great as I would like it to be, since up to this point the bulk of recognized biblical scholarship has been produced in the West. This situation is beginning to change; and I have no doubt that we are about to witness an influx of signficant scholarship emanating from the Majority World. And this is a most welcome development.

I am aware of the vast resources now available in biblical research through the Internet, especially for primary source material. Because the online venues for these resources are diverse and constantly changing I have chosen not to include them here. Students who wish to pursue these online resources should consult Roland H. Worth Jr., *Biblical Studies on the Internet: A Resource Guide,* 2d ed. (Jefferson, N.C.: McFarland, 2008). 378pp.

I hope this book will provide assistance to all who work in the area of biblical studies. But I developed this bibliography specifically for the benefit of my own students, and it is to them that I affectionately dedicate it.

My thanks go to Michael Stephens, reference book editor at Abingdon Press, who has been gracious and helpful at every point; to Asbury Theological Seminary, which provided a sabbatical for me to prepare this volume; and to my administrative assistant, Ms. Megan Longley, who gave excellent help in the production of this revised manuscript.

1

The Whole Bible

1.1   Bibliographic Helps: General

Highly Recommended

1.1.1   Allison, Joe. *Swords and Whetstones: A Guide to Christian Bible Study Resources*. 3d ed. Nappannee, Ind.: Evangel, 1999. 217pp.

An introduction to biblical studies resources that also explains clearly how to use each type of Bible reference work. Especially helpful is the guidance provided for selecting an English translation. Contains highly selective bibliography with annotations. Written from a conservative perspective for a primarily evangelical readership; is fair and balanced both in the works selected and in the evaluation of these works.

1.1.2   Bazylinski, Stanislaw. *A Guide to Biblical Research: Introductory Notes*. Rome: Pontifical Biblical Institute, 2006. 160pp.

Lists with some annotations works that are pertinent for researching an exegesis paper. Includes various original language editions of the biblical text, bibliographic research tools, and reference works (e.g., concordances, grammars, lexicons). Cites German, French, and Italian works in addition to those in English. Concludes with discussion of literary forms and practical suggestions for writing an exegesis paper.

1.1.3   Danker, Frederick W. *Multipurpose Tools for Bible Study*. 3d ed. Minneapolis: Fortress, 2003. 344pp.

Has been the benchmark of bibliographic guides to the Bible since the first edition in 1960. Contains specific descriptions of the various resources (including works from the entire history of the church, not simply the modern period), along with discussion on the use of these works in interpretation. The only serious limitation is its failure to list commentaries on specific biblical books, though it does discuss commentary series. A must for all Bible students.

1.1.4   Fitzmyer, Joseph A. *An Introductory Bibliography for the Study of Scripture*. Studia Biblica 3. 3d ed. Rome: Biblical Institute Press, 1990. 154pp.

From a leading Roman Catholic biblical scholar, it contains paragraph-long annotations of major scholarly works in the various areas of biblical studies but gives relatively little attention to commentaries on individual biblical books. Discusses works produced in a variety of languages, especially German and French; English works comprise fewer than half of those cited. Essential for academic research but of relatively limited usefulness for those engaged in regular teaching and preaching in the church.

1.1.5   Worth, Roland H., Jr. *Biblical Studies on the Internet: A Resource Guide*. 2d ed. Jefferson, N.C.: McFarland, 2008. 378pp.

Lists over forty-eight hundred resources at more than ten thousand Internet sites. Includes Bible translations (both English and non-English), editions of the biblical text in the original languages, a host of ancient documents related to the Bible, and a variety of secondary sources (mostly in English). An indispensable guide to this increasingly important source of information.

See also *Elenchus of Biblica* (§1.2.10)

Also Significant

1.1.6   Barber, Cyril J. *Best Books for Your Bible Study Library*. New York: Loizeaux, 2000. 95pp.

1.1.7   Glynn, John. *Commentary and Reference Survey: A Comprehensive Guide to Biblical and Theological Resources*. Grand Rapids: Kregel, 2007. 380pp.

1.1.8   Moo, Douglas J. *An Annotated Bibliography on the Bible and the Church*. Deerfield, Ill.: Trinity Evangelical Divinity School, 1986. 70pp.

2

1.1.9   Stuart, Douglas. *A Guide to Selecting and Using Bible Commentaries.*
          Waco, Tex.: Word, 1990. 131pp.

1.2   Periodicals

1.2.1   *African Journal of Biblical Studies.* 1986–. Semiannual.

          Produced by the Nigerian Association for Biblical Studies. The vast major-
          ity of contributors are from Africa. Most articles draw out significance of
          exegetical studies for the African context. Helpful for introducing North
          American students to African biblical studies and to the process of contex-
          tualizing results of biblical scholarship. Language: English. Book reviews:
          few.

1.2.2   *Bible Review.* 1985–. Quarterly.

          This journal, produced by the Biblical Archaeology Society in Washing-
          ton, D.C., provides studies in which some of the most prominent scholars
          address questions about biblical passages or biblical issues that trouble or
          concern nonspecialists. Articles represent almost all methods, and contrib-
          utors include scholars of virtually all faiths (and secularists who shun reli-
          gious commitment entirely). The orientation is, in fact, generally secular.
          It contains much informed and fresh insight, and is of value to specialists,
          but it is more useful to seminary students and trained pastors. Language:
          English. Book reviews: very few.

1.2.3   *The Bible Today: Scripture for Life and Ministry.* 1962–. 6 issues/year.

          Produced by the Order of St. Benedict in Collegeville, Minnesota, this
          Roman Catholic publication seeks to translate for the nonspecialist the
          results of serious scholarly investigation into the Bible, with special em-
          phasis on clarifying the meaning of difficult biblical passages and concepts.
          Although written for laypersons, the academic reputation of its contribu-
          tors and the high quality of its articles make it profitable for the seminary
          student and trained pastor. It is consistently reverent in handling the text
          and attentive in a pastoral way to issues of faith that are of concern to its
          Christian readers. Language: English. Book reviews: few and very brief
          (practically book notices).

1.2.4   *Biblica.* 1920–. Quarterly.

          Produced by the Pontifical Biblical Institute in Rome, it is one of the old-
          est and most prestigious journals given to serious biblical scholarship.

Articles deal meticulously with meaning and background of specific biblical passages, employing almost exclusively the traditional historical-critical method. Excellent for serious, in-depth study. Language: all European languages (Latin prominent in the earlier volumes), with English articles comprising approximately a third of the total. Book reviews: moderately few, but extensive in length. See also the related bibliographic annual, *Elenchus of Biblica* (§1.2.10)

1.2.5   *Biblical Interpretation: A Journal of Contemporary Approaches.* 1993–. 3 issues/year.

In response to the predominance of the historical-critical orientation of most periodicals in biblical studies, this journal, produced by Brill Academic Publishers in Leiden, the Netherlands, offers interpretations of particular texts and theoretical hermeneutical discussions centering on the new and emerging methods in interpretation, e.g., poststructuralism, semiotics, feminism, liberation hermeneutics, reader-oriented criticism, psychological and ecological readings. Contributions are consistently original and creative. Articles often illumine the methods employed more than the text itself, at least the text understood as canonical Scripture with its normative role in relation to the faith of the church. Yet there are exceptions, articles offering fresh, powerful, and compelling insights into the biblical text. Language: English. Book reviews: very few.

1.2.6   *Biblical Theology Bulletin: A Journal of Bible and Theology.* 1971–. Quarterly.

In spite of its name, this journal, produced by Biblical Theology Bulletin, Inc., in Wilmington, Delaware, does not deal primarily with larger issues of biblical theology (e.g., salvation history, kingdom of God) but rather explores the meaning of specific biblical passages and books using a variety of methods, especially new, emerging methods such as cultural anthropological and literary approaches. Articles are uneven in terms of their ability to serve as the basis of theological insights useful for preaching and teaching. In general, solid and helpful contributions by leading scholars in these emerging methods of interpretation. Language: English. Book reviews: few.

1.2.7   *Bulletin for Biblical Research.* 1991–. Annual.

The Institute for Biblical Research (IBR), which is the organization of evangelical biblical scholars responsible for producing this journal in Winona Lake, Indiana, accurately describes it as "both fully critical, yet supportive of the Christian faith." In many ways the American equivalent of the Tyndale Bulletin, its articles are in accord with the evangelical

4

convictions of the IBR but employ contemporary critical methods—in many cases in a masterful way. Unlike Tyndale Bulletin, however, it publishes mostly the work of established, senior scholars. Language: English. Book reviews: few.

1.2.8   *The Catholic Biblical Quarterly*. 1939–. Quarterly.

Next to the *Journal of Biblical Literature*, probably the most authoritative journal for serious academic study of the whole Bible. Published by the Catholic Biblical Association in Washington, D.C., its articles tend to avoid the kind of obscure and arcane issues that often occupy *JBL* and instead focus on significant questions of interpretation. Consequently, its articles rather consistently provide basis for theological reflection useful for preaching and teaching. Language: English. Book reviews: many.

1.2.9   *Currents in Biblical Research*. 1993–. Annual.

Formerly known as *Currents in Research*. Produced by Sheffield Academic Press in Sheffield, UK. Articles written by prominent scholars describe and critically assess new and emerging facets or developments within biblical studies. Each article contains extensive bibliography. Language: English.

1.2.10   *Elenchus of Biblica*. 24 vols. Rome: Biblical Institute Press, 1985–. Annual.

The most complete listing (nonannotated) available on works in biblical studies, produced by the Pontifical Biblical Institute in Rome. It includes both articles and books (with select citations of book reviews) in all areas of biblical studies and in all languages. The volumes are slow to appear, usually about four years behind schedule.

1.2.11   *The Expository Times*. 1889–. Monthly.

British publication produced by T&T Clark, Edinburgh, Scotland, attends to all the theological and pastoral disciplines and often contains helpful articles in biblical studies, including treatments of biblical themes and issues as well as exposition of specific passages. Contributors are often of global reputation but are almost exclusively from the British Isles. Language: English. Book reviews: few, but lengthy.

1.2.12   *Interpretation: A Journal of Bible and Theology*. 1946–. Quarterly.

Published by Union Presbyterian Seminary in Richmond, Virginia. From its inception has consistently emphasized the theological meaning of the text for the faith of the church. Articles model the ways in which theological and pastoral insights flow out of solid biblical exposition. Although the quality of the articles has in recent years become uneven, this journal seldom disappoints. Especially helpful are its "expository articles," in which scholars or gifted biblical preachers demonstrate how one might move from interpretation to proclamation of lectionary passages. Most highly recommended for those who regularly teach and preach in the context of the church or its institutions. Language: English. Book reviews: many.

1.2.13   *Journal of Biblical Literature.* 1881–. Quarterly.

Published by the Society of Biblical Literature in Atlanta, Georgia, arguably the world's foremost journal in biblical studies. Articles consistently reflect the highest academic standards and are original contributions to the biblical guild. Although articles generally do not draw out the theological significance of passages treated, some of them do contribute to an interpretation of the text that is useful for preaching and teaching. Yet many of the articles are arcane and deal with matters that do not clearly illumine the text as the church's Scripture. Language: English. Book reviews: none.

1.2.14   *Journal of Biblical and Pneumatological Research.* 2009–. Annually.

Published by Wipf & Stock in Eugene, Oregon. Contains articles written by Catholics, Protestants, and Pentecostals. In spite of the title of the journal, it deals exclusively with biblical studies and devotes only a little more than half of the articles specifically to the Spirit in the Bible. Articles employ a number of methods and emphasize the theological meaning of the text. Language: English. Book reviews: few, but lengthy.

1.2.15   *Review of Biblical Literature.* 1996–. Annual.

Published by the Society of Biblical Literature in Atlanta, Georgia, offers the most comprehensive review of books (including monographs, reference works, commentaries, dictionaries, editions of the biblical text and related ancient texts, and biblical translations) available. Reviews works published in all languages. Frequently provides multiple contrasting reviews of the same volume. Reviews are written by prominent scholars, are relatively extensive, and include description, analysis, and evaluation. Language: primarily English, with some reviews in German or French.

1.2.16   *Semeia: An Experimental Journal for Biblical Criticism.* 1974–. Quarterly.

Published by the Society of Biblical Literature in Atlanta, Georgia. Articles represent new and emerging methods of interpretation, especially structuralism, poststructuralism, feminist interpretation, etc. Typically avoids

theological reflection on the text in favor of illumining the new hermeneutical approaches on the one hand, and drawing out significance for
contemporary cultural and political applications on the other. Of marginal
value for teaching and preaching within the church. Language: English.
Book reviews: none.

1.2.17   *Tyndale Bulletin* (formerly *Tyndale House Bulletin*). 1950–. Semiannual.

Produced by Tyndale House of Cambridge, England, an evangelical academic study center. Most articles pertain to biblical studies, though some
represent other theological disciplines. The majority of contributors are
younger scholars. Articles are consistently informed and innovative, with
serious attention to theological issues. All conform to the evangelical confessional standards of Tyndale House but seek to engage seriously in the
critical study of the text. Language: English. Book reviews: few to none,
but with summaries of recent dissertations.

1.3   History of the Bible

Highly Recommended

1.3.1   Ackroyd, Peter R., and C. F. Evans, eds. *Cambridge History of the Bible*. 3
         vols. Cambridge: Cambridge University Press, 1988. 649/566/590pp.

The most thorough and authoritative history of the Bible in existence.
Articles produced by some of the world's most respected historians and
biblical scholars deal with all relevant aspects of the history of the development of the biblical text as well as its translation, canonization, use, and
influence from antiquity to the present. Should be in the library of every
seminary student and pastor.

1.3.2   Bratton, F. Gladstone. *A History of the Bible*. London: Robert Hale,
         1959. 287pp.

Something of a classic introduction to the history that surrounds the Bible. As such it deals with the history of the Hebrew people and the NT
church as well as with the history of the text of the Bible itself, especially
the canonization of the OT and NT, and the transmission of the Bible
from the Greek manuscripts through the early versions to the English
translations. Gives attention also to the history of exegesis. Designed for
the general reader, but a helpful introduction or refresher for the seminary
student or pastor.

1.3.3   Miller, Stephen M., and Robert V. Huber. *The Bible: A History*. Intercourse, Penn.: Good, 2004. 256pp.

Richly illustrated survey of the development of the biblical text and the history of the Bible's transmission. Gives significant attention to the impact of the Bible, primarily within the church.

1.3.4   Norton, David. *A History of the Bible as Literature*. 2 vols. Cambridge: Cambridge University Press, 1993. 375/493pp.

The only work in existence that thoroughly explores the relationship of the Bible, throughout its history, to the concept of literature. Addresses issues such as: In what sense have persons throughout history understood the Bible to be literature? How does the Bible relate to the various concepts of literature that have been operative over the past two millennia? Norton gives special attention to the reception of the King James Version as literature and to its role in the literary history of the English-speaking world. Informs understanding of the literary character of the Bible and the study of the Bible as literature, both of which have implications for several of the new and emerging interpretive methods, especially literary criticism.

1.3.5   Noss, Philip A., ed. *A History of Bible Translation*. Rome: Edizioni Di Storiae Litteratura, 2007. 521pp.

Produced by the Eugene A. Nida Institute for Biblical Scholarship of the American Bible Society, the first of a series of projected volumes pertaining to significant issues in Bible translation. Sixteen biblical scholars, linguists, and translation theoreticians contributed articles dealing with the changing ways in which Bible translation has been done and how Bible translation has been conceived from the Septuagint to contemporary African and Latin American translations.

1.3.6   Paget, James Carleton, and Joachim Schafer. *The New Cambridge History of the Bible: From the Beginnings to 600*. Cambridge: Cambridge University Press, 2013. 936pp; Marsden, Richard, and E. Ann Matter, *The New Cambridge History of the Bible: From 600 to 1450*. Cambridge: Cambridge University Press, 2012. 1068pp.

These two volumes are the first of a projected four-volume set that will trace the history of the Bible to the present. Deals with the transmission of the biblical text (including versions) and the reception of the Bible, treating not only various methods but also the influence of the Bible in poetry, fiction, law, and the visual arts. Attends to the study and reception of the Bible throughout the world, in the Eastern and Western church, and among Jews and Muslims.

1.3.7   Rogerson, John, ed. *The Oxford Illustrated History of the Bible*. Oxford: Oxford University Press, 2001. 416pp.

Leading scholars contributed concise discussions on matters pertaining to the development of the Bible, canonization, history of biblical interpretation, and contemporary use of the Bible (e.g., feminist scholarship and liberation theology). Copiously illustrated.

1.3.8   Trebolle Barrera, Julio. *The Jewish Bible and the Christian Bible: An Introduction to the History of the Bible*. Grand Rapids: Eerdmans, 1998. 573pp.

Thorough, informed, and current overview of the history of the Bible, dealing with the formation of the collections of canonical and apocryphal books, the transmission and translation of the Bible, and biblical interpretation in Judaism and Christianity, all with an eye toward the ways in which the social and cultural context illumines each of these aspects of the Bible's history. Contains numerous bibliographies of the most current scholarly work. Highly recommended for serious study.

Also Significant

1.3.9   Cunningham, Philip J. *Exploring Scripture: How the Bible Came to Be*. New York: Paulist, 1992. 216pp.

1.3.10   De Hamel, Christopher. *The Book: A History of the Bible*. London: Phaedon, 2001. 352 pp.

1.3.11   Ewert, David. *A General Introduction to the Bible: From Ancient Tablets to Modern Translations*. Grand Rapids: Zondervan, 1990. 284pp.

1.3.12   Koch, Klaus. *The Book of Books: The Growth of the Bible*. Philadelphia: Westminster, 1968. 192pp.

1.3.13   Pelikan, Jaroslav. *Whose Bible Is It? A History of the Scriputres through the Ages*. New York: Viking, 2005. 288pp.

1.3.14   Wegner, Paul D. *The Journey from Texts to Translations: The Origin and Development of the Bible*. Grand Rapids: Baker, 2000. 462pp.

1.4   History of the English Bible

Highly Recommended

1.4.1   Bailey, Lloyd R., ed. *The Word of God: A Guide to English Versions of the Bible*. Atlanta: John Knox, 1982. 228pp.

Noted biblical scholars (e.g., Bruce Metzger, James Smart, Eugene Nida) compare and contrast nine English versions (Revised Standard Version, New English Bible, New Jewish Version, Jerusalem Bible, New American Standard Bible, Good News Bible, Living Bible, New American Bible, New International Version), evaluating their relative worth on the basis of (1) quality of manuscripts employed, (2) basis of translation (etymology, context, cognate language, theological presuppositions), and (3) English usage (clarity, level, consistency). Concludes with annotated bibliography that lists book reviews and evaluative studies of each version discussed. Specific, informed, and very useful in evaluating the most popular contemporary versions.

1.4.2   Brake, Donald L. *A Visual History of the English Bible: The Tumultuous Tale of the World's Bestselling Book*. Grand Rapids: Baker, 2008. 349pp.

Engaging and richly illustrated description of the history of Bible translation into English. Gives primary attention to the early history through the King James Version. Emphasizes the commitment and risks of those involved in the translation of the English Bible, and the importance of their work for the life of the church.

1.4.3   Bruce, F. F. *The Books and Parchments: How We Got Our English Bible*. Rev. ed. Old Tappan, N.J.: Revell, 1984. 288pp.

Clearly written introduction to the history of the Bible in the form of brief treatments given to significant aspects of that history, including the Hebrew, Aramaic, and Greek languages, the significance of two testaments, the canon, the text of the OT, the Samaritan Pentateuch, the Targums, the Septuagint, the text of the NT, early versions of the NT, and the history of the English Bible. Produced by an unusually capable scholar who dealt confidently with each of these areas. Written for the general reader but may serve as a helpful survey for the seminary student or pastor.

1.4.4   ———. *History of the Bible in English*. New York: Oxford, 1978. 274pp.

Traces the history of the English Bible through its various translations from the very beginnings before Wycliffe through the Living Bible. Generally speaking, it is the most helpful survey of the history of the English Bible from the beginning through the 1970s, although its treatment of some of the major recent versions, especially the New American Standard Bible and the New International Version, is disappointing for its brevity.

1.4.5   Daniell, David. *The Bible in English: Its History and Significance.* New Haven, CT: Yale University Press, 2003. 899pp.

Detailed description of Bible translation in Britain and North America from 600 BCE to the present. Emphasizes cultural and religious contexts of the various translations and the impact of these translations upon both the church and the broader society.

1.4.6   Dewey, David. *A User's Guide to Bible Translations: Making the Most of Different Versions.* Downers Grove, Ill.: InterVarsity, 2004. 239pp.

Moves from a discussion of issues involved in translation (form-driven versus meaning-driven, formal equivalence versus dynamic equivalence, gender specific versus gender inclusive) to an assessment of major English translations. Insists that the choice of translation depends upon the use one has in mind, e.g., public reading, personal devotion, serious study.

1.4.7   Duthrie, Alan S. *How To Choose Your Bible Wisely.* 2d ed. Carlisle, UK: Paternoster, 1995. 244 pp.

Very helpful discussion of the major criteria that should be considered in evaluating the quality of an English translation. In the process assesses the most significant English translations.

1.4.8   Kerr, John Stevens. *Ancient Texts Alive Today: The Story of the English Bible.* Edited by Charles Houser. New York: American Bible Society, 1999. 229pp.

Concise description of the history of English translations from before William Tyndale through the Contemporary English Version. Replete with pictures and charts; presents a lively narrative that results not only in an understanding of the history and essential character of major translations, but also in a sense of the historical development of the task of English translation. Includes interesting biographical and historical details pertaining to the versions, especially the earlier ones, and concludes with a timeline of modern English Bibles.

1.4.9   Kubo, Sakae, and Walter Specht. *So Many Versions? Twentieth-Century English Versions of the Bible.* Rev. ed. Grand Rapids: Zondervan, 1983. 401pp.

11

Describes the aim, style, intended use, and target audience of each of the major twentieth-century translations through the Readers' Digest Bible, and provides a fair and trenchant evaluation of each. Concludes with an annotated list of all twentieth-century English translations, which provides essential information about those versions that were not treated more fully in the body of the book. Complements Bruce's volume (§1.4.4) in that it focuses on more recent versions, whereas Bruce emphasizes the earlier translations.

1.4.10   Lewis, Jack P. *The English Bible from KJV to NIV: A History and Evaluation.* 2d ed. Grand Rapids: Baker, 1991. 512pp.

Similar in purpose and goal to the volume by Kubo and Specht (§1.4.9), it describes the history, character, and aims of the translations and critically evaluates each. It differs from the aforementioned volume in that it contains a chapter on the King James Version, and discusses only thirteen twentieth-century translations. Lewis is thereby able to provide more depth in both description and evaluation than Kubo-Specht.

1.4.11   Metzger, Bruce M. *The Bible in Translation: Ancient and English Versions.* Grand Rapids: Baker, 2001. 200pp.

In spite of the subtitle, "Ancient and English Versions," Metzger dedicates only thirty-eight pages to ancient versions, thus giving by far the bulk of attention to English translations. Among the English translations, Metzger devotes the greatest attention to the Authorized Version, the Revised Standard Version and the New Revised Standard Version. Treatment of other contemporary English versions is extremely brief and tends to focus on details surrounding the emergence of the version. Whereas one might hope that Metzger would discuss the general character of each version, assessing its positive and negative qualities, one finds that Metzger typically cites the version's translation of one or two biblical passages with a view toward criticizing or applauding the translation of that limited unit. Useful as a historical chronicle of the various versions, but one should look to Bruce (§1.4.4) for more helpful assessment of strengths and weaknesses of each.

Also Significant

1.4.12   Chamberlin, William J. *Catalogue of English Bible Translations: A Classified Bibliography of Versions and Editions Including Books, Parts, and Old and New Testament Apocrypha and Apocryphal Books.* New York: Greenwood, 1991. 898pp.

1.4.13   Gilmore, Alec. *A Dictionary of the English Bible and Its Origins.* The Biblical Seminar 67. Sheffield: Sheffield Academic Press, 2000. 192pp.

1.4.14   Glassman, Eugene H. *The Translation Debate: What Makes a Bible Translation Good?* Downers Grove, Ill.: InterVarsity, 1981. 128pp.

1.4.15   Hargreaves, Cecil. *A Translator's Freedom: Modern English Bibles and Their Language.* The Biblical Seminar. Sheffield: JSOT, 1993. 206pp.

1.4.16   Kohlenberger, John R., III. *Words about the Word: A Guide to Choosing and Using Your Bible.* Regency Reference Library. Grand Rapids: Zondervan, 1987. 218pp.

1.4.17   Price, Ira M., William A. Irwin, and Allen P. Wikgren. *The Ancestry of Our English Bible: An Account of the Manuscripts, Texts, and Versions of the Bible.* 3d ed. New York: Harper & Row, 1956. 363pp.

1.4.18   Sheeley, Steven M., and Robert N. Nash Jr. *The Bible in English Translation: An Essential Guide.* Nashville: Abingdon, 1997. 116pp.

1.5   History of the Canon and History of Interpretation

See also EXEGETICAL METHOD/HERMENEUTICS (§1.12)

Highly Recommended

1.5.1   Abraham, William J. *Canon and Criterion in Christian Theology: From the Fathers to Feminism.* Oxford: Oxford University Press, 1998. 508pp.

A detailed and intellectually engaging study of the relationship between (biblical) canon and the criteria for determining doctrinal and ethical norms in the Christian faith. Written by a leading evangelical theologian, it traces the development of the canon in the early church and the subsequent functioning of the canon in the church in order to demonstrate the importance of distinguishing between the biblical canon itself and the church's complex and sophisticated use of that canon for its theological and moral life. Extremely helpful for probing the significance of the canon for the ongoing life of the church.

1.5.2   Barton, John. *Holy Writings, Sacred Text: The Canon in Early Christianity.* Louisville: Westminster John Knox, 1997. 210pp.

Presents a historical investigation into the development of the biblical canon in the church, addressing such issues as how the church came to accept as authoritative Scripture these and only these twenty-seven books that comprise the NT, and why the church placed the Hebrew Scriptures alongside these books. An excellent book for exploring the theological and historical problems of canonization of the Christian Scriptures.

1.5.3   Bruce, F. F. *The Canon of Scripture.* Downers Grove, Ill.: InterVarsity, 1988. 349pp.

Comprehensive survey of the history of the process of canonization of both the Old and New Testaments, with greater attention to the New. Especially illuminating are three final chapters that discuss canonical issues of continuing significance: criteria of canonicity, canon within the canon, and relationship of the canon to biblical criticism and interpretation (including "canonical criticism"). Highly recommended for general overview.

1.5.4   Campenhausen, Hans von. *The Formation of the Christian Bible.* Philadelphia: Fortress, 1972. 342pp.

A book that sets the standard in the study of the historical process of the formation of the canon. Campenhausen discusses the theological and historical problems of the Christian canon, and explores the pressures that led to the emergence of the canon, the forces that arose to challenge the formation of the canon, the outcome of the controversies surrounding the canon, and the theological significance of that outcome. Detailed, carefully documented, and original. The most authoritative treatment available.

1.5.5   Grant, Robert M., and David Tracy. *A Short History of the Interpretation of the Bible.* 2d ed. Philadelphia: Fortress, 1984. 213pp.

Offers a brief but solid history of interpretive method in the church from the NT itself (how Jesus and the NT writers treat the OT) through the 1970s, though gives bulk of attention to the early periods. Of special value are the final chapters, written by the noted Roman Catholic theologian David Tracy, which draw out the significance of this history for the theological interpretation of the Bible today.

1.5.6   Hayes, John H., ed. *Dictionary of Biblical Interpretation.* 2 vols. Nashville: Abingdon, 1999. 653/675pp.

By far the most comprehensive and current dictionary on biblical interpretation, it contains entries on the history of interpretation of the various biblical books (including apocryphal and deuterocanonical ones), on significant biblical interpreters throughout the history of the church, and on various interpretive methods and movements. Features almost four hundred contributors representing Jewish, Protestant, Orthodox, and Roman Catholic backgrounds. The range of essays is so broad that of necessity the individual articles tend to be quite brief; this drawback is somewhat mitigated by the bibliographies, which direct readers to additional research.

1.5.7   Margerie, Bertrand de. *An Introduction to the History of Exegesis.* 2 vols. Petersham, Mass.: St. Bede's, 1993, 1995. 277/154pp.

The first volume deals with the Greek fathers, while the second treats the Latin fathers. Analyzes the exegesis of the most significant fathers with a view toward calling the church to follow the model of the fathers, who sought to interpret the Bible within an avowedly confessional framework. Very selective in the number of fathers treated, especially in regard to the Latin fathers.

1.5.8   McDonald, Lee Martin. *The Biblical Canon: Its Origin, Transmission, and Authority.* Peabody, Mass.: Hendrickson, 2007. 546pp.

Thorough and critical investigation into the history of the canonical process, challenging many long-held assumptions. Emphasizes the diversity of opinion regarding decisions on canonical inclusion of books within both the Jewish and Christian communities. Insists that the establishment of the canon (especially the OT) was quite late. Draws out the significance of this history for the church's theology of Scripture.

1.5.9   McDonald, Lee Martin, and James A. Sanders, eds. *The Canon Debate.* Peabody, Mass.: Hendrickson, 2002. 662pp.

This book includes contributions from thirty-two scholars of international repute, all of whom are recognized authorities on that aspect of the canon about which they write in this volume. Includes the most current thinking on the wide range of issues related to the canon (both OT and NT) to be found in a single volume. Contributors represent a variety of positions on canonical issues and a spectrum of theological traditions.

1.5.10   McKenzie, Steven L., ed. *The Oxford Encyclopedia of Biblical Interpretation.* 2 vols. New York: Oxford University Press, 2013. 1164pp.

Contains 120 articles dealing with methods and topics of biblical interpretation with an emphasis upon the more recent approaches. Articles range from 3000 to 5000 words, and conclude with bibliographies.

1.5.11   Reventlow, Henning Graf. *History of Biblical Interpretation.* 4 vols. Atlanta: Society of Biblical Literature, 2009–2010. 243/313/278/471pp.

Traces the history of biblical interpretation from the first century to the twentieth, although it gives almost no attention to the twentieth century. Reflects upon the ways in which changing historical contexts of the church affected methods and approaches to biblical interpretation, and conversely how the message of the Bible impacted the church in succeeding generations.

Also Significant

1.5.12   Barr, James. *Holy Scripture: Canon, Authority, Criticism.* Philadelphia: Westminster, 1983. 175pp.

1.5.13   Bray, Gerald. *Biblical Interpretation: Past and Present.* Downers Grove, Ill.: InterVarsity, 1996. 608pp.

1.5.14   Elwell, Walter A., and J. D. Weaver. *Bible Interpreters of the Twentieth Century: A Selection of Evangelical Voices.* Grand Rapids: Baker, 1999. 445pp.

1.5.15   Evans, Craig. A., and Emanuel Tov, eds. *Exploring the Origins of the Bible: Canon Formation in Historical, Literary, and Theological Perspective.* Grand Rapids: Baker, 2008. 272pp.

1.5.16   Farrar, Frederick W. *History of Interpretation.* New York: Dutton, 1886. 553pp.

1.5.17   Frei, Hans. *The Eclipse of Biblical Narrative.* New Haven, Conn.: Yale, 1974. 355pp.

1.5.18   Froelich, Karlfried. *Biblical Interpretation in the Early Church. Sources of Early Christian Thought.* Philadelphia: Fortress, 1984. 135pp.

1.5.19   George, Timothy. *Reading Scripture with the Reformers.* Downers Grove, Ill: InterVarsity, 2011. 268 pp.

1.5.20   Hall, Christopher A. *Reading Scripture with the Church Fathers.* Downers Grove, Ill.: InterVarsity, 1998. 223pp.

1.5.21   Harrisville, Roy A., and Walter Sundberg. *The Bible in Modern Culture: Theology and Historical-Critical Method from Spinoza to Käsemann.* Grand Rapids: Eerdmans, 1995. 282pp.

1.5.22   Hauser, Alan J., and Duane F. Watson. *A History of Biblical Interpretation.* 2 vols. Grand Rapids: Eerdmans, 2002, 2009. 512/570pp.

1.5.23   Kugel, James L., and Rowan A. Greer. *Early Biblical Interpretation.* Library of Earliest Christianity. Philadelphia: Westminster, 1986. 214pp.

1.5.24   Lubac, Henri de. *Medieval Exegesis: The Four Senses of Scripture.* 2 vols. Ressourcement: Retrieval and Renewal in Catholic Thought. Grand Rapids: Eerdmans, 1998, 2000. 466/430pp.

1.5.25   McKim, Donald K. *Historical Handbook of Major Biblical Interpreters.* Downers Grove, Ill.: InterVarsity, 1998. 643pp.

1.5.26   Miller, John W. *The Origins of the Bible: Rethinking Canon History.* New York: Paulist, 1994. 250pp.

1.5.27   Noll, Mark. *Between Faith and Criticism: Evangelicals, Scholarship, and the Bible in America.* Society of Biblical Literature Confessional Perspective Series. Grand Rapids: Baker, 1986. 271pp.

1.5.28   Rogerson, J. W., and Judith M. Lieu, eds. *The Oxford Handbook of Biblical Studies.* Oxford: Oxford University Press, 2006. 896pp.

1.5.29   Sanders, James A. *From Sacred Story to Sacred Text: Canon as Paradigm.* Philadelphia: Fortress, 1986. 200pp.

1.5.30   Sandys-Wunsch, John. *What Have They Done to the Bible?: A History of Modern Biblical Interpretation.* Collegeville, Minn.: Michael Glazier, 2005. 378pp.

1.5.31   Silva, Moisés. *Has the Church Misread the Bible? The History of Interpretation in the Light of Contemporary Issues.* Grand Rapids: Zondervan, 1987. 136pp.

1.5.32   Simonetti, Manlio. *Biblical Interpretation in the Early Church: An Histori-cal Introduction to Patristic Exegesis.* Edited by Anders Bergquist and Markus Bockmuehl. Edinburgh: T&T Clark, 1994. 154pp.

1.5.33   Smalley, Beryl. *The Study of the Bible in the Middle Ages.* Notre Dame, Ind.: University of Notre Dame Press, 1964. 406pp.

1.5.34   Stokes, Mack B. *The Bible in the Wesleyan Heritage.* Nashville: Abingdon, 1979. 95pp.

1.5.35   Taylor, Mary Ann, ed. *Handbook of Women Biblical Interpreters: A His-torical and Biographical Guide.* Grand Rapids: Baker, 2012. 608pp.

1.5.36   Wansbrough, Henry. *The Use and Abuse of the Bible: A Brief History of Biblical Interpretation.* London: T&T Clark, 2010. 224 pp.

1.5.37   Young, Frances. *Biblical Exegesis and the Formation of Christian Culture.* Cambridge: Cambridge University Press, 2007. 340pp.

1.5.38   Zaman, Luc. *Bible and Canon: A Modern Historical Inquiry.* Studia Semitica Neerlandica, 50. Leiden: Brill, 2003. 714 pp.

1.6   Biblical History and Geography

See also BIBLE ATLASES (§1.7)

Highly Recommended

1.6.1   Aharoni, Yohanan. *The Land of the Bible: A Historical Geography.* Edited by A. F. Rainey. Rev. ed. Philadelphia: Westminster, 1979. 481pp.

Produced by a leading Israeli archaeologist, describes the history of the land of Palestine in general as well as the various regions, and even cities, roads, and highways. Presents both an introductory survey of the geogra-phy of the Holy Land and a chronologically ordered history of Palestine in the OT period, with special attention to the role of specific geographi-cal locations in the various stages of that history. Concludes with helpful indexes of biblical passages and of geographical names.

1.6.2   Chilton, Bruce, ed. *The Cambridge Companion to the Bible.* 2d ed. Cambridge: Cambridge University Press, 2008. 615pp.

Readable survey of the whole of the history of the Bible and its cultural environment from before the patriarchs through the first centuries of the church. Its breadth results in some lack of depth and detail in the discussions of the individual periods. Represents the general consensus of contemporary mainline critical scholarship in historical questions and reconstructions.

1.6.3   Coogan, Michael D., ed. *The Oxford History of the Biblical World.* New York: Oxford University Press, 2001. 643pp.

The most complete and authoritative history of the biblical world. In chronologically ordered chapters discusses the history, art, architecture, languages, culture, society, literature, and religion of the Bible, carefully synthesizing historical data and archaeological findings with the biblical text. Includes numerous prints, illustrations, and maps.

1.6.4   Drane, John W. *The World of the Bible.* Oxford: Lion, 2009. 256pp.

Explores the social, cultural, and religious contexts of the Bible from Sumerian culture to the Roman Empire, giving generally equal attention to these three types of context. Examines especially (royal) court, military, home, socioeconomic structures, cult and ritual. A rather short book, dealing with a wide range of subjects. Thus, space forbids developing any of them in much detail. A strength is that it depends almost entirely upon extra-biblical sources to illumine the Bible rather than drawing from descriptions within the Bible itself.

1.6.5   Finegan, Jack. *Myth and Mystery: An Introduction to the Pagan Religions of the Biblical World.* Grand Rapids: Baker, 1989. 335pp.

It is important to interpret biblical materials, which are theological texts, against the backdrop of the religious environment of the biblical world. This is the most authoritative examination of nine pagan religions influential during Old and New Testament times. Finegan discusses their beliefs, practices, writings, history, and relation to the biblical faith.

1.6.6   Turner, George Allen. *Historical Geography of the Holy Land.* Grand Rapids: Baker, 1973. 368pp.

A comprehensive synthesis of the history and geography of the Holy Land. Nowhere will one find clearer and more straightforward discussions of the regions and major specific geographical locations of Palestine and their

19

significance for the biblical account. Geared toward seminary students and trained pastors.

1.6.7   Vos, Howard F. *New Illustrated Bible Manners and Customs: How the People of the Bible Really Lived.* Nashville: Thomas Nelson, 1999. 661pp.

Moves chapter by chapter through biblical history, discussing in readable fashion various aspects of the history of Bible times, emphasizing everyday life. Although geared to a popular audience, contains much information that is directly helpful for the interpretation of specific passages, presented in an accessible format. Represents a conservative historical perspective.

Also Significant

1.6.8   Baly, Denis. *Basic Biblical Geography.* Philadelphia: Fortress, 1987. 80pp.

1.6.9   Barton, John. *The Biblical World.* 2 vols. New York: Routledge, 2002. 1115pp.

1.6.10   Corswant, Willy, and Edouard Urech. *A Dictionary of Life in Bible Times.* New York: Oxford University Press, 1960. 308pp.

1.6.11   DeVries, LaMoine F. *Cities of the Biblical World.* Peabody, Mass.: Hendrickson, 1997. 398pp.

1.6.12   Gray, John. *A History of Jerusalem.* London: Robert Hall, 1969. 336pp.

1.6.13   Harris, Robert L. *The World of the Bible.* London: Thames and Hudson, 1995. 192pp.

1.6.14   Harrison, R. K., ed. *Major Cities of the Biblical World.* New York: Thomas Nelson, 1985. 292pp.

1.6.15   Matthews, Victor H. *Manners and Customs in the Bible.* Rev. ed. Peabody, Mass.: Hendrickson, 1991. 283pp.

1.6.16   Page, Charles R. II, and Carl A. Volz. *The Land and the Book: An Introduction to the World of the Bible.* Nashville: Abingdon, 1993. 285pp.

1.6.17   Pfeiffer, Charles F., and Howard F. Vos. *The Wycliffe Historical Geography of Bible Lands.* Chicago: Moody, 1967. 588pp.

1.6.18   Shanks, Hershel, ed. *Ancient Israel: A Short History from Abraham to the Roman Destruction of the Temple.* Rev. ed. Washington, D.C.: Biblical Archaeology Society, 1999. 356pp.

1.6.19   Smith, George Adam. *The Historical Geography of the Holy Land.* 25th ed. London: Hodder & Stoughton, 1931. 512pp.

1.6.20   Thompson, J. A. *Handbook of Life in Bible Times.* Downers Grove, Ill.: InterVarsity, 1986. 384pp.

1.7   Bible Atlases

Highly Recommended

1.7.1   Aharoni, Yohanan, and Michael Avi-Yonah. *The Carta Biblical Atlas.* 3d ed. New York: Macmillan, 1993. 215pp.

Previously titled *The Macmillan Bible Atlas.* Completely revised from the second edition. Provides maps and illustrations covering 3000 BCE to 200 CE and dealing with settlements and mass migrations of populations; conquests and battles described in the Bible; economic developments, trade routes, and natural resources; movements of biblical characters within districts and cities; archaeological excavation; and growth of the church through the second century. Brief but specific and useful historical narrative accompanies each map. Along with Harper's (§1.7.6), most comprehensive Bible atlas available.

1.7.2   Bahat, Dan, and Chaim T. Rubinstein. *The Illustrated Atlas of Jerusalem.* New York: Simon & Schuster, 1990. 152pp.

Most comprehensive and authoritative atlas of this most important biblical site. Makes use of the latest archaeological discoveries. Presents maps, drawings, isometric reconstructions, and detailed descriptions of specific

21

features of Jerusalem and consistently relates these descriptions to biblical narrative and biblical history.

1.7.3   Beitzel, Barry J., ed. *Biblica: A Bible Atlas.* Vancouver: Raincoast, 2006. 575 pp.

This large volume is perhaps the most complete atlas in terms of maps and photographs, but does less in terms of cultural and religious background than Carta by Aharoni and Avi-Yonah (§1.7.1) or Harper's (§1.7.6). Devotes a great deal of space to retelling the biblical story, but helpfully relates maps and illustrations to the various biblical accounts. Compiled by twenty-seven globally recognized scholars.

1.7.4   Briscoe, Thomas V. *The Holman Bible Atlas.* Nashville: Broadman & Holman, 1998. 298pp.

Well-formatted and informed synthesis of maps, illustration, and historical and geographical discussions. Less comprehensive or authoritative than *The Carta Biblical Atlas* (§1.7.1) or *The Harper Atlas* (§1.7.6) but represents a responsible conservative complement to them.

1.7.5   Lawrence, Paul. *The IVP Atlas of Bible History.* Downers Grove, Ill: Inter-Varsity, 2006. 187pp.

Rehearses the narrative of biblical history with discussion of historical, geographical, and archaeological matters at each point. The historical narrative is based upon the biblical account itself rather than critical reconstructions and presents historical and archaeological discussions from a conservative perspective that seeks to support the reliability of the biblical witness. Richly illustrated with maps, drawings, and especially photographs.

1.7.6   Pritchard, James B. *The Harper Atlas of the Bible.* San Francisco: Harper, 1987. 254pp.

Among the most complete, comprehensive, and authoritative available. Compiled by fifty archaeologists, linguists, epigraphers, archaeological illustrators, geographers, interpreters, geologists, and historians, and containing 450 illustrations, with visual reconstructions of historical sites, e.g., Jerusalem as Jesus saw it. Text pertaining to historical background treats customs, beliefs, practices, texts, crafts, industries, weaponry, everyday life, etc. Combines geography, history, culture, and archaeology in dynamic synthesis with the biblical text. Comparable in quality to *The Carta Biblical Atlas* (§1.7.1).

1.7.7   Rainey, Anson F., and R. Steven Notley. *The Sacred Bridge: Carta's Atlas of the Biblical World.* Jerusalem: Carta, 2006. 448pp.

Helpfully discusses the methods and significance of historical geography for the study of ancient peoples and for biblical interpretation. Meticulously relates ancient texts (both biblical and extra-biblical) to the history, culture, and geography of the Levant, from the Bronze Age to the Bar Kochba Revolt. Discussions depend more upon texts than archaeology. Includes significant interaction with secondary literature.

Also Significant

1.7.8   Baly, Denis, and A. D. Tushingham. *Atlas of the Biblical World.* Cleveland: World, 1971. 208pp.

1.7.9   Bimson, J. J., J. P. Kane, J. H. Patterson, D. J. Wiseman, and D. R. W. Wood, eds. *New Bible Atlas.* Downers Grove, Ill.: InterVarsity, 1985. 128pp.

1.7.10   Currid, John D., and David P. Barrett, ed. *ESV Bible Atlas.* Wheaton, Ill: Crossway, 2010. 348pp.

1.7.11   Frank, Harry Thomas, ed. *Hammond's Atlas of the Bible Lands: An Illustrated Atlas of the Bible.* Rev. ed. Maplewood, N.J.: Hammond, 2000. 48pp.

1.7.12   Grollenberg, L. H. *Atlas of the Bible.* Edited by Joyce M. H. Reid and H. H. Rowley. London: Thomas Nelson, 1956. 165pp.

1.7.13   Kraeling, Emil Gottlieb Heinrich. *Rand McNally Bible Atlas.* Edited by Carl H. Kraeling. New York: Rand McNally, 1956. 485pp.

1.7.14   May, Herbert G. *Oxford Bible Atlas.* 3d ed. New York: Oxford University Press, 1984. 144pp.

1.7.15   Mittman, Siegried, and Götz Schmidt, *Tübinger Bibelatlas.* Stuttgart: Deutsche-Bibelgesellschaft, 2001. Maps. (This book does not include page numbers.)

1.7.16   Negenman, Jan H. *New Atlas of the Bible*. Edited by H. H. Rowley. New York: Doubleday, 1969. 208pp.

1.7.17   Pritchard, James B., ed. *The HarperCollins Concise Atlas of the Bible*. San Francisco: HarperSanFrancisco, 1997. 151pp.

1.7.18   Rasmussen, Carl. *The Zondervan NIV Atlas of the Bible*. Grand Rapids: Zondervan, 1989. 256pp.

1.7.19   Rogerson, John. *Atlas of the Bible*. New York: Facts on File Publications, 1985. 237pp.

1.7.20   Wright, G. Ernest, and Floyd V. Filson, eds. *The Westminster Historical Atlas to the Bible*. Rev. ed. Philadelphia: Westminster, 1956. 128pp.

1.8   Biblical Archaeology

See also EXEGETICAL METHOD/HERMENEUTICS (§1.12)

Highly Recommended

1.8.1   Bartlett, John R., ed. *Archaeology and Biblical Interpretation*. London: Routledge, 1997. 176pp.

The authors of the articles assembled here demonstrate how archaeology can illumine the social, political, and theological concerns of the biblical text, if used properly and with due caution. After an instructive introductory article by Bartlett ("What Has Archaeology to Do with the Bible—or Vice Versa?"), six scholars explore applications of archaeology to specific biblical texts or issues.

1.8.2   Charlesworth, James H., and Walter P. Weaver, eds. *What Has Archaeology to Do with Faith?* Faith and Scholarship Colloquies. Valley Forge, Pa.: Trinity Press International, 1992. 116pp.

Five prominent scholars explore the limits and potential of archaeology for interpreting the Bible and for faith. Probes the significance of archaeology for the study of Israelite history, the NT, and the historical Jesus, and argues for more intentionality in using archaeology to reconstruct ancient social history. Complements the volume edited by Bartlett (§1.8.1) in introducing readers to the relevance of archaeology for interpretation.

1.8.3   Hoffmeier, James K. *The Archaeology of the Bible*. Oxford: Lion, 2008. 192pp.

Moves through the Bible, discussing ways in which particular archaeological discoveries illumine historical descriptions in specific biblical passages. Avoids using archaeology to prove or disprove the historicity of the Bible. Rather uses archaeological discoveries to provide depth and precision to an understanding of the biblical accounts. Copiously illustrated.

1.8.4   Hoppe, Leslie J. *What Are They Saying about Biblical Archaeology?* New York: Paulist, 1984. 107pp.

Concise but illuminating introduction to contemporary issues in biblical archaeology. The first chapter ("Archaeology—Use and Abuse") and the last ("The Future of Biblical Archaeology") discuss theoretical issues, while the intervening chapters describe the process of excavation and explore how four current digs clarify the theoretical issues.

1.8.5   Kenyon, Kathleen M. *Archaeology in the Holy Land.* 5th ed. New York: Norton, 1979. 359pp.

A classic, written by an innovative and towering figure in the history of archaeology, this book presents both a description of her discoveries in various sites and her brilliant interpretation of these discoveries. Although this fifth edition represents a complete revision completed shortly before Kenyon's death, it is now somewhat dated in parts and should be supplemented with accounts of newer discoveries.

1.8.6   Master, Daniel, ed. *Oxford Encyclopedia of the Bible and Archaeology.* 2 vols. New York: Oxford University Press, 2013. 1188pp.

Articles attempt to draw out the significance of archaeological discoveries for the social organization of Israel or the ANE and for the interpretation of the biblical text. Methodologically sophisticated and comprehensive, and highly illuminating.

1.8.7   Mazar, Amihai. *Archaeology of the Land of the Bible: 10,000–586 B.C.E.* Anchor Bible Reference Library. Garden City, N.Y.: Doubleday, 1990. 576pp.

Comprehensive, current, and informed description of archaeological research of Palestine relating to the OT and dealing with the period of

25

10,000 BCE to the Babylonian Captivity. It is careful to represent differences of scholarly opinion. Gives some (secondary) consideration to the implications of the archaeological discoveries discussed for biblical history. A most helpful survey.

1.8.8   Morrey, P. R. S. *A Century of Biblical Archaeology.* Louisville: Westminster John Knox, 1991. 189pp.

A most comprehensive and accessible critical history of biblical archaeology. Explores especially the relationship between archaeologists and biblical scholars, made complex by their different views on the purpose of biblical archaeology. Provides valuable information on major schools, scholars, and excavations in archaeology since 1890.

1.8.9   Rousseau, John J., and Rami Arav (with Carol Meyers). *Jesus and His World: An Archaeological and Cultural Dictionary.* Philadelphia: Fortress, 1994. 189pp.

Entries arranged alphabetically treat various subjects (e.g., coins, magic, medicine), places, and persons that pertain to Jesus and the Gospels, in each case including Scripture references, general information, archaeological data, and implications for Jesus research, concluding with a select bibliography. Very accessible, readable, and illuminating background material.

1.8.10   Stern, Ephraim. *The New Encyclopedia of Archaeological Excavations in the Holy Land.* 4 vols. New York: Simon & Schuster, 1993. 1551pp.

Most comprehensive, detailed, scholarly dictionary of archaeological excavations available. Discussions are highly technical, but contributors consistently relate archaeological discoveries to relevant biblical passages (and an index to biblical passages is included). Generously illustrated with charts, maps, and photographs.

Periodicals

1.8.11   *Archaeology in the Biblical World.* Shafter, Calif.: Near East Archaeological Society, 1991–.

1.8.12   *Artifax.* Brighton, Minn: Institute for Biblical Archaeology; Near East Archaeological Society, 1985–.

1.8.13   *The Biblical Archaeological Review.* Washington, D.C.: Biblical Archaeology Society, 1975–.

1.8.14 *The Bulletin of the American Schools of Oriental Research.* Ann Arbor, Mich.: American Schools of Oriental Research, 1919–.

1.8.15 *Israel Exploration Journal.* Jerusalem: Israel Exploration Society and the Institute of Archaeology of Hebrew University, 1951–.

1.8.16 *Near Eastern Archaeology* (originally *The Biblical Archaeologist*). Boston: American Schools of Oriental Research, 1938–.

Also Significant

1.8.17 Albright, William Foxwell. *The Archaeology of Palestine.* Rev. ed. Harmondsworth, UK: Penguin, 1960. 271pp.

1.8.18 Bartlett, John R., ed. *Archaeology & Biblical Interpretation.* London: Routledge, 1997. 176pp.

1.8.19 Campbell, Edward F., and David Noel Freedman. *The Biblical Archaeologist Reader.* Vols. 2–3. New York: Doubleday, 1961–1970. 420/424pp.

1.8.20 ———. *The Biblical Archaeologist Reader.* Vol. 4. New York: Sheffield, 1983. 390pp.

1.8.21 Cline, Eric H. *Biblical Archaeology: A Very Short Introduction.* Oxford: Oxford University Press, 2009. 168pp.

1.8.22 Coogan, Michael D., Cheryl J. Exum, and Lawrence E. Stager, eds. *Scripture and Other Artifacts: Essays on the Bible and Archaeology in Honor of Philip J. King.* Louisville: Westminster John Knox, 1994. 452pp.

1.8.23 Currid, John D. *Doing Archaeology in the Land of the Bible: A Basic Guide.* Grand Rapids: Baker, 1999. 666pp.

1.8.24 Dever, William G. *What Did the Biblical Writers Know and When Did They Know It? What Archaeology Can Tell Us about the Reality of Ancient Israel.* Grand Rapids: Eerdmans, 2001. 275pp.

1.8.25   Finegan, Jack. *The Archaeology of the New Testament: The Life of Jesus and the Beginning of the Early Church.* Rev. ed. Princeton, N.J.: Princeton University Press, 1992. 409pp.

1.8.26   Frendo, Anthony J. *Pre-Exilic Israel, the Hebrew Bible, and Archaeology: Integrating Text and Artifact.* New York: T&T Clark, 2011. 120pp.

1.8.27   Fritz, Volkmar. *An Introduction to Biblical Archaeology.* Journal for the Study of the Old Testament Supplement Series 172. Sheffield: JSOT, 1994. 223pp.

1.8.28   Hoerth, Alfred, and John McRay. *Bible Archaeology: An Exploration of the History and Culture of Early Civilizations.* Grand Rapids: Baker, 2005. 288pp.

1.8.29   Hoffmeier, James K., and Alan Millard, eds. *The Future of Biblical Archaeology: Reassessing Methodologies and Assumptions.* Grand Rapids: Eerdmans, 2004. 385pp.

1.8.30   Lance, H. Darrell. *The Old Testament and the Archaeologist.* Guides to Biblical Scholarship. Philadelphia: Fortress, 1981. 98pp.

1.8.31   Meyers, Eric M., ed. *The Oxford Encyclopedia of Archaeology in the Near East.* 5 vols. Oxford: Oxford University Press, 1997. 2592pp.

1.8.32   Negev, Avraham, ed. *Archaeological Encyclopedia of the Holy Land.* Revised by Shimon Gibson. New York: Continuum, 2001. 559pp.

1.8.33   Rast, Walter E. *Through the Ages in Palestinian Archaeology: An Introductory Handbook.* Philadelphia: Trinity Press International, 1992. 221pp.

1.8.34   Stern, Ephraim. *Archaeology of the Land of the Bible.* Vol. 2. The Assyrian, Babylonian, and Persian Periods (733–332 B.C.E.). Anchor Bible Reference Library. New York: Doubleday, 2001. 592pp.

1.8.35   Thompson, J. A. *The Bible and Archaeology.* 3d ed. Grand Rapids: Eerdmans, 1982. 474pp.

1.8.36   Wright, G. Ernest. *Biblical Archaeology*. Rev. ed. Philadelphia: Westminster, 1962. 291pp.

1.8.37   Wright, G. Ernest, and David Noel Freedman. *The Biblical Archaeologist Reader*. Vol. 1. New York: Doubleday, 1961–1970. 342pp.

1.9   Concordances to the English Bible

Highly Recommended

1.9.1   Goodrick, Edward W., and John R. Kohlenberger III. *Zondervan NIV Exhaustive Concordance*. 2d ed. Grand Rapids: Zondervan, 1999. 1647pp.

Only concordance based on the NIV that includes every occurrence of every word. Contains dictionary index that defines every Hebrew, Aramaic, and Greek words in the Bible, including frequency counts for each original language word and for each of its English translations. Uses numbering system developed by the authors (which seeks to replace the old Strong's numbering system), and indexes this new numbering system to Strong's.

1.9.2   Metzger, Bruce M. *New Revised Standard Version Exhaustive Concordance*. Nashville: Thomas Nelson, 1991. 1828pp. + indexes.

Compiled by chairman of the NRSV translation committee, contains every occurrence of every word in the NRSV. Includes topical index, referencing more than eight thousand biblical persons, places, things, concepts, events, and doctrines. Comparable to Kohlenberger's NRSV Concordance (§1.9.10), but the topical index in this volume is more complete. A deficiency in both is that neither employs a system whereby the reader can identify the Greek, Hebrew, or Aramaic word lying behind the NRSV translation.

1.9.3   Mounce, William D. *The Crossway Comprehensive Concordance of the Holy Bible: English Standard Version*. Wheaton, Ill: Crossway, 2002. 1163pp.

Lists all passages for the fourteen thousand words that appear in the English Standard Version, with the exception of 115 very common ones (e.g., "a," and "in"), which are listed at the front. Each citation appears in approximately eight words of context so as to give the reader some sense of the use of the term in the passage. Like Metzger and Kohlenberger

(§§1.9.2, 1.9.10) no system is employed allowing the reader to identify the Greek, Hebrew, or Aramaic word lying behind the ESV translation.

1.9.4 Strong, James. *The Strongest Strong's Exhaustive Concordance of the Bible*, revised by John R. Kohlenberger III and James A. Swanson. Grand Rapids: Zondervan, 2001. 1742pp.

For over a century the most widely used concordance to the King James Version was Strong's. Contains the well-known Strong's numbering system, which assigns a number to each Greek, Hebrew, or Aramaic word used in the Bible, with the result that the reader can, by using the index provided, locate passages where individual Greek, Hebrew, or Aramaic words appear. Since several significant original-language reference works are coded to the Strong's numbers, this concordance can serve as the basis for the use of these original-language resources by persons who do not know Greek or Hebrew. In this revised edition, the database has been compiled and verified by computer technology, and it features new Hebrew and Greek dictionaries.

1.9.5 Thomas, Robert L., ed. *The Strongest NASB Exhaustive Concordance.* Grand Rapids: Zondervan, 2004. 1582 pp.

Updates the *Zondervan NASB Exhaustive Concordance.* Contains every occurrence of every word in the updated NASB, indexed to Greek, Hebrew, and Aramaic words lying behind the English translation, using Strong's numbering system. Includes Greek and Hebrew-Aramaic dictionary.

Also Significant

1.9.6 Cruden, Alexander. *Cruden's Complete Concordance to the Old and New Testaments.* Peabody, Mass.: Hendrickson, 1988. 783pp. (Originally published in 1737.)

1.9.7 Ellison, John W. *Nelson's Complete Concordance of the Revised Standard Version of the Bible.* New York: Nelson, 1957. 2157pp.

1.9.8 Hazard, M. C. *A Complete Concordance to the American Standard Version of the Holy Bible.* New York: Thomas Nelson, 1922. 1234pp.

1.9.9 Kohlenberger, John R., III. *The NRSV Concordance: Unabridged.* Grand Rapids: Zondervan, 1991. 1483pp. + indexes.

1.9.10   Manser, Martin. *The NIV Comprehensive Concordance.* London: Hodder & Stoughton, 2001. 1121pp.

1.9.11   Whitaker, Richard E. *RSV Analytical Concordance.* Grand Rapids: Eerdmans, 1988. 1548pp.

1.9.12   Young, Robert. *Analytical Concordance to the Bible.* Rev. ed. Nashville: Thomas Nelson, 1982. 1090pp. + indexes.

1.10   Topical Concordances

Highly Recommended

1.10.1   Day, A. Colin. *Roget's Thesaurus of the Bible.* San Francisco: Harper, 1992. 927pp.

Employs Roget's familiar category concept (known to most readers through *Roget's International Thesaurus*) that groups together related subjects (both similar and opposite). Readers can use subject categories to find relevant biblical references, or can use the Scripture index to find appropriate subject categories. Not tied to one translation, but based on Day's own paraphrase, representing his eclectic examination of several versions (and of the Greek and Hebrew). Not as complete in either categories or citations as Kohlenberger's Nave's, but since even Kohlenberger's volume is not absolutely complete it is well to supplement Kohlenberger's volume with this one.

1.10.2   Kohlenberger, John R., III. *Zondervan NIV Nave's Topical Bible.* Grand Rapids: Zondervan, 1992. 1152pp.

Kohlenberger's extensive revision and expansion of the classic produced by Orville J. Nave more than a century ago, it is the most complete topical concordance to the Bible in existence. Invaluable for locating all biblical passages pertaining to a given topic.

Also Significant

1.10.3   Hitchcock, Roswell D. *Baker's Topical Bible.* Rev. ed. Grand Rapids: Baker, 1975. 685pp.

1.10.4   Joy, Charles R. *Harper's Topical Concordance*. Rev. ed. New York: Harper & Row, 1962. 628pp.

1.10.5   Viening, Edward, ed. *The Zondervan Topical Bible*. Grand Rapids: Zondervan, 1969. 1114pp.

1.11 Bible Dictionaries

Highly Recommended

1.11.1   Bromiley, Geoffrey W., ed. *International Standard Bible Encyclopedia*. Rev. ed. 4 vols. Grand Rapids: Eerdmans, 1979–1988. 1005/1175/1060/1211pp.

First revision since 1929 of the classic encyclopedia that originally appeared in 1915. Although fully revised, it does include some of the monumental articles from earlier editions. Some entries include very selective bibliographies. Along with the *Anchor Bible Dictionary* (§1.11.2), the most useful dictionary available. Generally more conservative and often more concise than the *Anchor*.

1.11.2   Freedman, David Noel, ed. *The Anchor Bible Dictionary*. 6 vols. New York: Doubleday, 1992. 1232/1100/1135/1162/1230/1176pp.

Almost universally considered the standard multivolume Bible dictionary in English. Contributors include the most recognized scholars in the world, and represent a broad theological spectrum. All articles of significant length include brief but helpful bibliographies. Although the most comprehensive dictionary in English, it evinces some notable omissions. It is therefore well to supplement this dictionary with others, especially the *International Standard Bible Encyclopedia* (§1.11.1).

1.11.3   ———, ed. *Eerdmans Dictionary of the Bible*. Grand Rapids: Eerdmans, 2000. 1425pp.

Contains five thousand articles, written by approximately six hundred scholars, although contributors include many graduate students along with some of the world's most recognized authorities. Comparable to *HarperCollins* (§1.11.5), and along with the latter the most current, wide-ranging, and generally useful single-volume dictionary. The quality of the articles, however, is more uneven than is the case with *HarperCollins*.

1.11.4   Klauck, Hans-Josef et al., eds. *Encyclopedia of the Bible and Its Reception*. 30 vols. projected; 2 vols. currently available. Berlin: de Gruyter, 2009–.

A massive project, with thirty volumes anticipated by 2018. Over six hundred scholars of global reputation contributed articles just under "A." Is distinguished from other Bible dictionaries by its attention not simply to historical and methodological matters, but also to the history of influence (*Wirkungsgeschichte*), use, and reception in Judaism, Christianity, Islam and other religions, literature, art, music, and film. Although articles on more narrow topics parallel the kinds of entries found in other major Bible dictionaries, those dealing with significant topics offer separate discussions (often written by a number of different scholars) on a range of issues; the article on Amos, e.g., deals with Hebrew Bible/OT, New Testament, Greco-Roman Antiquity, Christianity, Islam, Literature, visual arts, and music.

1.11.5   Powell, Mark Allan, ed. *HarperCollins Bible Dictionary*. Rev. ed. New York: HarperCollins, 2011. 1168pp.

Commissioned by the Society of Biblical Literature, and containing four thousand articles by Roman Catholic, Jewish, mainline Protestant, and evangelical scholars, probably the most comprehensive and authoritative single-volume Bible dictionary. Nevertheless, it shares with all one-volume dictionaries the significant limitations of breadth and detail over against the multivolume ones.

1.11.6   Sakenfeld, Katharine Doob, ed. *The New Interpreter's Dictionary of the Bible*. 5 vols. Nashville: Abingdon, 2006–2009. 843/1012/936/950/1075pp.

Replaces the original *Interpreter's Dictionary of the Bible* (§1.11.1) not as a revision but rather a completely new work. Discusses all persons and places mentioned in the Bible, as well as cultural and religious matters, and methods of interpretation. Especially helpful are the articles pertaining to the various biblical books. Has a greater concern for theological and ethical issues than is found in the *Anchor Bible Dictionary* (§1.11.2). The nine hundred contributors represent a wide cultural and theological spectrum. Contributors naturally represent their own perspective, but typically present alternative views with respect and sympathy.

1.11.7   Tenney, Merrill C., and Moisés Silva. *The Zondervan Encyclopedia of the Bible*. Rev. ed. 5 vols. Grand Rapids: Zondervan, 2009. Volumes average 1000pp.

Informative, comprehensive, and thoroughly evangelical. Includes articles on all sorts of matters relating to the Bible and biblical study, while giving particular emphasis to the key themes and doctrines of the Bible. Describes varying viewpoints on major theological and historical issues and seeks to evaluate these viewpoints fairly, doing so from a conservative Protestant perspective. Represents solid scholarship, but written for the nonspecialist. Richly illustrated.

Also Significant

1.11.8   Butler, Trent C., ed. *Holman Bible Dictionary*. Nashville: Holman, 1991. 1450pp.

1.11.9   Buttrick, George Arthur, ed. *The Interpreter's Dictionary of the Bible*. 4 vols. plus Supplementary Volume. Nashville: Abingdon, 1962, 1976. 876/1030/878/964/998pp.

1.11.10   Douglas, J. D., and N. Hillyer, eds. *The Illustrated Bible Dictionary*. 3 vols. Downers Grove, Ill.: InterVarsity, 1986. 1726pp.

1.11.11   Elwell, Walter A., ed. *Baker Encyclopedia of the Bible*. 2 vols. Grand Rapids: Baker, 1988. 2210pp.

1.11.12   Hastings, James, ed. *Dictionary of the Bible*. 5 vols. Edinburgh: T&T Clark, 1898. 864/870/896/994/936pp.

1.11.13   Marshall, I. Howard, A. R. Millard, and J. I. Packer, eds. *New Bible Dictionary*. 3d ed. Downers Grove, Ill.: InterVarsity, 1996. 1298pp.

1.11.14   Mills, Watson E., ed. *Mercer Dictionary of the Bible*. Macon, Ga.: Mercer University Press, 1990. 993pp.

1.12   Exegetical Method/Hermeneutics

Highly Recommended

1.12.1   Bauer, David R., and Robert A. Traina, *Inductive Bible Study: A Comprehensive Guide to the Practice of Hermeneutics*. Grand Rapids: Baker Academic, 2011. 446pp.

The standard resource for the "inductive method" of biblical study that presents a practical, comprehensive, and holistic approach to the study of the Bible, and one that is methodologically rigorous in its attempt to allow the Bible to speak on its own terms. A thorough manual of Bible study that moves from observation through interpretation to the evaluation and contemporary appropriation of passages, with emphasis upon the final form of the text as the church's Scripture. Concerned also with correlating the teaching of various passages into a broader biblical theology.

1.12.2   Caird, G. B. *The Language and Imagery of the Bible.* Philadelphia: Westminster, 1980. 280pp.

A classic exploration of the ways in which an understanding of the function of language informs the interpretation of Scripture. Unlike many current studies of biblical linguistics that are based on recent, and in some cases questionable, trends, this work moves out from established and solid linguistic research.

1.12.3   Carson, D. A. *Exegetical Fallacies.* 2d ed. Grand Rapids: Baker, 1996. 148pp.

Practical and eminently usable discussion of the most common exegetical mistakes in the form of word-study fallacies, grammatical fallacies, logical fallacies, and presuppositional and historical fallacies. Indispensable for every seminary student, pastor, and teacher.

1.12.4   Coggins, R. J., and J. L. Houlden, eds. *A Dictionary of Biblical Interpretation.* Philadelphia: Trinity Press International, 1990. 748pp.

Deals with the ways the Bible has been interpreted throughout history and today. The articles, written by distinguished biblical scholars from Europe and North America and representing a cross-section of theological perspectives, are devoted to the history of interpretation of each book of the Bible, various interpretive methods and techniques, the main phases of biblical interpretation, major interpretive schools and movements, and significant interpreters of the Bible, both ancient and modern. Articles conclude with brief bibliographies.

1.12.5   Cotterell, Peter, and Max Turner. *Linguistics and Biblical Interpretation.* Downers Grove, Ill.: InterVarsity, 1989. 348pp.

Collaborative project by a linguist and an exegete, this book provides a solid introduction to the most current insights into the exegesis of Scripture from the perspective of contemporary linguistics. Deals with concept of meaning, and particularly meaning of words; significance to be assigned to author, text, and reader in pursuit of meaning of biblical passages; and significance of role of the broader discourse in the interpretation of a specific passage. By giving attention to newer developments in linguistics, it complements Caird's fine classic treatment (§1.12.2).

1.12.6 Hayes, John H., and Carl R. Holladay. *Biblical Exegesis: A Beginner's Handbook.* 3d ed. Louisville: Westminster John Knox, 2007. 236pp.

Written by leading OT and NT scholars, probably the most recognized basic introduction to exegetical method of the Bible as a whole. Provides orientation to the major aspects of interpretation from a mainstream critical approach. Although this edition gives some attention to the emerging methods, e.g., canonical criticism, and cultural, economic, ethnic, gender and sexual perspectives, it focuses primarily on the traditional grammatical- and historical-critical approaches. Includes a helpful appendix on the use of electronic technologies in exegesis.

1.12.7 McKenzie, Steven L., and Stephen R. Haynes, eds. *To Each Its Own Meaning: An Introduction to Biblical Criticisms and Their Application.* Louisville: Westminster John Knox, 1993. 251pp.

Informative introduction to the most significant methods of biblical criticism, giving attention to both historical and literary approaches. Each chapter is written by a leading practitioner of the method and addresses five issues: (1) description, history, and assumptions; (2) relation to other methods; (3) examples of the application of the method to specific passages; (4) drawbacks; (5) suggested further reading. Chapters suffer somewhat from brevity, but still the most useful introduction to the range of contemporary approaches.

1.12.8 Osborne, Grant R. *The Hermeneutical Spiral.* Rev. ed. Downers Grove, Ill.: InterVarsity, 2006, 624pp.

The most comprehensive, informed, and readable introduction to biblical interpretation from an evangelical perspective. Insists that biblical hermeneutics involve a constant spiral from text to contemporary application with the result that the interpreter progressively comes closer to the intended meaning of the biblical author. Deals with all major aspects of hermeneutics but gives special attention to the role of genre and to applied hermeneutics (i.e., biblical, systematic, contextual, and homiletical theology). Two appendixes address contemporary philosophical challenges to the notion of "fixed meanings" in biblical texts.

1.12.9 Thiselton, Anthony C. *New Horizons in Hermeneutics: The Theory and Practice of Transforming Biblical Reading.* Grand Rapids: Zondervan, 1992. 703pp.

A philosophically and historically informed textbook in advanced hermeneutics, and yet one that is concerned with the use of the Bible in the church and with practical questions about how readers engage biblical texts. Describes and evaluates all the major theoretical models and approaches in contemporary hermeneutics and shows how these models find expression in specific approaches to biblical passages and issues in biblical interpretation. Indispensable for a thorough understanding of contemporary hermeneutics.

1.12.10   Webb, William J. *Slaves, Women & Homosexuals: Exploring the Hermeneutics of Cultural Analysis.* Downers Grove, Ill: InterVarsity, 2001. 301pp.

Sets forth a thoughtful, comprehensive, and practical framework for identifying those aspects of biblical teachings that have continuing relevance for contemporary application from those that are so attached to their original cultural contexts that they cannot legitimately be taken up and directly applied. Appeals especially to the principle of redemptiveness as developed within the Bible itself. Uses the issues of slavery, women (in the family structure and in ministry), and homosexuality as test cases for the principles presented in the book.

Also Significant

1.12.11   Adam, A. K. M., Stephen E. Fowl, Kevin J. Vanhoozer, and Francis Watson. *Reading Scripture with the Church: Toward a Hermeneutic for Theological Interpretation.* Grand Rapids: Baker, 2006. 155pp.

1.12.12   Alter, Robert. *The World of Biblical Literature.* San Francisco: Harper, 1993. 225pp.

1.12.13   Barr, James. *The Semantics of Biblical Language.* London: SCM, 1961. 313pp.

1.12.14   Bartholomew, Craig, Colin Greene, and Karl Möller, *After Pentecost: Language & Biblical Interpretation.* Scripture and Hermeneutics Series, vol. 2. Grand Rapids: Zondervan, 2001. 425 pp.

1.12.15   ———, eds. *Renewing Biblical Interpretation.* Scripture and Hermeneutics Series, vol. 1. Grand Rapids: Zondervan, 2000. 366pp.

1.12.16 Bartholomew, Craig, C. Stephen Evans, Mary Healy, and Murray Rae, eds. *Behind the Text: History and Biblical Interpretation*. Scripture and Hermeneutics Series, vol. 4. Grand Rapids: Zondervan, 2003. 553pp.

1.12.17 Bartholomew, Craig, Scott Hahn, Robin Parry, Christopher Seitz, and Al Wolters, eds. *Canon and Biblical Interpretation*. Scripture and Hermeneutics Series, vol. 7. Grand Rapids: Zondervan, 2006. 445pp.

1.12.18 Barton, John, ed. *The Cambridge Companion to Biblical Interpretation*. Cambridge: Cambridge University Press, 1998. 338pp.

1.12.19 Dockery, David S. *Biblical Interpretation Then and Now: Contemporary Hermeneutics in the Light of the Early Church*. Grand Rapids: Baker, 1992. 247pp.

1.12.20 Fee, Gordon D., and Douglas Stuart. *How to Read the Bible for All Its Worth*. 3d ed. Grand Rapids: Zondervan, 2003. 287pp.

1.12.21 Goldingay, John. *Models for the Interpretation of Scripture*. Grand Rapids: Eerdmans, 1995. 328pp.

1.12.22 Goldsworthy, Graeme. *Gospel-Centered Hermeneutics: Foundations and Principles of Evangelical Biblical Interpretation*. Downers Grove, Ill: InterVarsity, 2006. 341pp.

1.12.23 Gorman, Michael J. *Elements of Biblical Exegesis: A Basic Guide for Students and Ministers*. Rev. ed. Peabody, Mass.: Hendrickson, 2009. 286pp.

1.12.24 Kaiser, Walter C., Jr. *Toward an Exegetical Theology: Biblical Exegesis for Preaching and Teaching*. Grand Rapids: Baker, 1981. 268pp.

1.12.25 Kaiser, Walter C., Jr., and Moisés Silva. *An Introduction to Biblical Hermeneutics: The Search for Meaning*. Rev. ed. Grand Rapids: Zondervan, 2007. 350pp.

1.12.26 Keener, Craig, and M. Daniel Carroll R., eds. *Global Voices: Reading the Bible in the Majority World*. Peabody, Mass.: Hendrickson, 2013. 144pp.

1.12.27 Klein, William W., Craig L. Blomberg, and Robert L. Hubbard. *Introduction to Biblical Interpretation*. Dallas: Word, 1993. 518pp.

1.12.28 Kuist, Howard T. *These Words upon Thy Heart: Scripture and the Christian Response*. Richmond, Va.: John Knox, 1947. 189pp.

1.12.29 Krentz, Edgar. *The Historical-Critical Method*. Guides to Biblical Scholarship. Philadelphia: Fortress, 1975. 88pp.

1.12.30 McCown, Wayne, and James Massey, eds. *God's Word for Today: An Inquiry into Hermeneutics from a Biblical Theological Perspective*. Wesleyan Theological Perspectives 2. Anderson, Ind.: Warner, 1982. 264pp.

1.12.31 Morgan, Robert, and John Barton. *Biblical Interpretation*. Oxford Bible Series. Oxford: Oxford University Press, 1988. 342pp.

1.12.32 Mulholland, M. Robert, Jr. *Shaped by the Word: The Power of Scripture in Spiritual Formation*. Rev. ed. Nashville: Upper Room, 2000. 176pp.

1.12.33 Porter, Stanley E., and Beth M. Stovell, eds. *Biblical Hermeneutics: Five Views*. Downers Grove, Ill: InterVarsity, 2012. 224pp.

1.12.34 Ramm, Bernard L. *Protestant Biblical Interpretation: A Textbook of Hermeneutics for Conservative Protestants*. 3d ed. Grand Rapids: Baker, 1970. 298pp.

1.12.35 Ricoeur, Paul. *Essays on Biblical Interpretation*. Philadelphia: Fortress, 1980. 182pp.

1.12.36 Scalise, Charles J. *From Scripture to Theology: A Canonical Journey into Hermeneutics*. Downers Grove, Ill: InterVarsity, 1996. 150pp.

1.12.37 ———. *Hermenetuics as Theological Prolegomena*. Macon, Ga: Mercer, 1994. 155pp.

1.12.38 Segovia, Fernando F., and Mary Ann Tolbert, eds. *Reading from This Place: Social Location and Biblical Interpretation in Global Perspective*. 2 vols. Minneapolis: Fortress, 1995. 321/365pp.

1.12.39   Silva, Moisés. *Biblical Words and Their Meaning: An Introduction to Lexical Semantics*. Rev. ed. Grand Rapids: Zondervan, 1994. 224pp.

1.12.40   ———. *God, Language, and Scripture: Reading the Bible in Light of General Linguistics*. Foundations of Contemporary Hermeneutics. Grand Rapids: Zondervan, 1990. 160pp.

1.12.41   Soulen, Richard N. *Handbook of Biblical Criticism*. 4th ed. Louisville: Westminster John Knox, 2011. 258pp.

1.12.42   Sternberg, Meir. *The Poetics of Biblical Narrative: Ideological Literature and the Drama of Reading*. Bloomington: Indiana University Press, 1985. 580pp.

1.12.43   Stuhlmacher, Peter. *Historical Criticism and the Theological Interpretation of Scripture*. Philadelphia: Fortress, 1977. 93pp.

1.12.44   Tate, W. Randolph. *Biblical Interpretation: An Integrated Approach*. 3d ed. Peabody, Mass.: Hendrickson, 2008. 380pp.

1.12.45   ———. *Handbook for Biblical Interpretation: An Essential Guide to Methods, Terms, and Concepts*. 2d ed. Grand Rapids: Baker, 2012. 544pp.

1.12.46   Terry, Milton S. *Biblical Hermeneutics*. New York: Eaton and Mains, 1911. 782pp.

1.12.47   Thompson, David L. *Bible Study That Works*. Rev. ed. Nappanee, Ind.: Evangel, 1994. 128pp.

1.12.48   Traina, Robert A. *Methodical Bible Study: A New Approach to Hermeneutics*. New York: Ganis & Harris, 1952. 269pp.

1.12.49   Vanhoozer, Kevin J. *Is There a Meaning in This Text? The Bible, the Reader, and the Morality of Literary Knowledge*. Grand Rapids: Zondervan, 1998. 496pp.

1.12.50   Wink, Walter. *Transforming Bible Study*. 2d ed. Nashville: Abingdon, 1989. 176pp.

1.12.51   Zimmerman, Jens. *Recovering Theological Hermeneutics: An Incarnational-Trinitarian Theory of Interpretation.* Grand Rapids: Baker, 2004. 345pp.

1.13   Biblical Theology and the Theological Use of the Bible

See also OLD TESTAMENT: EXEGETICAL METHOD/HERME-NEUTICS (§2.13); NEW TESTAMENT: EXEGETICAL METHOD/HERMENEUTICS (§4.12)

Highly Recommended

1.13.1   Alexander, T. Desmond, Brian S. Rosner, D. A. Carson, and Graeme Goldsworthy, eds. *New Dictionary of Biblical Theology: Exploring the Unity and Diversity of Scripture.* Downers Grove, Ill.: InterVarsity, 2000. 866pp.

The most comprehensive current dictionary on biblical theology from an evangelical perspective. Part 1 includes twelve major articles dealing with key issues of biblical theology; part 2 contains articles on major sections of the Bible as well as on the theology of the individual biblical books; and part 3 consists of articles on major biblical themes. Emphasizes the unity of the Bible's theology over against the tendency in some circles to stress diversity and perceived disunity between the biblical witnesses. The breadth of issues treated requires that many of the articles be given brief and somewhat cursory treatment. Written with an eye toward teaching and preaching within the context of the church.

1.13.2   Barr, James. *The Concept of Biblical Theology: An Old Testament Perspective.* Minneapolis: Fortress, 1999. 715pp.

Offers a comprehensive overview of biblical theology by tracing the development of the discipline of biblical theology, describing and critiquing the major contributors (e.g., von Rad, Childs, Brueggemann), and providing his own analysis of such key issues as the typologies for doing biblical theology, the role of the Apocrypha and Pseudepigrapha, the relationship between the OT and NT, and the biblical theology movement. As its subtitle suggests, gives relatively greater attention to the OT than the NT. Moreover, Barr is stronger in critique than in offering his own compelling program. Nevertheless, the best critical description of the history of biblical theology.

1.13.3   Bauer, Johannes Baptist, ed. *Encyclopedia of Biblical Theology: The Complete Sacramentum Verbi*. Rev. ed. New York: Crossroad, 1981. 1141pp.

Articles discuss the theologically most significant biblical words, with the intention of revealing the modes of thought of the biblical writers themselves. Contributors are among the most prominent scholars in the German-speaking world. Comparable in quality and in purpose to the *New Dictionary of Biblical Theology* (§1.13.1) but contributors represent critical German scholarship rather than American and British evangelicalism. Moreover, since this volume contains articles dealing only with biblical concepts it is more focused than the *New Dictionary*, and its individual articles tend to be more comprehensive and detailed.

1.13.4   Bright, John. *The Kingdom of God*. Nashville: Abingdon, 1953. 288pp.

This prominent OT scholar compellingly argues that the central and unifying theological concept in the whole of the Bible is the kingdom of God. He presents an articulate, cohesive, and insightful exposition of this concept. A model for the study of a biblical concept throughout the canon.

1.13.5   Childs, Brevard S. *Biblical Theology of the Old and New Testaments: Theological Reflection on the Christian Bible*. Minneapolis: Fortress, 1993. 745pp.

The first comprehensive biblical theology to appear in a generation. Argues that the fundamental issue in biblical theology is the relationship between the testaments, and that both testaments bear witness to Jesus Christ, but each in its distinctive way. Introductory chapters outline the history of biblical theology and set forth a new program for doing biblical theology. Then follow examples of exegesis done in the service of biblical theology and discussions of the major themes of the Christian Bible. The volume ends with discussion of what is involved in a holistic theological reading of the Christian Scriptures. The most significant recent contribution to biblical theology.

1.13.6   Cullmann, Oscar. *Salvation in History*. New York: Harper & Row, 1967. 352pp.

Written by a prominent New Testament scholar who emphasized the role of "salvation history"; i.e., that the history of God's redemptive acts on behalf of Israel coming to culmination in Jesus Christ is the central concern of the whole of biblical revelation. As such, the historical manifestation of Christ is the center and defining point of all history and of all human existence. This book offers the most compelling presentation of the salvation-history model of biblical theology, and is an excellent conceptual synthesis of the entire biblical revelation.

1.13.7   Marshall, I. Howard. *Beyond the Bible: Moving from Scripture to Theology.* Grand Rapids: Baker, 2004. 136pp.

Explores the issues involved in the church's need to move beyond the Bible to its systematic theology. In the process Marshall presents his own approach for doing so, a modified foundationalism that seeks to allow the Bible itself to suggest the trajectory to systematic theology. The book concludes with responses from Kevin Vanhoozer and Stanley Porter.

1.13.8   Mead, James K. *Biblical Theology: Issues, Methods, and Themes.* Louisville: Westminster John Knox, 2007. 328pp.

Perhaps the most helpful introduction to the discipline of biblical theology at the beginning of the twenty-first century. Discusses the problems and challenges of biblical theology, the history of the discipline, the most significant approaches to biblical theology, and the prospects for the future of biblical theology.

1.13.9   Vanhoozer, Kevin J., ed. *Dictionary for Theological Interpretation of the Bible.* Grand Rapids: Baker, 2005. 896pp.

Attempts to bridge the "ugly ditch" between biblical studies and the faithful life of the church by probing the connection between the biblical presentation and the theological significance of each of the biblical books and by examining the various hermeneutical approaches, major interpreters and interpretive communities, and a range of doctrines and themes.

1.13.10   Watson, Francis. *Truth and Text: Redefining Biblical Theology.* Grand Rapids: Eerdmans, 1997. 344pp.

Rejects the tendency in recent times to divorce biblical studies from systematic theology, arguing that biblical theology must be an interdisciplinary approach that maintains the essential distinctives of the OT, the NT, and systematics, but at the same time relates them in a holistic process of ascertaining Christian truth. From this perspective, Watson discusses in the first part of the volume certain specific issues in hermeneutics from an explicitly theological perspective, and in the second part he explores the Christian theological use of the OT. Challenging, groundbreaking work pertaining to the way in which the Bible must function theologically in the church.

Also Significant

1.13.11   Achtemeier, Paul J., and Elizabeth Achtemeier. *The Old Testament Roots of Our Faith.* Rev. ed. Peabody, Mass.: Hendrickson, 1995. 142pp.

1.13.12   Childs, Brevard S. *Biblical Theology: A Proposal.* Facets. Minneapolis: Fortress, 2002. 96pp.

1.13.13   ———. *Biblical Theology in Crisis.* Philadelphia: Fortress, 1970. 255pp.

1.13.14   Feldmeier, Reinhard, and Hermann Spieckermann. *God of the Living: A Biblical Theology.* Waco, TX: Baylor University Press, 2011. 612pp.

1.13.15   Gerhardsson, Birger. *The Ethos of the Bible.* Philadelphia: Fortress, 1981. 152pp.

1.13.16   Goldsworthy, Graeme. *Christ-Centered Biblical Theology: Hermeneutical Foundations and Principles.* Downers Grove, Ill: InterVarsity, 2012. 251pp.

1.13.17   Hafemann, Scott J., ed. *Biblical Theology: Retrospect and Prospect.* Downers Grove, Ill.: InterVarsity, 2002. 304pp.

1.13.18   Hafemann, Scott J., and Paul R. House, eds. *Central Themes in Biblical Theology: Mapping Unity in Diversity.* Grand Rapids: Baker, 2007. 329pp.

1.13.19   Hanson, Paul D. *The Diversity of Scripture: A Theological Interpretation.* Overtures to Biblical Theology. Philadelphia: Fortress, 1982. 157pp.

1.13.20   Kaiser, Walter C., Jr. *The Promise-Plan of God: A Biblical Theology of the Old and New Testaments.* Grand Rapids: Zondervan, 2008. 419pp.

1.13.21   Klink, Edward W., III, and Darian R. Lockett. *Understanding Biblical Theology: A Comparison of Theory and Practice.* Grand Rapids: Zondervan, 2012. 192pp.

1.13.22   Kraftchick, Steven J., Charles D. Myers Jr., and Ben C. Ollenburger, eds. *Biblical Theology: Problems and Perspectives, in Honor of J. Christiaan Beker.* Nashville: Abingdon, 1995. 336pp.

1.13.23   Léon-Dufour, Xavier. *Dictionary of Biblical Theology.* 2d ed. New York: Seabury, 1973. 617pp.

1.13.24   Meadors, Gary T., ed. *Four Views on Moving Beyond the Bible to Theology.* Grand Rapids: Zondervan, 2009. 369pp.

1.13.25   Nürnberg, Klaus. *Theology of the Biblical Witness: An Evolutionary Approach.* Münster: LIT, 2002. 439pp.

1.13.26   O'Collins, Gerald, and Daniel Kendall. *The Bible for Theology: Ten Principles for the Theological Use of Scripture.* New York: Paulist, 1997. 208pp.

1.13.27   Perdue, Leo G., Robert Morgan, and Benjamin D. Sommer. *Biblical Theology: Introducing the Conversation.* Nashville: Abingdon, 2009. 337pp.

1.13.28   Reumann, John. *The Promise and Practice of Biblical Theology.* Philadelphia: Fortress, 1991. 214pp.

1.13.29   Schreiner, Thomas R. *The King in His Beauty: A Biblical Theology of the Old and New Testaments.* Grand Rapids: Baker, 2013. 752pp.

1.13.30   Scobie, Charles H. H. *The Ways of Our God: An Approach to Biblical Theology.* Grand Rapids: Eerdmans, 2003. 1038pp.

1.13.31   Seitz, Christopher. *The Character of Christian Scripture: The Significance of a Two-Testament Scripture.* Grand Rapids: Baker, 2011. 218pp.

1.13.32   Stuhlmacher, Peter. *How to Do Biblical Theology.* Allison Park, Pa.: Pickwick, 1995. 95pp.

1.13.33   Treier, Daniel J. *Introducing Theological Interpretation of Scripture: Recovering a Christian Practice.* Grand Rapids: Baker, 2008. 221pp.

1.13.34   Turner, George Allen. *The Vision Which Transforms: Is Christian Perfection Scriptural?* Kansas City, Mo.: Beacon Hill, 1964. 348pp.

1.13.35   Vos, Geerhardus. *Biblical Theology: Old and New Testaments.* Grand Rapids: Eerdmans, 1948. 426pp.

45

1.13.36   Watson, Francis. *Text, Church, and World: Biblical Interpretation in Theological Perspective*. Grand Rapids: Eerdmans, 1994. 366pp.

1.14   Biblical Ethics

Highly Recommended

1.14.1   Birch, Bruce C., and Larry L. Rasmussen. *Bible and Ethics in the Christian Life*. Rev. ed. Minneapolis: Augsburg, 1989. 239pp.

The result of collaboration between an ethicist (Rasmussen) and a biblical scholar (Birch), this volume attempts to bridge the gap between biblical studies and ethics by clarifying the major issues that are involved and by offering specific guidance for the church's use of the Bible for its ethical decisions. Deals with the task and process of using the Bible for ethics rather than discussing specific contemporary ethical issues. A most helpful, readable introduction.

1.14.2   Green, Joel B., ed. *Dictionary of Scripture and Ethics*. Grand Rapids: Baker, 2011. 889pp.

The most comprehensive reference work available on the Bible and ethics. Begins with major introductory essays on "Ethics in Scripture," "Scripture in Ethics: A History," and "Scripture in Ethics: Methodological Issues," followed by an alphabetical listing of articles on the relation of ethics to Scripture, ethics within Scripture, and issues in Christian ethics. Each article concludes with a brief bibliography. Contributors represent both biblical scholars and ethicists.

1.14.3   McDonald, J. I. H. *Biblical Interpretation and Christian Ethics*. Cambridge: Cambridge University Press, 1993. 305pp.

Probes the issues involved in using the Bible for ethical decision making by tracing the history of the enterprise from the liberalism of the eighteenth and nineteenth centuries, through the emphasis on an eschatological ethic that was prominent at the beginning of the twentieth century, to the present stress on the ways in which the cultural and personal participation of the reader of the Bible fundamentally determines how one can and should use the Bible as a guide for ethics. Includes many examples that employ specific ethical issues. Assumes something of an evolutionary model according to which the earlier periods are judged in light of the most recent developments and these recent developments are given the greatest approval. Nevertheless, extremely helpful critical review of the history of the relation between biblical interpretation and ethics, and one that greatly illumines the task of deriving ethics from Scripture.

1.14.4   Siker, Jeffrey S. *Scripture and Ethics: Twentieth-Century Portraits.* New York: Oxford, 1997. 294pp.

Describes how the Bible has actually functioned in theological ethics in the twentieth century by exploring how eight of the century's most influential theologians have appropriated Scripture for ethics; these include Reinhold Niebuhr, H. Richard Niebuhr, Bernard Häring, Paul Ramsey, Stanley Hauerwas, Gustavo Gutierrez, James Cone, and Rosemary Radford Reuther. In each case Siker explores which biblical passages were used, the ways in which these texts were employed, the view of the Bible's authority, the hermeneutic employed, and the practical ethical results. Each chapter includes critical evaluation. Although one might quibble about the choice of theologians selected in this book, still it is helpful not only as historical review but as the basis for clarification of the issues and for the constructing of one's own approach. Might be supplemented by Spohn's volume (§1.14.11), which includes other prominent theologians (e.g., Bonhoeffer) but treats them more briefly and less critically than does Siker's approach.

Also Significant

1.14.5   Bretzke, James T. *Bibliography on Scripture and Christian Ethics.* Studies in Religion and Theology. Lewiston, Pa.: Mellen, 1997. 364pp.

1.14.6   Brown, William P., ed. *Character & Scripture: Moral Formation, Community, and Biblical Interpretation.* Grand Rapids: Eerdmans, 2002. 440pp.

1.14.7   ———. *The Ethos of the Cosmos: The Genesis of Moral Imagination in the Bible.* Grand Rapids: Eerdmans, 1999. 458pp.

1.14.8   Everding, H. Edward, Jr., and Dana W. Wilbanks. *Decision-Making and the Bible.* Valley Forge, Pa.: Judson, 1975. 160pp.

1.14.9   Ogletree, Thomas W. *The Use of the Bible in Christian Ethics.* Philadelphia: Westminster, 1983. 220pp.

1.14.10 Sleeper, C. Freeman. *The Bible and the Moral Life*. Louisville: Westminster John Knox, 1992. 181pp.

1.14.11 Spohn, William C. *What Are They Saying about Scripture and Ethics?* Rev. ed. New York: Paulist, 1995. 142pp.

1.14.12 Swartley, Willard M. *Slavery, Sabbath, War, and Women: Case Issues in Biblical Interpretation*. Scottsdale, Pa.: Herald, 1983. 366pp.

1.15 Bible Commentaries: One-Volume

Highly Recommended

1.15.1 Brown, Raymond E., Joseph A. Fitzmyer, and Roland E. Murphy, eds. *The New Jerome Biblical Commentary*. Englewood Cliffs, N.J.: Prentice-Hall, 1990. 1484pp.

The best single-volume commentary available from the Roman Catholic tradition, with articles written by leading Roman Catholic scholars. Includes introductory topical articles dealing with background issues. Interpretations employ critical approaches, especially source, form, redaction, and textual criticism, and give attention to the range of interpretations among Roman Catholic scholars. More technical and with less emphasis on theology and application than is the case with most single-volume commentaries, but the consistently high quality of the scholarship makes this a most impressive and, in respect to critical and historical issues, helpful volume.

1.15.2 Carpenter, Eugene, and Wayne McCown, eds. *Asbury Bible Commentary*. Grand Rapids: Zondervan, 1992. 1246pp.

Represents the best current biblical scholarship from the Wesleyan tradition. Although the articles are somewhat uneven in quality, most of them are (given the limits of space) remarkably insightful in their exposition of the theological message of the text and are useful even to students outside of the Wesleyan tradition. The general articles stress theological and hermeneutical issues rather than historical or cultural ones; especially helpful is the discussion on the place and functions of Scripture (in the Wesleyan tradition).

1.15.3 Gaventa, Bevery Roberts, and David Peterson, eds. *The New Interpreter's Bible One Volume Commentary*. Nashville: Abingdon, 2010. 1068pp.

An extremely helpful guide to the basic meaning and function of passages for teaching and preaching in the church. For each book of the Bible (and the Apocrypha), provides an overview of contents and outline, followed by passage-by-passage explanation, concluding with a brief bibliography. Reference is made to the Hebrew and Greek, but with clear explanation. Interprets passages in light of historical background, higher-critical considerations, book and canonical contexts. Volume concludes with general articles on matters such as the canon of the OT, Hebrew legal literature, and cultures of the Greco-Roman world. Contributors represent a theological group who are moderately critical, and committed to the central role of the Bible in the life of the church. Thus, they have a concern for the theological meaning of the text.

1.15.4   Mays, James Luther, ed. *HarperCollins Bible Commentary*. Rev. ed. San Francisco: HarperSanFrancisco, 2000. 1203pp.

Commissioned by the Society of Biblical Literature, this volume is an authoritative single-volume commentary. Includes commentary on the OT Apocrypha. Contains helpful background articles on the literary, cultural, and historical context of the Bible. Somewhat less technical and more concerned to ascertain the essential meaning and function of passages than is *The New Jerome Biblical Commentary* (§1.15.1), but not necessarily more theological than the latter.

1.15.5   Tukunboh, Adeyemo, ed. *Africa Bible Commentary.* Grand Rapids: Zondervan, 2006. 1585pp.

Written by seventy African scholars, all evangelical and involved in ministry within the church. Produced for a broad range of readers: pastors, seminarians, theologians, lay preachers, and Christian educators. Commentary moves through the Bible passage by passage, with little attention to the structure of books or passages, but with constant references to related passages throughout the canon. Contributors attempt to explain the original sense of the text, yet their expositions are informed by their experience with African culture and religion. The text is applied to Christians in an African context. Helpful for non-African readers by providing insight into interpretation by those in another culture and exposure to the applicatory moves by those in an African context.

Also Significant

1.15.6   Bruce, F. F. *The International Bible Commentary with the New International Version*. Grand Rapids: Zondervan, 1986. 1269pp.

1.15.7   Burge, Gary M., and Andrew E. Hill, eds. *The Baker Illustrated Bible Commentary.* Grand Rapids: Baker, 2012. 1635pp.

1.15.8   Carson, D. A., R. T. France, Gordon J. Wenham, J. A. Motyer, eds. *New Bible Commentary: 21st Century Edition.* Downers Grove, Ill.: InterVarsity, 1994. 1455pp.

1.15.9   Elwell, Walter A., ed. *Evangelical Commentary on the Bible.* Grand Rapids: Baker, 1989. 1229pp.

1.15.10   Farmer, William R., ed. *International Bible Commentary: A Catholic and Ecumenical Commentary for the Twenty-first Century.* Collegeville, Minn.: Liturgical Press, 1998. 1918pp.

1.15.11   Mills, Watson E., and Richard F. Wilson, eds. *Mercer Commentary on the Bible.* Macon, Ga.: Mercer University Press, 1995. 1347pp.

1.15.12   Radmacher, Earl D., ed. *Nelson's New Illustrated Bible Commentary.* Nashville: Thomas Nelson, 1999. 1804pp.

1.16   Bible Commentaries: Multivolume

Highly Recommended

1.16.1   Calvin, John. *Calvin's Commentaries.* 45 vols. in 22. Grand Rapids: Baker, 1979. (Originally published in Latin and French, ca. 1550–1555.) Volumes average 500pp.

Bible students should consult commentaries from a variety of periods of the church, and Calvin was the most authoritative, comprehensive, informed, and insightful commentator of the Reformation period. Calvin is uniformly clear and concise, with a keen theological interest and a pastoral concern.

1.16.2   Gaebelein, Frank E., and J. D. Douglas, eds. *The Expositor's Bible Commentary.* 12 vols. Grand Rapids: Zondervan, 1979. Volumes average 600pp.

The most comprehensive and academically solid multivolume commentary from a thoroughly conservative evangelical perspective. Contributors represent both the Reformed and Wesleyan-Arminian traditions. The commentary stresses the basic meaning of passages by focusing on the significance of the original language (primarily in terms of lexicography, but also with some concern for grammatical structure and syntax), historical background, and relation to other biblical passages. Brief "notes" discuss more technical text-critical, terminological, hermeneutical, and theological issues. Little explicit attention given to theological implications or application.

1.16.3   Keck, Leander E. et al., eds. *The New Interpreter's Bible*. 12 vols. Nashville: Abingdon, 1994–2002. Volumes average 1000pp.

The most comprehensive and respected of the multivolume commentaries. Written by leading biblical scholars, contributions are readable and accessible to pastors and professional academicians alike. Includes comment on the apocryphal/deuterocanonical books. On each passage, provides "commentary" (exegetical "close reading" employing various methods, e.g., historical-critical, literary, sociological) and "reflection" (significance for contemporary faith and life). In contrast to the original edition of *The Interpreter's Bible* (§1.16.4), the reflection here grows directly out of what is said in the commentary. Contributors represent a broad spectrum of Christian traditions (including evangelical).

Also Significant

1.16.4   Buttrick, George Arthur, ed. *The Interpreter's Bible (IB)*. 12 vols. Nashville: Abingdon, 1952. Volumes average 1000pp. (Replaced by *The New Interpreter's Bible* [§1.16.3].)

1.16.5   Carter, Charles W., ed. *The Wesleyan Bible Commentary*. 7 vols. Grand Rapids: Eerdmans, 1964–1969. Volumes average 650pp.

1.16.6   Clarke, Adam. *Clarke's Commentary*. 8 vols. London: Butterworth, 1810–1825. Volumes average 1000pp.

1.16.7   Lange, John Peter et al. *A Commentary on the Holy Scriptures: Critical, Doctrinal, and Homiletical*. Translated from the German, and edited, with additions, by Philip Schaff et al. 24 vols. New York: Scribners, 1865–1879. Volumes average 800pp.

1.16.8   Patte, Daniel, ed. *Global Bible Commentary*. Nashville: Abingdon, 2004. 570pp.

1.16.9   Purkiser, W. T., Ralph Earle, and A. F. Harper, eds. *Beacon Bible Commentary*. 10 vols. Kansas City, Mo.: Beacon Hill, 1969. Volumes average 600pp.

1.17   Bible Commentaries: Series

Highly Recommended

1.17.1   Ancient Christian Commentary on Scripture (ACCS). Edited by Thomas C. Oden. 29 vols. Downers Grove, Ill.: InterVarsity, 1998–2009. Volumes average 250pp.

Recently scholars have recognized the value of ancient commentary, especially from the Fathers. Much of this material that has been unavailable or hard to find has now become accessible through this series. Each passage receives one or more brief quotations from the Fathers, with selection on the basis of depth of insight, value for theological instruction, "rhetorical power," representation of "consensual exegesis" of the early church, enrichment for preaching and teaching, and inclusion of commentators from various early Eastern, Western, and African churches. Each quote is referenced so that readers can examine it in its context. Volumes are appearing in rapid succession.

1.17.2   Ancient Christian Texts. Edited by Thomas C. Oden and Gerald L. Bray. 11 vols. currently available. Downers Gover, Ill.: InterVarsity, 2009–. Volumes average 275pp.

Companion series to Ancient Christian Commentary on Scripture (§1.17.1). Whereas the earlier series provided short excerpts from various ancient interpreters this series gives over each biblical book to a single ancient writer. The series includes full-length commentaries or sermons based on entire books or extended passages by writers such as Ambriosiaster, John of Damascas, and Origen.

1.17.3   Asia Bible Commentary Series. Edited by Bruce J. Nichols. 14 vols. currently available. Manila: Asia Theological Association, 2007–. Volumes average 375pp.

Reliable, informed commentaries written by Asian evangelical scholars and produced especially for seminary students and pastors to facilitate understanding of the message of the text and its significance for Christians in an Asian context. Emphasizes meaning of passages within their literary, canonical, and historical contexts, often with specific reference to application to Asian Christians. Series makes fine Asian scholarship accessible to those in other cultural locations.

1.17.4   Brazos Theological Commentary on the Bible. Edited by R. R. Reno et al. 18 vols. currently available. Grand Rapids: Brazos, 2005–. Volumes average 275pp.

The purpose of the series is to provide an interpretation of the Bible as the church's Scripture informed by dogmatic theology. Accordingly constant reference is made to the theological tradition of the church from the Fathers to the present. Volumes vary greatly in terms of helpfulness for the interpretation of the biblical text. Some contributors use dialogue with the theological tradition of the church to elucidate well the sense of the text, while others use motifs or topics mentioned in a passage as a springboard for theological reflection that has little to do with the communicative intent of the biblical passage under consideration.

1.17.5   The Church's Bible. Edited by Robert Louis Wilken. 4 vols. currently available. Grand Rapids, Eerdmans, 2003–. Volumes average 340pp.

Like the Ancient Christian Commentary on Scripture (§1.17.1), this series seeks to acquaint modern readers with interpretations from the early church. This series differs from the Ancient Christian Commentary by including writers through the first Christian millennium (rather than to 750 CE) and limiting contributions to commentaries or homilies on entire biblical books. This series also includes longer excerpts than does the Ancient Christian Commentary. Volumes are appearing very slowly.

1.17.6   The Concordia Commentary Series. Edited by Dean O. Wenthe. 25 vols. currently available. St. Louis, Mo.: Concordia, 2005–. Volumes average 600pp.

Written for pastors and teachers from a conservative Lutheran perspective. Interprets individual passages within a broadly canonical setting out of the conviction that Scripture's unity centers around its witness to Jesus Christ. Attends to the original languages; but is made understandable to those who have no knowledge of these languages. Gives explicit attention to contemporary application. Some readers may discern a tendency at points to read the NT into the OT or to allow Lutheran theology to direct interpretation.

1.17.7   Cornerstone Biblical Commentary (CBC). Edited by Philip W. Comfort. 18 vols. Carol Stream, Ill: Tyndale House, 2005–2012. Volumes average 500pp.

Contributors represent a range of theological traditions within evangelicalism. The "Notes" include discussion on linguistic, historical, or contextual matters; while the "Commentary" offers lucid interpretation, with some attention to theological significance. Generally two to three biblical books are treated within each volume; and the text of the New Living Translation is printed within the commentary. These considerations suggest that space for commentary is limited. Yet the authors are able to include the most pertinent explanation, and sometimes offer truly original insights into the text.

1.17.8   The Expositor's Bible. Edited by W. Robertson Nicoll. 25 vols. New York: Armstrong, 1903. Volumes average 400pp.

A classic work written by the most prominent British biblical scholars at the turn of the twentieth century. Combines the most solid exegetical insights with theological and pastoral concerns. Excellent for exposure to aspects of the text that might be missed by persons whose focus is determined almost exclusively by the framework of the twenty-first century.

1.17.9   International Theological Commentary (ITC). Edited by Fredrick Carlson Holmgren and George A. F. Knight. 28 vols. Grand Rapids: Eerdmans, 1983–1998. Volumes average 185pp.

Contributors represent critical scholars from twenty countries. After brief introduction to the biblical book with discussion of authorship, date, etc., commentary moves section by section, setting forth basic meaning of passage in its literary context, noting most significant exegetical and historical issues, but giving primary attention to theological meaning and contemporary significance. Responsible and reliable, but also brief and therefore tends toward either superficial or highly selective treatment.

1.17.10   The New American Commentary: An Exegetical and Theological Exposition of Holy Scripture (NAC). Edited by David S. Dockery. 31 vols. presently available. Nashville: Broadman, 1991–. Volumes average 450pp.

Contributors represent some of the most significant conservative biblical scholars from the Baptist tradition in America. Assumes inerrancy of Scripture. Emphasizes most important exegetical issues involving theological meaning of the text, which in turn leads to contemporary application and suggestions for preaching and teaching. Written primarily for pastors and interested laypersons. Footnotes reference major current works in biblical studies.

1.17.11   New Beacon Bible Commentary. Edited by Alex Varughese, Roger Hahn, and George Lyons. 46 vols. (13 vols. currently available.) Kansas City, Mo.: Beacon Hill, 2008–. Volumes average 275pp.

Written by scholars within the evangelical Wesleyan tradition (with the majority of contributors from the Church of the Nazarene). Although this series employs the New International Version, the focus is upon the exegesis of the text from the original languages. Introductions to each book include discussion of authorship, date, hermeneutical issues, and theology. The commentary itself has three sections. "Behind the Text" explores historical background, context, and other literary features. "In the Text" provides verse-by-verse explanation on the basis of grammatical, lexical, contextual, and canonical considerations. "From the Text" offers theological significance, history of interpretation, and contemporary appropriation. Reliable and helpful for pastors and teachers.

1.17.12   New International Biblical Commentary. Edited by Robert L. Hubbard Jr. and Robert K. Johnston. 29 vols. presently available (including all of New Testament). Peabody, Mass.: Hendrickson, 1988–. Volumes average 400pp.

Written by prominent biblical scholars who respect the text as the church's Scripture and are concerned with preaching and teaching within the church. Directed primarily at general readers, with section-by-section comments discussing the basic meaning of the text in its literary, historical, and canonical contexts. Includes few brief technical notes on text-critical issues and language. Contains select bibliography.

1.17.13   The NIV Application Commentary. Edited by Terry Muck. 40 vols. currently available. Grand Rapids: Zondervan, 1994–. Volumes average 325pp.

Represents evangelical perspective, with many leading evangelical biblical scholars among the contributors. Attempts to assist readers in moving from original meaning to contemporary application in informed and responsible ways. Treats each passage in terms of "original significance" (original meaning derived from language, historical background, context, etc.), "bridging contexts" (which reflects on the process of applying the ancient passage to today's world), and "contemporary significance" (which identifies contemporary situations that are comparable to those encountered in the text and explores various possible applications). Generally very useful for teaching and preaching, though quality of both interpretation and application varies from volume to volume. Clearly written, accessible to nonspecialists. Series is now complete in the NT; OT volumes continue to appear.

1.17.14 Reformation Commentary on the Scriptures. Edited by Timothy George. 28 vols. (3 vols. currently available.) Downers Grove, Ill.: InterVarsity, 2011–. Volumes average 450pp.

A sequel to Ancient Christian Commentary on the Scriptures (§1.17.1), this series moves through biblical books passage by passage, offering brief comments from various leaders of the Reformation. Seeks to include a broad range of Reformation writers from the mid-fifteenth century to the mid-seventeenth century. Lutheran, Reformed, Anabaptist, and Anglican voices are represented. While Luther, Calvin, Melancthon, and Bullinger are well represented, other less familiar persons are also included, sometimes for the first time in English translation. Helpful in making available material that is widely dispersed and often not very accessible. The comments are necessarily brief and highly selective.

1.17.15 The Two Horizons Commentary. Edited by J. Gordon McConville and Craig Bartholomew (Old Testament) and Joel B. Green and Max Turner (New Testament). 8 vols. currently available. Grand Rapids: Eerdmans, 2005–. Volumes average 250pp.

Seeks to combine traditional grammatical-historical considerations with theological significance as derived from conversation with the church's reading of its Scripture past and present. Attends to the role of individual biblical books within the theology of the entire canon and their employment and influence within historical and systematic theology. The specific manner in which theological significance is developed varies from volume to volume. Complements well the majority of scholarly commentaries that tend to give relatively little attention to interaction with the theological tradition of the church.

Series Whose Individual Volumes Are Frequently Included in Lists on Specific Books

1.17.16 The Anchor Bible: A New Translation with Introduction and Commentary. Edited by William Foxwell Albright and David Noel Freedman. Garden City, N.Y.: Doubleday, 1964–.

1.17.17   Hermeneia: A Critical and Historical Commentary on the Bible. Edited by Frank Moore Cross and Helmut Koester. Minneapolis: Fortress, 1971–.

1.17.18   The International Critical Commentary. Original series edited by S. R. Driver, Alfred Plummer, and Charles A. Briggs, 1895–1951. New series edited by J. A. Emerton, C. E. B. Cranfield, and Graham N. Stanton. Edinburgh: T&T Clark, 1975–.

1.17.19   Interpretation: A Bible Commentary for Teaching and Preaching. Edited by James Luther Mays. Louisville: Westminster John Knox, 1983–2005.

1.17.20   New Century Bible. Edited by Ronald E. Clements and Matthew Black. Grand Rapids: Eerdmans, 1967–.

1.17.21   Smyth & Helwys Commentary. Edited by R. Scott Nash. Macon, Ga.: Smyth & Helwys. 2000–.

1.17.22   Word Biblical Commentaries. Edited by Bruce M. Metzger. Nashville: Thomas Nelson, 1982–.

With commentary series, it is generally advisable to select individual volumes rather than purchase the whole set; individual volumes tend to vary in terms of quality and usefulness.

1.17.23   Extended commentary by select church fathers (e.g., St. Augustine and St. John Chrysostom) is available in *The Nicene and Post-Nicene Fathers*. Series 1, 14 vols., edited by Philip Schaff. Series 2, 14 vols., edited by Philip Schaff and Henry Wace. Peabody, Mass.: Hendrickson, 1994.

2
The Old Testament

2.1   Bibliographic Helps

See also PERIODICALS (§2.2); HISTORY OF THE CANON AND HISTORY OF INTERPRETATION (§2.3); OLD TESTAMENT INTRODUCTIONS (§2.14)

Highly Recommended

2.1.1   Brooke, George J., ed. *Society for Old Testament Study Booklist, 2002.* Sheffield: JSOT, 2002. 240pp.

Published annually by the Society of Old Testament Studies, includes annotations of various books pertaining to OT study, including archaeology, history, geography, sociology, texts and versions, exegesis, literary criticism, introductions, life and thought of surrounding peoples, Apocrypha and postbiblical studies, philosophy, and grammar. Annotations written by leading OT scholars (mostly British). Annotations are concise but descriptive and evaluative.

2.1.2   Childs, Brevard S. *Old Testament Books for Pastor and Teacher.* Philadelphia: Westminster, 1977. 120pp.

Select annotated bibliography dealing with various types of resources for OT study, but with emphasis on commentaries. Provides practical assistance for pastors in the building of their libraries, but is of value for scholars as well. Prioritizes and critically evaluates works on the basis of their usefulness for preaching and teaching in the church. Gives attention to older works (including ancient ones) as well as modern. Although some-what dated, it remains indispensable.

2.1.3   Longman, Tremper, III. *Old Testament Commentary Survey.* 5th ed. Grand Rapids: Baker, 2013. 176pp.

Highly selective annotated bibliography of works pertaining to various aspects of OT study, including introductions, surveys, theologies, diction-aries, translations, and computer software, but focuses especially on com-mentaries. Annotations include description of purpose, audience, and use, and critically evaluate the work on the basis of value for pastor's library, grading each work according to a five-star system. Written from conserva-tive evangelical stance, but includes works from various theological per-spectives. Annotations are fair, balanced, and very useful.

2.1.4   Mills, Watson E., ed. *Bibliographies for Biblical Research: Old Testament Series.* 17 vols. Lewiston, N.Y.: Mellen, 2002. Volumes average 100pp.

Invaluable to anyone searching for scholarly treatments of an OT pas-sage. Cites journal articles, essays in collected works, monographs, and commentaries throughout the twentieth century, although preference is given to more recent works; the citations from the last third of the century greatly outnumber those from the first third. Selection is made on the basis of helpfulness in understanding the biblical text and biblical backgrounds. Lists works in all European languages, without annotations. The final vol-ume is given over to an author index.

2.1.5   ———. *Bibliographies for Biblical Research: Periodical Literature for the Study of the Old Testament.* 17 vols. Lewiston, N.Y.: Mellen, 2002. Vol-umes average 90pp.

Similar in format to *Bibliographies for Biblical Research: Old Testament Se-ries* (§2.1.4), citing works published in periodical literature throughout the twentieth century, but limited to journal articles (arranged by chapter and verse citation). Many of the same articles appear in these two works, but without complete overlap in that some articles are cited in only one of these two resources. Cites English, French, German, and Italian articles. The final volume is given over to an author index.

Also Significant

2.1.6   Barker, Kenneth L., Bruce K. Waltke, and Roy B. Zuck. *Bibliography for Old Testament Exegesis and Exposition.* 4th ed. Dallas: Dallas Theological Seminary, 1979. 66pp.

2.1.7   Hostetter, Edwin C. *Old Testament Introduction*. IBR Bibliographies 11. Grand Rapids: Baker, 1995. 106pp.

2.1.8   Zannoni, Arthur E. *The Old Testament: A Bibliography*. Collegeville, Minn.: Michael Glazier, 1992. 277pp.

2.2   Periodicals

2.2.1   *Journal for the Study of the Old Testament*. 1976–. Quarterly.

Published by the Department of Biblical Studies at the University of Sheffield. Contributors employ various approaches, including the older, established ones (e.g., redaction criticism), but especially the emerging methods (e.g., literary criticism). Serious academic explorations of the meaning of the text. Gives little to no attention to historical background, archaeology, or surrounding cultures. Also gives little specific attention to theological issues. Contributors largely from the British Isles. Language: English. Book reviews: none.

2.2.2   *Old Testament Abstracts*. 1978–. 3 issues/year.

Published by the Catholic Biblical Association in Washington, D.C., contains abstracts of articles and books pertaining to the OT and related fields. Each issue lists more than three hundred journal articles (from approximately three hundred journals) and about fifty books. Annotations are brief, but helpful, and are descriptive rather than evaluative.

2.2.3   *Vetus Testamentum*. 1951–. Quarterly.

Published by Brill Academic Publishers at Leiden, the Netherlands; academic, technical, and authoritative. Employs a variety of critical methods in the study of the biblical text and other matters pertinent to OT study. Little explicit attention given to theological issues. Languages: English, French, German, and Dutch. Book reviews: few.

2.3   History of the Canon and History of Interpretation

See also INTRODUCTIONS (§2.14)

Highly Recommended

2.3.1   Baker, David W., and Bill T. Arnold, eds. *The Face of Old Testament Studies: A Survey of Contemporary Approaches*. Grand Rapids: Baker Academic, 1999. 512pp.

Fine introduction to recent developments in various areas of OT study. Focuses upon mainline critical scholarship, but includes more conservative voices. Contributors are generally evangelical; and all adopt a reverential perspective towards the text and its claims.

2.3.2　Beckwith, Roger T. *The Old Testament Canon of the New Testament Church and Its Background in Early Judaism.* Grand Rapids: Eerdmans, 1985. 529pp.

The most comprehensive and informed study available on the several issues involved in the church's canon of OT Scriptures. Treats in the process the notion of the canon and the process of canonization in early Judaism. Deals with the historical development of the debate on the canon, the concept of canon, the structure of the canon, and the disputes pertaining to included and excluded books. Indispensable for any study of these issues.

2.3.3　Clements, Ronald E. *One Hundred Years of Old Testament Interpretation.* Philadelphia: Westminster, 1976. 152pp.

Readable narrative history of scholarship from Wellhausen to 1976 pertaining to major areas of OT study (Pentateuch, historical books, prophets, psalms, wisdom literature, and OT theology), giving approximately equal attention to each of these areas. Emphasizes the interdependence of critical methods, and argues that these critical methods were intended to be instruments of faith and can be used to shed light on the nature of biblical faith. Mostly descriptive, but with some modest evaluation. Should be supplemented with *The Hebrew Bible and Its Modern Interpreters* (§2.3.5) and *Text in Context* (§2.3.6) for more recent work.

2.3.4　Gignilliat, Mark S. *A Brief History of Old Testament Criticism: From Benedict Spinoza to Brevard Childs.* Grand Rapids: Zondervan, 2012. 186pp.

Presents seven significant OT scholars, each representing a major trend in OT study over the past three hundred years. The chapters discuss biographical, philosophical, methodological, and hermeneutical matters. Places the work of the scholar (and the movement he represents) in the context of the broader history of ideas. Written by an evangelical who deals with the various scholars in a fair and accurate manner. Each chapter concludes with a brief bibliography. A fine introduction to the modern history of OT interpretation.

2.3.5　Knight, Douglas A., and Gene M. Tucker, eds. *The Hebrew Bible and Its Modern Interpreters.* The Bible and Its Modern Interpreters. Chico, Calif.: Scholars, 1985. 516pp.

Commissioned by the Society of Biblical Literature and containing contributions from leading (primarily North American) OT scholars representing the mainline critical consensus, this volume charts developments in major aspects of critical OT study since 1945. Its chapters are arranged topically, and each chapter concludes with a fairly extensive bibliography. More emphasis on historical and literary than theological features. Must reading for recent developments in OT studies.

2.3.6 Mayes, A. D. H., ed. *Text in Context: Essays by Members of the Society for Old Testament Study.* Oxford: Oxford University Press, 2000. 477pp.

Similar in scope and aim to *The Hebrew Bible and Its Modern Interpreters* (§2.3.4), but with more attention to emerging approaches and issues, e.g., the role of the reader, feminism, ethnicity. Some of the most prominent OT scholars in the world address various topics of contemporary OT study. Each chapter concludes with an extensive bibliography. Most articles are quite technical, assuming some significant background on the part of the reader.

2.3.7 Saebo, Magne, ed. *Hebrew Bible/Old Testament: The History of Its Interpretation.* 3 vols. (Vols. 1–2 presently available.) Göttingen: Vandenhoeck & Ruprecht, 1996–. 847pp.

By far the most complete and authoritative study of the history of the interpretation of the OT within the OT itself, in Judaism, and in Christianity (including the use of the OT within the NT). Written by leaders in their respective fields, these articles are original contributions based on painstaking study of the primary sources. Includes extensive bibliographies, listing works in Latin, German, French, and English. Essential for any complete study of this area.

Also Significant

2.3.8 Chapman, Stephen B. *The Law and the Prophets: A Study in Old Testament Canon Formation.* Forschungen zum Alten Testament 27. Tübingen: Mohr Siebeck, 2000. 356pp.

2.3.9 Davies, Philip R. *Scribes and Schools: The Canonization of the Hebrew Scriptures.* Library of Ancient Israel. Louisville: Westminster John Knox, 1998. 219pp.

2.3.10 Evans, Craig A., and James A. Sanders, eds. *The Function of Scripture in Early Jewish and Christian Tradition.* Journal for the Study of the New

Testament Supplement Series 154; Studies in Scripture in Early Judaism and Christianity 6. Sheffield: Sheffield Academic Press, 1998. 350pp.

2.3.11 Exum, J. Cheryl, and David J. A. Clines, eds. *The New Literary Criticism and the Hebrew Bible*. Valley Forge, Pa.: Trinity Press International, 1993. 276pp.

2.3.12 Fishbane, Michael. *Biblical Interpretation in Ancient Israel*. Oxford: Clarendon, 1985. 617pp.

2.3.13 Halbertal, Moshe. *People of the Book: Canon, Meaning, and Authority*. Cambridge, Mass.: Harvard University Press, 1997. 185pp.

2.3.14 Kraeling, Emil G. *The Old Testament since the Reformation*. New York: Harper, 1955. 320pp.

2.3.15 Levenson, Jon D. *The Hebrew Bible, the Old Testament, and Historical Criticism: Jews and Christians in Biblical Studies*. Philadelphia: Westminster, 1993. 192pp.

2.3.16 Rogerson, John. *Old Testament Criticism in the Nineteenth Century*. Philadelphia: Fortress, 1985. 320pp.

2.3.17 Saebo, Magne. *On the Way to Canon: Creative Tradition History in the Old Testament*. Journal for the Study of the Old Testament Supplement Series 191. Sheffield: Sheffield Academic Press, 1998. 401pp.

2.3.18 Sanders, James A. *Torah and Canon*. Philadelphia: Fortress, 1972. 121pp.

2.3.19 Sarna, Nahum. *Studies in Biblical Interpretation*. JPS Scholar of Distinction Series. Philadelphia: Jewish Publication Society, 2000. 452pp.

2.3.20 Sundberg, Albert C. *The Old Testament of the Early Church*. Cambridge, Mass.: Harvard University Press, 1964. 190pp.

2.3.21 Vasholz, Robert I. *The Old Testament Canon in the Old Testament Church: The Internal Rationale for Old Testament Canonicity*. Ancient Near Eastern Texts and Studies 7. Lewiston, N.Y.: Edwin Mellen, 1990. 105pp.

2.4   History and Geography

Highly Recommended

2.4.1   Ahlström, Gösta W. *The History of Ancient Palestine*. Edited by Diana Edelman. Minneapolis: Fortress, 1993. 990pp.

Learned, massive, and detailed history of the peoples of Palestine from earliest times to the conquest of Alexander. Employs all available source material (textual, epigraphic, archaeological) to reconstruct the major epochs and events so as to analyze the social, political, military, and economic conditions of Palestine as contextual background for the history of Israel. Ahlström belonged to the "Uppsala" or "Scandinavian" school of OT historical criticism, with its unique and (in the judgment of some) eccentric positions, yet was an independent thinker who moved beyond the accepted positions of any specific school. His historical reconstruction will often appear at odds with the OT text, since he attempts to be "free from the bias of the biblical writers." Nevertheless, a very helpful resource for interpreting the OT in its environment.

2.4.2   Albertz, Rainer. *A History of Israelite Religion in the Old Testament Period*. 2 vols. Old Testament Library. Louisville: Westminster John Knox, 1994. 738pp.

Combines general history of Israel and Judah with the history specifically of Israel's religion in an attempt to explore the interaction between historical events, religious experiences, and theological responses as various groups within Israel and Judah gave religious expression to historical and social situations. Adopts a thoroughly critical approach, sometimes following the more established critical lines of (for example) Noth, and sometimes more recent critical movements, but affirms the early dating of many texts over against the view that we have virtually nothing from the preexilic period. Readers will sometimes be disappointed that he seeks to explain religious phenomena almost entirely in terms of historical events and social realities without giving place to the transcendent activity of God. But insofar as even the OT writers assume the importance of social and historical context, this work will be helpful in understanding the faith of the OT in that light.

2.4.3   Bright, John. *A History of Israel*. 4th ed. Philadelphia: Westminster, 2000. 533pp.

Revised with a helpful appendix by William P. Brown, this is the most authoritative and accessible history of Israel from the "Albright school," which engaged in critical historical reconstruction but was more inclined to identify substantive connections between the archaeological and historical evidence and the perspectives of the OT texts than certain other schools. The result is a history that is at once both critical and relatively conservative. Perhaps the best overall introduction to the history of Israel for the interpreter of the OT.

2.4.4   Hess, Richard S. *Israelite Religions: An Archaeological and Biblical Survey.* Grand Rapids: Baker, 2007. 432pp.

Attempts to make accessible to the nonspecialist the results of the plethora of recent discoveries and scholarship regarding the various forms of Israelite religion throughout the OT period, and the relationship between the extra-biblical data and the OT. Of necessity, Hess's citation of data is selective, but also balanced and reasonable. Written from an evangelical perspective that tends to emphasize the distinctiveness of Israelite religion over against those of other ANE peoples.

2.4.5   Matthews, Victor H., and Don C. Benjamin. *Social World of Ancient Israel: 1250–587 B.C.E.* Peabody, Mass.: Hendrickson, 1993. 832pp.

Historical/cultural background information is obviously essential for biblical interpretation, and interpreters often find it difficult to locate the most relevant background information for specific passages. This volume offers a readable, nontechnical presentation of such data for each passage of the OT. The fact that the whole of OT background is treated in a single-volume commentary results in the information being highly selective. Moreover, it sometimes presents only general background information derived from other OT passages rather than specific cultural insights from archaeological or cultural studies. Nevertheless it is usually quite helpful and the only single-volume resource of its kind available. For fuller treatment, students should consult Walton, *Zondervan Illustrated Bible Backgrounds Commentary* (§2.4.8).

2.4.6   Miller, Patrick D., Jr. *The Religion of Ancient Israel.* Library of Ancient Israel. Louisville: Westminster John Knox, 2000. 335pp.

Readable, informed, and current discussion of the history of Israel's religion according to major themes and institutions: deity and the divine world; types of religion; sacrifice and offering; holiness and purity; and leadership. Written with a view toward informing the actual interpretation of the OT text.

2.4.7   Vaux, Roland de. *Ancient Israel: Its Life and Institutions.* 2 vols. New York: McGraw-Hill, 1965. 592pp.

From a leading Roman Catholic biblical historian and archaeologist associated with the famous École Biblique in Jerusalem, this work is something of a classic treatment of the social and religious life of ancient Israel, focusing on the principal institutions that provided the framework for Israel's life. Draws heavily on data from the OT itself, which he tends to treat as historically reliable, and relates these data to archaeological evidence and the history of Israel's neighbors. Readable, reliable, and useful resource for deeper understanding of specific passages as well as of the OT as a whole.

2.4.8   Walton, John H., ed. *Zondervan Illustrated Bible Backgrounds Commentary.* 4 vols. Grand Rapids: Zondervan, 2009. Volumes average 550pp.

Despite its title, deals only with the OT. Writing from an evangelical perspective, the thirty contributors employ comparative study of the OT and ANE in a cautious manner. Moves through the OT passage by passage, presenting archaeological findings, historical and geographical background, and information regarding manners and customs. Makes use of most current scholarship, presenting findings in an accessible manner, with many photographs. Goal throughout is to illumine the biblical text.

2.4.9   Wellhausen, Julius. *Prolegomena to the History of Israel: With a Reprint of the Article "Israel" from the Encylopaedia Britannica.* Edinburgh: A. & C. Black, 1885; reprint, Gloucester, Mass.: Peter Smith, 1973. 552pp.

Probably the most influential work ever written on the history of Israel. Responsible for establishing the basic direction of OT study until the present, although some of its specific positions have been modified or largely abandoned. Important not so much for the assistance it can give in the interpretation of the final form of the text, for in fact its value for preaching and teaching in the church is extremely limited. Rather, its significance is in its role in the development of the discipline of OT study.

Also Significant

2.4.10   Clements, Ronald E., ed. *The World of Ancient Israel: Sociological, Anthropological, and Political Perspectives.* Cambridge: Cambridge University Press, 1991. 436pp.

2.4.11   Fohrer, Georg. *A History of Israelite Religion.* Nashville: Abingdon, 1972. 416pp.

2.4.12   Hayes, John H., and J. Maxwell Miller, eds. *Israelite and Judaean History.* Old Testament Library. Philadelphia: Westminster, 1977. 736pp.

2.4.13   Kaufmann, Yehezkel. *The Religion of Israel: From Its Beginnings to the Babylonian Exile.* New York: Schocken, 1960. 486pp.

2.4.14   King, Philip J., and Lawrence E. Stager. *Life in Biblical Israel.* Library of Ancient Israel. Louisville: Westminster John Knox, 2001. 440pp.

2.4.15   Long, V. Philips, ed. *Israel's Past in Present Research: Essays on Ancient Israelite Historiography.* Winona Lake, Ind.: Eisenbrauns, 1999. 612pp.

2.4.16   Long, V. Philips, David W. Baker, and Gordon J. Wenham, eds. *Windows into Old Testament History: Evidence, Argument, and the Crisis of Biblical Israel.* Grand Rapids: Eerdmans, 2002. 200pp.

2.4.17   Matthews, Victor H., and James C. Moyer. *The Old Testament: Text and Context.* 3d ed. Grand Rapids: Baker, 2012. 322pp.

2.4.18   McDermott, John J. *What Are They Saying about the Formation of Israel?* New York: Paulist, 1998. 113pp.

2.4.19   Noth, Martin. *The History of Israel.* 2d ed. New York: Harper & Row, 1960. 487pp.

2.4.20   Oswalt, John N. *The Bible among the Myths: Unique Revelation or Just Ancient Literature?* Grand Rapids: Zondervan, 2009. 204pp.

2.4.21   Provan, Iain W., V. Philips Long, and Tremper Longman III. *A Biblical History of Israel.* Louisville: Westminster John Knox, 2003. 426pp.

2.4.22   Schmidt, Werner H. *The Faith of the Old Testament: A History.* Philadelphia: Westminster, 1983. 302pp.

2.4.23   Wood, Leon. *A Survey of Israel's History.* Revised by D. McBride. Grand Rapids: Zondervan, 1986. 416pp.

2.5 Ancient Near Eastern Literature and Art

Highly Recommended

2.5.1   Hallo, William W., and K. Lawson Younger Jr., eds. *The Context of Scripture.* 3 vols. Leiden: Brill, 1997–2002. 599/433/406pp.

A work that promises to be the authoritative standard in this area well into the twenty-first century. The first volume includes ANE texts that pertain to the OT. The selection is broad, balanced, and representative, and includes the most recent discoveries and fresh translations of long-familiar texts. The second volume deals with monumental inscriptions from the biblical world. In both of these volumes there are cross-references to OT passages, but little specific discussion of the relationship to the OT. Includes critical footnotes and extensive bibliographies of works in English, German, and French. The third volume includes indexes and develops connections between these materials and the OT.

2.5.2   Matthews, Victor H., and Don C. Benjamin. *Old Testament Parallels: Laws and Stories from the Ancient Near East.* 3d ed. New York: Paulist, 2006. 430pp.

Probably the most readable, accessible, and current anthology of ANE parallels to OT passages. The translations are fresh and understandable to contemporary English speakers (indeed, they border on paraphrase). The book moves through the OT canonically, presenting parallels according to their relationship to specific biblical passages. In addition to the citation of the ANE text itself, each entry includes a brief discussion of the ANE passage and an explanation of its relationship to the biblical passage; the authors identify similarities and differences between the ANE passage and the biblical text so as to note the distinctive features of the biblical perspective. Excellent introduction to the most significant ANE parallels.

2.5.3   Pritchard, James B., ed. *Ancient Near Eastern Texts Relating to the Old Testament.* 3d ed. with supplement. Princeton, NJ: Princeton University Press, 1969. 710pp

Complete, authoritative, meticulously accurate translation of ANE texts pertaining to the OT. Very little introduction to the texts or discussion regarding their relationship to and significance for OT passages. The text and translations are technically accurate, but not as reader-friendly or understandable as those presented by Matthews and Benjamin (§2.5.2).

Excellent for the scholar and others trained in the field, but not as useful for nonspecialists.

2.5.4 Sparks, Kenton L. *Ancient Texts for the Study of the Hebrew Bible: A Guide to the Background Literature*. Peabody, Mass: Hendrickson, 2005. 514pp.

An invaluable introduction to and bibliography of ANE primary sources relevant to the study of the OT. Volume is arranged according to genre. Does not include any actual texts, but discusses the content, history, and scholarly debates concerning the most pertinent texts for each genre (e.g., Mesopotamian Hymns, Prayers, and Laments), then provides bibliography of both text and translations, and of the secondary literature.

2.5.5 Walton, John H. *Ancient Israelite Literature in Its Cultural Context: A Survey of Parallels between Biblical and Ancient Near Eastern Texts*. Library of Biblical Interpretation. Grand Rapids: Zondervan, 1990. 256pp.

Not so much an anthology of ANE parallels as a survey of texts that have typically been identified as parallels to OT passages, and a discussion of the considerations involved in deciding whether such a text is truly parallel, and if so, how it should be used to interpret the OT and to understand Israel's faith. Written from a consciously conservative perspective, but fair, balanced, and judicious. Notes common elements between Israel and its neighbors but emphasizes the distinctiveness of Israel's faith.

Note also the series Society of Biblical Literature Writings from the Ancient World (edited by Theodore J. Lewis; Atlanta: Scholars Press, 1990–), which presents current, readable translations of a variety of texts from ANE cultures from Sumerian civilization to the age of Alexander. Each volume deals with a specific type of text from a particular area (e.g., letters from ancient Egypt) and contains an introduction describing the texts presented, but there is little explicit attention given to the relationship to the biblical material. Now the standard comprehensive reference work for ANE texts. Thus far, nineteen volumes have appeared.

Also Significant

2.5.6 Arnold, Bill T., and Bryan E. Beyer. *Readings from the Ancient Near East: Primary Sources for Old Testament Study*. Encountering Biblical Studies. Grand Rapids: Baker, 2001. 256pp.

2.5.7   Beyerlin, Walter, ed. *Near Eastern Religious Texts Relating to the Old Testament*. Old Testament Library. Philadelphia: Westminster, 1978. 288pp.

2.5.8   Pritchard, James B., ed. *The Ancient Near East: An Anthology of Texts and Pictures*. Princeton, N.J.: Princeton University Press, 2011. 474pp. + 138pp. of plates.

2.6 Editions of the Old Testament

Highly Recommended

2.6.1   Dotan, Aron, ed. *Biblia Hebraica Leningradensia: Prepared according to the Vocalization, Accents, and Masora of Aaron ben Moses ben Asher in the Leningrad Codex*. Edited by Aron Dotan. Peabody, Mass.: Hendrickson, 2001.

This printed edition of the Leningrad Codex (L), an important eleventh-century manuscript of the Masoretic Text, has no Masora (a traditional apparatus devised by medieval Hebrew scribes) and no critical apparatus but follows L with a high degree of accuracy and clearly indicates when it departs from L for certain specified reasons.

2.6.2   Elliger, K., and W. Rudolph, eds. *Biblia Hebraica Stuttgartensia*. 2d ed., edited by W. Rudolph and H. P. Rüger. Stuttgart: Deutsche Bibelgesellschaft, 1977.

The edition of the Hebrew Bible most widely used by scholars and students. Based on earlier editions by R. Kittel and others, its text is an edition of the Leningrad Codex (L), an important eleventh-century manuscript of the Masoretic Text. Also included are an edition of L's version of the Masora and a modern critical apparatus.

2.6.3   Rahlfs, Alfred and Robert Hanhart, ed. *Biblia Graeca: Septuaginta*. Rev. ed. Stuttgart: Deutsche Bibelgesellschaft, 2007. 941pp.

The most commonly used edition of the Septuagint. Based primarily on the three major uncials Vaticanus, Sinaiticus, Alexandrinus. Contains brief and basic text-critical apparatus. Originally produced by Rahlfs in 1935, it has been revised by Hanhart in 2006, with more than a thousand corrections and expansions.

2.6.4   Ziegler, Joseph et al., eds. *Septuaginta: Vetus Testamentum Graecum.* 16 vols. Göttingen: Vandenhoeck & Ruprecht, 1930–1999. Volumes vary greatly in size, averaging around 300pp.

Often called the "Göttingen Septuagint," this is the standard critical edition of those books that have been published. When complete, it will contain sixteen "volumes" comprising half again as many physical volumes. Ziegler edited the earliest volumes, but the subsequent volumes were edited by various scholars. Each volume contains an introduction (in German), the text of the Septuagint, and a much more complete and detailed textual apparatus than that which appears in Rahlfs.

The *Biblia Hebraica Quinta* is being produced by the German Bible Society at the initiative of the United Bible Societies. It is intended to supersede the *Biblia Hebraica Stuttgartensia* (§2.6.2). In contrast to the *Biblia Hebraica Stuttgartensia* this new edition will produce the entire text of the Leningrad Codex without departure. It is presently available from the German Bible Society and from Hendrickson only in individual fascicles on certain books of the Old Testament (2004–2012); but it will eventually be published in a single volume, with an accompanying volume providing commentary on the critical apparatus. The German Bible Society anticipates completion of the project by 2020.

Also Significant

2.6.5   Brenton, Lancelot C. L. *The Septuagint with Apocrypha: Greek and English.* Peabody, Mass.: Hendrickson, 1986.

2.6.6   Pietersma, Albert, and Benjamin G. Wright, eds. *A New English Translation of the Septuagint and the other Greek Translations Traditionally Included under That Title.* New York: Oxford University Press, 2007. 1027pp.

2.7   Hebrew Grammars

Highly Recommended

2.7.1   Arnold, Bill T., and John H. Choi. *A Guide to Biblical Hebrew Syntax.* Cambridge: Cambridge University Press, 2003. 228pp.

A current and usable intermediate grammar. The first three parts deal with individual words (nouns, verbs, participles), while the fourth part addresses clauses and sentences. It is replete with pertinent and clear examples. While more concise than Joüon-Muraoka (§2.7.3) and than Waltke-O'Connor (§2.7.5), it is more accessible for repeated referencing and for mastering the essentials of intermediate-level competency in Hebrew.

2.7.2   Beckman, John C. *Williams' Hebrew Syntax*, 3d ed. Toronto: University of Toronto Press, 2007. 264pp.

Beckman has completely revised and expanded *Hebrew Syntax: An Outline*, by Ronald J. Williams, originally published in 1967. Addresses syntax exclusively, without attention to morphology and phonology. Provides clear examples, with English translation. A significant benefit is the inclusion of footnotes that reference fuller treatments in five of the major grammars.

2.7.3   Joüon, Paul, and T. Muraoka. *A Grammar of Biblical Hebrew*. 2 vols. Subsidia Biblica 14.1–2. Rome: Biblical Institute Press, 1991. 779pp.

Comprehensive reference grammar for intermediate-level Hebrew, though on the detailed and technical end of the range of intermediate Hebrew texts. Comparable to Waltke-O'Connor (§2.7.5), though treats all branches of Hebrew grammar, including phonetics/phonology and morphology, whereas Waltke-O'Connor deals almost exclusively with syntax. Consequently does not deal as fully with syntax as Waltke-O'Connor, and the latter should be used to complement this volume. Footnotes interact with current scholarly discussions on major issues. Includes a fairly extensive bibliography.

2.7.4   Kautzsch, E., ed. *Gesenius' Hebrew Grammar*. 2d ed. Rev. by A. E. Cowley. Oxford: Clarendon, 1909. 598pp.

The classic and still most authoritative standard grammar of biblical Hebrew, although portions are becoming dated, and therefore it should be used in connection with more recent works, especially Waltke-O'Connor (§2.7.5). Indispensable for thorough, serious study of Hebrew grammar.

2.7.5   Waltke, Bruce K., and M. O'Connor. *An Introduction to Biblical Hebrew Syntax*. Winona Lake, Ind.: Eisenbrauns, 1990. 765pp.

Focuses almost entirely on syntax; and its discussions of syntactical issues are consistently clear, with numerous helpful examples from the OT. Its introductory discussions on the history of the study of Hebrew grammar and on basic methodological issues are also very helpful. At a few points its explanation of syntax can be usefully supplemented by Joüon (§2.7.3).

Also Significant

2.7.6   Blau, Joshua. *Phonology and Morphology of Biblical Hebrew: An Introduction.* Winona Lake, Ind: Eisenbrauns, 2010. 369pp.

2.7.7   Bodine, Walter R., ed. *Linguistics and Biblical Hebrew.* Winona Lake, Ind.: Eisenbrauns, 1992. 323pp.

2.7.8   Chisholm, Robert B. *From Exegesis to Exposition: A Practical Guide to Using Biblical Hebrew.* Grand Rapids: Baker, 1998. 304pp.

2.7.9   Davidson, A. B. *Hebrew Syntax.* 3d ed. Edinburgh: T&T Clark, 1924. 233pp.

2.7.10   Driver, S. R. *A Treatise on the Use of the Tenses in Hebrew.* 3d ed. Oxford: Clarendon, 1892. 306pp.

2.7.11   Gogel, Sandra Landis. *A Grammar of Epigraphic Hebrew.* Atlanta: Scholars, 1998. 522pp.

2.7.12   Horsnell, Malcolm J. A. *A Review and Reference Grammar for Biblical Hebrew.* Rev. ed. Hamilton, Ont.: McMaster University Press, 1999. 463pp.

2.7.13   Merwe, Christo H. J. van der, Jackie A. Naudé, and Jan H. Kroeze. *A Biblical Hebrew Reference Grammar.* Sheffield: Sheffield Academic Press, 1999. 403pp.

2.7.14   Waldman, Nahum M. *The Recent Study of Hebrew: A Survey of the Literature with Selected Bibliography.* Winona Lake, Ind.: Eisenbrauns, 1989. 464pp.

Popular Beginning Grammars

2.7.15   Cook, John A., and Robert D. Holmstedt. *Beginning Biblical Hebrew: A Grammar and Illustrated Reader.* Grand Rapids: Baker, 2013. 352pp.

2.7.16   Kelley, Page H. *Biblical Hebrew: An Introductory Grammar.* Grand Rapids: Eerdmans, 1992. 453pp.

2.7.17   Lambdin, T. O. *Introduction to Biblical Hebrew.* New York: Scribners, 1971. 345pp.

2.7.18   LaSor, William Sanford. *Handbook of Biblical Hebrew.* 2 vols. Grand Rapids: Eerdmans, 1988. 189/249pp.

2.7.19   Marks, John H., and Virgil Rogers. *A Beginner's Handbook to Biblical Hebrew.* Nashville: Abingdon, 1958. 174pp.

2.7.20   Martin, James D. *Davidson's Introductory Hebrew Grammar,* 27th ed. Edinburgh: T&T Clark, 1993. 225pp.

2.7.21   Seow, C. L. *A Grammar for Biblical Hebrew.* Rev. ed. Nashville: Abingdon, 1995. 366pp.

2.7.22   Weingreen, J. *A Practical Grammar for Classical Hebrew.* 2d ed. Oxford: Clarendon, 1959. 316pp.

2.8   Hebrew Lexicons

Highly Recommended

2.8.1   Armstrong, Terry A., Douglas L. Busby, and Cyril F. Carr. *A Reader's Hebrew-English Lexicon of the Old Testament.* 4 vols. in 3. Grand Rapids: Zondervan, 1982–1988. 230/220/296pp.

Companion volume to Kubo's *Reader's Greek-English Lexicon of the New Testament* (§4.8.2). Designed for the student or pastor, offers assistance in rapid reading of the Hebrew Bible by listing, according to passage, words that occur fifty times or fewer in the OT. Definitions are brief, and are based on Brown-Driver-Briggs (§2.8.2). Each entry indicates also the page number in BDB where the definition can be found, and frequencies of the word both in the biblical book and in the OT as a whole. Contains many errors, but still a helpful resource.

2.8.2   Brown, Francis, S. R. Driver, and Charles A. Briggs. *A Hebrew and English Lexicon of the Old Testament*. Oxford: Oxford University Press, 1907. Reprint, Peabody, Mass.: Hendrickson, 1979 (indexed to Strong's). 1185pp.

A classic work, and among the most authoritative, based on Gesenius's dictionary. Now somewhat dated, and rather difficult to use given the arrangement, system of abbreviations, and even print format. An index, available separately (§2.8.8), helps greatly. Still a significant resource for serious study of the Hebrew Bible.

2.8.3   Clines, David J. A., ed. *The Dictionary of Classical Hebrew*. 8 vols. Sheffield: Sheffield Academic Press, 1993–2011. Volumes average 650pp.

Touted to be the the the first dictionary of classical over against only biblical Hebrew. Treats every known Hebrew word not only in the OT but in inscriptions, the Dead Sea Scrolls, Ben Sira, etc., from the beginning of the Hebrew language until 200 CE; and cites every occurrence of each word (except for the most common). Volumes 2 through 8 include a bibliography.

2.8.4   Davidson, Benjamin. *The Analytical Hebrew and Chaldee Lexicon*. 2d ed. Peabody, Mass.: Hendrickson, 1992. 784pp.

Originally published in 1850, lists, parses, and identifies the root of every word in the Hebrew Bible. Gives basic definitions of each root. Regularly alludes to relevant morphological and grammatical discussions found at the beginning of the volume. Somewhat dated insofar as it is based on a less reliable edition of the Hebrew text than more recent works, but remains extremely helpful as a parsing guide, especially for unusual or irregular forms.

2.8.5   Holladay, William L. *A Concise Hebrew and Aramaic Lexicon of the Old Testament*. Grand Rapids: Eerdmans, 1971. 425pp.

Probably the most reader-friendly and accessible of the more recent, up-to-date lexicons. Based on Koehler-Barmgartner (§2.8.6) and produced for English-speaking audiences before Koehler-Barmgartner had been fully published in English in revised form, this abridgment retains its value for reliable, quick-reference definition. Recognizing that most students are less familiar with Aramaic than with Hebrew, it offers fuller treatment of Aramaic words, including identification of number, person, and gender of verbs.

2.8.6   Koehler, Ludwig, and Walter Baumgartner. *The Hebrew and Aramaic Lexicon of the Old Testament*. Revised by Walter Baumgartner and Johann Jakob Stamm. Translated and edited under the supervision of M. E. J. Richardson. 3d ed. 5 vols. Leiden: Brill, 1994–2000. 2094pp.

Now the standard dictionary for the OT and related literature in Hebrew and Aramaic. In contrast to older works, like Brown-Driver-Briggs (§2.8.2), it lists entries in alphabetical order rather than according to verbal roots, thus making this lexicon easier to use and saving much time. It incorporates data and insights from recent discoveries and the most recent research into these languages.

Also Significant

2.8.7   Clines, David J. A., ed. *The Concise Dictionary of Classical Hebrew.* Sheffield: Sheffield Phoenix, 2009. 510pp.

2.8.8   Einspahr, Bruce. *Index to Brown, Driver & Briggs Hebrew Lexicon.* Chicago: Moody, 1980. 456pp.

2.8.9   Fohrer, Georg, ed. *Hebrew and Aramaic Dictionary of the Old Testament.* Berlin: Walter De Gruyter, 1973. 332pp.

2.8.10   Girdlestone, Robert B. *Synonyms of the Old Testament: Their Bearing on Christian Doctrine.* 3d ed. Revised and edited by Donald R. White. Grand Rapids: Baker, 1983. 388pp.

2.8.11   Klein, Ernest. *A Comprehensive Etymological Dictionary of the Hebrew Language for Readers of English.* New York: Macmillan, 1987. 721pp.

The United Bible Societies is sponsoring the Semantic Dictionary of Biblical Hebrew project (edited by Reinier de Blois with the assistance of Enio R. Mueller), which is producing the "Hebrew-English Lexicon of the Old Testament Based on Semantic Domains," a work corresponding to Louw and Nida, *Greek-English Lexicon of the New Testament Based on Semantic Domains* (§4.8.4). This work is still in process; but the material is appearing incrementally and is accessible at http://www.sdbh.org.

2.9   Theological Dictionaries (Wordbooks)

Highly Recommended

2.9.1   Botterweck, G. Johannes, Helmer Ringgren, and Heinz-Josef Fabry, eds. *Theological Dictionary of the Old Testament.* 15 vols. Grand Rapids: Eerdmans, 1974-2006. Volumes average 650pp.

Companion to *Theological Dictionary of the New Testament* (§4.9.3), this magisterial work offers in-depth discussions of key Hebrew and Aramaic terms in the OT. Each entry focuses on meaning, moving from general, everyday senses to full understanding of theological significance. Each key word is related to its larger linguistic and semantic fields, and attention is given to cognate terms and concepts in surrounding ANE cultures. Attention is given also to use in Qumran and the Septuagint. Contributors represent a wide range of nations and religious traditions, though most are European and North American, and virtually all assume the general critical consensus of the historical and textual development of the OT and thus make use of form- and tradition-critical insights. Contains extensive bibliographies. The standard work in this category.

2.9.2   Jenni, Ernst, and Claus Westermann, eds. *Theological Lexicon of the Old Testament.* 3 vols. Peabody, Mass.: Hendrickson, 1997. 1638pp.

Mainline critical alternative to conservative-evangelical theological dictionaries such as those edited by VanGemeren (§2.9.3) and Harris-Archer-Waltke (§2.9.5), etc. Articles produced by some of most prominent OT scholars from the German-speaking world. Includes significant interaction with history of interpretation, and includes fairly extensive bibliographies (most works cited are in German, though some in English or French). Emphasizes insights from form- and tradition-criticism, and therefore discussions sometimes focus on the function of the word in sources or traditions that lie behind the OT text rather than in the final form of the text. For those who do not know Hebrew, or do not know it well, words are numerically coded to Strong's numbers.

2.9.3   VanGemeren, Willem A., ed. *New International Dictionary of Old Testament Theology and Exegesis.* 5 vols. Grand Rapids: Zondervan, 1997. Volumes average 1100pp.

This counterpart to *New International Dictionary of New Testament Theology* (§4.9.2) is designed to provide both scholars and nonspecialists understanding of the basic meaning of key OT terms as well as their fuller theological significance. Briefer and more basic than *Theological Dictionary of the Old Testament* (§2.9.1) and representing a conservative-evangelical perspective over against *TDOT* and *Theological Lexicon of the Old Testament* (§2.9.2), although contributors represent a spectrum that includes both Wesleyan and Reformed scholars. Contains brief bibliographies. Solid, informed, and reliable.

See also the discussions of OT terms found in Gerhard Kittel and Gerhard Friedrich, eds., *Theological Dictionary of the New Testament* (§4.9.3) and the discussions of OT passages and concepts found in Karl Barth, *Church Dogmatics* (14 vols.; Edinburgh: T&T Clark, 1975–1977).

Also Significant

2.9.4   Baker, Warren, and Eugene Carpenter. *Complete Word Study Dictionary of the Old Testament.* Chatanooga: AMG, 2003. 2138pp.

2.9.5   Harris, R. Laird, G. L. Archer, and Bruce K. Waltke, eds. *Theological Wordbook of the Old Testament.* 2 vols. Chicago: Moody, 1980. 1124pp.

2.9.6   Unger, Merrill F., and William White, eds. *Nelson's Expository Dictionary of the Old Testament.* Nashville: Thomas Nelson, 1980. 509pp.

2.10   Concordances to the Hebrew Bible

Highly Recommended

2.10.1   Even-Shoshan, Abraham. *A New Concordance of the Old Testament.* Jerusalem: Kiryat Sepher; Grand Rapids: Baker, 1984. 1242pp.

Most complete, current, and accessible Hebrew concordance among those that employ the Hebrew exclusively and make no use of English translation. Includes several features that make it simpler to use than Lisowsky or Mandelkern. Entries cite synonyms and related words. Includes not just single words, but also collocations (phrases). Employs certain "space-saving" devices for high-frequency words, and these can cause confusion. For this reason, the user should consult the introduction by John Sailhamer (§2.10.7).

2.10.2   Kohlenberger, John R., III. *The Hebrew-English Concordance to the Old Testament: With the New International Version.* Grand Rapids: Zondervan, 1998. 2192pp.

Lists all occurrences of a Hebrew word (even where there is no English equivalent in the NIV or other standard translations). Uses Goodrick-Kohlenberger numbering system, which is keyed to major lexicons, e.g., Brown, Driver, Briggs; Koehler-Barmgartner; and Holladay. Also includes cross-references to Strong's numbers. Each entry gives the various ways the Hebrew word is translated by the NIV, transliteration, part of speech, frequency count, related words, context lines, textual variants, and (in verbs) identification of stem. Contains also concise Hebrew-English and Aramaic-English dictionary. Reliable, current, full of helpful information, and user-friendly.

2.10.3 Wigram, George V. *The Englishman's Hebrew Concordance of the Old Testament*. Peabody, Mass.: Hendrickson, 1996. 1680pp.

First published in the middle of the nineteenth century, now somewhat dated in terms of the quality of the Hebrew text employed and suffers from some omissions. Still, accessible and user-friendly and generally reliable. Numerically coded to Strong's.

Also Significant

2.10.4 Andersen, Francis I. *The Vocabulary of the Old Testament*. Rome: Pontifical Biblical Institute Press, 1989. 721pp.

2.10.5 Lisowsky, Gerhard. *Konkordanz zum Hebräischen Alten Testament*. 2d ed. Stuttgart: Wurttembergische Bibelanstalt, 1958. 1672pp.

2.10.6 Mandelkern, Solomon. *Veteris Testamenti Concordantiae: Hebraica atqua Chaldaicae*. Tel Aviv: Sumptibus Schocken Hierosolymis, 1971. 1532pp.

2.10.7 Sailhamer, John. *Introduction to A New Concordance of the Old Testament*. Grand Rapids: Baker, 1987. 37pp.

2.11   Textual Criticism

Highly Recommended

2.11.1 Brotzman, Ellis R. *Old Testament Textual Criticism: A Practical Introduction*. Grand Rapids: Baker, 1994. 208pp.

Most readable and accessible introduction to all the major aspects of OT textual criticism, including a history of the transmission of the OT in Hebrew, a description of the ancient versions of the OT, guidance for the use of *Biblia Hebraica Stuttgartensia* (§2.6.2), a discussion of the role of the

Dead Sea Scrolls, an explanation of scribal errors, a study of the principles and practice of textual criticism, and an illustrative application of textual criticism directed at the book of Ruth. Includes a select bibliography.

2.11.2   McCarter, P. Kyle. *Textual Criticism: Recovering the Text of the Hebrew Bible*. Guides to Biblical Scholarship. Philadelphia: Fortress, 1986. 94pp.

Like Brotzman (§2.11.1), an introduction to the discipline of textual criticism, but more narrow in focus, emphasizing the types of textual corruption and the main considerations in adjudicating between variant readings. Also somewhat more theoretical, less concerned to lead the reader through the actual process of doing textual criticism. Yet contains many illuminating examples. A useful supplement to Brotzman.

2.11.3   Tov, Emanuel. *Textual Criticism of the Hebrew Bible*. Philadelphia: Fortress, 1993. 456pp.

An introduction to OT textual criticism, but more thorough and technical than Brotzman (§2.11.1) or McCarter (§2.11.2), and indeed more than an introduction in that its discussions on specific issues often pertain to current scholarly debate and carry that debate forward. Especially valuable for its descriptions of texts and versions. Probably the most authoritative treatment of OT textual criticism, but the reader should be aware that some of Tov's specific perspectives and conclusions are debatable and are not universally shared by scholars in the field.

2.11.4   Wurthwein, E. *The Text of the Old Testament: An Introduction to the Biblia Hebraica*. Rev. ed. Grand Rapids: Eerdmans, 1994. 293pp.

Probably the most readable introduction to the major texts of the OT, with special attention to the Masoretic text, the Septuagint, the Peshitta, and the Dead Sea Scrolls. Also helpful is the chapter that discusses the theological significance of textual criticism.

Also Significant

2.11.5   Kelley, Page H., Daniel S. Mynatt, and Timothy G. Crawford, eds. *The Masorah of Biblia Hebraica Stuttgartensia: Introduction and Annotated Glossary*. Grand Rapids: Eerdmans, 1998. 241pp.

2.11.6   Klein, Ralph W. *Textual Criticism of the Old Testament: The Septuagint after Qumran*. Guides to Biblical Scholarship. Philadelphia: Fortress, 1974. 84pp.

2.11.7   Tov, Emanuel. *The Text-Critical Use of the Septuagint in Biblical Research.* 2d ed. Jerusalem Biblical Studies 8. Jerusalem: Simor, 1997. 289pp.

2.11.8   Weingreen, J. *Introduction to the Critical Study of the Text of the Hebrew Bible.* Oxford: Clarendon, 1982. 103pp.

2.11.9   Wonneberger, Reinhard. *Understanding BHS: A Manual for Users of Biblica Hebraica Stuttgartensia.* 2d ed. Subsidia Biblica 8. Rome: Biblical Institute Press, 1990. 104pp.

2.12   Septuagint

See also TEXTUAL CRITICISM (§2.11); EDITIONS OF THE OLD TESTAMENT (§2.6)

Highly Recommended

2.12.1   Conybeare, F. C., and St. George Stock. *Grammar of Septuagint Greek: With Selected Readings, Vocabularies, and Updated Indexes.* Peabody, Mass.: Hendrickson, 1988. 382pp.

This reprint of the original 1905 volume adds indexes of ancient sources (including biblical passages) and Greek words, and glossaries. Although an older work, still indispensable for translation and study of the Greek of the Septuagint. Contains discussion (somewhat dated) of origin, inspiration, date, and Greek of the Septuagint; analysis of accidence and syntax of Septuagintal grammar, with numerous examples; and selected readings from the Septuagint with introductions and textual and grammatical notes.

2.12.2   Fernandez Marcos, Natalio. *The Septuagint in Context: Introduction to the Greek Versions of the Bible.* Leiden: Brill, 2001. 394pp.

A more technical introduction to the Septuagint than Jobes and Silva (§2.12.5), and one that focuses on the various contexts of the Septuagint, e.g., the linguistic, cultural, and historical contexts of its emergence and the relation of the Septuagint to the Hebrew Bible and to the Christian tradition. Actually deals not exclusively with the Septuagint, but with all the major Greek translations of the OT through Origen's Hexapla and the Lucianic Recension, and even deals with secondary versions such as the Old Latin and the Coptic versions, these secondary versions being useful for reconstructing the old Greek translations. Each chapter concludes with a brief and current bibliography.

2.12.3 Hatch, Edwin, and Henry A. Redpath. *A Concordance to the Septuagint and the Other Greek Versions of the Old Testament.* 2 vols. Oxford: Clarendon, 1897–1906. 1504pp. + supp.

This work, now a century old, continues to be the most reliable and comprehensive concordance to the Septuagint. Includes complete listing of every word appearing in the three major manuscripts of the Septuagint (Alexandrinus, Vaticanus, and Sinaiticus) and Sixtine edition of 1587, identifies in every instance the Hebrew word standing behind it, and includes the most significant textual variants. The citations are long enough to show the grammatical construction of the word and the words with which it is usually associated. In the absence of Bible software programs that will conduct exhaustive searches, this is an indispensable work.

2.12.4 Jellicoe, Sidney. *The Septuagint and Modern Study.* Oxford: Oxford University Press, 1968. 423pp.

Generally regarded as something of a classic in Septuagintal studies. Attempts to consolidate in one volume the significant amount of scholarship in the study of the Septuagint since the magisterial works of Swete and Ottley (§2.12.22, not "highly recommended" because of its age). The value of this volume is its comprehensive and at points detailed description of the recent history of Septuagintal studies, a value that is, of course, somewhat mitigated by the fact that this volume appeared in 1968.

2.12.5 Jobes, Karen H., and Moisés Silva. *Invitation to the Septuagint.* Grand Rapids: Baker, 2000. 351pp.

Readable introduction to the Septuagint designed for the nonspecialist yet containing current discussions of interest also to the scholar. Explores the importance of the Septuagint for the interpretation of both the OT and NT, describes the various Greek versions of the OT, evaluates the current printed editions, discusses textual criticism of the Septuagint, explores the use of the Septuagint for OT textual criticism, examines its relationship to the Dead Sea Scrolls, and gives examples of the interpretation of specific Septuagint passages (these examples require basic knowledge of Greek and Hebrew). Includes extremely brief bibliography.

2.12.6 Lust, J., E. Eynikel, and K. Hauspie (with the collaboration of G. Chamberlain), eds. *A Greek-English Lexicon of the Septuagint.* 2 vols. Stuttgart: Deutsche Bibelgesellschaft, 1992, 1996. 528pp.

The only lexicon of the Septuagint available in English. Lists every word that appears in Rahlfs's edition of the Septuagint, giving brief definitions, identifying up to five references to biblical texts in which the word occurs, and providing brief bibliography for most entries. The second volume contains an extensive bibliography on the Septuagint.

2.12.7   McLay, R. Timothy. *The Use of the Septuagint in New Testament Research.* Grand Rapids: Eerdmans, 2003. 207pp.

Employs a sophisticated understanding of translation theory to discuss major methodological issues involved in the use of the Septuagint by the NT writers, including the often difficult task of deciding whether the Septuagint was actually employed in a given instance. In spite of its title, gives relatively little attention to examining the specific citations of the Septuagint within the NT or to exploring the influence of the Septuagint upon the NT.

2.12.8   Muraoka, T. *A Greek-English Lexicon of the Septuagint.* Louvain: Peeters, 2009. 757pp.

Covers the entirety of the Septuagint, including the deuterocanonical books and words found in the various versions of the Septuagint. Recognizes the complexities of compiling a lexicon on the basis of translation from a Semitic original, and considers ways in which the Greek words were used in "daughter versions based on the Septuagint" and in patristic commentaries on the Septuagint rather than understanding the Greek of the Septuagint primarily in terms of its relation to the Hebrew Bible, as does Lust. Generally superior to Lust in terms of methodological sophistication and comprehensiveness. Includes an extensive bibliography on Septuagintal studies.

2.12.9   Taylor, Bernard A. *The Analytical Lexicon to the Septuagint: A Complete Parsing Guide.* Grand Rapids: Zondervan, 1994. 460pp.

Designed to assist beginning students in reading the Septuagint in the original Greek, but helpful also for more advanced students who might need assistance with rare or irregular forms. Parses every Greek word found in Rahlfs's edition of the Septuagint. The word "lexicon" in the title is somewhat misleading, since this volume gives no definition of terms. One should consult Lust's lexicon (§2.12.6) for definitions.

Periodical

2.12.10   *The Journal of Septuagint and Cognate Studies.* (Formerly Bulletin of the International Organization for Septuagint and Cognate Studies.) Winona Lake, Ind.: Eisenbrauns, 1968–.

Also Significant

2.12.11   Brock, Sebastian P., Charles T. Fritzsch, and Sidney Jellicoe. *A Classified Bibliography of the LXX.* Philadelphia: Fortress, 1974. 217pp.

2.12.12   Dines, Jennifer M. *The Septuagint.* London: T&T Clark, 2004. 196pp.

2.12.13   Dogniez, Cécile. *Bibliography of the Septuagint: 1970–1993.* Vetus Testamentum Supplemental Series 60. Leiden: Brill, 1995. 325pp.

2.12.14   Hatch, Edwin. *Essays in Biblical Greek.* Oxford: Oxford University Press, 1889. 293pp.

2.12.15   Hengel, Martin. *The Septuagint as Christian Scripture in Prehistory and the Problem of Its Canon.* Old Testament Studies. Edinburgh: T&T Clark, 2001. 256pp.

2.12.16   Kraus, Wolfgang, and R. Glenn Wooden, eds. *Septuagint Research: Issues and Challenges in the Study of the Greek Jewish Scriptures.* Society of Biblical Literature Septuagint and Cognate Studies, no. 53. Atlanta: Society of Biblical Literature, 2005. 414pp.

2.12.17   Morrish, George. *A Concordance to the Septuagint.* Grand Rapids: Zondervan, 1976. 284pp.

2.12.18   Muraoka, T. *A Greek-Hebrew/Aramaic Two-Way Index to the Septuagint.* Louvain: Peeters, 2010. 383pp.

2.12.19   Olofsson, Staffan. *God Is My Rock: A Study of Translation Technique and Theological Exegesis in the Septuagint.* Stockholm: Almqvist & Wiksell, 1990. 208pp.

2.12.20   Orlinsky, Harry M., ed. *Studies in the Septuagint: Origins, Recension, and Interpretations: Selected Essays with a Prolegomena by Sidney Jellicoe.* New York: Ktav, 1974. 609pp.

2.12.21   Pietersma, Albert, and Benjamin G. Wright, eds. *A New English Translation of the Septuagint and the Other Greek Translations Traditionally*

Included under That Title. New York: Oxford University Press, 2007. 1027pp.

2.12.22   Swete, Henry Barclay. *An Introduction to the Old Testament in Greek.* Revised by R. R. Ottley. Cambridge: Cambridge University Press, 1914. 626pp.

2.12.23   Thackeray, H. St. J. *A Grammar of the Old Testament in Greek: According to the Septuagint.* Cambridge: Cambridge University Press, 1909. 325pp.

2.12.24   Walters, Peter, and D. W. Gooding. *The Text of the Septuagint: Its Corruptions and Their Emendation.* Cambridge: Cambridge University Press, 1973. 418pp.

2.13   Exegetical Method/Hermeneutics

Highly Recommended

2.13.1   Achtemeier, Elizabeth. *Preaching from the Old Testament.* Louisville: Westminster John Knox, 1989. 187pp.

Written by a prominent authority on both the OT and preaching, this book presents solid theoretical foundation, practical guidelines, and engaging and illuminating examples of the Christian use of the OT. Emphasizes that the continuity between the testaments is based on the continuous activity of God's salvation-historical activity coming to fulfillment in Christ. Especially helpful are her discussions pertaining to Christian preaching from various types of OT material: narrative, law, prophets, psalms, wisdom.

2.13.2   Alter, Robert. *The Art of Biblical Narrative.* San Francisco: Harper, 1983. 195pp.

The pioneering work in the literary approach (now often called "narrative-critical") to the study of the OT. Employs engaging examples to demonstrate the value of and, to some extent, the techniques for making use of insights from the literary study of narrative for the interpretation of the OT.

2.13.3   Armerding, Carl. E. *The Old Testament and Criticism.* Grand Rapids: Eerdmans, 1983. 134pp.

Though now somewhat dated in its discussion of various types of OT criticism, and though quite brief, this book is a thoughtful, lucid appeal from a conservative biblical scholar for an evangelical appreciation for and use of OT criticism. Armerding also offers a critique of the use of criticism by certain mainstream scholars.

2.13.4   Barton, John. *Reading the Old Testament: Method in Biblical Study*. Rev. ed. Louisville: Westminster John Knox, 1996. 294pp.

Lucid introduction to the various methods currently employed in OT study. It probes the purpose of the various methods, their interrelationship, and critiques each one. Special attention is given to the emerging literary approaches, and their relationship to the more traditional methods of source, form, and redaction criticism. Contains extremely brief bibliography at the end of each chapter, and a selective bibliography at the conclusion of the book.

2.13.5   Goldingay, John. *Models for Interpretation of Scripture*. Grand Rapids: Eerdmans, 1995. 328pp.

An insightful and practical examination of what is involved in interpreting the several types of OT material, taking into account the various methods that have been and continue to be employed, and demonstrating how the concerns of these various methods can be brought together in a holistic approach. Gives attention both to foundational theoretical issues and to the demands of Christian proclamation.

2.13.6   Hoffmeier, James K., and Dennis R. Magary, eds. *Do Historical Matters Matter to Faith?: A Critical Appraisal of Modern and Postmodern Approaches to Scripture*. Wheaton, Ill.: Crossway, 2012. 542pp.

Intended to be a rejoinder to Sparks, *God's Word in Human Words* (§2.13.7), and those like him who call for an embrace of the results of mainline critical OT scholarship. The present volume argues from theological, hermeneutical, and historical considerations for the inerrancy of the OT not only in its theological teaching but also in matters pertaining to history and science. Although it contains a section on the NT, the focus is upon OT criticism.

2.13.7   Sparks, Kenton. *God's Word in Human Words: An Evangelical Appropriation of Critical Biblical Scholarship*. Grand Rapids: Baker, 2008. 415pp.

Employs detailed philosophical, historical, and exegetical argumentation to insist that evangelicals must accept the methods and findings of mainline critical OT scholarship in order to be true to the facts and to avoid

87

the charge of obscurantism. Adopts an "accommodationist" model, which avers that God, acting according to full incarnation, has chosen to reveal God's Word through the weak and often mistaken views of the human authors of Scripture. Although written particularly for evangelicals, this volume and the one edited by Hoffmeier and Magary (§2.13.6) deal with issues in OT hermeneutics that are pertinent to students of the Bible in general.

2.13.8   Stuart, Douglas. *Old Testament Exegesis: A Primer for Students and Pastors.* 4th ed. Louisville: Westminster John Knox, 2009. 193pp.

An introduction to the task of OT exegesis for the seminary student and pastor. Assumes very little regarding biblical and hermeneutical background. Clearly written and eminently practical guide for the basic steps involved in the interpretation of the text with a view toward preaching and teaching. The fourth edition contains suggestions on the use of online resources.

Also Significant

2.13.9   Achtemeier, Elizabeth. *The Old Testament and the Proclamation of the Gospel.* Philadelphia: Westminster, 1973. 224pp.

2.13.10   Alter, Robert. *The Art of Biblical Poetry.* San Francisco: Harper, 1987. 228pp.

2.13.11   Bar-Efrat, Shimon. *Narrative Art in the Bible.* Journal for the Study of the Old Testament Supplemental Series 70; Bible and Literature Series 17. Sheffield: Sheffield Academic Press, 1997. 295pp.

2.13.12   Bos, Rein. *We Have Heard That God Is With You: Preaching the Old Testament.* Grand Rapids: Eerdmans, 2008. 384pp.

2.13.13   Broyles, Craig C., ed. *Interpreting the Old Testament: A Guide for Exegesis.* Grand Rapids: Baker, 2001. 272pp.

2.13.14   Brueggemann, Walter. *Interpretation and Obedience: From Faithful Reading to Faithful Living.* Minneapolis: Fortress, 1991. 325pp.

2.13.15   Exum, J. Cheryl, and David J. A. Clines, eds. *The New Literary Criticism and the Hebrew Bible.* Sheffield: JSOT, 1993. 276pp.

2.13.16   Goldingay, John. *Approaches to Old Testament Interpretation.* Rev. ed. Downers Grove, Ill.: InterVarsity, 1990. 207pp.

2.13.17   ———. *Key Questions about Biblical Interpretation: Old Testament Answers.* Grand Rapids: Baker, 2011. 384pp.

2.13.18   Gowan, Donald E. *Reclaiming the Old Testament for the Christian Pulpit.* Atlanta: John Knox, 1980. 163pp.

2.13.19   Greidanus, Sidney. *Preaching Christ from the Old Testament: A Contemporary Hermeneutical Method.* Grand Rapids: Eerdmans, 1999. 373pp.

2.13.20   Gunn, David M., and Danna Nolan Fewell. *Narrative in the Hebrew Bible.* Oxford Bible Series. Oxford: Oxford University Press, 1993. 263pp.

2.13.21   Hayes, John H., ed. *Old Testament Form Criticism.* San Antonio, Tex.: Trinity University Press, 1974. 289pp.

2.13.22   Holmgren, Fredrick C. *The Old Testament and the Significance of Jesus: Embracing Change, Maintaining Christian Identity.* Sources for Biblical and Theological Study 2. Grand Rapids: Eerdmans, 1999. 204pp.

2.13.23   House, Paul R., ed. *Beyond Form Criticism: Essays in Old Testament Literary Criticism.* Winona Lake, Ind.: Eisenbrauns, 1992. 446pp.

2.13.24   Koch, Klaus. *The Growth of the Biblical Tradition: The Form-Critical Method.* New York: Scribner's, 1969. 233pp.

2.13.25   Kugel, James L. *The Idea of Biblical Poetry: Parallelism and Its History.* New Haven, Conn.: Yale University Press, 1981. 339pp.

2.13.26   McCurley, Foster R. *Wrestling with the Word: Christian Preaching from the Hebrew Bible.* Valley Forge, Pa.: Trinity Press International, 1996. 243pp.

2.13.27   Rad, Gerhard von. *Biblical Interpretations in Preaching.* Nashville: Abingdon, 1977. 125pp.

2.13.28   Smith, George Adam. *Modern Criticism and the Preaching of the Old Testament.* 3d ed. New York: Armstrong, 1902. 325pp.

2.13.29   Steck, Odil Hannes. *Old Testament Exegesis: A Guide to Methodology.* Society of Biblical Literature Resources for Biblical Study 33. Atlanta: Scholars, 1995. 208pp.

The following volumes in the Guides to Biblical Scholarship series are relevant:

2.13.30   Habel, Norman C. *Literary Criticism of the Old Testament.* Philadelphia: Fortress, 1971. 86pp.

2.13.31   Hens-Piazza, Gina. *The New Historicism.* Minneapolis: Fortress, 2002. 94pp.

2.13.32   Kille, D. Andrew. *Psychological Biblical Criticism.* Minneapolis: Fortress, 2001. 161pp.

2.13.33   Miller, J. Maxwell. *The Old Testament and the Historian.* Philadelphia: Fortress, 1976. 87pp.

2.13.34   Niditch, Susan. *Folklore and the Hebrew Bible.* Minneapolis: Fortress, 1983. 117pp.

2.13.35   Overholt, Thomas W. *Cultural Anthropology and the Old Testament.* Minneapolis: Fortress, 1996. 116pp.

2.13.36   Petersen, David L., and Kent Harold Richards. *Interpreting Hebrew Poetry.* Minneapolis: Fortress, 1992. 117pp.

2.13.37   Rast, Walter E. *Tradition History and the Old Testament.* Philadelphia: Fortress, 1972. 82pp.

2.13.38   Robertson, David. *The Old Testament and the Literary Critic.* Philadelphia: Fortress, 1977. 87pp.

2.13.39   Sanders, James A. *Canon and Community: A Guide to Canonical Criticism*. Philadelphia: Fortress, 1984. 78pp.

2.13.40   Trible, Phyllis. *Rhetorical Criticism: Context, Method, and the Book of Jonah*. Minneapolis: Fortress, 1994. 264pp.

2.13.41   Tucker, Gene M. *Form Criticism of the Old Testament*. Philadelphia: Fortress, 1971. 84pp.

2.13.42   Wilson, Robert R. *Sociological Approaches to the Old Testament*. Philadelphia: Fortress, 1984. 83pp.

2.14   Old Testament Introductions

Highly Recommended

2.14.1   Anderson, Bernhard W. *Understanding the Old Testament*. 4th ed. Upper Saddle River, N.J.: Prentice-Hall, 1998. 635pp.

This basic introduction to the OT moves in the direction of a "survey" of the OT, but contains more technical historical, hermeneutical, and literary discussion than typically found in surveys. Moves chronologically from the beginnings of Israel's existence as a people to the threshold to the NT period. Employs a narrative style that weaves together in a lively and readable fashion historical, literary, and theological concerns. Generally assumes conclusions of mainline critical scholarship, but is critically and theologically moderate in comparison with much recent OT study.

2.14.2   Brueggemann, Walter, and Tod Linafelt. *An Introduction to the Old Testament: The Canon and Christian Imagination*. 2d ed. Louisville: Westminster John Knox, 2012. 504pp.

Treats each book of the OT in its final canonical form according to literary, historical, and theological considerations with a view towards its meaning for the church's faith and life. Complements the more traditional historical-critical OT introductions. The literary features of the canonical text are informed by political, ideological, and religious background, which together invite imaginative interaction with the theological meaning of the individual biblical books and the OT in its entirety read as the canon of the church. For Brueggemann this imaginative interaction does not merely conform to the theological tradition of the church but may at times challenge or expand it. Explicitly draws out theological and pastoral significance for the contemporary life of the church.

2.14.3   Childs, Brevard S. *Introduction to the Old Testament as Scripture*. Philadelphia: Fortress, 1979. 688pp.

A classic work and extremely significant in the history of twentieth century OT scholarship both for the cogent description at the beginning of this volume of the "canonical approach" to OT study for which Childs is famous and for the fact that this volume, written from the perspective of the canonical approach, is a new type of OT introduction. There is virtually no attention here to many issues that are normally addressed in introductions, e.g., historical development of Israel, archaeology. Rather, the emphasis is on the "canonical form" of the text (essentially the final form), and the ways in which the history of the tradition that lies behind the final form and the history of OT interpretation can illumine the canonical form and the church's theological and pastoral appropriation of that canonical text.

2.14.4   Dillard, Raymond B., and Tremper Longman III. *An Introduction to the Old Testament*. Rev. ed. Grand Rapids: Zondervan, 2006. 528pp.

Lucid, basic introduction that concentrates on the final form of the text as the church's Scripture, and consequently gives relatively little attention to source analysis or the history of the development of individual books. Emphasizes "special introduction" (study of individual books) rather than "general introduction" (topics pertaining to the OT as a whole, e.g., textual criticism or the canon). In the process, concentrates on three issues: (1) historical background, (2) literary analysis, (3) theological message. Written from a conservative perspective, but offering fair and open interaction with less conservative historical criticism.

2.14.5   Eissfeldt, Otto. *The Old Testament: An Introduction*. New York: Harper & Row, 1965. 861pp.

Most thorough, detailed, authoritative introduction representing the results of German critical scholarship (which had definitive global influence) in the latter half of the twentieth century. Also discusses the Apocrypha, Pseudepigrapha, and the Dead Sea Scrolls. Now somewhat dated; it should be supplemented with more recent critical studies (e.g., Schmidt [§2.14.7]). Complemented by Harrison (§2.14.6), which presents the conservative rejoinder to many of the conclusions found here.

2.14.6   Harrison, R. K. *Introduction to the Old Testament*. Grand Rapids: Eerdmans, 1969. 1325pp.

In many ways a conservative corollary to Eissfeldt (§2.14.5). Written by perhaps the most prominent conservative OT scholar of his generation, a massive, learned, and detailed introduction that discusses virtually every major aspect of OT. Includes the Apocrypha. Employs a type of historical-critical study, but consistently arrives at conservative positions. Now dated; it should be supplemented by more recent treatments (e.g., Dillard and Longman [§2.14.4]).

2.14.7   Schmidt, Werner H. *Old Testament Introduction.* 2d ed. Louisville: Westminster John Knox, 1995. 452pp.

Lucid presentation of contemporary critical perspectives on major issues of OT history, source analysis, origin and development of OT books, and theology and hermeneutics. Schmidt offers the "consensus" view on the various questions, and thus puts forth little of his own original thinking. Discussions tend to be quite brief, but still a helpful basic orientation.

Also Significant

2.14.8   Birch, Bruce C., Walter Brueggemann, Terence E. Fretheim, and David L. Petersen. *A Theological Introduction to the Old Testament.* 2d ed. Nashville: Abingdon, 2005. 485pp.

2.14.9   Coggins, Richard. *Introducing the Old Testament.* Oxford Bible Series. 2d ed. Oxford: Oxford University Press, 2001. 192pp.

2.14.10   Coogan, Michael D. *The Old Testament: A Historical and Literary Introduction to the Hebrew Scriptures.* 2d ed. New York: Oxford University Press, 2011. 562pp.

2.14.11   Crenshaw, James L. *Old Testament Story and Faith: A Literary and Theological Introduction.* Peabody, Mass.: Hendrickson, 1992. 472pp.

2.14.12   Drane, John. *Introducing the Old Testament.* 3d ed. Minneapolis: Fortress, 2011. 380pp.

2.14.13   Gottwald, Norman K. *The Hebrew Bible: A Socio-Literary Introduction.* Philadelphia: Fortress, 1985. 702pp.

2.14.14   Orr, James. *The Problem of the Old Testament Considered with Reference to Recent Criticism.* New York: Scribners, 1906. 562pp.

2.14.15   Peckham, Brian. *History and Prophecy: Its Development of Late Judean Literary Traditions.* New York: Doubleday, 1993. 880pp.

2.14.16   Rendtorff, Rolf. *The Old Testament: An Introduction.* Philadelphia: Fortress, 1985. 308pp.

2.14.17   Sandmel, Samuel. *The Hebrew Scriptures: An Introduction to Their Literature and Religious Ideas.* Oxford: Oxford University Press, 1978. 546pp.

2.14.18   Schultz, Samuel. *The Old Testament Speaks.* 4th ed. New York: Harper, 1990. 440pp.

2.14.19   Smith, W. Robertson. *The Old Testament in the Jewish Church.* 3d ed. London: A. & C. Black, 1926. 458pp.

2.14.20   Young, Edward J. *An Introduction to the Old Testament.* Revised ed. Grand Rapids: Eerdmans, 1964. 432pp.

2.15   Old Testament Theology

Highly Recommended

2.15.1   Bright, John. *The Authority of the Old Testament.* Nashville: Abingdon, 1967.

Probably the most definitive treatment of the theological and practical issues of the authority of the OT for the Christian church. Deals especially with the use of the OT in Christian preaching, and includes illuminating examples of Christian preaching from some of the most difficult and problematic OT passages.

2.15.2   Brueggemann, Walter. *Theology of the Old Testament: Testimony, Dispute, Advocacy.* Minneapolis: Fortress, 1997. 777pp.

Massive, learned, and creative, attempts to move OT theology beyond the ruling paradigms of preceding generations into the new era of postmodernism. As such, emphasizes the pluralistic testimonies to Yahweh in the OT and interaction between those testimonies. Understands the object of the study of OT theology to be the dynamic process of theological dispute between competing visions of God found within the OT rather than the content of the theological claims of the OT themselves. Helpful for considering how the contemporary cultural environment affects the doing of OT theology, but less helpful for understanding that theology itself.

2.15.3   Childs, Brevard S. *Old Testament Theology in a Canonical Context*. Philadelphia: Fortress, 1985. 255pp.

Here Childs applies his canonical approach to OT study (as set forth paradigmatically at the beginning of his *Introduction to the Old Testament as Scripture* [§2.14.3]) to the writing of an OT theology. Thus it focuses on the canonical writings rather than events or experiences behind them. Understands the OT specifically as part of Christian theology, and thus engages in a distinctively Christian reading of the OT, and one that is at times implicitly informed by Child's own Reformed tradition. Extremely relevant and practical for Christian reflection on the various major themes and aspects of OT theology.

2.15.4   Eichrodt, Walther. *Theology of the Old Testament*. 2 vols. Old Testament Library. Philadelphia: Westminster, 1967. 542/573pp.

Produced by one of the most prominent OT scholars in the twentieth century, a classic and standard work that emphasizes that Israel's faith was essentially unique among its neighbors and was self-consistent (over against the pluralistic view of Brueggemann [§2.15.2]). Finds the unity of OT theology in the concept of "covenant." Deals with OT theology on the basis of the final form of the text, and treats it synchronically, i.e., as it stands in the OT with little regard to historical development. If one were to buy just one OT theology, this might be the best.

2.15.5   Goldingay, John. *Old Testament Theology*. 3 vols. Downers Grove, Ill.: InterVarsity, 2003–2009. 940/891/912pp.

Arguably the most comprehensive and sweeping OT theology to appear in a generation. Written by an evangelical who accepts many of the conclusions of critical scholarship. Focusing upon the final form of the text, it is based on careful exegetical work that does not explicitly appear in the discussions themselves but is frequently referenced in footnotes. The first volume interprets the story of God's relationship with Israel and is something of a theological commentary on the narrative of the OT; the second volume addresses matters of faith and hope and treats major theological concepts in turn; while the third volume addresses the ethos and ethics of the OT in terms of the kinds of relationships the OT inculcates. Careful to avoid reading NT or Christian ideas into the OT, yet attends to the ways in which OT theology culminates in Jesus Christ and the Christian gospel.

2.15.6   Hasel, Gerhard F. *Old Testament Theology: Basic Issues in the Current Debate.* 4th ed. Grand Rapids: Eerdmans, 1991. 262pp.

Surveys the various approaches to OT theology pursued especially in twentieth-centruy works, and critically examines them in order to identify both positive and negative aspects. As a result of this study, Hasel presents his own method, emphasizing the nature of the biblical materials themselves without depending on external categories. Contains extensive bibliography.

2.15.7   Hayes, John H., and Frederick Prussner. *Old Testament Theology: Its History and Development.* Atlanta: John Knox, 1985. 290pp.

Similar in purpose and character to the volume by Hasel (§2.15.6), but more concerned with the major figures and historical development of the discipline of OT theology, with relatively less attention to OT theology's major issues or methods. Contains rather extensive bibliographies for each section. Most comprehensive and current history of OT theology available.

2.15.8   Rad, Gerhard von. *Old Testament Theology.* 2 vols. New York: Harper & Row, 1962. 483/470pp.

A monumental work by arguably the greatest OT scholar of the twentieth century. Argues that the theology of the OT reflects Israel's experience of God's acts of salvation, and that OT theology moves progressively forward to full realization in Christ according to a process in which Israel constantly re-interpreted ("re-actualization") earlier traditions in light of contemporary concerns. As such, he depends much on tradition-critical reconstruction. Rich in profound insight even for those who do not accept his critical conclusions or his specific method.

Also Significant

2.15.9   Anderson, Bernhard W. *Contours of Old Testament Theology.* Minneapolis: Fortress, 1999. 358pp.

2.15.10   ———. *From Creation to New Creation: Old Testament Perspectives.* Overtures to Biblical Theology. Minneapolis: Fortress, 1994. 256pp.

2.15.11   Barth, Christoph. *God with Us: A Theological Introduction to the Old Testament*. Grand Rapids: Eerdmans, 1991. 403pp.

2.15.12   Becker, Joachim. *Messianic Expectation in the Old Testament*. Edinburgh: T&T Clark, 1977. 96pp.

2.15.13   Brueggemann, Walter. *Old Testament Theology: An Introduction*. Nashville: Abingdon, 2008. 433pp.

2.15.14   Collins, John J. *Encounters with Biblical Theology*. Minneapolis: Fortress, 2005. 243pp.

2.15.15   Davidson, A. B. *The Theology of the Old Testament*. International Theological Library. Edinburgh: T&T Clark, 1904. 553pp.

2.15.16   Gerstenberger, Erhard S. *Theologies in the Old Testament*. Minneapolis: Fortress, 2002. 384pp.

2.15.17   Goldingay, John. *Theological Diversity and the Authority of the Old Testament*. Grand Rapids: Eerdmans, 1987. 308pp.

2.15.18   Holladay, William L. *Long Ago God Spoke: How Christians May Hear the Old Testament Today*. Minneapolis: Fortress, 1995. 355pp.

2.15.19   House, Paul R. *Old Testament Theology*. Downers Grove, Ill: InterVarsity, 1998. 655pp.

2.15.20   Kaiser, Walter C., Jr. *Toward an Old Testament Theology*. Grand Rapids: Zondervan, 1978. 303pp.

2.15.21   Knierim, Rolf P. *The Task of Old Testament Theology: Substance, Method, and Cases*. Grand Rapids: Eerdmans, 1995. 390pp.

2.15.22   Martens, Elmer A. *Old Testament Theology*. IBR Bibliographies 13. Grand Rapids: Baker, 1997. 138pp.

2.15.23   Moberly, R. W. L. *Old Testament Theology: Reading the Hebrew Bible as Christian Scripture*. Grand Rapids: Baker Academic, 2013. 320pp.

2.15.24 Ollenburger, Ben C., ed. *Old Testament Theology: Flowering and Future.* Rev. ed. Winona Lake, Ind: Eisenbrauns, 2004. 544pp.

2.15.25 Perdue, Leo G. *The Collapse of History: Reconstructing Old Testament Theology.* Overtures to Biblical Theology. Minneapolis: Fortress, 1994. 317pp.

2.15.26 Preuss, Horst Dietrich. *Old Testament Theology.* 2 vols. Louisville: Westminster John Knox, 1995, 1996. 372/438pp.

2.15.27 Richter, Sandra L. *The Epic of Eden: A Christian Entry into the Old Testament.* Downers Grove, Ill.: InterVarsity, 2008. 263pp.

2.15.28 Routledge, Robin. *Old Testament Theology: A Thematic Approach.* Downers Grove, Ill.: InterVarsity, 2008. 384pp.

2.15.29 Sailhamer, John H. *Introduction to Old Testament Theology: A Canonical Approach.* Grand Rapids: Zondervan, 1995. 327pp.

2.15.30 Satterthwaite, Philip E., Richard S. Hess, and Gordon J. Wenham, eds. *The Lord's Anointed: Interpretation of Old Testament Messianic Texts.* Grand Rapids: Baker, 1995. 320pp.

2.15.31 Seitz, Christopher R. *Word without End: The Old Testament as Abiding Theological Witness.* Grand Rapids: Eerdmans, 1998. 355pp.

2.15.32 Snaith, Norman H. *The Distinctive Ideas of the Old Testament.* New York: Schocken, 1964. 193pp.

2.15.33 Vanhoozer, Kevin J., ed. *Theological Interpretation of the Old Testament: A Book-by-Book Survey.* Grand Rapids: Baker, 2005. 336pp.

2.15.34 Vriezen, Theodorus Christiaan. *An Outline of Old Testament Theology.* 2d ed. Newton, Mass.: Branford, 1970. 479pp.

2.15.35 Waltke, Bruce K. *An Old Testament Theology: An Exegetical, Canonical, and Thematic Approach.* Grand Rapids: Zondervan, 2006. 1040pp.

2.15.36   Westermann, Claus. *Elements of Old Testament Theology.* Atlanta: John
            Knox, 1982. 261pp.

2.15.37   Wright, Christopher J. H. *Knowing Jesus through the Old Testament.*
            Downers Grove, Ill.: InterVarsity, 1995. 256pp.

2.15.38   Wright, G. Ernest. *God Who Acts: Biblical Theology as Recital.* Studies in
            Biblical Theology 8. London: SCM, 1952. 132pp.

2.15.39   Zimmerli, Walther. *Old Testament Theology in Outline.* Atlanta: John
            Knox, 1978. 258pp.

2.16   Old Testament Ethics

Highly Recommended

2.16.1   Birch, Bruce C. *Let Justice Roll Down: The Old Testament, Ethics, and the
           Christian Life.* Louisville: Westminster John Knox, 1991. 383pp.

           Written by a leading authority in biblical (and especially OT) ethics, this
           volume is not a description of ethical thinking or systems within the OT
           itself, but rather a hermeneutical exploration of the use of the OT for
           contemporary Christian ethics. Its emphasis is therefore methodological.
           Although Birch makes serious use of exegesis employing the historical-
           critical method, he focuses on the canonical shape of the text (and in the
           process reads the OT in light of the NT). He moves through the OT,
           discussing the issues involved in the ethical use of its various parts.

2.16.2   Janzen, Waldemar. *Old Testament Ethics: A Paradigmatic Approach.* Louis-
           ville: Westminster John Knox, 1994. 236pp.

           Identifies five models of the good life in the OT (priestly, wisdom, royal,
           prophetic, familial) and argues that each of these includes stories that
           are paradigmatic for OT ethics in general, and that each of these models
           comes to full expression in the portrait of Jesus in the NT. These models
           reflect various genres of the OT and thus support Janzen's major claim
           that the whole of the OT, and not just certain genres (e.g., law), is relevant
           for ethics. Suggestive and engaging, although more dependent on Janzen's
           unique construal of passages and his distinctive hermeneutical perspective
           than is Birch's work (§2.16.1).

2.16.3   Wright, Christopher J. H. *Old Testament Ethics for the People of God.* Downers Grove, Ill.: InterVarsity, 2004. 520pp.

Wright here develops his own model for doing OT ethics, which he set forth originally in *An Eye for an Eye* (§2.16.12). Moves from an examination of the essential perspectives the OT establishes for its ethics, to an exploration of the major issues in OT ethics, culminating in a discussion of methodological issues. The choice of major issues Wright chooses to explore is not particularly objectionable, yet he does not justify the selection. Lucid, engaging, and practical. Best overall introduction to the study of OT ethics.

Also Significant

2.16.4   Barton, John. *Ethics and the Old Testament.* Harrisburg, Pa.: Trinity Press International, 1998. 100pp.

2.16.5   ———. *Understanding Old Testament Ethics: Approaches and Explorations.* Louisville: Westminster John Knox, 2003. 212pp.

2.16.6   Birch, Bruce C. *What Does the Lord Require? The Old Testament Call to Social Witness.* Louisville: Westminster John Knox, 1985. 116pp.

2.16.7   Carrol R., M. Daniel, and Jacqueline E. Lapsley, eds. *Character Ethics and the Old Testament: Moral Dimensions of Scripture.* Louisville: Westminster John Knox, 2007. 260pp.

2.16.8   Crenshaw, James L., and John T. Willis, eds. *Essays in Old Testament Ethics.* New York: Ktav, 1974. 284pp.

2.16.9   Green, Joel B., and Jaqueline E. Lapsey, eds. *The Old Testament and Ethics: A Book-by-Book Survey.* Grand Rapids: Baker Academic, 2013. 240pp.

2.16.10   Kaiser, Walter C., Jr. *Toward Old Testament Ethics.* Grand Rapids: Zondervan, 1983. 345pp.

2.16.11   Rodd, Cyril S. *Glimpses of a Strange Land: Studies in Old Testament Ethics.* Old Testament Studies. Edinburgh: T&T Clark, 2000. 384pp.

2.16.12   Wright, Christopher J. H. *An Eye for an Eye: The Place of Old Testament Ethics Today.* Downers Grove, Ill.: InterVarsity, 1983. 224pp.

2.17   Old Testament Commentaries: Multivolume

2.17.1   Keil, Carl Friedrich, and Franz Delitzsch. *Commentary on the Old Testament.* 10 vols. Peabody, Mass.: Hendrickson, 1996. Reprinted from the English edition originally published by T&T Clark, Edinburgh, 1860–1891. Volumes average 800pp.

Learned commentary on every passage of the OT from two of the most prominent nineteenth-century German OT scholars, representing an evangelical and generally conservative position. Gives serious attention to details of the Hebrew text, but equally concerned with historical and literary context and theological significance. Especially useful in providing solid exposition for parts of the OT for which there are relatively few helpful commentaries. Now dated, and should be used in combination with more recent contributions. This retypeset edition corrects typographical errors, uses current abbreviations, and incorporates other changes to improve readability.

2.17.2   Wesley, John. *Explanatory Notes upon the Old Testament.* 3 vols. Bristol, UK: William Pine, 1765–1766. 2613pp.

Comparable to Wesley's better-known *Explanatory Notes upon the New Testament* (§4.18.5), the founder of Methodism offers terse commentary for the "unlettered" reader of the Bible. Very basic comment, with frequent insights pertaining to the relation of the text to other biblical passages, fulfillment in Christ, and significance for Christian living. More helpful for exposure to eighteenth-century British commentary and to Wesley's interpretive methods and conclusions than for its critical interpretation of the details of the text in their historical and literary contexts.

2.18   Old Testament Commentaries: Series

Highly Recommended

2.18.1   Abingdon Old Testament Commentaries. Edited by Patrick D. Miller Jr. 14 vols. currently. Nashville: Abingdon, 2001–. Volumes average 300pp.

Produced for theological students and informed ministers, offers straightforward interpretation of extended units of the text from a moderately critical perspective. After an introduction discussing the historical setting of the book, the commentary offers a "literary analysis," setting forth the structure, rhetorical devices, and genre of the passage, followed by "exegetical analysis," which provides a careful, though brief, interpretation, which is in turn followed by "theological and ethical analysis," which seeks to intersect the interpretation with contemporary issues and challenges. Each volume concludes with an annotated bibliography. Handy, reliable, and helpful for preaching and teaching.

2.18.2   Forms of Old Testament Literature. Edited by Rolf Knierim, Gene M. Tucker, and Marvin A. Sweeney. 17 vols. presently available. Grand Rapids: Eerdmans, 1981–. Volumes average 250pp.

Highly technical volumes offer form-critical analysis of individual portions of biblical books. Examines the structure, genre, setting, and intention of each passage. The emphasis on critical analysis means that the lion's share of attention is given to sources lying behind the final text and to the editorial process of including individual portions within the composition of the whole. With some exceptions, gives little attention to the theological meaning of the final form of the text.

Series Whose Individual Volumes Are Frequently Included in Lists on Specific Books

2.18.3   Apollos Old Testament Commentary. Edited by David W. Baker and Gordon J. Wenham. Downers Grove, Ill.: InterVarsity, 2002–.

2.18.4   Baker Exegetical Commentary on the Old Testament. Edited by Tremper Longman III. Grand Rapids: Baker, 2005–.

2.18.5   Berit Olam: Studies in Hebrew Narrative & Poetry. Edited by David W. Cotter. Collegeville, MN: Michael Glazier, 1996–.

2.18.6   Daily Study Bible: Old Testament. Edited by John C. L. Gibson. 24 vols. Louisville: Westminster John Knox, 1981–1987.

2.18.7   Historical Commentary on the Old Testament. Edited by Cornelius Houtman, Willem S. Prinsloo, Wilfred G. E. Watson, and Al Wolters. Leuven: Peeters, 1993–.

2.18.8   New International Commentary on the Old Testament. Edited by R. K.
Harrison and Robert L. Hubbard Jr. Grand Rapids: Eerdmans, 1976–.

2.18.9   Old Testament Library. Edited by Peter R. Ackroyd, Bernhard Anderson,
James Barr, James Luther Mays, and G. Ernest Wright. Original series.
Louisville: Westminster John Knox, 1962–1988; William P. Brown,
Carol A. Newsome, and David L. Petersen. New Series. Louisville: West-
minster John Knox, 1991–.

2.19   The Pentateuch: General Works

Highly Recommended

2.19.1   Alexander, T. Desmond, and David W. Baker, eds. *Dictionary of the Old
Testament Pentateuch: A Compendium of Contemporary Biblical Scholarship.* Downers Grove, Ill.: InterVarsity, 2003. 954pp.

The first OT volume in a series of dictionaries published by InterVarsity
Press on specific portions of the Bible (previous volumes had been limited
to the NT). Articles written by evangelicals or those friendly to evangelical
concerns who are generally open to the critical study of the OT and committed to a fair appraisal of critical methods and conclusions. Deals with a
wide range of topics and issues pertaining to the Pentateuch. Articles range
from one thousand to ten thousand words in length. Each concludes with
a bibliography.

2.19.2   Blenkinsopp, Joseph. *The Pentateuch: An Introduction to the First Five
Books of the Bible.* Anchor Bible Reference Library. New York: Doubleday, 1992. 273pp.

Readable, comprehensive study from a leading OT scholar. Describes and
evaluates recent developments in the source-critical analysis of the Pentateuch, and argues for a modified form of the documentary hypothesis.
Employs source analysis, historical background, and a close reading of the
final form of the text to arrive at a holistic interpretation, presented passage by passage through the Pentateuch. Probably the best overall introduction to the Pentateuch. Includes extensive bibliography.

2.19.3   Brueggemann, Walter, and Hans Walter Wolff. *The Vitality of Old Testament Traditions.* 2d ed. Atlanta: John Knox, 1982. 180pp.

Two prominent OT scholars address the theology of the major sources (according to the general critical consensus) of the Pentateuch: Yahwist, Elohist, Deuteronomist, and Priestly. The discussions are lucid and engaging and provide insight also into the theology of the final form of the text, and thus are useful even to those who are skeptical regarding these sources.

2.19.4   Clines, David J. A. *The Theme of the Pentateuch.* 2d ed. Journal for the Study of the Old Testament Supplemental Series 10. Sheffield: JSOT, 1997. 176pp.

The brevity of this book belies its value as an illuminating study of the identification and exposition of the unifying theme of the Pentateuch, which Clines takes to be the partial fulfillment (and therefore also partial nonfulfillment) of the promise of blessing to the patriarchs. Includes a sustained reading of the Pentateuch from the perspective of this central theme. Clines focuses on the final form of the text, while relating his method and conclusions to the dominant theories of the history of tradition that lies behind the final text.

2.19.5   Crüsemann, Frank. *The Torah: Theology and Social History of Old Testament Law.* Minneapolis: Fortress, 1996. 460pp.

Most comprehensive treatment available of OT law. Traces the development of the commandments of the Pentateuch from their earliest formulation to their inclusion in oral and written sources to their role in the final form of the Pentateuch. Attends to historical background, social context, and theological significance.

2.19.6   Livingston, G. Herbert. *The Pentateuch in Its Cultural Environment.* 2d ed. Grand Rapids: Baker, 1987. 322pp.

A most comprehensive, learned, and balanced treatment of the various aspects of the Pentateuch (historical, literary, theological) from a conservative perspective. Offers informed and lucid discussions, replete with illustrations, photos, and maps. Each section concludes with select bibliography. Very useful as an introduction to the study of the Pentateuch, valuable even to those who do not share its conservative orientation.

2.19.7   Sailhamer, John H. *The Pentateuch as Narrative: A Biblical-Theological Commentary.* Grand Rapids: Zondervan, 1992. 522pp.

Solid commentary on the final form of the Pentateuch from a conservative perspective. Treats the Pentateuch as a continuous narrative, and thus makes very little of the distinction between the five books and gives no attention to the sources that might lie behind the final text. Argues that the author of the Pentateuch (possibly Moses) had lived under the Law of the Covenant given at Sinai and had come to recognize that it could not produce true faith in Yahweh and thus looked forward to the hope of the new covenant that would be established entirely on God's faithfulness. Despite its avowedly narrative approach, draws very little on current narrative-critical theory and suffers somewhat from its general lack of attention to historical background. Still, offers helpful theological insights into the final form of the text.

Also Significant

2.19.8   Alexander, T. Desmond. *From Paradise to the Promised Land: An Introduction to the Main Themes of the Pentateuch.* 3d ed. Grand Rapids: Baker, 2012. 360pp.

2.19.9   Buber, Martin. *Moses: The Revelation and the Covenant.* New York: Harper, 1958. 226pp.

2.19.10   Campbell, Antony F., and Mark A. O'Brien. *Sources of the Pentateuch: Texts, Introductions, Annotations.* Minneapolis: Fortress, 1993. 266pp.

2.19.11   Coats, George W. *Moses: Heroic Man, Man of God.* Journal for the Study of the Old Testament Supplement Series 57. Sheffield: JSOT, 1988. 250pp.

2.19.12   Fretheim, Terence E. *The Pentateuch.* Interpreting Biblical Texts. Nashville: Abingdon, 1996. 183pp.

2.19.13   Hamilton, Victor P. *Handbook on the Pentateuch.* 2d ed. Grand Rapids: Baker, 2005. 468pp.

2.19.14   Lohfink, Norbert. *Theology of the Pentateuch: Themes of the Priestly Narrative and Deuteronomy.* Minneapolis: Fortress, 1994. 314pp.

2.19.15   McCarthy, D. J. *Old Testament Covenant: A Survey of Current Opinions.* Growing Points in Theology. Atlanta: John Knox, 1972. 112pp.

2.19.16   Nicholson, Ernest. *The Pentateuch in the Twentieth Century: The Legacy of Julius Wellhausen.* Oxford: Clarendon, 1998. 294pp.

2.19.17   Noth, Martin. *A History of Pentateuchal Traditions.* Atlanta: Scholars, 1981. 296pp.

2.19.18   ———. *Laws in the Pentateuch and Other Studies.* London: SCM, 1966. 289pp.

2.19.19   Patrick, Dale. *Old Testament Law.* Atlanta: John Knox, 1985. 278pp.

2.19.20   Rad, Gerhard von. *The Problem of the Hexateuch and Other Essays.* London: SCM, 1966. 340pp.

2.19.21   Rofé, Alexander. *Introduction to the Composition of the Pentateuch.* Sheffield: Sheffield Academic Press, 1999. 152pp.

2.19.22   Sailhamer, John H. *The Meaning of the Pentateuch: Revelation, Composition and Interpretation.* Downers Grove, Ill.: InterVarsity, 2009. 632pp.

2.19.23   Sherwood, Stephen K. *Leviticus, Numbers, and Deuteronomy.* Berit Olam. Collegeville, Minn.: Michael Glazier, 2002. 320pp.

2.19.24   Sparks, Kenton L. *The Pentateuch: An Annotated Bibliography.* IBR Bibliographies 1. Grand Rapids: Baker, 2002. 160pp.

2.19.25   Suelzer, A. *The Pentateuch: A Study in Salvation History.* New York: Herder & Herder, 1964. 224pp.

2.19.26   Whybray, R. N. *Introduction to the Pentateuch.* Grand Rapids: Eerdmans, 1995. 146pp.

2.20   Genesis

Highly Recommended

2.20.1   Arnold, Bill T. *Genesis.* New Cambridge Bible Commentary. Cambridge: Cambridge University Press, 2009. 409pp.

Combines a diachronic approach that reads Genesis in terms of ANE proto-histories with a synchronic reading that interprets individual passages within the literary (Genesis and Pentateuch) context. Although the commentary is relatively brief, includes the most relevant information and develops the most significant features of the text for a robust theological interpretation.

2.20.2   Brueggemann, Walter. *Genesis*. Interpretation: A Bible Commentary for Teaching and Preaching. Atlanta: John Knox, 1982. 384pp.

One of the best in the Interpretation series, this volume focuses on the theological witness of the final form of the text. Sets forth engaging, profound, and practical theological insights based on careful exegesis. Elegantly written, and almost poetic in places.

2.20.3   Hamilton, Victor P. *The Book of Genesis*. 2 vols. New International Commentary on the Old Testament. Grand Rapids: Eerdmans, 1990, 1995. 522/774pp.

Thorough, current commentary from an evangelical perspective by a prominent OT scholar in the Wesleyan tradition. Affirms literary and theological unity of the book, and thus does not deal with multiple layers of tradition. Emphasizes the development throughout Genesis of the book's main theme: God's gracious promise of blessing and reconciliation in the face of sin and evil. Each section concludes with discussion of the use of that portion of Genesis in the NT.

2.20.4   Hendel, Ronald, ed. *Reading Genesis: Ten Methods*. Cambridge: Cambridge University Press, 2010. 230pp.

Offers a panorama of the ways in which Genesis has been read over the centuries and continues to be read today. Includes both ancient ways of reading, critical methods, and contemporary models. The term "methods" in the subtitle is a bit misleading, since not all of the chapters deal with methods in the narrow sense of the term but some pertain to the appropriation of Genesis (as, e.g., in modern literature). Provides profound insight into aspects of Genesis and introduces the reader to various interpretive strategies.

2.20.5   Rad, Gerhard von. *Genesis: A Commentary*. Rev. ed. Old Testament Library. Philadelphia: Westminster, 1972. 440pp.

One of the finest commentaries ever written on any biblical book, this is a masterpiece of brilliant literary analysis that leads to engaging theological insight. Although at a few points the commentary depends on von Rad's critical reconstruction of sources, generally the focus is on the final form of the text.

2.20.6 Wenham, Gordon J. *Genesis.* 2 vols. Word Biblical Commentary. Waco, Tex.: Word, 1987, 1994. 352/517pp.

Employs lucid, terse style to communicate a wealth of information pertaining to text-critical analysis, compositional sources, and theological significance. Engages in broad interaction with current research and consistently reaches conclusions that are well informed and judicious. Draws insights from historical background and tradition history, but in the service of an interpretation of the final text that takes its compositional artistry seriously. Represents the best of British evangelical scholarship.

2.20.7 Westermann, Claus. *Genesis: A Commentary.* 3 vols. Continental Commentary. Minneapolis: Augsburg, 1984–1986. 636/604/269pp.

Most complete, comprehensive, and erudite commentary on Genesis ever produced. Encyclopedic in treatment of text-critical issues, historical and archaeological background, linguistic matters, and history of interpretation. Technical in content, but readable in form. Makes use of source-critical insights, but focuses on final shape of the text. Gives serious attention to theological significance.

Also Significant

2.20.8 Cassuto, Umberto. *Commentary on the Book of Genesis.* 2 vols. Jerusalem: Magnes, 1961–1964. 323/386pp.

2.20.9 Cotter, David W. *Genesis.* Berit Olam. Collegeville, MN: Liturgical, 2003. 366pp.

2.20.10 Delitzsch, Franz. *A New Commentary on Genesis.* 2 vols. 5th ed. Edinburgh: T&T Clark, 1899. 412/408pp.

2.20.11 Driver, S. R. *The Book of Genesis.* Westminster Commentaries. London: Methuen, 1904. 420pp.

2.20.12 Evans, Craig A., Joel N. Lohr, and David L. Petersen, eds. *The Book of Genesis: Composition, Reception, and Interpretation.* Supplements to Vetus Testamentum *The Formation and Interpretation of Old Testament Literature,* vol. 152. Leiden: Brill, 2012. 763pp.

2.20.13 Fokkelman, J. P. *Narrative Art in Genesis: Specimens of Stylistic and Structural Analysis.* 2d ed. Sheffield: JSOT, 1991. 244pp.

2.20.14 Gunkel, Hermann. *Genesis.* Mercer Library of Biblical Studies. Macon, Ga.: Mercer University Press, 1997. (Original German edition, 1910.) 477pp.

2.20.15 Sarna, Nahum. *Understanding Genesis.* New York: McGraw-Hill, 1966. 267pp.

2.20.16 Skinner, John. *A Critical and Exegetical Commentary on the Book of Genesis.* 2d ed. International Critical Commentary. Edinburgh: T&T Clark, 1930. 551pp.

2.20.17 Speiser, Ephraim A. *Genesis.* 3d ed. Anchor Bible. Garden City, N.Y.: Doubleday, 1964. 378pp.

2.20.18 Waltke, Bruce K., and Cathi J. Fredricks. *Genesis: A Commentary.* Grand Rapids: Zondervan, 2001. 656pp.

2.21 Exodus

Highly Recommended

2.21.1 Childs, Brevard S. *The Book of Exodus: A Critical, Theological Commentary.* Old Testament Library. Philadelphia: Westminster, 1974. 659pp.

A new type of commentary, one that puts into practice Childs's "canonical approach," as set forth at the beginning of his *Introduction to the Old Testament as Scripture* (§2.14.3). Childs employs insights from a philological examination of the language of the text, the growth of the tradition through its various stages to the final (canonical) shape, the function of the passage in its literary context, its role in the canon of the OT, and the history of Jewish and Christian exegesis in order to interpret the theological significance of the text as Scripture for the church. Probably the most authoritative commentary on Exodus, and the most helpful for teaching and preaching.

2.21.2 Dozeman, Thomas B. *Exodus.* Eerdmans Critical Commentary. Grand Rapids: Eerdmans, 2009. 868pp.

Massive, technical commentary that interprets Exodus as a theological document whose meaning is informed by consideration of ANE background. Attends especially to the role of Exodus within the Pentateuch and the entire Christian canon. Considers the book of Exodus to be not history, but a religious document expressing the faith of Israel. Rejects many of the details of the Documentary Hypothesis in favor of a two-stage composition (Pre-P History and P-History). Commentary depends upon this compositional theory throughout, and therefore its usefulness is somewhat limited for those who do not accept this critical reconstruction. Engages in constant and lively interaction with contemporary scholarship.

2.21.3 ———, ed. *Methods for Exodus*. Methods in Biblical Interpretation. Cambridge: Cambridge University Press, 2010. 254pp.

Introduces both older and emerging methods in OT interpretation and applies these methods to the book of Exodus. Thus illumines both the various exegetical approaches and the text of Exodus. Deals with literary and rhetorical criticism, genre criticism, source and redaction criticism, liberation criticism, feminist criticism, and postcolonial biblical criticism. Seeks to demonstrate how these individual interpretive approaches relate to each other and how they can complement one another with a view toward obtaining a holistic understanding of Exodus. Employs Exodus 1–2 and 19–20 as test cases throughout.

2.21.4 Durham, John I. *Exodus*. Word Biblical Commentary. Waco, Tex.: Word, 1987. 516pp.

Emphasizes the theological unity of Exodus in its canonical form, and finds the book's unity in its central theme, viz., Yahweh as present in the midst of his people Israel. Interpretation focuses on language and literary context, with little attention given to growth of the tradition, historical background or archaeological discoveries, since Durham regards most attempts to reconstruct actual historical events or earlier traditions to be hopelessly speculative. Deals seriously with theological issues as they are encountered in the text, but gives little explicit attention to theological implications or contemporary application.

2.21.5 Fretheim, Terence E. *Exodus*. Interpretation: A Bible Commentary for Teaching and Preaching. Louisville: Westminster John Knox, 1991. 321pp.

Outstanding example of engaging and profound theological reflection on issues of contemporary concern based on careful exegesis of the text. Deals especially with issues of the relationship between history and faith, theology of creation, the knowledge of God, images of God, Exodus as

110

a paradigm for liberation, theology of worship, and the role of law and covenant for Israel's identity. Complements the more "traditional" commentaries that are heavy on technical matters, but give little attention to contemporary theological significance.

2.21.6   Gowan, Donald E. *Theology in Exodus: Biblical Theology in the Form of a Commentary*. Philadelphia: Westminster, 1994. 297pp.

Like Childs's commentary (§2.21.1), this book is intended to chart new methodological paths. Whereas Childs attempted to write a new kind of commentary, Gowan attempted a new type of biblical theology, viz., one that emerges out of a careful reading of the text in its literary (i.e., book) and canonical contexts. Organized like a commentary, but asks a single question: What does this book say about God? Traces the major affirmations about God through the rest of Scripture and into Judaism and Christianity. Somewhat restrictive, in that the theology of the book is broader than the doctrine of God, yet certainly God is the primary concern, and this restriction establishes and maintains focus.

2.21.7   Hamilton, Victor P. *Exodus: An Exegetical Commentary*. Grand Rapids: Baker, 2011. 721pp.

Eminently helpful for preaching and teaching on Exodus within the church. Does not address in much detail issues of historicity, but does consider selectively historical background and gives significant attention to Hebrew terms. Engages in a theological reading of the text that interprets Exodus in light of the rest of the OT and considers its meaning also from the perspective of the NT.

Also Significant

2.21.8   Cassuto, Umberto. *A Commentary on the Book of Exodus*. Jerusalem: Magnes, 1967. 509pp.

2.21.9   Driver, S. R. *The Book of Exodus*. Cambridge Bible for Schools and Colleges. Cambridge: Cambridge University Press, 1911. 443pp.

2.21.10   Houtman, Cornelius. *Exodus*. 3 vols. Historical Commentary on the Old Testament. Kampen: Kok, 1993–2000. 554/466/737pp.

2.21.11   Knight, George A. F. *Theology as Narration: A Commentary on the Book of Exodus*. Edinburgh: Handsel, 1976. 209pp.

111

2.21.12   Larsson, Gören. *Bound for Freedom: The Book of Exodus in Jewish and Christian Traditions.* Peabody, Mass.: Hendrickson, 1999. 334pp.

2.21.13   Meyer, Lester. *The Message of Exodus: A Theological Commentary.* Minneapolis: Augsburg, 1983. 171pp.

2.21.14   Meyers, Carol. *Exodus.* New Cambridge Bible Commentary. Cambridge: Cambridge University Press, 2005. 311pp.

2.21.15   Noth, Martin. *Exodus.* Old Testament Library. Philadelphia: Westminster, 1962. 283pp.

2.21.16   Propp, William H. C. *Exodus 1–18.* Anchor Bible. New York: Doubleday, 1998. 680pp.

2.21.17   ———. *Exodus 19–40.* Anchor Yale Bible Commentary. New Haven, Conn.: Yale University Press, 2006.

2.21.18   Sarna, Nahum. *Exploring Exodus: The Heritage of Biblical Israel.* New York: Schocken, 1986. 277pp.

2.22   Leviticus

Highly Recommended

2.22.1   Balentine, Samuel E. *Leviticus.* Interpretation: A Bible Commentary for Teaching and Preaching. Louisville: Westminster John Knox, 2002. 220pp.

Although acknowledging a complex compositional history, focuses upon the final form of the text. Employs insights from ritual theory and other anthropological studies to explore the role and significance of ritual and worship within Leviticus for the whole of the community of faith in ancient Israel and for the church today. Interprets individual passages in terms of their role within the book and the OT more generally. Gives some limited attention to the relationship between passages in Leviticus and the NT.

2.22.2   Hartley, John E. *Leviticus.* Word Biblical Commentary. Dallas: Word, 1992. 496pp.

Careful attention by this evangelical scholar to exegetical detail combined with emphasis on theological issues and implications make this volume extremely helpful for preaching and teaching on a portion of the canon that resists easy or immediate application to contemporary concerns. Identifies the central issue of Leviticus as the significance of pure worship and holy living, with a subordinate (though still important) issue pertaining to leadership and the relationship between priest and laity. Contends that the book contains a core of laws originating with Moses that has been supplemented by applications of these laws pertinent to later generations of Israelites.

2.22.3   Milgrom, Jacob. *Leviticus.* 3 vols. Anchor Bible. New York: Doubleday, 1991, 2000, 2001. 2714pp.

Technical, detailed, and encyclopedic treatment of text-critical, source-critical, linguistic, and historical considerations, with serious interaction with the history of interpretation, especially ancient interpretation (e.g., rabbis and interpretation implicit in the Septuagint versions). Written by a Jewish scholar, these volumes offer exposure to critical Jewish scholarship, but of course do not relate Leviticus to the NT or Christian fulfillment. Finds the center of the book in the presence of Yahweh dwelling in the midst of camp and congregation as the basis of the unique privilege and responsibility of Israel, a people thus called to worship and service. Excellent for serious study of the development of traditions and the original meaning and function of the text, but less helpful for theological implications and discussion of contemporary application.

2.22.4   Wenham, Gordon J. *The Book of Leviticus.* New International Commentary on the Old Testament. Grand Rapids: Eerdmans, 1979. 362pp.

Like Hartley (§2.22.2), Wenham gives careful attention to the language of the text and to issues of historical background, with a view toward development of theological issues and suggestions regarding contemporary Christian application. Refuses to take a position on critical issues of the book's origins, and thus remains independent of any specific theory of authorship, sources, and date. Briefer, less technical, with less bibliography than Hartley's, but still quite helpful for both serious academic work and tasks of preaching and teaching.

Also Significant

2.22.5   Bonar, A. A. *A Commentary on the Book of Leviticus: Expository and Practical.* 2d ed. London: Nisbet, 1863. 513pp.

2.22.6   Budd, Philip J. *Leviticus.* New Century Bible. Grand Rapids: Eerdmans, 1996. 395pp.

2.22.7   Carmichael, Calum M. *Illuminating Leviticus: A Study of Its Laws and Institutions in Light of Biblical Narratives.* Baltimore: Johns Hopkins University Press, 2006. 212pp.

2.22.8   Douglas, Mary. *Leviticus as Literature.* Oxford: Oxford University Press, 1999. 280pp.

2.22.9   Gerstenberger, Erhard S. *Leviticus: A Commentary.* Old Testament Library. Louisville: Westminster John Knox, 1996. 450pp.

2.22.10   Harrison, R. K. *Leviticus.* Tyndale Old Testament Commentaries. Downers Grove, Ill.: InterVarsity, 1980. 252pp.

2.22.11   Kiuchi, Nobuyoshi. *Leviticus.* Apollos Old Testament Commentary. Downers Grove, Ill.: IVP, 2007. 538pp.

2.22.12   Milgrom, Jacob. *Leviticus: A Book of Ritual and Ethics.* Continental Commentaries. Minneapolis: Fortress, 2004. 388pp.

2.22.13   Noth, Martin. *Leviticus: A Commentary.* Rev. ed. Old Testament Library. Philadelphia: Westminster, 1977. 208pp.

2.22.14   Warning, Wilfried. *Literary Artistry in Leviticus.* Leiden: Brill, 1999. 256pp.

2.22.15   Watts, James W. *Ritual and Rhetoric in Leviticus: From Sacrifice to Scripture.* Cambridge: Cambridge University Press, 2007. 257pp.

2.23   Numbers

Highly Recommended

2.23.1   Ashley, Timothy R. *The Book of Numbers.* New International Commentary on the Old Testament. Grand Rapids: Eerdmans, 1993. 667pp.

Careful attention to the details of the text, especially linguistic details. This commentary from an evangelical scholar grants the reality of a long process of transmission of tradition toward the final form, but asserts that because this process is unrecoverable with any degree of certainty we should focus on the final form of the text. Identifies the overall theological and pastoral purpose as a call to exact obedience to God. Helpful for dealing with technical matters essential for interpretation, but offers relatively little explicit comment on theological significance of passages.

2.23.2   Budd, Philip J. *Numbers*. Word Biblical Commentary. Waco, Tex.: Word, 1984. 409pp.

Informed and current, lucid in style though with a focus on technical linguistic and tradition-critical issues. Treats Numbers as composed in its final form by priestly writers in the early postexilic period as part of the priestly redaction of the whole Pentateuch, yet argues that Numbers has its own unity and distinct themes and theology, one that concerns especially the Levitical order and the tent of meeting. Commentary focuses on the ways the priestly writers edited received tradition in order to address concerns that Israel faced in the sixth century BCE. This emphasis might mitigate somewhat the value of commentary for those who disagree with this historical or methodological perspective. Gives serious attention to the theology of the text.

2.23.3   Levine, Baruch A. *Numbers*. 2 vols. Anchor Bible. New York: Doubleday, 1993, 2000. 528/613pp.

Meticulous, detailed commentary by a leading Jewish Pentateuchal scholar. Focuses on technical linguistic and historical issues. Like Budd (§2.23.2), emphasizes the role of priestly traditions and priestly editorial activity in the sixth century BCE, but without the concern for theological issues found in Budd's volume. Helpful for serious exploration of technical matters pertaining to interpretation, less so for theological reflection.

2.23.4   Olson, Dennis T. *Numbers*. Interpretation: A Bible Commentary for Teaching and Preaching. Louisville: Westminster John Knox, 1996. 196pp.

Readable, reliable exposition of the meaning of the text in its final form, with engaging and creative connections to the NT and contemporary issues facing the church. Important complement to the majority of commentaries on Numbers, which give little attention to theology and virtually no attention to contemporary application. Does suffer some from brevity.

Also Significant

2.23.5   Gray, George Buchanan. *A Critical and Exegetical Commentary on Numbers.* International Critical Commentary. Edinburgh: T&T Clark, 1903. 489pp.

2.23.6   Harrison, R. K. *Numbers: An Exegetical Commentary.* Grand Rapids: Baker, 1992. 542pp.

2.23.7   Ibn Ezra, with annotations by H. Norman Strickman and Arthur M. Silver. *Commentary on the Pentateuch: Numbers.* New York: Menorah, 1999. 270pp.

2.23.8   Lee, Won W. *Punishment and Forgiveness in Israel's Migratory Campaign.* Grand Rapids: Eerdmans, 2003. 308pp.

2.23.9   Maarsingh, B. *Numbers.* Text and Interpretation: A Practical Commentary. Grand Rapids: Eerdmans, 1987. 122pp.

2.23.10   Olson, Dennis T. *The Death of the Old and the Birth of the New: The Framework of the Book of Numbers and the Pentateuch.* Brown Judaic Studies 71. Chico, Calif.: Scholars, 1985. 253pp.

2.23.11   Riggans, Walter. *Numbers.* Daily Study Bible. Philadelphia: Westminster, 1983. 251pp.

2.23.12   Wenham, Gordon J. *Numbers.* Tyndale Old Testament Commentaries. Downers Grove, Ill.: InterVarsity, 1981. 240pp.

2.24   Deuteronomy

See also THE FORMER PROPHETS: GENERAL WORKS (§2.25)

Highly Recommended

2.24.1   Christensen, Duane. *Deuteronomy.* 2d ed. 2 vols. Word Biblical Commentary. Nashville: Thomas Nelson, 2001, 2002. 915pp.

Argues the unusual thesis that Deuteronomy is a didactic poem, intended to be recited publicly to music within a liturgical setting, and thus emphasizes the artistic and literary structures of Deuteronomy, comparing them to modern epic poetry and music. While acknowledging the role of Moses in the traditions found in this book, focuses on the post-Mosaic formation and liturgical use of the book. Many readers will find Christensen's thesis unpersuasive, but all readers will find its theological reflections and probes into contemporary relevance and application useful.

2.24.2   Clements, Ronald E. *God's Chosen People: A Theological Interpretation of the Book of Deuteronomy*. London: SCM, 1968. 126pp.

Brief but solid and illuminating discussion of the major theological themes in Deuteronomy, within the context of the historical production of the book (reforms under Josiah) and its place in OT theology. Useful as an introduction to Deuteronomy's theology.

2.24.3   Craigie, Peter C. *The Book of Deuteronomy*. New International Commentary on the Old Testament. Grand Rapids: Eerdmans, 1976. 424pp.

Clear and solid commentary espousing a conservative position regarding date and unity: Deuteronomy is a record of the words of Moses as Israel gathered for a ceremonial renewal of the Sinai covenant before entering Canaan. Craigie grants it might have been edited in Joshua's time. Finds the theme to be the covenant, and this theme forms the basis for the book's contemporary significance to the people of the new covenant. Gives careful attention to the language of the text, book context, and historical background.

2.24.4   Miller, Patrick D., Jr. *Deuteronomy*. Interpretation: A Bible Commentary for Teaching and Preaching. Louisville: Westminster John Knox, 1990. 253pp.

The best commentary available for the theological meaning of Deuteronomy. Deals with the original significance of the text at the time of its production (sixth century BCE), and uses this discussion as the basis for canonical reflection on its relation to other OT and NT passages, and for creative and compelling theological reflection that has practical ramifications for contemporary Christian life.

2.24.5   Nelson, Richard D. *Deuteronomy: A Commentary*. Old Testament Library. Louisville: Westminster John Knox, 2002. 424pp.

Informed and judicious commentary, attending to historical background, linguistic analysis, literary structure and other rhetorical features pertaining to the final form of the text, the history of composition (i.e., the stages of the book's development), and the significance of the book for the original audience (who lived during the reigns of Manasseh and Josiah). Is concerned to present the distinctive theology of Deuteronomy, especially the call to reform, the centralization of sacrifice, the repudiation of competing religions, election, and covenant. Commentary is thus ambitious in scope. This ambitious scope is both a strength and a weakness, for Nelson struggles in a commentary of this length to treat each of these concerns thoroughly and to relate them in significant ways to one another.

2.24.6   Rad, Gerhard von. *Deuteronomy.* Old Testament Library. Philadelphia: Westminster, 1966. 210pp.

Authoritative and learned; argues that the central concern of the book is loyalty to the one God and worship at one place. Maintains that the book was composed of a vast array of traditions connected with the holy war and that it emerged at the end of eighth century BCE in response to an unparalleled threat to the existence of Israel and its worship. The commentary carefully explains the text within this framework. Provides many helpful insights, yet is somewhat constrained by its brevity and by the narrow (and by no means universally accepted) view of the book's origin. Offers less theological reflection than does his commentary on Genesis (§2.20.5).

Also Significant

2.24.7   Driver, S. R. *A Critical and Exegetical Commentary on Deuteronomy.* International Critical Commentary. Edinburgh: T&T Clark, 1895. 434pp.

2.24.8   Firth, David G., and Philip S. Johnston. *Interpreting Deuteronomy: Issues and Approaches.* Downers Grove, Ill.: InterVarsity, 2012. 288pp.

2.24.9   McConville, J. Gordon. *Deuteronomy.* Apollos Old Testament Commentary. Downers Grove, Ill.: InterVarsity, 2002. 448pp.

2.24.10   Millar, J. Gary. *Now Choose Life: Theology and Ethics in Deuteronomy.* New Studies in Biblical Theology. Grand Rapids: Eerdmans, 1998. 216pp.

2.24.11   Olson, Dennis T. *Deuteronomy and the Death of Moses.* Overtures to Biblical Theology. Philadelphia: Fortress, 1994. 191pp.

2.24.12   Rad, Gerhard von. *Studies in Deuteronomy. Studies in Biblical Theology.* London: SCM, 1953. 96pp.

2.24.13   Rofé, Alexander. *Deuteronomy: Issues and Interpretation.* Old Testament Studies. Edinburgh: T&T Clark, 2001. 224pp.

2.24.14   Thompson, J. A. *Deuteronomy.* Tyndale Old Testament Commentaries. Downers Grove, Ill.: InterVarsity, 1974. 320pp.

2.24.15   Tigay, Jeffrey. *Deuteronomy.* JPS Torah Commentary. Philadelphia: Jewish Publication Society, 1996. 538pp.

2.24.16   Vogt, Peter T. *Deuteronomic Theology and the Significance of Torah: A Reappraisal.* Winona Lake, Ind.: Eisenbrauns, 2006. 242pp.

2.24.17   Weinfeld, Moshe. *Deuteronomy 1–11.* Anchor Bible. New York: Doubleday, 1991. 455pp.

2.24.18   Welch, Adam C. *Deuteronomy: The Framework to the Code.* London: Oxford University Press, 1932. 215pp.

2.25   The Former Prophets: General Works

See also THE PENTATEUCH: GENERAL WORKS (§2.19)

Highly Recommended

2.25.1   Arnold, Bill T., and H. G. M. Williamson, eds. *Dictionary of the Old Testament Historical Books.* Downers Grove, Ill.: InterVarsity, 2005. 1060pp.

A companion volume to *Dictionary of the Old Testament Pentateuch* (§2.19.1), this volume treats in some detail all pertinent matters pertaining to the Deuteronomic History (Joshua–2 Kings) and the Chronicler's History (Chronicles–Esther). A welcome feature of this dictionary is its concern for the two aspects of history: the events as they actually occurred, and historiography as the selective and interpretive process of presenting the narrative of events. Largely evangelical in orientation, this dictionary sets forth the various major views on issues and deals with alternative perspectives with fairness and sympathy.

2.25.2 Bendavid, Abba. *Maqbilot baMiqra [Parallels in the Bible]*. Jerusalem: Carta, 1972. 219pp.

Reliable and accessible synopsis between the Books of Chronicles and Samuel/Kings as well as other relevant biblical parallels. Less extensive than Vanuttelli (§2.25.8), especially in the area of textual criticism and the Septuagint. Usable for those who have a firm basic knowledge of Hebrew.

2.25.3 Endres, John C., William R. Millar, and John Barclay Burns, eds. *Chronicles and Its Synoptic Parallels in Samuel, Kings, and Related Biblical Texts*. Collegeville, Minn.: Liturgical Press, 1998. 356pp.

Probably the most current and accessible synopsis of the historical books. Includes a helpful introduction to the history of synopses or harmonies of the historical books and the use of these resources, followed by the synopsis proper, in which the text from Chronicles appears on the left column with parallels on the right. Includes a new "synoptic" translation that seeks to reflect points of similarity in the original Hebrew between Chronicles and parallel passages that might be missed by the standard versions.

2.25.4 Fretheim, Terence E. *Deuteronomic History*. Interpreting Biblical Texts. Nashville: Abingdon, 1983. 160pp.

Engaging and practical guide for theological interpretation and contemporary application of the Deuteronomic History, which Fretheim believes was produced for exiles in Babylonian captivity. After dealing briefly but specifically with the most relevant introductory matters (e.g., historicity and the overall theology of the Deuteronomic History), Fretheim presents models of interpretation and application of four key passages, one each from Joshua, Judges, Samuel, and Kings.

2.25.5 McConville, J. Gordon. *Grace in the End: A Study in Deuteronomic Theology*. Studies in Old Testament Biblical Theology. Grand Rapids: Zondervan, 1993. 176pp.

Illuminating review of recent scholarly contributions to both the critical issues and theology of the book of Deuteronomy and the Deuteronomic History. McConville includes his own conclusions regarding the theological message of this corpus, which asserts God's continuing grace to Israel in spite of Israel's constant sin and rebellion.

2.25.6   Nelson, Richard D. *The Historical Books.* Interpreting Biblical Texts. Nashville: Abingdon, 1998. 190pp.

Basic introduction to the study of the Historical Books (including both the Deuteronomic and Chronistic histories), dealing with the concept of history and historical writing in the ancient, and especially biblical, world, and major interpretive methods employed in the study of these books. Moves from meaning of individual books to their role in the overall theological program of the Deuteronomic History and/or the Chronicler's History. Emphasizes theological meaning of the final form of the text.

2.25.7   Polzin, Robert. *Moses and the Deuteronomist: A Literary Study of the Deuteronomic History.* New York: Seabury, 1980. 226pp.

The first volume of a proposed four-part study of the Deuteronomic History (two others are available, §2.29.7; §2.29.8) that employs contemporary reader-response theory to grasp the meaning of the narrative in its final form. Recognizes the existence of earlier sources and a complex process of redaction lying behind the extant text, but argues that the final form is a coherent narrative and should be read as such. Provides many illuminating insights, but should be supplemented with more traditional verse-by-verse commentaries on the specific books that offer fuller and more sustained treatment of individual passages. This commentary covers Deuteronomy through Judges.

2.25.8   Vannutelli, Primus. *Libri Synoptici Veteris Testamenti seu Librorum Regum et Chronicorum Loci Paralleli.* Rome: Pontifical Biblical Institute Press, 1931–1934. 701pp.

Most complete and authoritative synoptic parallel between Chronicles and Samuel/Kings (and other parallel biblical material) available. Includes both Hebrew and Greek (Septuagint) texts, and contains extensive text-critical apparatus. But it is accessible only to those who read the biblical languages, and is somewhat difficult to find, since it has been long out of print. Students who wish to consult a Hebrew synopsis that is more accessible and less expensive (though also less extensive) might consider Abba Bendavid (2.25.2).

Also Significant

2.25.9   Auld, A. Graeme. *Kings without Privilege: David and Moses in the Story of the Bible's Kings.* Edinburgh: T&T Clark, 1994. 203pp.

2.25.10　Campbell, Antony F., and Mark A. O'Brien. *Unfolding the Deutero-nomistic History: Origins, Upgrades, Present Text.* Minneapolis: Augsburg Fortress, 2000. 505pp.

2.25.11　Gerbrandt, Gerald Eddie. *Kingship according to the Deuteronomistic History.* Society of Biblical Literature Dissertation Series 87. Atlanta: Scholars, 1986. 229pp.

2.25.12　Hamilton, Victor P. *Handbook on the Historical Books.* Grand Rapids: Baker, 2001. 560pp.

2.25.13　Mayes, A. D. H. *The Story of Israel between Settlement and Exile: A Redactional Study of the Deuteronomistic History.* London: SCM, 1983. 202pp.

2.25.14　Newsome, James. *A Synoptic Harmony of Samuel, Kings, and Chronicles with Related Passages from Psalms, Isaiah, Jeremiah and Ezra.* Grand Rapids: Baker, 1986. 275pp.

2.25.15　Noth, Martin. *The Deuteronomistic History.* Journal for the Study of the Old Testament Supplement Series 15. Sheffield: JSOT, 1981. 153pp.

2.25.16　Römer, Thomas. *The So-Called Deuteronomistic History: A Sociological, Historical and Literary Introduction.* London: T&T Clark, 2007. 202pp.

2.25.17　Weinfeld, Moshe. *Deuteronomy and the Deuteronomistic School.* Oxford: Clarendon, 1972. 467pp.

2.26　Joshua

Highly Recommended

2.26.1　Auld, A. Graeme. *Joshua, Judges, and Ruth.* Daily Study Bible. Philadelphia: Westminster, 1984. 282pp.

A remarkably perceptive and helpful volume, in spite of its brevity and the amount of biblical material it attempts to cover. Written by a leading authority in this part of the canon, this volume is based on solid and informed exegesis but emphasizes the continuing theological, and indeed, pastoral significance of the final form of the text for Christian thought and life.

2.26.2   Butler, Trent C. *Joshua*. Word Biblical Commentary. Waco, Tex.: Word, 1983. 304pp.

An informed and judicious commentary focusing on the technical issues surrounding this biblical book, including text-critical issues, the oral stages of tradition lying behind the extant text, and the theological purposes of the final compiler. Butler deals with these issues separately and together in a holistic interpretation of passages that focus on their final form. Technical, but richly suggestive in issues of theological significance.

2.26.3   Creach, Jerome. *Joshua*. Interpretation: A Bible Commentary for Teaching and Preaching. Louisville: John Knox, 2003. 135pp.

Like other volumes in the Interpretation series, focuses upon the final form of the text. It deals with historical reconstruction and the history of composition only insofar as these matters illumine the canonical text. Focuses upon those portions of Joshua that have more theological significance, especially chs. 1–12 and 23–24. Deals more with the role of passages within OT theology than within the canon-as-a-whole, and accordingly relates the meaning of the text to the NT and Christian faith in only a limited way. The commentary suffers some from brevity.

2.26.4   Hawk, L. Daniel. *Joshua*. Berit Olam: Studies in Hebrew Narrative and Poetry. Collegeville, Minn.: Liturgical Press, 2000. 303pp.

A careful, sensitive interpretation of the final form of Joshua, employing with sophistication the principles of the emerging literary methods of OT interpretation. Insists that the book is in fact unified and intentional in its literary design, but that the book's theological program is complex, concerned to present Israel's identity not in terms of racial or ethnic realities or the possession of the land or cultic practices, but rather in terms of a people constantly living at the point of decision in the face of the gracious (though also judgmental) word of God.

2.26.5   Nelson, Richard D. *Joshua*. Old Testament Library. Louisville: Westminster John Knox, 1997. 310pp.

Informed, current commentary dealing with all the major issues of this biblical book, including the significant text-critical differences between the Hebrew and Greek (Septuagint) forms of the text, tradition-critical considerations, and the Deuteronomic redactions that pertain to the final composition. Emphasizes especially the meaning of passages within the context of Deuteronomy and the whole Deuteronomic History.

2.26.6   Woudstra, M. H. *The Book of Joshua*. New International Commentary on the Old Testament. Grand Rapids: Eerdmans, 1981. 396pp.

Solid and theologically illuminating commentary from a conservative perspective that avers that the book was written close to the events recorded. Considers the central theological theme to be the fulfillment of God's promises to the patriarchs regarding the land, and identifies how other subordinate themes contribute to this main one. Thus, emphasizes both historical accuracy and theological coherence. Theological insights frequently reflect an evangelical Reformed perspective, but are helpful even for those who belong to other theological traditions.

Also Significant

2.26.7   Auld, A. Graeme. *Joshua Retold: Synoptic Perspectives*. Old Testament Studies. Edinburgh: T&T Clark, 1998. 179pp.

2.26.8   Boling, Robert G., and G. Ernest Wright. *Joshua*. Anchor Bible. Garden City, N.Y.: Doubleday, 1982. 580pp.

2.26.9   Gray, John. *Joshua, Judges, and Ruth*. Rev. ed. New Century Bible. Grand Rapids: Eerdmans, 1986. 325pp.

2.26.10   Hawk, L. Daniel. *Every Promise Fulfilled: Contesting Plots in Joshua*. Literary Currents in Biblical Interpretation. Louisville: Westminster John Knox, 1991. 172pp.

2.26.11   Hess, Richard S. *Joshua: An Introduction and Commentary*. Tyndale Old Testament Commentaries. Downers Grove, Ill.: InterVarsity, 1996. 320pp.

2.26.12   Mitchell, Gordon. *Together in the Land: A Reading of the Book of Joshua*. Journal for the Study of the Old Testament Supplemental Series 134. Sheffield: JSOT, 1993. 219pp.

2.26.13   Noort, Ed., ed. *The Book of Joshua and the Land of Israel*. Bibliotheca Ephemeridum Theologicarum Lovaniensium, no. 250. Louvain: Peeters, 2012. 712pp.

2.26.14   Soggin, J. Alberto. *Joshua.* Old Testament Library. Philadelphia: Westminster, 1972. 245pp.

2.27   Judges

See also JOSHUA (§2.26)

Highly Recommended

2.27.1   Buber, Martin. *The Kingship of God.* New York: Harper & Row, 1967.
228pp.

Brilliant theological discussions of major issues in the book of Judges from
one of the twentieth century's foremost Jewish philosophers and theologians. Discusses textual and historical problems in the book, but always in
the context of the book's broader theological concern, which emphasizes
the establishment of God's people as those who are in dialogue with God
through their various experiences, and who are called and empowered
through this dialogue to live under God's kingship.

2.27.2   Butler, Trent. *Judges.* Word Biblical Commentary. Nashville: Thomas
Nelson, 2009. 537pp.

Massive, erudite commentary that attends to the historical events re-
counted, but gives primary emphasis to the meaning of the narrative. Recognizes the role of satire, irony, and even humor as key communicative
devices in Judges. Interacts with the history of interpretation, but gives
almost exclusive attention to modern scholarship over against the pre-
critical periods. Although technical and detailed in the exegesis of individual passages, it manages constantly to maintain concern for the broad issues of the entire narrative, identifying the major theme of Judges to be the
sovereignty of God and the proper response of worship from God's people.
Gives very little attention to connections with the NT and makes little
reference to significance for the Christian faith as the church's Scripture.

2.27.3   Cundall, Arthur E., and Leon Morris. *Judges and Ruth: An Introduction
and Commentary.* Tyndale Old Testament Commentaries. Downers
Grove, Ill.: InterVarsity, 1968. 318pp.

Written from a conservative perspective. Dates the final composition of
Judges to the period of the early monarchy, and insists on the historical

accuracy of the record. Attends to theological and pastoral significance and to the relation of passages to other biblical texts and motifs. Sometimes uncritically mixes historical reconstruction of events with the witness of the canonical text according to its own narrative world. Since, however, there are few commentaries on Judges that deal seriously at all with theological issues, this volume is generally recommended.

2.27.4   McCann, J. Clinton. *Judges*. Interpretation: A Bible Commentary for Teaching and Preaching. Louisville: Westminster John Knox, 2002. 146pp.

This commentary is very helpful for the theological interpretation of Judges. Focuses on the final form of the text, but the introduction provides brief yet helpful discussion of critical issues and historical background, as well as Judges' role in the canon and its major theological motifs. McCann employs insights from the introduction in his comments throughout. Commentary consistently draws out significance for the contemporary church and world in a way that is not at all forced, but entirely natural. A longer commentary than this on the book of Judges would have been justified and would have allowed McCann to develop his fine treatment in an even more satisfying way.

2.27.5   Niditch, Susan. *Judges*. The Old Testament Library. Louisville: Westminster John Knox, 2008. 289pp.

Interprets Judges from the perspective of oral-traditional cultural analysis and folklore studies and is thus primarily concerned to discern how the stories of Judges would have been heard by ancient Israelites at successive stages of the reception of the book. The commentary itself is little interested in theology and gives no consideration to its function within the canon. The emphasis throughout is upon cultural anthropology and social history. This approach does illumine certain aspects of the text and often introduces insights that are original and sometimes helpful for interpretation.

2.27.6   Webb, Barry G. *The Book of Judges*. The New International Commentary on the Old Testament. Grand Rapids: Eerdmans, 2012. 555pp.

Overall the most useful commentary available on Judges. Although it focuses upon the ways in which the rhetoric of the text directs the communicative sense of the narrative, this commentary is not "narrative-critical" in the narrow sense. Rather, it is eclectic, making use of historical and critical considerations insofar as the text requires them for understanding. Examines also how the function of Judges within the Christian canon informs its sense. Elegantly written. A real jewel.

Also Significant

2.27.7   Boling, Robert G. *Judges*. Anchor Bible. Garden City, N.Y.: Doubleday, 1975. 338pp.

2.27.8   Burney, C. F. *Judges and Kings*. 2d ed. London: Rivingtons, 1919. 384pp.

2.27.9   Gunn, David M. *Judges*. Blackwell Bible Commentaries. Malden, Mass.: Blackwell, 2005. 329pp.

2.27.10   Klein, Lillian R. *The Triumph of Irony in the Book of Judges*. Journal for the Study of the Old Testament Supplement Series 68. Sheffield: Almond, 1988. 280pp.

2.27.11   Lindars, Barnabas. *Judges 1–5: A New Translation and Commentary*. Edited by A. D. H. Mays. Edinburgh: T&T Clark, 1995. 302pp.

2.27.12   Matthews, Victor H. *Judges and Ruth*. New Cambridge Bible Commentary. Cambridge: Cambridge University Press, 2004. 270pp.

2.27.13   Moore, George Foot. *A Critical and Exegetical Commentary on Judges*. International Critical Commentary. Edinburgh: T&T Clark, 1895. 476pp.

2.27.14   O'Connell, Robert H. *The Rhetoric of the Book of Judges*. Leiden: Brill, 1996. 541pp.

2.27.15   Schneider, Tammi J. *Judges*. Berit Olam: Studies in Hebrew Narrative and Poetry. Collegeville, Minn.: Liturgical Press, 2000. 317pp.

2.27.16   Webb, Barry G. *The Book of Judges: An Integrated Reading*. Journal for the Study of the Old Testament Supplement Series 46. Sheffield: JSOT, 1987. 280pp.

2.27.17   Wong, Gregory T. K. *Compositional Strategy in the Book of Judges: An Inductive, Rhetorical Study*. Leiden: Brill, 2006. 287pp.

2.27.18   Yee, Gale A., ed. *Judges and Method: New Approaches in Biblical Studies*. Minneapolis: Fortress, 1995. 186pp.

2.28   Ruth

See also JOSHUA (§2.26); JUDGES (§2.27)

Highly Recommended

2.28.1   Bush, Frederic. *Ruth and Esther.* Word Biblical Commentary. Dallas: Word, 1996. 514pp.

Drawing heavily on recent work on genre studies and discourse analysis as well as narrative poetics, explores the theme, purpose, theology, and dates of these books and interprets their individual passages in great depth. It is the most detailed, complete, and technical of the major commentaries on these books, and is probably the best overall commentary on Esther, although it could be more explicit in theological reflection and more intentional in presenting possibilities for contemporary application.

2.28.2   Campbell, Edward F. *Ruth.* Anchor Bible. Garden City, N.Y.: Doubleday, 1975. 188pp.

Probably the best commentary on Ruth, and one of the best volumes in the Anchor Bible series. Combines sensitive and profound narrative analysis, discussion of ancient customs, and insights from word origins and the nuances to produce a holistic and engaging interpretation, rich in theological reflection. Emphasizes the hidden and subtle, yet determinative, role of God in the book, which Campbell considers a historical novelette composed around the time of Solomon. Accessible to students but also invaluable to scholars.

2.28.3   Hals, Ronald M. *The Theology of the Book of Ruth.* Facet Books. Philadelphia: Fortress, 1966. 81pp.

Lucid, careful, and insightful study of the theology (i.e., specifically the doctrine of God) in Ruth, comparing it with similar stories in the OT, and concluding that both form and content suggest that Ruth was written during the "Solomonic enlightenment." A must for preaching or teaching on Ruth.

2.28.4   Hubbard, Robert L., Jr. *The Book of Ruth.* New International Commentary on the Old Testament. Grand Rapids: Eerdmans, 1988. 317pp.

Gives attention to historical background and linguistic analysis, but focuses especially on the author's use of literary artistry to develop significant theological themes and to draw the reader into the story and effect changes in the reader at the affective as well as cognitive levels. Argues that Ruth was composed to counter opposition to the Davidic monarchy during Solomon's reign. Gives relatively less attention than does Bush (§2.28.1) to technical matters (e.g., careful analysis of the Hebrew), but more attention to the tracing of major theological themes through the narrative and to contemporary application.

2.28.5 LaCocque, André. *Ruth*. Continental Commentary. Minneapolis: Fortress, 2004. 187pp.

Unlike Hals (§2.28.3) or Hubbard (§2.28.4) insists that the book was written by a woman in the days of the "ethnic purging" of Ezra and Nehemiah as a way of understanding and implementing Torah by emphasizing generous inclusive love, a perspective that would be adopted by Jesus. Thus adopts a "socio-legal" approach, utilizing the insights of literary criticism and feminism to inform the social setting and the legal reorientation that are considered essential for construing the book. Erudite, penetrating, and highly insightful. Challenges the consensus about Ruth at a number of points and thus complements well the other major commentaries.

Also Significant

2.28.6 Beattie, D. R. G. *Jewish Exegesis of the Book of Ruth*. Journal for the Study of the Old Testament Supplement Series 2. Sheffield: JSOT, 1977. 251pp.

2.28.7 Caspi, Mishael. *The Book of Ruth: An Annotated Bibliography*. New York: Garland, 1994. 133pp.

2.28.8 Fewell, Danna Nolan, and David Miller Gunn. *Compromising Redemption: Relating Characters in the Book of Ruth*. Literary Currents in Biblical Interpretation. Louisville: Westminster John Knox, 1990. 141pp.

2.28.9 Gowan, Murray D. *The Book of Ruth: Its Structure, Theme, and Purpose*. Leicester, UK: Apollos, 1992. 240pp.

2.28.10 Linafelt, Tod, and Timothy K. Beal. *Ruth and Esther*. Berit Olam. Collegeville, Minn.: Liturgical Press, 1999. 130pp.

2.28.11   Nielsen, Kirsten. *Ruth.* Old Testament Library. Louisville: Westminster John Knox, 1997. 103pp.

2.28.12   Sakenfeld, Katharine Doob. *Ruth.* Interpretation: A Bible Commentary for Teaching and Preaching. Louisville: Westminster John Knox, 1999. 91pp.

2.28.13   Sasson, Jack M. *Ruth: A New Translation with a Philological Commentary and a Formalist-Folklorist Interpretation.* 2d ed. Sheffield: Sheffield Academic Press, 1995. 292pp.

2.29   Books of Samuel

Highly Recommended

2.29.1   Auld, A. Graeme. *I & II Samuel.* Old Testament Library. Louisville: Westminster John Knox, 2011. 686.

Massive, erudite commentary that focuses upon the text of the books of Samuel rather than attempting to reconstruct the events these books report. Provides a sensitive and illuminating reading of the narrative informed by technical analysis of the Hebrew. Insists that these books are concerned exclusively with David. Gives little attention to the theological message of the text and no attention to the role of these books within the Christian canon.

2.29.2   Firth, David G. *1 & 2 Samuel.* Apollos Old Testament Commentary. Downers Grove, Ill.: InterVarsity, 2009. 614pp.

May be described as a "narrative-theological commentary" in that it attends to the rhetoric of the final form of the text as an index to the text's theological claims. Locates these theological claims within the OT and relates them to the NT. In contrast to much postmodern interpretation, identifies Yahweh and the acts of Yahweh as the central concern of these books rather than certain figures (e.g., David) or political agenda.

2.29.3   Fokkelman, J. P. *Narrative Art and Poetry in the Books of Samuel: A Full Interpretation Based on Stylistic and Structural Analyses.* 4 vols. Studia Semitica Neerlandica. Winona Lake, Ind.: Eisenbrauns, 1981–1993. 517/796/441/651pp.

Massive, detailed attempt to combine modern literary study and OT exegesis, focusing on the final form of the text as an integrated narrative. Treats
the text at three levels, each building upon the preceding: (1) literary analysis
exploring the narrative artistry of the passage; (2) psychological analysis exploring the narrator's probing of the deep dimensions of human life; and (3)
"psychagogical" analysis exploring the ways in which contemporary readers
engage the text spiritually or existentially. The first of these levels receives the
most attention. Methodological perspective biases the interpretation toward
a human-centered over against God-centered reading, but volumes offer
(perhaps inadvertently) much theological insight, since they deal seriously
with narratives that are concerned primarily with God.

2.29.4   Hertzberg, Hans Wilhelm. *I and II Samuel: A Commentary.* Old Testament Library. Philadelphia: Westminster, 1964. 416pp.

Overall the best commentary on these books. Elegant, compelling, engaging interpretation focusing on the theological message of the text, while
giving some brief attention to the structure of passages and the history of
the formation of passages from earlier sources. A must for those interested
in rich and profound theological treatment in the service of preaching and
teaching.

2.29.5   McCarter, P. Kyle. *1 Samuel.* Anchor Bible. Garden City, N.Y.: Doubleday, 1980. 474pp.

This volume, like McCarter's commentary on 2 Samuel (§2.29.6), offers a
most complete and detailed examination of text-critical (significant especially for the books of Samuel), historical, source-critical, archaeological,
and linguistic matters, all essential for ascertaining the meaning of the text.
Tends to deal with the text as an amalgam of traditions and redactional
processes rather than as an integrated narrative that functions within the
canon of the church, and therefore does relatively little with theological
reflection.

2.29.6   ———. *2 Samuel.* Anchor Bible. Garden City, N.Y.: Doubleday, 1984.
553pp.

See comments under McCarter's 1 Samuel (§2.29.5).

2.29.7   Polzin, Robert. *David and the Deuteronomist: 2 Samuel.* Indiana Studies
in Biblical Literature. Bloomington: University of Indiana Press, 1993.
245pp.

Sequel to Polzin's *Moses and the Deuteronomist.* See description of the series
presented under that title (§2.25.7).

2.29.8   ———. *Samuel and the Deuteronomist: A Literary Study of the Deutero-nomic History: 1 Samuel.* San Francisco: Harper & Row, 1989. 296pp.

Sequel to Polzin's *Moses and the Deuteronomist.* See description of the series presented under that title (§2.25.7) in the Former Prophets.

2.29.9   Tsumura, David Toshio. *The First Book of Samuel.* New International Commentary on the Old Testament. Grand Rapids: Eerdmans, 2007. 698pp.

Written by a specialist in Semitic languages and ancient Canaanite religion, this commentary is much more technical than is typically the case with volumes in this series. It is highly authoritative, and a volume that all scholarship must take with utmost seriousness. Gives little attention to theological significance of the text and is therefore of somewhat limited value for teaching and preaching in the church.

2.29.10   Welch, Adam C. *Kings and Prophets of Israel.* London: Lutterworth, 1952. 264pp.

Presents biographical sketches of Saul and David as well as Hosea, Amos, and Isaiah. Mentioned here because Welch's treatment of Saul and David is rich in expositional insight from the books of Samuel. In spite of its age, remains an eminently rewarding study of the Saul and David narratives.

Also Significant

2.29.11   Anderson, Arnold. *2 Samuel.* Word Biblical Commentary. Waco, Tex.: Word, 1989. 301pp.

2.29.12   Baldwin, Joyce G. *1 and 2 Samuel.* Tyndale Old Testament Commentaries. Downers Grove, Ill.: InterVarsity, 1988. 299pp.

2.29.13   Brueggemann, Walter. *David's Truth in Israel's Imagination and Memory.* 2d ed. Minneapolis: Fortress, 2002. 144pp.

2.29.14   ———. *First and Second Samuel.* Interpretation: A Bible Commentary for Teaching and Preaching. Louisville: Westminster John Knox, 1990. 362pp.

2.29.15   Cartledge, Tony W. *1 and 2 Samuel.* Smyth & Helwys Bible Commentary. Macon, Ga.: Smyth & Helwys, 2001. 748pp.

2.29.16   Driver, S. R. *Notes on the Hebrew Text of the Books of Samuel.* Oxford: Clarendon, 1890. 296pp.

2.29.17   Edelman, Diana Vikander. *King Saul in the Historiography of Judah.* Journal for the Study of the Old Testament Supplement Series 121. Sheffield: JSOT, 1991. 347pp.

2.29.18   Gordon, Robert P. *I and II Samuel: A Commentary.* Grand Rapids: Zondervan, 1988. 375pp.

2.29.19   Gunn, David M. *The Fate of King Saul: An Interpretation of a Biblical Story.* Journal for the Study of the Old Testament Supplemental Series 14. Sheffield: JSOT, 1980. 181pp.

2.29.20   ———. *The Story of King David: Genre and Interpretation.* Journal for the Study of the Old Testament Supplement Series 6. Sheffield: JSOT, 1978. 164pp.

2.29.21   Jobling, David. *1 Samuel.* Berit Olam: Studies in Hebrew Narrative and Poetry. Collegeville, Minn.: Liturgical Press, 1998. 330pp.

2.29.22   Klein, Ralph W. *1 Samuel.* Word Biblical Commentary. Waco, Tex.: Word, 1983. 307pp.

2.29.23   Long, V. Philips. *The Reign and Rejection of King Saul: A Case for Literary and Theological Coherence.* Society of Biblical Literature Dissertation Series 118. Atlanta: Scholars, 1989. 276pp.

2.29.24   Miscall, Peter D. *1 Samuel: A Literary Reading.* Indiana Studies in Biblical Literature. Bloomington: Indiana University Press, 1986. 198pp.

2.29.25   Payne, David F. *I and II Samuel.* Daily Study Bible. Philadelphia: Westminster, 1982. 277pp.

2.29.26   Smith, Henry Preserved. *A Critical and Exegetical Commentary on the Books of Samuel.* International Critical Commentary. Edinburgh: T&T Clark, 1899. 421pp.

2.30   Books of Kings

See also BOOKS OF SAMUEL (§2.29)

Highly Recommended

2.30.1   Brueggemann, Walter. *1 and 2 Kings*. Smith & Helwys Bible Commentary. Macon, Ga.: Smyth & Helwys, 2000. 645pp.

Primarily for theological students and pastors, but useful for a broad audience, from interested laypersons to scholars. Format is user friendly, with sidebars providing additional historical, theological, bibliographic, and homiletical discussions. Commentary focuses on the theological meaning of the final form of the text, which emerges from careful attention to narrative artistry, but without excessively technical language. Proceeds passage by passage, focusing on Solomon, Elijah, Elisha, and Josiah as models of faith. Each section of commentary is followed by "connections," comprising applications to contemporary personal, church, and national life. Brueggemann is interested in dynamics of (political) power, and that issue (which is certainly significant in these books) is emphasized. This tendency to focus on the human characters tends to de-emphasize the actions of Yahweh, which are arguably the primary concern of these books.

2.30.2   Cohn, Robert L. *2 Kings*. Berit Olam: Studies in Hebrew Narrative and Poetry. Collegeville, Minn.: Liturgical Press, 2000. 186pp.

Like the companion volume on 1 Kings by Walsh (§2.30.9), probes the literary impact of the text in its final form. Cohn recognizes the existence of sources and employs some insights from source and redaction criticism to illumine the final narrative, but the emphasis is almost exclusively on the extant text. Perhaps even more than Walsh, Cohn is careful to interpret individual passages in light of the book's overall narrative and purpose, yet gives less attention to the structure of specific passages and their linguistic nuances than does Walsh. Both Cohn and Walsh give little explicit attention to theological significance and virtually none to contemporary appropriation. Suffers somewhat from its brevity, but still extremely helpful for the interpretation of the text in its final form.

2.30.3   Ellul, Jacques. *The Politics of God and the Politics of Man*. Grand Rapids: Eerdmans, 1972. 198pp.

Written by one of the most perceptive theological thinkers of the twentieth century, this volume is not a commentary in the accepted sense of the term, but rather a series of profound and probing theological reflections pertaining to the contemporary appropriation of selected narratives from the book of Kings. Focuses on matters such as the relationship between God's work and political action, the appropriateness of God's people to be involved in social action, the nature of prophetic activity, the concept of success, and the acceptance of a utilitarian perspective. A model for rich and original theologizing and application of the Bible, and particularly Kings.

2.30.4   Fritz, Volkmar. *1 & 2 Kings*. Continental Commentary. Minneapolis: Fortress, 2003. 448pp.

Originally published in German in 1996, the English translation appeared in 2003. Although adopting the notion of Deuteronomic History the author is uninterested in tracing the compositional development of Kings. Yet gives some attention to redactional layers. The author is an authority on Palestinian archaeology and ANE societies, and thus the commentary emphasizes these matters of background. This is the strength of the commentary. It deals relatively little with theological matters, and when it does the discussion is quite basic and offers little in the way of profound insights.

2.30.5   Gray, John. *I and II Kings: A Commentary*. 3d ed. Old Testament Library. Louisville: Westminster John Knox, 1985. 813pp.

Definitive treatment of the range of technical issues pertaining to these books, especially text-critical considerations, analysis of Hebrew terms and constructions, matters of historical background, and redaction of earlier sources. Gives serious attention to narrative development and to the theology of the text. Especially helpful in its interaction with the history of interpretation, particularly critical scholarship.

2.30.6   Hobbs, T. R. *2 Kings*. Word Biblical Commentary. Waco, Tex.: Word, 1985. 387pp.

Argues that 2 Kings was written by a single author who composed a carefully crafted literary product that evinces a pastoral concern to give to the exilic community of Judah a new understanding of their past and hope for their future under the sovereign faithfulness of God. Emphasizes the role of the prophet, the power of the word of God, and the divine demand for obedience to the law as the condition for the continuation of the Davidic covenant. Carefully considers the author's selectivity and editing of his sources, the nuance of Hebrew terms and constructions, historical background, intercanonical connections (including NT passages and themes), and theological significance.

2.30.7   Nelson, Richard D. *First and Second Kings.* Interpretation: A Bible
Commentary for Teaching and Preaching. Atlanta: John Knox, 1987.
273pp.

Lucid and engaging examination of the literary impact of the final form of
Kings leading to a discovery of its theological message for the community
of faith. Attends to the role of the theological claims of the text of Kings
within the biblical canon as a whole. Concerned also to probe the significance of these passages for contemporary Christian existence. One of the
most solid, original, and compelling volumes in the Interpretation series,
and the most helpful commentary available for teaching and preaching the
Books of Kings.

2.30.8   Sweeney, Marvin A. *I & II Kings.* Old Testament Library. Louisville:
Westminster John Knox, 2007. 476pp.

Argues that the present form of the book is the result of a five-stage
redaction beginning with a Solomonic edition in the late tenth century
BCE and ending with an exilic edition in the mid-sixth century BCE.
Each of these stages represents its own theological, ideological, and political agenda, and therefore an apt interpretation must consider the
historiographical perspective of the redactional stage that is represented
in any passage. This, then, is a rather thoroughgoing redaction-critical
commentary. It is of value in presenting historical background to the
various passages, even if one does not accept the precise compositional
history herein adopted. In spite of its concern to locate passages in terms
of the theological context of the redactor, commentary provides little
theological insight.

2.30.9   Walsh, Jerome T. *1 Kings.* Berit Olam: Studies in Hebrew Narrative and
Poetry. Collegeville, Minn.: Liturgical Press, 1996. 393pp.

Employing the literary approach known as "narrative criticism," focuses
on the meaning of the narrative itself in its final form over against a concern for historical events or the identification of sources or the history of
the development of the traditions. Attends to the structure of passages,
verbal techniques employed (uses Hebrew, but does not require a knowledge of Hebrew on the part of the reader), narrator, plot, point of view,
and characterization. This careful reading of the text is most useful for an
understanding of the impact of the text in its final form and hence for
teaching and preaching, even though Walsh does little with canonical connections or reflections on theological significance.

Also Significant

2.30.10   Auld, A. Graeme. *I and II Kings*. Daily Study Bible. Philadelphia: Westminster, 1986. 258pp.

2.30.11   Burney, C. F. *Notes on the Hebrew Text of the Books of Kings*. Oxford:
Clarendon, 1903. 384pp.

2.30.12   Cogan, Mordechai. *I Kings*. Anchor Bible. New York: Doubleday, 2001.
336pp.

2.30.13   Cogan, Mordechai, and Hayim Tadmor. *II Kings*. Anchor Bible. New
York: Doubleday, 1988. 371pp.

2.30.14   DeVries, Simon J. *1 Kings*. Word Biblical Commentary. Waco, Tex.:
Word, 1985. 286pp.

2.30.15   Halpern, Baruch, and André Lemaire, eds. *The Books of Kings: Sources,
Composition, Historiography and Reception*. Leiden: Brill, 2010. 710pp.

2.30.16   Jones, G. H. *1 and 2 Kings*. 2 vols. New Century Bible Commentary.
Grand Rapids: Eerdmans, 1984. 666pp.

2.30.17   Knoppers, Gary N. *Two Nations under God: The Deuteronomistic History
of Solomon and the Dual Monarchies*. 2 vols. Harvard Semitic Museum
Monographs 52–53. Atlanta: Scholars, 1993. 302/348pp.

2.30.18   Linville, James Richard. *Israel in the Book of Kings: The Past as a Project of
Social Identity*. Journal for the Study of the Old Testament Supplement
Series 272. Sheffield: Sheffield Academic Press, 1998. 331pp.

2.30.19   McKenzie, Steven L. *The Trouble with Kings: The Composition of the Book
of Kings in the Deuteronomistic History*. Leiden: Brill, 1991. 186pp.

2.30.20   Montgomery, James A., and Henry Snyder Gehman. *A Critical and
Exegetical Commentary on the Books of Kings*. International Critical Commentary. Edinburgh: T&T Clark, 1951. 575pp.

2.30.21   Skinner, John. *Kings*. New Century Bible. New York: Henry Frowde, 1904. 459pp.

2.30.22   Wiseman, Donald J. *1 and 2 Kings*. Tyndale Old Testament Commentaries. Downers Grove, Ill.: InterVarsity, 1993. 318pp.

2.31   Books of Chronicles

Highly Recommended

2.31.1   Ackroyd, Peter R. *The Chronicler in His Age*. Journal for the Study of the Old Testament Supplement Series 101. Sheffield: JSOT, 1991. 397pp.

Comprehensive, informed, and judicious study of the books of Chronicles, dealing with all major issues, especially the social and religious environment in which these books were composed. Relates this historical background to the theology of the Chronicler. Considers the Chronicler as a redactor of earlier traditions and as an exegete. Extremely helpful for the theological interpretation of these books.

2.31.2   Braun, Roddy. *1 Chronicles*. Word Biblical Commentary. Waco, Tex.: Word, 1986. 311pp.

Solid and reliable, though not particularly original or imaginative. Gives significant attention to historical background, the role of passages within their book context, and relation to parallel passages in Samuel/Kings. Gives also some attention to the Chronicler's unique contributions to an understanding of Israel's history and to OT theology. Relates theological concerns of the Chronicler to issues of contemporary Christian existence, but tends to do so briefly and generally.

2.31.3   Dillard, Raymond B. *2 Chronicles*. Word Biblical Commentary. Waco, Tex.: Word, 1987. 323pp.

Lucid and somewhat more engaging in terms of probing the theological significance of the text than is Braun's commentary on 1 Chronicles. Especially strong in showing the ways in which the Chronicler interacted with other canonical materials, and in demonstrating the work of the Chronicler as both historian and theologian. Uses the "Explanation" section to relate the theology of Chronicles to the rest of the canon and especially its development in the NT. Contains virtually no introduction; depends on the introductory material in Braun (§2.31.2).

2.31.4   Japhet, Sara. *1 and 2 Chronicles: A Commentary.* Old Testament Library. Louisville: Westminster John Knox, 1993. 1077pp.

Massive, detailed, and probably the most authoritative commentary on these books. Argues for the unity of the work composed by a single author with a definite literary method and theological purpose. Emphasizes the structure, form, and linguistic aspects of passages as well as the author's redaction of earlier sources. Gives relatively little attention to theological claims in the commentary proper, but does briefly discuss the theology of Chronicles in the introduction.

2.31.5   ————. *The Ideology of the Book of Chronicles and Its Place in Biblical Thought.* Beiträge zur Erforschung des Alten Testaments und des Antiken Judentums 9. 2d ed. Frankfurt: Peter Lang, 1997. 553pp.

Helpful supplement to Japhet's fine commentary, which gives little treatment to theological matters. Probes in an informed, balanced, and judicious fashion every major aspect of the theology of the books of Chronicles. This prominent Jewish scholar gives special attention to the relationship of the theology of Chronicles to that of Samuel/Kings and to roughly contemporary biblical materials (e.g., Jeremiah or Ezra/Nehemiah).

2.31.6   Klein, Ralph W. *1 Chronicles.* Hermeneia: A Critical and Historical Commentary on the Bible. Minneapolis: Fortress, 2006. 561pp.

Like Knoppers (§2.31.8), a highly technical commentary that provides much information regarding text-critical matters, historical background, and the redaction of Kings by the Chronicler (employing a text of Kings different from the Masoretic) so as to speak into the situation of fourth-century Judah. Although consistently relates passages in 1 Chronicles to other OT material gives practically no explicit attention to the theological meaning of the text.

2.31.7   ————. *2 Chronicles.* Hermeneia: A Critical and Historical Commentary on the Bible. Minneapolis: Fortress, 2012. 592pp.

See above under Klein, *1 Chronicles* (§2.31.6).

2.31.8   Knoppers, Gary N. *I Chronicles 1–9; I Chronicles 10–29.* 2 vols. Anchor Bible. New York: Doubleday, 2003, 2004. 1045pp.

The most comprehensive commentary on technical and historical matters pertaining to 1 Chronicles. The 240-page introduction and bibliography themselves make these volumes invaluable for the study of the book. Emphasizes text-critical considerations, the writer's use of early (biblical) materials, the relationship between Chronicles and early Hellenistic historiography, and the ways in which the reshaping of Israel's history by Chronicles redefines that history in a way designed to speak to the postexilic audience. Indispensable for technical matters of text and background, but like most volumes in the Anchor Bible series gives little attention to the theology of the text.

2.31.9   Selman, Martin J. *1 and 2 Chronicles: An Introduction and Commentary.* 2 vols. Tyndale Old Testament Commentaries. Downers Grove, Ill.: InterVarsity, 1994. 551pp.

Lucid and engaging commentary that emphasizes the Chronicler as a pastoral theologian who expounded the Bible as he knew it so as to communicate a divine word of healing and reaffirm hope of restoration and of the fulfillment of God's promises. Not as technically oriented as Japheth's commentary or the Word volumes, but more focused on core interpretive issues and matters of concern to most contemporary expositors.

2.31.10   Tuell, Steven S. *First and Second Chronicles.* Interpretation: A Bible Commentary for Teaching and Preaching. Louisville: John Knox, 2001. 252pp.

Focusing on the final form of the text, Tuell argues that the books of Chronicles represented an attempt to read Scripture (especially the Deuteronomic History) in such a way that it would speak anew to the generation of the Chronicler. This new reading of Scripture involved especially a fuller appreciation of God's plan and purposes through the history of Israel, with special reference to David and his line. All of this was intended to lead the postexilic readers of Chronicles to recognize that God was now at work among them as ordinary people in ordinary ways in their own ordinary times. Tuell concludes that Chronicles was written as part of a larger historical work that included Ezra and Nehemiah, and he thus interprets Chronicles in light of those books. But Tuell gives primary attention to the ways the Chronicler adapts earlier biblical tradition to fulfill his own theological purpose. This volume gives much less attention than do most in this series to theological implications for Christians or to contemporary appropriation.

2.31.11   Williamson, H. G. M. *I and II Chronicles.* New Century Bible. Grand Rapids: Eerdmans, 1982. 428pp.

Comparable to Selman (§2.31.9) for accessibility and straightforward discussion of crucial matters for the meaning of the text. Especially helpful are Williamson's introductions to each passage, in which he discusses the history of interpretation and gives judicious conclusions regarding history and theology. Interacts more with other interpreters than does Selman, but does less than Selman to relate passages in Chronicles to other parts of the canon, especially the NT.

Also Significant

2.31.12   Curtis, Edward Lewis, and Albert Alonzo Madsen. *A Critical and Exegetical Commentary on the Books of Chronicles.* International Critical Commentary. Edinburgh: T&T Clark, 1910. 534pp.

2.31.13   Dyck, Jonathan E. *The Theocratic Ideology of the Chronicler.* Biblical Interpretation Series. Leiden: Brill, 1998. 256pp.

2.31.14   Graham, M. Patrick, and Steven L. McKenzie, eds. *The Chronicler as Author: Studies in Text and Texture.* Journal for the Study of the Old Testament Supplemental Series 263. Sheffield: Sheffield Academic Press, 1999. 422pp.

2.31.15   Hahn, Scott W. *The Kingdom of God as Liturgical Empire: A Theological Commentary on 1–2 Chronicles.* Grand Rapids: Baker, 2012. 240pp.

2.31.16   Johnstone, William. *1 and 2 Chronicles.* 2 vols. Journal for the Study of the Old Testament Supplemental Series 253. Sheffield: Sheffield Academic Press, 1997. 411/300pp.

2.31.17   Kalimi, Isaac. *An Ancient Israelite Historian: Studies in the Chronicler, His Time, Place and Writing.* Assen, Netherlands: Van Gorcum, 2005. 212pp.

2.31.18   McKenzie, Steven L. *The Chronicler's Use of the Deuteronomistic History.* Harvard Semitic Monographs 33. Atlanta: Scholars, 1985. 219pp.

2.31.19   Myers, Jacob M. *I Chronicles.* Anchor Bible. 2d ed. Garden City, N.Y.: Doubleday, 1973. 239pp.

2.31.20   ———. *2 Chronicles.* Anchor Bible. 2d ed. Garden City, N.Y.: Doubleday, 1973. 268pp.

2.31.21   Noth, Martin. *The Chronicler's History.* Journal for the Study of the Old
Testament Supplement Series 50. Sheffield: JSOT Press, 1987. 200pp.

2.31.22   Welch, Adam C. *The Work of the Chronicler: Its Purpose and Date.* London: British Academy, 1939. 163pp.

2.32   Ezra and Nehemiah

Highly Recommended

2.32.1   Blenkinsopp, Joseph. *Ezra-Nehemiah: A Commentary.* Old Testament
Library. Louisville: Westminster John Knox, 1988. 366pp.

Perhaps the most authoritative commentary on these books. Gives careful
attention to historical background, development of traditions, and relationship to other biblical books and passages from the same period. Uses
these data to probe the beginnings of emergent Judaism. Argues strongly
(against the tide of recent scholarship) for a close connection between
these books and Chronicles. Helpful for basic understanding of the text,
but gives relatively little attention to theological issues.

2.32.2   Davis, Gordon F. *Ezra and Nehemiah.* Berit Olam: Studies in Hebrew
Narrative and Poetry. Collegeville, Minn.: Liturgical Press, 1999. 148pp.

Employs "rhetorical criticism," i.e., a careful analysis of the literary strategies of the final form of the text on ten key passages in order to ascertain
the theological goal of this literary strategy and how the book accomplishes
that goal. This approach illumines both the original intention of these
books and their continuing significance to readers in every age, including
our own. Concerned especially to draw out the theological application of
faithfulness on the part of the community of God and of leadership and
preaching in the church today. A more sophisticated and intentional employment of current rhetorical-critical methods than Throntveit (§2.32.4).

2.32.3   Fensham, F. Charles. *The Books of Ezra and Nehemiah.* New International
Commentary on the Old Testament. Grand Rapids: Eerdmans, 1982.
288pp.

Lucid and engaging commentary from a conservative perspective, arguing for the historical accuracy of these books, which Fensham takes to
have been written by the Chronicler. Emphasizes ANE context, historical and religious background, and the development of postexilic Judaism.

Less technical and comprehensive than Blenkinsopp (§3.32.1), but gives greater attention to religious concerns of the text in ways that help the reader identify points of contemporary significance.

2.32.4   Throntveit, Mark A. *Ezra-Nehemiah.* Interpretation: A Bible Commentary for Teaching and Preaching. Louisville: Westminster John Knox, 1992. 127pp.

Although Throntveit discusses historical issues in the introduction, the commentary itself focuses on the ways in which the reader construes meaning from the story in its final narrative form so as to derive theological insight from the text. The commentary emphasizes the structure of passages and narrative development. Theological insights grow out of these literary probes, but Throntveit gives little explicit attention to contemporary theological significance or the relation of religious ideas in these passages to other parts of the biblical canon. Still, a helpful complement to most other commentaries on Ezra-Nehemiah, which deal almost entirely with historical questions.

2.32.5   Williamson, H. G. M. *Ezra, Nehemiah.* Word Biblical Commentary. Waco, Tex.: Word, 1985. 417pp.

Careful and erudite, focusing on technical issues of historical reconstruction, literary sources, literary forms, and nuances of Hebrew terms and constructions. Argues that these books were not written by the Chronicler but arose from the same community. Traces three stages of development: (1) primary sources contemporaneous with events described (fifth century BCE); (2) Ezra memoir and Nehemiah memoir (400 BCE); and (3) final redaction (300 BCE). Probes the theological purpose of each of these levels, especially the Ezra and Nehemiah memoirs. Especially helpful for historical, linguistic, and literary aspects of the text, with some value for theological reflection. But usefulness of commentary is somewhat mitigated by dependence on very specific (and somewhat speculative) reconstructions.

Also Significant

2.32.6   Allen, Leslie C., and Timothy S. Laniak. *Ezra, Nehemiah, Esther.* New International Biblical Commentary. Peabody, Mass.: Hendrickson, 2003. 290pp.

2.32.7   Batten, Loring W. *A Critical and Exegetical Commentary on the Books of Ezra and Nehemiah.* International Critical Commentary. Edinburgh: T&T Clark, 1913. 384pp.

2.32.8   Blenkinsopp, Joseph. *Judaism, The First Phase: The Place of Ezra and Nehemiah in the Origins of Judaism.* Grand Rapids: Eerdmans, 2009. 262pp.

2.32.9   Boda, Mark, and Paul L. Reddit, eds. *Unity and Disunity in Ezra-Nehemiah.* Hebrew Bible Monograph, no. 17. Sheffield: Phoenix, 2008. 384pp.

2.32.10   Clines, David J. A. *Ezra, Nehemiah, Esther.* New Century Bible. Grand Rapids: Eerdmans, 1984. 342pp.

2.32.11   Kidner, Derek. *Ezra and Nehemiah.* Tyndale Old Testament Commentaries. Downers Grove, Ill.: InterVarsity, 1979. 174pp.

2.32.12   McConville, J. G. *Ezra, Nehemiah, and Esther.* Daily Study Bible. Philadelphia: Westminster, 1985. 197pp.

2.32.13   Myers, Jacob M. *Ezra, Nehemiah.* Anchor Bible. Garden City, N.Y.: Doubleday, 1965. 268pp.

2.33   Esther

See also EZRA AND NEHEMIAH (§2.32); RUTH (§2.28)

Highly Recommended

2.33.1   Baldwin, Joyce G. *Esther.* Tyndale Old Testament Commentaries. Downers Grove, Ill.: InterVarsity, 1984. 126pp.

Complement to the other volumes listed in that it interprets Esther as part of the Christian canon and discusses its significance for a Christian audience. Adopts a conservative position that espouses the historicity of the story. Contains a helpful and quite lengthy introduction, while the commentary itself is brief and laconic.

2.33.2   Bechtel, Carol M. *Esther.* Interpretation: A Bible Commentary for Teaching and Preaching. Louisville: John Knox, 2002. 101pp.

Introduction deals with historical setting, literary structure, and theology, especially the theological motifs of proportion and balance in life, living faithfully in the midst of a faithless culture, and significance of the written word (the last an emphasis often missed, but certainly present in view of its prominence in the summary of Esther 9). Although introduction contains discussion of the Christian use of Esther in preaching and teaching, the commentary itself gives little attention to these matters, but offers almost exclusively a sensitive literary examination of the flow of the narrative. Suffers slightly from extreme brevity.

2.33.3   Berlin, Adele. *Esther.* JPS Bible Commentary. Philadelphia: Jewish Publication Society, 2001. 110pp.

Offers a coherent and largely compelling interpretation, emphasizing how literary features point to the book's distinctive character and message. Understands Esther to belong to the literary form of comedy, and argues that the author drew heavily on literary motifs associated with Persia. Thus, commentary examines motifs about Persia especially from the Greek writings of the period with a view to the connotations their appearance in Esther would have for the ancient reader. But emphasizes also that it is a Jewish book, and part of the Jewish canon, and thus commentary is concerned to read Esther in the light of earlier canonical materials and later Jewish interpretation, especially the rabbis.

2.33.4   Fox, Michael V. *Character and Ideology in the Book of Esther.* 2d ed. Grand Rapids: Eerdmans, 2001. 352pp.

Engaging and illuminating study that focuses on the ways in which the presentation of characters in Esther reveals the assumptions, ideas, values, and teachings of the author. Insists that Esther is presented as a model for life in the Diaspora. Commentary proper is followed by discussions on historicity and dating, genres, structures, each of the major characters, God, the world, and the three textual versions of Esther. Fox's treatment of God (in this book that does not explicitly mention God) is especially helpful.

2.33.5   Grossman, Jonathan. *Esther: The Outer Narrative and the Hidden Reading.* Siphrut: Literature and Theology of the Hebrew Scriptures. Winona Lake, Ind.: Eisenbrauns, 2011. 255pp.

A careful and sophisticated narrative reading of Esther, employing the literary approach of Bakhtin, but not exclusively indebted to any specific literary theory. Insists that Esther offers a surface narrative that points beyond itself to a deeper and somewhat hidden message, one that centers on

145

the actions of God. Offers a consistent, original, and compelling reading based upon solid evidence within the book itself, including careful attention to the Hebrew. Recognizes that the intended audience of Esther knows the religious tradition of the earlier canonical materials and is expected to bring these connections to bear in the interpretation of Esther, and thus this volume demonstrates how connections with the Hebrew Scriptures illumine the meaning of the text.

2.33.6   Levenson, Jon D. *Esther*. Old Testament Library. Louisville: Westminster John Knox, 1997. 142pp.

Methodologically comprehensive treatment in that this prominent Jewish scholar examines the interplay between the longer Greek version of Esther and the shorter Hebrew one, tracks the narrative development of the story, draws heavily on historical and linguistic background, relates passages in Esther to other OT material, extensively cites ancient Jewish interpretation of the book, and interacts vigorously with more recent history of interpretation. Remarkably, Levenson brings these diverse data together into a coherent and illuminating interpretation.

Also Significant

2.33.7   Berg, Sandra Beth. *The Book of Esther: Motifs, Themes, and Structure.* Society of Biblical Literature Dissertation Series 44. Missoula, Mont.: Scholars, 1979. 219pp.

2.33.8   Carruthers, Jo. *Esther through the Centuries.* Blackwell Bible Commentaries. Malden, Mass.: Blackwell, 2008. 303pp.

2.33.9   Clines, David J. A. *The Esther Scroll: The Story of the Story.* Journal for the Study of the Old Testament Supplement Series 30. Sheffield: JSOT, 1984. 260pp.

2.33.10   Craig, Kenneth. *Reading Esther: A Case for the Literary Carnivalesque.* Literary Currents in Biblical Interpretation. Louisville: Westminster John Knox, 1995. 192pp.

2.33.11   Day, Linda. *Three Faces of a Queen: Characterization in the Books of Esther.* Journal for the Study of the Old Testament Supplement Series 186. Sheffield: Sheffield Academic Press, 1995. 254pp.

2.33.12   Lubetski, Edith, and Meier Lubetski. *The Book of Esther: A Classified Bibliography.* Sheffield: Phoenix, 2008. 268pp.

2.33.13   Moore, Carey. *Esther.* Anchor Bible. Garden City, N.Y.: Doubleday, 1971. 117pp.

2.33.14   Paton, Lewis B. *Critical and Exegetical Commentary on the Book of Esther.* International Critical Commentary. Edinburgh: T&T Clark, 1908. 339pp.

2.33.15   Reid, Debra. *Esther.* Tyndale Old Testament Commentaries. Downers Grove, Ill.: InterVarsity, 2008. 168pp.

2.34   Wisdom Literature: General Works

Highly Recommended

2.34.1   Blenkinsopp, Joseph. *Wisdom and Law in the Old Testament: The Ordering of Life in Israel and Early Judaism.* Rev. ed. Oxford Bible Series. Oxford: Oxford University Press, 1995. 197pp.

Comprehensive and original study of two major streams of tradition, law and wisdom, in terms of their respective origins, their points of connection, their role in the ordering of life within the Jewish people, and their eventual synthesis in the latest OT writings and in the intertestamental period. Emphasizes continuity between Jewish thought and NT theology. Gives special attention to literary genres and social settings as key interpretive contexts for understanding wisdom (and law).

2.34.2   Crenshaw, James L. *Old Testament Wisdom: An Introduction.* Rev. ed. Louisville: Westminster John Knox, 1998. 255pp.

Produced by a leading authority on OT wisdom, this introductory textbook is accessible to beginning students but its acute insights and wealth of current information make it valuable also for the scholar. Remarkably comprehensive, it covers the world of wisdom (language and literary forms) and the self-understanding of the wisdom teachers, the development of wisdom traditions (with special emphasis on role of Solomon), each wisdom book in the OT and intertestamental writings (identifying the central themes of each), and the continuing significance of the wisdom tradition for contemporary life. A final chapter treats the relationship between OT wisdom and wisdom texts from Egypt and Mesopotamia.

2.34.3 Longman, Tremper, III, and Peter Enns. *Dictionary of the Old Testament Wisdom, Poetry, and Writings*. Downers Grove, Ill.: InterVarsity, 2008. 967pp.

The same quality and approach of the other dictionaries in this series (§§2.19.1, 2.25.1). Includes discussion of Ruth and Esther and the Psalms, along with those OT books typically identified as "wisdom literature." Offers a major article on each of these biblical books, along with additional articles on ANE background and the history of interpretation for each of them. Also includes articles on major characters, theological themes, methods, and literary features.

2.34.4 Murphy, Roland E. *The Tree of Life: An Exploration of Biblical Wisdom Literature*. 2d ed. Grand Rapids: Eerdmans, 1996. 233pp.

Traces the quest for wisdom within the OT and deuterocanonical writings. After a general introduction, devotes a separate chapter each to Proverbs, Job, Ecclesiastes, Ben Sira, and Wisdom of Solomon. Concludes with a series of chapters synthesizing the major aspects of the presentation of wisdom within these materials, including a fine discussion on wisdom and theology. Supplement contains significant interaction with recent interpreters.

2.34.5 Perdue, Leo G. *Wisdom and Creation: The Theology of the Wisdom Literature*. Nashville: Abingdon, 1994. 420pp.

Most comprehensive and insightful study available on the theology of the wisdom tradition. Probes the theology of wisdom literature in the OT and deuterocanonical materials around the theme of creation, emphasizing the relationship between two sets of creation images: creation of the world and creation of humanity. Employs the theme of creation as basis of coherence in wisdom theology without forcing all wisdom texts into a creation "straight-jacket." Emphasis on creation is important for biblical theology especially within the Christian tradition, which often minimizes the role of creation in favor of a spiritual redemption of the individual and so fails to do full justice to God's work in and purposes for the cosmos.

Also Significant

2.34.6 Alter, Robert. *The Wisdom Books: Job, Proverbs, and Ecclesiastes: A Translation with Commentary*. New York: Norton, 2010. 394pp.

2.34.7   Bergant, Dianne. *What Are They Saying about Wisdom Literature?* New York: Paulist, 1984. 96pp.

2.34.8   Berry, Donald K. *An Introduction to Wisdom and Poetry in the Old Testament.* Nashville: Broadman & Holman, 1995. 463pp.

2.34.9   Brown, William P. *Character in Crisis: A Fresh Approach to the Wisdom Literature of the Old Testament.* Grand Rapids: Eerdmans, 1996. 179pp.

2.34.10   Brueggemann, Walter. *In Man We Trust: The Neglected Side of Biblical Faith.* Richmond, Va.: John Knox, 1972. 144pp.

2.34.11   Clements, Ronald E. *Wisdom in Theology.* Grand Rapids: Eerdmans, 1992. 188pp.

2.34.12   Enns, Peter. *Poetry and Wisdom.* IBR Bibliographies 3. Grand Rapids: Baker, 1998. 171pp.

2.34.13   Noth, Martin, and D. Winton Thomas, eds. *Wisdom in Israel and in the Ancient Near East.* Supplement to Vetus Testamentum 3. Leiden: Brill, 1953. 301pp.

2.34.14   Rad, Gerhard von. *Wisdom in Israel.* Nashville: Abingdon, 1972. 330pp.

2.34.15   Scott, R. B. Y. *The Way of Wisdom in the Old Testament.* New York: Macmillan, 1971. 238pp.

2.34.16   Westermann, Claus. *Roots of Wisdom: The Oldest Proverbs of Israel and Other Peoples.* Louisville: Westminster John Knox, 1995.

2.35   Job

Highly Recommended

2.35.1   Andersen, Francis I. *Job.* Tyndale Old Testament Commentaries. Downers Grove, Ill.: InterVarsity, 1976. 294pp.

Among the most substantive and authoritative volumes in the Tyndale series, written by a scholar who would in subsequent years become a leading commentator on various OT books. The seventy-page introduction presents readable and informed discussion of all major aspects of Job. Commentary itself emphasizes ANE historical background and insights from other OT material. Interacts significantly with the history of interpretation, and seriously engages theological meaning. Remarkable for the amount of relevant information packed into a small volume.

2.35.2   Clines, David J. A. *Job*. 3 vols. Word Biblical Commentary. Nashville: Thomas Nelson, 1990, 2006, 2011. 1539pp.

By far the most detailed and meticulous commentary on Job, and yet consistently concerned to demonstrate how each detail plays an essential role in the complex argument of the whole book. Comprehensive in treatment, dealing with textual, linguistic, historical, and theological issues. Emphasizes especially the interplay of the distinct viewpoints of major speakers in Job. Contains massive bibliographies.

2.35.3   Habel, Norman C. *The Book of Job: A Commentary.* Old Testament Library. Louisville: Westminster John Knox, 1985. 586pp.

Comprehensive commentary that engages in a careful, close reading of the text that emphasizes the interplay of literary artistry and theological issues. Rejects stages of development in the book's history in favor of understanding Job as a literary whole that masterfully interweaves prose and poetry in such a way as to express theological truth creatively. Focuses more on literary matters, e.g., narrative plot and literary structures, than does Clines. Original and insightful, of much value for preaching and teaching.

2.35.4   Hartley, John E. *Job*. New International Commentary on the Old Testament. Grand Rapids: Eerdmans, 1988. 591pp.

Solid, readable commentary that gives attention to text-critical and technical linguistic matters, but focuses especially on salient issues that are at the heart of the interpretation of the text itself. Emphasizes the role of passages within broader-book context and the connection of passages in Job to other OT and Jewish writings so as to explore the place of these passages and of the entire book within the witness of the whole Bible (especially the OT, but with some attention to significance for the NT as well).

2.35.5   Janzen, J. Gerald. *Job*. Interpretation: A Bible Commentary for Teaching and Preaching. Louisville: Westminster John Knox, 1985. 273pp.

Treats the final form of the text as a complex literary entity that requires the reader to track carefully the literary dynamics of the book in order thereby to confront both theological and existential issues. Is concerned to relate Job to the history of Israel's religion, and to psychological, spiritual, and existential realities that persons in all periods and in all places continue to confront. By giving attention to both of these aspects, Janzen points to contemporary application of the text both for the community of faith as a corporate body and for individual believers. Readers should be aware, however, of the potential for allowing contemporary existential concerns to be read back into the text.

2.35.6   Longman, Tremper, III. *Job.* Baker Commentary on the Old Testament Wisdom and Psalms. Grand Rapids: Baker, 2012. 491pp.

Eminently accessible commentary written by a seasoned OT scholar primarily for ministers and seminary students. Draws out the theological significance of the text both in comments and in "Theological Implications" that follow the comments on each passage. Of special value are the forty-four "reflective essays" that discuss in some detail the major themes that run through the speeches in Job.

Also Significant

2.35.7   Dailey, Thomas F. *Job.* Bibliographies for Biblical Research: Old Testament Series 13. Lewiston, N.Y.: Mellen Biblical Press, 1997. 148pp.

2.35.8   Dhorme, Edouard Paul. *A Commentary on the Book of Job.* London: Thomas Nelson, 1967. 675pp.

2.35.9   Hoffman, Yair. *A Blemished Perfection: The Book of Job in Context.* Journal for the Study of the Old Testament Supplement Series 213. Sheffield: JSOT, 1996. 360pp.

2.35.10   Newsome, Carol A. *The Book of Job: A Contest of Moral Imaginations.* Oxford: Oxford University Press, 2003. 301pp.

2.35.11   Perdue, Leo G., and W. Clark Gilpin, eds. *The Voice from the Whirlwind: Interpreting the Book of Job.* Nashville: Abingdon, 1991. 264pp.

2.35.12   Pope, Marvin H. *Job*. Anchor Bible. 3d ed. Garden City, N.Y.: Double-
          day, 1973. 405pp.

2.35.13   Rowley, H. H. *Job*. Rev. ed. New Century Bible Commentary. Grand
          Rapids: Eerdmans, 1980. 281pp.

2.35.14   Schifferdecker, Kathryn. *Out of the Whirlwind: Creation Theology in the
          Book of Job*. Harvard Theological Studies, no. 61. Cambridge, Mass.:
          Harvard University Press, 2008. 217pp.

2.35.15   Seow, C. L. *Job 1–21: Interpretation and Commentary*. Illuminations.
          Grand Rapids: Eerdmans, 2012. 922pp.

2.35.16   Simundson, Daniel J. *The Message of Job: A Theological Commentary*.
          Augsburg Old Testament Studies. Minneapolis: Augsburg, 1985. 159pp.

2.35.17   Westermann, Claus. *The Structure of the Book of Job: A Form-Critical
          Analysis*. Philadelphia: Fortress, 1981. 148pp.

2.36   Psalms

Highly Recommended

2.36.1   Allen, Leslie C. *Psalms 101–150*. Rev. ed. Word Biblical Commentary.
          Nashville: Thomas Nelson, 2002. 384pp.

          This commentary, along with the two companion volumes on the Psalms
          in the Word Biblical Commentary (see Craigie [§2.36.2] and Tate
          [§2.36.10]), is a detailed treatment of each psalm, dealing with techni-
          cal textual and linguistic matters, but giving primary attention to the
          form, structure, and original liturgical setting or devotional function of
          the psalm in Israel. Gives little attention to the role of individual psalms
          within the final canonical book of Psalms, but does attend to theologi-
          cal significance, the use of the psalm elsewhere in the canon, connections
          of thought between the psalm and other biblical passages (including NT
          ones), and contemporary Christian application. This volume contains an
          introduction to the Psalms that is assumed in the volumes by Tate and
          Allen. Although written by three separate scholars, these volumes are re-
          markably consistent in purpose and perspective.

2.36.2   Craigie, Peter C. *Psalms 1–50.* Word Biblical Commentary. Waco, Tex.: Word, 1983. 375pp.

See Allen (§2.36.1).

2.36.3   Goldingay, John. *Psalms.* Baker Commentary on the Old Testament Wisdom and Psalms. 3 vols. Grand Rapids: Baker, 2006, 2007, 2008. 639/744/812pp.

Informed, erudite commentary that is nonetheless accessible to the non-specialist and is in fact written primarily for ministers and seminary students. Includes a lengthy introduction to the Psalter that addresses especially matters that pertain to function of the psalms in the life of the church and the believer. Attends carefully to the structure and key terms and motifs of each psalm, followed by a discussion of theological implications, where matters pertaining to Christian faith are briefly addressed. Gives relatively little attention to the composition of the entire Psalter and the relationship of individual psalms to each other.

2.36.4   Hossfeld, Frank-Lother, and Erich Zenger. *Psalms 2.* Hermeneia: A Critical and Historical Commentary on the Bible. Minneapolis: Fortress, 2005. 553pp. *Psalms 3.* Hermeneia: A Critical and Historical Commentary on the Bible. Minneapolis: Fortress, 2011. 712pp.

Most current and authoritative treatment of the Psalms. For each psalm discusses text-critical matters, history of interpretation, genre, structure, origin, date, purpose, reception (including quotation and allusion within the NT), and theological significance for the church. In addition, includes a bibliography (mostly English, German, and French titles) for each psalm. Pays special attention to the role of each psalm within the Psalter. A downside is that the commentary deals with such a broad range of issues that it is unable to develop any of them in depth. Moreover, the interpretation is much influenced by a specific understanding of the redaction and composition of the Psalter, which may limit somewhat its value for those who are not persuaded by these compositional views. *Psalms 2* treats Psalms 51–100; and *Psalms 3* treats Psalms 101–150. The first volume, dealing with Psalms 1–50 and including an introduction to the Psalter, is still awaited.

2.36.5   Kirkpatrick, A. F. *The Book of Psalms.* Cambridge: Cambridge University Press, 1910. 852pp.

Erudite classic commentary of enduring worth despite its age. Discusses background, structure, and significance of each psalm, and provides trenchant comment on each phrase of the psalm. Adopts a conservative critical position, arguing that David was largely responsible for the origin of the Psalter. Interprets the psalms in terms of the original significance for psalmist and intended audience, but relates that original significance to the rest of the canon, to NT teachings, and to Christian application.

2.36.6   Kraus, Hans-Joachim. *Psalms: A Commentary.* 2 vols. Minneapolis: Augsburg, 1988, 1989. 559/587pp.

Represents the best of contemporary critical German scholarship on the Psalms. After a lengthy and comprehensive introduction, deals with each psalm by providing a select bibliography (mostly German and French titles), original translation, linguistic notes, identification of the psalm according to form-critical categories and discussion of significance of form, commentary on each verse (emphasizing linguistic, literary, and historical elements), and the theological thrust of the psalm (from a Christian, and more specifically Lutheran, perspective). Emphasizes the original setting of the psalm and gives no serious attention to the role of a psalm within the book of Psalms. Requires basic knowledge of Hebrew for full use.

2.36.7   ———. *Theology of the Psalms.* Minneapolis: Augsburg, 1986. 235pp.

Draws on Kraus's interpretation of the Psalter presented in his commentaries (§2.36.6), but can be used without reference to the commentaries. Argues that the theological thrust of the psalms is "Israel in the presence of God," and analyzes how the major issues in the psalms (e.g., God of Israel, worship, suffering and joy, king and temple, response to hostility) develop this central thrust. Involves somewhat technical discussions of the origin and development of each theological concept in ancient Israel in relation to the religious environment of the ANE. Of special value is the discussion of the use of the Psalms in the NT.

2.36.8   Mays, James Luther. *The Lord Reigns: A Theological Handbook to the Psalms.* Philadelphia: Westminster, 1994. 159pp.

A most helpful discussion of the theological value of the psalms for the Christian church. Insists that the theological foundation for all the psalms is the confession that "the Lord reigns," and thus the Psalter provides the framework for life within the kingdom of God. Mays employs insights from the history of original composition and the history of the use of the psalms to shed light on practical issues that pertain especially to the devotional, liturgical, and confessional lives of Christians.

2.36.9   ———. *Psalms.* Interpretation: A Bible Commentary for Teaching and Preaching. Louisville: Westminster John Knox, 1994. 457pp.

Insightful and original commentary from a recognized authority on the Psalter. Adopts a two-track approach: (a) provides a concise description of certain psalms, and (b) offers fuller exposition of those psalms that are prominent in worship, used in the NT, significant for the church's theology, or play an important role in the Psalter as a whole. In this way Mays can give detailed treatment to the more important psalms, while giving at least a broad interpretation of each of the others. For those treated more fully, Mays employs literary structure, original setting, and role within the Psalter as a basis for a robust Christian reading, probing the theological and religious aspects of most concern to contemporary Christians.

2.36.10   Tate, Marvin. *Psalms 51–100*. Word Biblical Commentary. Dallas: Word, 1990. 578pp.

See Allen (§2.36.1).

2.36.11   Terrien, Samuel. *The Psalms: Strophic Structure and Theological Commentary*. Eerdmans Critical Commentary. Grand Rapids: Eerdmans, 2003. 971pp.

Insightful, original commentary that employs ANE background, considerations of the Hebrew, and especially the form and structure of the psalm to lead to theological reflection. A contribution, but also a potential limitation, of the commentary is the identification (and implementation for interpretation) of specific strophic structures that not all scholars have found compelling. The theological reflection tends to be quite penetrating and pertinent to modern believers.

Also Significant

2.36.12   Anderson, Bernhard W. *Out of the Depths: The Psalms Speak for Us Today*. 3d ed. Philadelphia: Westminster, 2000. 249pp.

2.36.13   Briggs, Charles Augustus, and Emilie Grace Briggs. *A Critical and Exegetical Commentary on the Book of Psalms*. International Critical Commentary. 2 vols. Edinburgh: T&T Clark, 1906–1907.

2.36.14   Brueggemann, Walter. *The Message of the Psalms: A Theological Commentary*. Augsburg Old Testament Studies. Minneapolis: Augsburg, 1984. 206pp.

2.36.15   Bullock, C. Hassell. *Encountering the Book of Psalms: A Literary and Theological Introduction*. Encountering Biblical Studies. Grand Rapids: Baker, 2001. 256pp.

2.36.16   Crenshaw, James L. *The Psalms: An Introduction*. Grand Rapids: Eerdmans, 2001. 187pp.

2.36.17   Dahood, Mitchell. *Psalms*. 3 vols. Anchor Bible. Garden City, N.Y.:
Doubleday, 1965–1970. 329/399/490pp.

2.36.18   Firth, David G., and Philip S. Johnston. *Interpreting the Psalms: Issues
and Approaches*. Downers Grove, Ill.: InterVarsity, 2005. 345pp.

2.36.19   Gillingham, Susan E. *Psalms Through the Centuries: Volume 1*. Blackwell
Bible Commentaries. Malden, Mass.: Blackwell, 2003. 382pp.

2.36.20   Gunkel, Hermann. *The Psalms: A Form-Critical Introduction*. Facet Books
Biblical Series 19. Philadelphia: Fortress, 1967. 52pp.

2.36.21   Gunkel, Hermann, and Joachim Begrich. *An Introduction to the Psalms:
The Genres of the Religious Lyric of Israel*. Mercer Library of Biblical Studies. Macon, Ga.: Mercer, 1998. 388pp. (Originally published in German
in 1933.)

2.36.22   Holladay, William L. *The Psalms through Three Thousand Years: Prayerbook
of a Cloud of Witnesses*. Philadelphia: Fortress, 1993. 395pp.

2.36.23   Kidner, Derek. *Psalms: An Introduction and Commentary*. 2 vols. Tyndale
Old Testament Commentaries. Downers Grove, Ill.: InterVarsity, 1975.
492pp.

2.36.24   McCann, J. Clinton, Jr., ed. *The Shape and Shaping of the Psalter*. Journal
for the Study of the Old Testament Supplement Series 159. Sheffield:
JSOT, 1993. 130pp.

2.36.25   ———. *A Theological Introduction to the Book of Psalms*. Nashville:
Abingdon, 1994. 204pp.

2.36.26   Miller, Patrick D., Jr. *Interpreting the Psalms*. Philadelphia: Fortress,
1986. 165pp.

2.36.27   Mowinkel, Sigmund. *The Psalms in Israel's Worship*. 2 vols. Nashville: Abingdon, 1963. 303pp.

2.36.28   Perowne, John. *The Book of Psalms*. London: D. Ball, 1878–1879. 523pp.

2.36.29   Schaefer, Konrad. *Psalms*. Berit Olam: Studies in Hebrew Narrative and Poetry. Collegeville, Minn.: Liturgical Press, 2001. 448pp.

2.36.30   Weiser, Artur. *The Psalms*. Old Testament Library. Philadelphia: Westminster, 1962. 841pp.

2.36.31   Westermann, Claus. *The Psalms: Structure, Content, and Message*. Minneapolis: Augsburg, 1990. 128pp.

2.36.32   Zenger, Erich. *A God of Vengeance?: Understanding the Psalms of Divine Wrath*. Louisville: Westminster John Knox, 1996. 104pp.

2.37   Proverbs

Highly Recommended

2.37.1   Boström, Lennart. *The God of the Sages: The Portrayal of God in the Book of Proverbs*. Coniectanea Biblica: Old Testament Series 29. Stockholm: Almqvist & Wiksell, 1990. 260pp.

Insofar as commentaries on Proverbs generally give inadequate attention to the book's theology, this volume is a welcome contribution. While focusing on the doctrine of God, Boström discusses also such theological issues as creation, order of the world, retribution, and theodicy. Recognizes the complexity of Proverbs' portrait of God as both transcendent sovereign Lord and an imminent God who relates intimately to humans and is seriously involved in the world. Explores both continuity and discontinuity between theology of Proverbs and that of the wisdom traditions of Israel's neighbors.

2.37.2   Clifford, Richard J. *Proverbs*. Old Testament Library. Louisville: Westminster John Knox, 1999. 286pp.

While attending to such matters as philology, textual criticism, and comparison with wisdom material from Israel's neighbors, the focus and distinctive value of this commentary is its attention to the rhetoric of Proverbs, i.e., ways in which the language, structure, and literary features engage the reader to encourage and guide the quest for wisdom (which is taken to be the purpose and main theme of the book). This commentary is more engaging to the modern reader than most others, since it focuses on matters that the text invites the reader to ponder. Yet insofar as it emphasizes Proverbs' relationship to the secular wisdom tradition of the ANE, it gives no serious consideration to its role within the OT canon or to its witness specifically to the creator God of Israel, or to its contribution to Jewish and Christian theology.

2.37.3   Fox, Michael V. *Proverbs 1–9; Proverbs 10–31*. 2 vols. Anchor Yale Bible. New Haven, CT: Yale University Press. 2000, 2009. 5205pp.

This leading Jewish authority on OT wisdom presents a thorough verse-by-verse commentary, with emphasis on the meaning of key terms, connections with other OT passages, ANE parallels, interaction with the history of interpretation, and the stages of tradition leading to the final text. Especially helpful are excurses on the most significant issues encountered in the text. The second volume, dealing with the remainder of Proverbs and including a more comprehensive discussion of historical and ideological issues, is awaited.

2.37.4   Longman, Tremper, III. *Proverbs*. Baker Commentary on the Old Testament Wisdom and Psalms. 2006. 608pp.

A helpful commentary for the Christian use of the book of Proverbs, especially for the nonspecialist. Interprets Proverbs in light of ANE wisdom traditions and the OT Scriptures, with limited reference to the Hebrew. Insists that the proverbs are not simply good advice derived from experience, but have real theological content. In contrast to Waltke (§2.37.7), sees no deep structure in the arrangements of the proverbs, but concludes that the proverbs are presented randomly. An appendix includes brief discussions of some of the major topics in Proverbs. Concludes each section of Proverbs with a discussion of "Theological Implications," which tends to be short and somewhat superficial, but does offer some suggestions for beginning to think about Christian appropriation.

2.37.5   McKane, William. *Proverbs*. Old Testament Library. Philadelphia: Westminster, 1970. 670pp.

Interprets Proverbs by examining especially (a) its relation to Egyptian and Babylonian-Assyrian wisdom literature; (b) a careful and original reclassification of literary forms employed in Proverbs (a reclassification not universally accepted by scholars); and (c) ancient Palestinian background. This threefold emphasis is a strength but also a weakness, since it results in little attention to other interpretive evidence, to the function of Proverbs within the canon, or to theological significance.

2.37.6   Perdue, Leo G. *Proverbs*. Interpretation: A Bible Commentary for Teaching and Preaching. Louisville: Westminster John Knox, 2000. 289pp.

Divides Proverbs into eight collections, composed at different times by a variety of sages. Emphasizes especially the role of social setting, and (unlike most commentaries) the literary structure of smaller units as well as the entire book in the interpretation of individual passages. The introduction gives an exceptionally clear and accessible presentation of the history of wisdom tradition, the sages responsible for the proverbs, the development of the wisdom collections toward the formation of the final book, the role of Proverbs within the canon, and its contribution to Christian theology and life. The commentary itself, however, treats the theology of the text according to its religious significance specifically for the original audience and gives little attention to possible theological appropriation by contemporary Christians.

2.37.7   Waltke, Bruce K. *The Book of Proverbs Chapters 1–15*. New International Commentary on the Old Testament. Grand Rapids: Eerdmans, 2004. 693pp.

Detailed, learned commentary from a conservative evangelical perspective. Argues that Solomon composed and compiled the proverbs in chs. 1–24. Attends primarily to the Hebrew language and to the scriptural canon (including the NT), with less attention to ANE parallels than is found in most other technical commentaries. Like Longman (§2.37.4), insists on the essentially theological character of Proverbs. At times may read NT ideas into Proverbs, as when he discerns concern for eternal judgment. Identifies a "deep structure" in the arrangement of the proverbs in chs. 10–24, which affects the interpretation of this portion of the book.

Also Significant

2.37.8   Hidenbrandt, Ted. *Book of Proverbs: A Classified Bibliography*. Sheffield: Phoenix, 2007. 250pp.

2.37.9   Kidner, Derek. *Proverbs*. Tyndale Old Testament Commentaries. Downers Grove, Ill.: InterVarsity, 1964. 192pp.

2.37.10   Philip, Johannes Nel. *The Structure and Ethos of the Wisdom Admonitions in Proverbs*. Berlin: Walter De Gruyter, 1982. 142pp.

2.37.11   Scott, R. B. Y. *Proverbs and Ecclesiastes*. Anchor Bible. Garden City, N.Y.: Doubleday, 1965. 255pp.

2.37.12   Toy, C. H. *A Critical and Exegetical Commentary on the Book of Proverbs*. International Critical Commentary. Edinburgh: T&T Clark, 1899. 554pp.

2.37.13   Weeks, Stuart. *Early Israelite Wisdom*. Oxford Theological Monographs. Oxford: Oxford University Press, 1994. 212pp.

2.37.14   Westermann, Claus. *Roots of Wisdom: The Oldest Proverbs of Israel and Other Peoples*. Philadelphia: Westminster, 1995. 178pp.

2.37.15   Whybray, R. N. *The Book of Proverbs: A Survey of Modern Study*. History of Biblical Interpretation Series 1. Leiden: Brill, 1995. 184pp.

2.37.16   ———. *Proverbs*. New Century Bible Commentary. Grand Rapids: Eerdmans, 1994. 446pp.

2.38   Ecclesiastes (Qohelet)

See also PROVERBS (§2.37); SONG OF SOLOMON (§2.39)

Highly Recommended

2.38.1   Bartholomew, Craig G. *Ecclesiastes*. Baker Commentary on the Old Testament Wisdom and Psalms. Grand Rapids: Baker, 2009. 448pp.

This volume demonstrates that a commentary can be both accessible to theological students and informed ministers and original, profound, and even groundbreaking. Bartholomew is one of the leading thinkers in biblical hermeneutics, and he brings his methodological sophistication to bear on a biblical book that requires such skill for its construal. Argues that two contrasting voices are in conversation throughout Ecclesiastes: Qohelet, which represents the traditional, orthodox God-centered wisdom tradition of Israel, and an opposing one representing a human-centered perspective that accords with Greek thought. The message of Ecclesiastes plays off of this tension. Solid exegesis in conversation with ancient and modern writers leads to profound theological insights that connect with spiritual and existential experience of believers and others in our modern world.

2.38.2   Brown, William P. *Ecclesiastes.* Interpretation: A Bible Commentary for Teaching and Preaching. Louisville: Westminster John Knox, 2000. 143pp.

Creative, lucid, and engaging. Rather than attempting to press a kind of logical and theological coherence that Brown believes is absent from Ecclesiastes, he shows how the ambivalence of the text witnesses to enduring spiritual and theological truth. Gives attention to Ecclesiastes's distinctive thought, but helps the reader discern the place of this book within the larger witness of Scripture. Engages as a Christian believer in constant dialogue with the strange and challenging perspective of Ecclesiastes. The epilogue, "Qoheleth's Place in Christian Faith and Life," is itself worth the prices of the volume.

2.38.3   Crenshaw, James L. *Ecclesiastes: A Commentary.* Old Testament Library. Louisville: Westminster John Knox, 1987. 192pp.

Crenshaw brings his comprehensive knowledge of OT wisdom to bear on the language and historical background of the book (the two emphases of his commentary). The commentary is thus illuminating of technical matters, but does little to engage the reader who desires to probe theological and existential issues. The introduction offers a lucid and enlightening orientation to the book's most significant aspects, including its teachings (from which Crenshaw excludes the "secondary addition" of 12:8–14).

2.38.4   Krüger, Thomas. *Qoheleth.* Hermeneia: A Critical and Historical Commentary on the Bible. Minneapolis: Fortress, 2004. 306pp.

Learned and highly technical commentary that aids greatly in the interpretation of details within Ecclesiastes but gives less attention to fitting individual passages into the larger flow of the book; thus readers can become lost in the morass of information. Like many recent commentators, insists that tensions within the book must be allowed to stand and that such tensions are integral to the book's message. But rejects the notion of contradictory voices in favor of "critical wisdom," which seeks to find the truth through an exploration of contradictions. Deals with theological issues as they are pursued within the book, but (as with most volumes in this series) does not explore their significance for contemporary persons.

161

2.38.5   Lohfink, Norbert. *Qoheleth*. Continental Commentary. Minneapolis: Fortress, 2003. 158pp.

Informed and erudite interpretation that understands the major contribution of Ecclesiastes to be an affirmation of the realities of present earthly existence and a view of God that does not limit God to a narrow Israelite perspective and refuses to privilege a covenant model. It thus offers a somewhat unique perspective in the Hebrew Bible, one that connects with both believers and unbelievers today. In contrast to Bartholomew (§2.38.1), insists that there is one voice presented by the book. Verse-by-verse comments are brief, but careful exegesis is regularly joined with reflection on the present significance of the teaching of the passage. Suffers some from its brevity.

2.38.6   Longman, Tremper, III. *The Book of Ecclesiastes*. New International Commentary on the Old Testament. Grand Rapids: Eerdmans, 1998. 306pp.

Writes from a conservative perspective, but rejects Solomonic authorship. Posits a later writer who adopts the persona of Solomon and is responsible for 1:12–12:7, and a second unnamed wisdom teacher who provides a frame to the book (1:1-11 and 12:8-14) and qualifies and clarifies the intervening material. Thus, in contrast to most commentators, insists that 12:8-14 is not merely a secondary addition, but critical for understanding the book's message. Longman's major contribution is to show how Qohelet's claim that everything is meaningless fits into the rest of biblical revelation. Excellent in moving from original significance of the text to Christian theological reflection and contemporary application.

2.38.7   Murphy, Roland E. *Ecclesiastes*. Word Biblical Commentary. Dallas: Word, 1992. 165pp.

Prominent Roman Catholic OT scholar offers a serious examination of the book's most vexing problems and passages by careful analysis of the text in conversation with the history of interpretation, leading to judicious and informed conclusions. Concise and accessible discussion of textual, linguistic, and historical issues, always in the service of understanding as precisely as possible the author's thought. Attempts to identify the specific theological meaning of larger passages in the book, often moving on to discuss concerns of contemporary (Christian) readers. Sees more fundamental coherence in the book than most modern commentators, who make much of inconsistencies in Ecclesiastes.

2.38.8   Seow, C. L. *Ecclesiastes*. Anchor Bible. New York: Doubleday, 1997. 419pp.

Arguably the most current and comprehensive treatment presently available. Offers detailed technical discussion in the "Notes," while providing fresh and persuasive interpretation accessible to the general reader in the "Comments." Presents a helpful description of Ecclesiastes' theology in the introduction, but the commentary itself generally avoids theological issues, and does nothing to probe the ideological and existential struggle readers (including modern ones) have with the apparently fatalistic perspective of Ecclesiastes. Gives little attention to potential for Christian application.

Also Significant

2.38.9   Bartholomew, Craig G. *Reading Ecclesiastes: Old Testament Exegesis and Hermeneutical Theory.* Rome: Editrice Pontificio Instituto, 1998. 319pp.

2.38.10   Barton, George A. *A Critical and Exegetical Commentary on the Book of Ecclesiastes.* International Critical Commentary. Edinburgh: T&T Clark, 1908. 212pp.

2.38.11   Christianson, Eric S. *Ecclesiastes through the Centuries.* Blackwell Bible Commentaries. Malden, Mass.: Blackwell, 2007. 314pp.

2.38.12   ———. *A Time to Tell: Narrative Strategies in Ecclesiastes.* Journal for the Study of the Old Testament Supplement Series 280. Sheffield: Sheffield Academic Press, 1998. 299pp.

2.38.13   Eaton, Michael A. *Ecclesiastes: An Introduction and Commentary.* Tyndale Old Testament Commentaries. Downers Grove, Ill.: InterVarsity, 1983. 159pp.

2.38.14   Ellul, Jacques. *Reason for Being: A Meditation on Ecclesiastes.* Grand Rapids: Eerdmans, 1990. 306pp.

2.38.15   Fox, Michael V. *A Time to Tear Down and a Time to Build Up: A Rereading of Ecclesiastes.* Grand Rapids: Eerdmans, 1999. 421pp.

2.38.16   Gordis, Robert. *Koheleth: The Man and His World.* 3d ed. New York: Block, 1968. 421pp.

2.38.17   Whitley, Charles F. *Koheleth: His Language and Thought*. Beiheft zur Zeitschrift für die alttestamentliche Wissenschaft 148. Berlin: Walter De Gruyter, 1979. 199pp.

2.38.18   Whybray, R. N. *Ecclesiastes*. New Century Bible Commentary. Grand Rapids: Eerdmans, 1989. 179pp.

2.39   Song of Solomon

See also ECCLESIASTES (QOHELET) (§2.38)

Highly Recommended

2.39.1   Carr, G. Lloyd. *The Song of Solomon: An Introduction and Commentary*. Tyndale Old Testament Commentaries. Downers Grove, Ill.: InterVarsity, 1983. 175pp.

Because of the problem of vocabulary and syntax in the Song of Solomon, this volume gives greater attention to technical matters than is typical for this series. But all technical discussion is pursued explicitly for the purpose of explicating the most salient issues for the text's meaning. According to Carr, the book celebrates and gives guidance to human love, especially in its emotional and sexual aspects. Carr traces this theme throughout his commentary, and thus the commentary tends to be more consistently theologically oriented than most other Song of Solomon commentaries. Considers that the poem was essentially completed at the time of Solomon (and is thus one of the very few modern commentators who link it to Solomon), but revised during the time of the divided monarchy.

2.39.2   Exum, J. Cheryl. *Song of Songs*. Old Testament Library. Louisville: Westminster John Knox, 2005. 263pp.

Insists that the book presents in a most visual and therefore emotive fashion the transcendent and transformative experience of human (and especially romantic) love. Finds the center of the book at 8:6 ("love is as strong as death") and interprets the entire book according to this overriding thesis. Most adept at combining insights from the Hebrew language, ANE culture, and ancient erotic lyrical poetry to bring out the richness and power of the poem. Does rather little with theological aspects.

2.39.3   Garrett, Duane, and Paul R. House. *Song of Songs/Lamentations*. Word Biblical Commentary. Nashville: Thomas Nelson, 2004. 478pp.

The portion on Song of Songs was written by Garrett. In contrast to most recent commentators, argues that the book was written during the Solomonic period from within Solomon's court, perhaps by Solomon himself. The book contains several songs, but they are unified around a detailed chiastic structure, with the songs alternating between a soprano (female) and tenor (male) voice. The center of the chiasm, and thus the critical passage of the book, is deemed to be 4:12–5:1. Finds the basic meaning in the celebration of sexual love, but with certain potential for the relationship between Christians (and the church) and Christ. Discusses theological significance in the introduction, but gives little attention to it in the commentary proper. Contains fine discussion of the history of interpretation into the modern period.

The portion on Lamentations was written by House. He argues that Lamentations was written by a single author who composed separate poems and placed them in order. The book was written at the time of Jeremiah, though not necessarily by him. Offers a clear, reliable, learned interpretation, and relates it to broader themes in OT theology.

2.39.4   Hess, Richard S. *Song of Songs*. Baker Commentary on the Old Testament Wisdom and Psalms. Grand Rapids: Baker, 2005. 285pp.

Like other volumes in this series, intended primarily for theological students and informed ministers, but also makes a contribution to the scholarly discussion. In contrast to Exum (§2.39.2) and Garrett (§2.39.3), refuses to identify one passage as the critical center that holds the key to the entire message of the book. Rejects any allowance of allegorical possibilities in favor of an affirmation of human sexual love as good coming from the good God; it celebrates physical love and committed relationship as a gift from the Creator. The message of the book thus resonates with the view of human sexuality embraced by the entire Bible, both OT and NT. Commentary itself demonstrates reliable scholarship, with attention to the Hebrew and ANE customs and poetry. While appreciating Hess's attempt to relate the Song to theological themes throughout the canon, one might wish to find more sophisticated discussion of the implications of the book's participation in the canon so as to provide a hermeneutical basis for introducing God into a book in which God is not explicitly featured.

2.39.5   Keel, Othmar. *The Song of Songs*. Continental Commentary. Philadelphia: Fortress, 1994. 308pp.

A careful analysis of the meaning of the language of this book, drawing especially on literary forms employed, the significance of metaphorical and symbolic language, and parallels from Palestine, Egypt, and Mesopotamia. Gives special attention to iconographic parallels, and thus is replete with illustrations from the ANE. Introduction contains helpful discussion of theological significance, but commentary proper offers little theological reflection.

2.39.6 Longman, Tremper, III. *Song of Songs*. New International Commentary on the Old Testament. Grand Rapids: Eerdmans, 2001. 238pp.

This prominent evangelical OT scholar, known especially for his work on literary aspects of biblical interpretation, offers a comprehensive and careful examination of this book, which Longman takes to be an anthology of several originally independent poems, most of which are post-Solomonic. In spite of its varied origins, the Song of Songs coheres in its final form, and Longman focuses almost exclusively on this final form, finding here a celebration of the love between husband and wife and thus a celebration of male-female relationship that is analogous to God's love for his people. Contains critical discussion of the history of interpretation and a helpful section on the theology of the book, where Longman explores its relation to the rest of the OT and (to a limited extent) to the NT. Commentary itself emphasizes examination of the Hebrew (gives more attention to lexical than to syntactical matters), literary forms, and ANE parallels. In spite of its attention to technical matters, is accessible to nonspecialists.

2.39.7 Murphy, Roland E. *The Song of Songs*. Hermeneia: A Critical and Historical Commentary on the Bible. Philadelphia: Fortress, 1990. 237pp.

Informed, careful, and judicious examination of the language and background of the text. Lengthy introduction deals with significant aspects of the book, including the history of interpretation and major possibilities for its theological use. Murphy sees the Song, understood within the framework of the biblical canon, as expressing a theology of human sexuality, with emphasis on the emotional experiences of love. All of this contributes to Scripture's affirmation that human love, and particularly sexual love, is part of God's gracious design for his human creation.

2.39.8 Pope, Marvin H. *Song of Songs*. Anchor Bible. Garden City, N.Y.: Doubleday, 1977. 743pp.

Massive, learned, detailed, and technical commentary focusing on the text, language, historical background, and history of interpretation. Considers the poem to be a celebration of sexual love, which in its depth reveals the nature of all human love and in its transcendence points to divine love. Finds the bases for this poem to be in fertility religions of the ANE, the sacred marriage rite, and the funeral feast. Rejects allegorical interpretations, but recognizes that these interpretations sometimes contain helpful theological insight and therefore cites traditional Jewish and Christian allegorical interpretations for each passage.

Also Significant

2.39.9   Barbiero, Gianni. *Song of Songs: A Close Reading.* Supplements to Vetus Testamentum, no. 144. Leiden: Brill, 2011. 542pp.

2.39.10   Bergant, Dianne. *The Song of Songs.* Berit Olam: Studies in Hebrew Narrative and Poetry. Collegeville, Minn.: Liturgical Press, 2001. 138pp.

2.39.11   Gordis, Robert. *The Song of Songs and Lamentations.* New York: Ktav, 1974. 203pp.

2.39.12   Jenson, Robert W. *Song of Songs.* Interpretation: A Bible Commentary for Teaching and Preaching. Louisville: John Knox, 2005. 106pp.

2.39.13   LaCocque, André. *Romance She Wrote: A Hermeneutical Essay on Song of Songs.* Harrisburg, Pa.: Trinity Press International, 1998. 240pp.

2.39.14   Stadelmann, Luis I. J. *Love and Politics: A New Commentary on the Song of Songs.* New York: Paulist, 1992. 243pp.

2.40   Prophetic Literature: General Works

Highly Recommended

2.40.1   Blenkinsopp, Joseph. *A History of Prophecy in Israel: From the Settlement in the Land to the Hellenistic Period.* Rev. ed. Louisville: Westminster John Knox, 1993. 291pp.

A critical history of the phenomenon of prophecy in Israel, from the settlement through early Judaism. Treats the origin and development of Israelite prophecy against the background of the political, social, and religious environment of the ANE and the role of the prophetic materials in the OT canon. Emphasizes lines of continuity, but considers also distinctive character of each prophet and diverging courses of development. Accepts generally held critical views regarding sources and dates.

2.40.2   Boda, Mark J., and J. Gordon McConville, eds. *Dictionary of the Old Testament Prophets: A Compendium of Contemporary Scholarship.* Downers Grove, Ill.: InterVarsity, 2012. 966pp.

The most recent volume in the series of dictionaries produced by InterVarsity given over to specific areas of the biblical canon. The only full-scale reference work devoted entirely to the OT prophets. Remarkably wide-ranging in subjects, including both texts and topics found in the prophets, as well as matters pertaining to prophecy, major traditional and contemporary methodologies employed in the interpretation of the prophets, history of reception of the various prophetic books, and the use of these books within the NT. Contributors tend to be moderately critical, but represent a rather wide range of perspectives, and include both Christian and Jewish scholars. While representing their own perspectives, contributors usually show appreciation and respect for alternative points of view.

2.40.3   Gowan, Donald E. *Theology of the Prophetic Books: The Death and Resurrection of Israel.* Louisville: Westminster John Knox, 1998. 250pp.

Clearly written and illuminating study of the theology of each of the prophetic books, taking seriously the way the prophet's own historical context influenced his message and how later prophets built on earlier ones. Insists that the individual prophetic messages are all variations of the overarching prophetic theme of the death and resurrection of Israel, which can serve as the bridge to Christian appropriation.

2.40.4   Heschel, Abraham. *The Prophets.* 2 vols. New York: Harper, 1969. 235/287pp.

Something of a modern classic, this work by a prominent Jewish scholar of an earlier generation is an elegant, insightful, and sympathetic exploration into the phenomenon of Israel's prophecy, including presuppositions, character of prophetic inspiration, prophetic consciousness, and the major theological concerns of the prophets. Treats all of these matters with religious and spiritual sensitivity. Emphasizes the uniqueness of prophecy in Israel over against prophetic phenomena among Israel's neighbors.

2.40.5   Koch, Klaus. *The Prophets.* 2 vols. Philadelphia: Fortress, 1982, 1983. 182/216pp.

Lucid and comprehensive description of Israelite prophecy in general and of each of the prophetic books in particular (the latter receiving the bulk of attention). Discusses each of the literary prophets in terms of historical, religious, and social background, and the method and forms of his prophecy so as to illumine the prophet's message. Emphasizes lines of development between the prophets. Provides depth, clarification, and perspective to the theological message of the prophets. Accepts generally held critical views regarding sources and dates, but recognizes the speculative character of much literary reconstruction and is therefore generally reluctant to dismiss large passages as later additions or interpolations.

2.40.6   VanGemeren, Willem A. *Interpreting the Prophetic Word: An Introduction to the Prophetic Literature of the Old Testament.* Grand Rapids: Zondervan, 1990. 545pp.

Written by a leading evangelical scholar, this volume provides a conservative alternative to many of the critical conclusions regarding dates and sources assumed by most other scholars listed here. Emphasizes historical background, literary form and structure, and theological message of each prophetic book. Notes how each book contributes to biblical revelation as a whole, and constantly draws connections between these books and NT fulfillment.

Also Significant

2.40.7   Brueggemann, Walter. *The Prophetic Imagination.* 2d ed. Minneapolis: Fortress, 2001. 151pp.

2.40.8   Clements, Ronald E. *Old Testament Prophecy: From Oracles to Canon.* Louisville: Westminster John Knox, 1996. 278pp.

2.40.9   Gordon, Robert P., ed. *The Place Is Too Small for Us: The Israelite Prophets in Recent Scholarship.* Sources for Biblical and Theological Study 5. Winona Lake, Ind.: Eisenbrauns, 1995. 638pp.

2.40.10   Lindblom, Johannes. *Prophecy in Ancient Israel.* Oxford: Blackwell, 1962. 472pp.

2.40.11   Matthews, Victor H. *Social World of the Hebrew Prophets.* Peabody, Mass.: Hendrickson, 2001. 217pp.

2.40.12   Mays, James Luther, and Paul J. Achtemeier, eds. *Interpreting the Prophets.* Philadelphia: Fortress, 1987. 287pp.

2.40.13   Nissinen, Martti, ed. *Prophecy in Its Ancient Near Eastern Context: Mesopotamian, Biblical, and Arabian Perspectives.* Society of Biblical Literature Symposium Series 15. Atlanta: Scholars, 2000. 160pp.

2.40.14 Rad, Gerhard von. *The Message of the Prophets*. London: SCM, 1968. 289pp.

2.40.15 Robinson, T. H. *Prophecy and Prophets in Ancient Israel*. 2d ed. London: Duckworth, 1953. 231pp.

2.40.16 Sandy, D. Brent. *Prophecy and Apocalyptic: An Annotated Bibliography*. Grand Rapids: Baker, 2007. 240pp.

2.40.17 Sawyer, John F. A. *Prophecy and the Biblical Prophets*. Rev. ed. Oxford Biblical Series. Oxford: Oxford University Press, 1993. 180pp.

2.40.18 Scott, R. B. Y. *The Relevance of the Prophets*. Rev. ed. New York: Macmillan, 1968. 248pp.

2.40.19 Seitz, Christopher R. *The Goodly Fellowship of the Prophets: The Achievement of Association in Canon Formation*. Grand Rapids: Baker, 2009. 136pp.

2.40.20 ———. *Prophecy and Hermeneutics: Toward a New Introduction to the Prophets*. Grand Rapids: Baker, 2007. 264pp.

2.40.21 Steck, Odil Hannes. *The Prophetic Books and Their Theological Witness*. St. Louis, Mo.: Chalice, 2000. 246pp.

2.40.22 Westermann, Claus. *Basic Forms of Prophetic Speech*. Philadelphia: Westminster, 1991. 222pp.

2.40.23 Wilson, Robert R. *Prophecy and Society in Ancient Israel*. Philadelphia: Fortress, 1980. 322pp.

2.40.24 Young, Edward J. *My Servants the Prophets*. Grand Rapids: Eerdmans, 1952. 231pp.

2.40.25 Zimmerli, Walther. *The Fiery Throne: The Prophets and Old Testament Theology*. Edited by K. C. Hanson. Minneapolis: Fortress, 2003. 179pp.

2.41 Isaiah

Highly Recommended

2.41.1   Blenkinsopp, Joseph. *Isaiah 1–39; Isaiah 40–55; Isaiah 56–66.*
3 vols. Anchor Bible. New York: Doubleday, 2000, 2002, 2003.
524/528/348pp.

The most current and judicious example of a type of commentary on Isaiah (represented also in the massive commentaries by Kaiser [§§2.41.20, 2.41.21], Westermann [§2.41.26], and Wildberger [§2.41.10]) that carefully identifies earlier traditions and probes the centuries-long editorial process that led to the composition of First (chs. 1–39), Second (chs. 40–55), and Third (chs. 56–66) Isaiah. Rich in linguistic analysis, historical background, and ANE parallels, but little concerned with theological issues of the text. Helpful for full discussion of technical matters, but should be supplemented with commentaries that give greater attention to the final form of the text and adopt a more intentional theological perspective.

2.41.2   Childs, Brevard S. *Isaiah.* Old Testament Library. Louisville: Westminster John Knox, 2001. 555pp.

Argues for theological unity of the book, resulting from a redactional process according to which the influence of Second Isaiah (chs. 40–55) was responsible for reshaping First Isaiah (chs. 1–39) and largely determined Third Isaiah (chs. 56–66). Childs insists that a recognition of this compositional growth enriches the theological witness of the book in its final canonical shape. Thus he argues against a "synchronic" reading that simply takes the text as it stands without any concern for the stages of tradition, but argues also against a focus on the stages of tradition or redactional processes as ends in themselves. Consistently presses for his approach over against these two alternatives throughout the commentary. Commentary also attends to development of thought within the book, and offers acute theological insights. Focuses on Isaiah's own discrete theological witness, but in a few instances relates Isaiah to other OT materials and probes significance for NT faith.

2.41.3   ———. *The Struggle to Understand Isaiah as Christian Scripture.* Grand Rapids: Eerdmans, 2004. 332pp.

Childs uses Isaiah as a case study of the church's reception and use of its Scriptures. After a brief examination of Isaiah in the LXX and the NT, Childs deals with the church's employment of Isaiah in successive periods:

patristic, Reformation, modern. Despite differences, Childs discovers a "family resemblance" in interpretation around faithfulness to Jesus Christ. Childs explores hermeneutical issues from the perspective of his well-known "canonical approach."

2.41.4   Goldingay, John, and David Payne. *A Critical and Exegetical Commentary on Isaiah 40–55*. 2 vols. International Critical Commentary. London: T&T Clark, 2006. 369/381pp.

As one would expect from the International Critical Commentary, a detailed and highly technical commentary. Deals with Isaiah 40–55 as a discrete unit within the book of Isaiah, and thus attempts to interpret it in terms of its time and audience (sixth–century BCE Babylon). Yet also attends to its synchronic function within the book of Isaiah as we have it, especially how it is to be understood in light of its relationship with Isaiah 1–39. Gives no real attention to theological meaning, a deficiency that Goldingay attempts to address in *The Message of Isaiah 40–55*, listed below. (§2.41.17)

2.41.5   Hanson, Paul D. *Isaiah 40–66*. Interpretation: A Bible Commentary for Teaching and Preaching. Louisville: Westminster John Knox, 1995. 255pp.

In contrast to the companion volume on chs. 1–39 by Seitz, this commentary isolates Second (chs. 40–55) and Third (chs. 56–66) Isaiah from chs. 1–39, and emphasizes the historical setting of these materials for their interpretation rather than their literary structure or their role within the final form of the entire book. Yet this commentary emphasizes the theological concerns of the writers, and frequently makes explicit connections with moral, religious, and spiritual challenges that face contemporary readers.

2.41.6   Oswalt, John N. *The Book of Isaiah*. 2 vols. New International Commentary on the Old Testament. Grand Rapids: Eerdmans, 1986, 1998. 746/755pp.

Argues strongly for the traditional position that the entire book represents the prophecy of Isaiah of Jerusalem. Chapters 1–39 were written for Isaiah's contemporaries in the eighth century BCE; chs. 40–55 presuppose the exile of the sixth century; and ch. 56–66 presuppose the eventual return from exile. Chapters 40–66 thus contain predictive prophecy from Isaiah. Introduction contains comprehensive and illuminating discussion of the book's theology and its function within the canon. Commentary deals extensively with textual, linguistic, literary, and historical matters, but emphasizes structure of passages, their function within the broader book, and their relation to other biblical materials, including the NT. Probes theological significance from an evangelical Christian perspective. Most helpful for preaching and teaching.

2.41.7   Seitz, Christopher R. *Isaiah 1–39*. Interpretation: A Bible Commentary for Teaching and Preaching. Louisville: Westminster John Knox, 1993. 271pp.

Limited to chs. 1–39, but Seitz interprets these chapters in terms of the final form of the entire book and focuses on the structure of passages and their function within the book as the basis for their theological meaning. Constantly reflects on hermeneutical issues facing Christian interpreters of Isaiah, and deftly models the movement from the theological claims of the original compilers of the book to contemporary Christian appropriation.

2.41.8   ———, ed. *Reading and Preaching the Book of Isaiah*. Philadelphia: Fortress, 1988. 126pp.

Several leading OT scholars probe the character, original meaning, and theological significance of the various portions of Isaiah with a view toward exploring the issues involved in Christian proclamation of these passages. Contains two essays on chs.1–39, two essays on chs. 40–55, and one essay on chs. 56–66. Concludes with a final chapter on reading the entire book as a holistic theological unity.

2.41.9   Watts, John D. W. *Isaiah*. 2 vols. Word Biblical Commentary. Waco, Tex.: Word, 1985, 1987. 449/385pp.

Maintains that the overall concern of Isaiah is God's inauguration of a new age for his people, when servanthood rather than authoritarian domination will be the mark of election. Israel's rejection of Isaiah's message is the basis for Isaiah's vision of the realization of this divine purpose in the future. Understands the book to be, in form, an example of "vision genre," and hence argues that its dramatic presentation is similar to a play, with scenes, stage direction, and twelve acts. The prophecy of Isaiah of Jerusalem forms the core of the book, but was supplemented by extensive additions until the book reached its final composition in the Persian period. Even those who do not accept Watts's literary and historical hypotheses will benefit from his detailed discussion of text and language, his informed and judicious interpretations, and his attention to the text's theological claims. Especially helpful are his excurses (in-depth discussions) of significant issues.

2.41.10   Wildberger, Hans. *Isaiah: A Commentary*. 3 vols. Continental Commentary. Minneapolis: Fortress, 1991, 1997, 2002. 524/624/781pp.

Extremely thorough (indeed, encyclopedic), erudite, and technical commentary on "First Isaiah," representing the German critical tradition. Interpretation informed by Ancient Near Eastern background, text-critical issues, analysis of the Hebrew, considerations of the formation of the book of Isaiah from Isaiah himself through post-Isaianic redaction, and the history of interpretation. Commentary on each passage concludes with "Purpose and Thrust," which offers brief theological reflections of the text as Christian Scripture. Introductory matters, including a fine discussion of the book of Isaiah, are treated at the end of the third volume. Wildberger died in 1986, well before this English translation was published, but the extensive bibliography in the third volume was updated through 2001.

2.41.11 Williamson, H. G. M. *A Critical and Exegetical Commentary on Isaiah 1–27.* 3 vols. Volume 1 on Isaiah 1–5 currently available. International Critical Commentary. London: T&T Clark, 2006. 410pp.

Detailed, highly technical commentary by a seasoned OT scholar. Includes a translation that reflects Williamson's text-critical, philological, and poetic conclusions; a verse-by-verse discussion of text-critical and philological issues; an exploration of the form and structure of the larger passage, along with an examination of its role within the final form of Isaiah and within the compositional history of Isaiah; and an exegesis of the passage, emphasizing the meaning of the passage within the composition of the book of Isaiah. Solid and reliable. This first volume contains no introduction to Isaiah or even to Isaiah 1–27. Such an introduction will presumably be part of the third volume.

Also Significant

2.41.12 Achtemeier, Elizabeth. *The Community and Message of Isaiah 55–66: A Theological Commentary.* Minneapolis: Augsburg, 1982. 157pp.

2.41.13 Baltzer, Klaus. *Deutero-Isaiah.* Hermeneia: A Critical and Historical Commentary on the Bible. Minneapolis: Fortress, 2001. 400pp.

2.41.14 Clements, Ronald E. *Isaiah 1–39.* New Century Bible Commentary. Grand Rapids: Eerdmans, 1981. 301pp.

2.41.15 Conrad, Edgar W. *Reading Isaiah.* Overtures to Biblical Theology. Philadelphia: Fortress, 1991. 185pp.

2.41.16   Firth, David G., and H. G. M. Williamson, eds. *Interpreting Isaiah: Issues and Approaches.* Downers Grove, Ill.: InterVarsity, 2009. 287pp.

2.41.17   Goldingay, John. *The Message of Isaiah 40–55: A Literary-Theological Commentary.* London: T&T Clark, 2005. 578pp.

2.41.18   Gray, George Buchanan. *A Critical and Exegetical Commentary on the Book of Isaiah: I-XXXIX.* International Critical Commentary. Edinburgh: T&T Clark, 1912. 472pp.

2.41.19   Hayes, John H. *Isaiah, the Eighth Century Prophet: His Times and His Preaching.* Nashville: Abingdon, 1987. 416pp.

2.41.20   Kaiser, Otto. *Isaiah 1–12: A Commentary.* 2d ed. Old Testament Library. Philadelphia: Westminster, 1983. 272pp.

2.41.21   ———. *Isaiah 13–39: A Commentary.* Old Testament Library. Philadelphia: Westminster, 1974. 412pp.

2.41.22   McKenzie, John L. *Second Isaiah.* Anchor Bible. Garden City, N.Y.: Doubleday, 1968. 225pp.

2.41.23   Motyer, J. Alec. *The Prophecy of Isaiah: An Introduction and Commentary.* Downers Grove, Ill.: InterVarsity, 1993. 544pp.

2.41.24   North, Christopher R. *The Suffering Servant in Deutero-Isaiah: An Historical and Critical Study.* 2d ed. London: Oxford University Press, 1948. 264pp.

2.41.25   Sawyer, John F. A. *The Fifth Gospel: Isaiah in the History of Christianity.* Cambridge: Cambridge University Press, 1996. 281pp.

2.41.26   Westermann, Claus. *Isaiah 40–66.* Old Testament Library. Philadelphia: Westminster, 1969. 429pp.

2.41.27   Whybray, R. N. *Isaiah 40–66.* New Century Bible. London: Oliphants, 1975. 301pp.

2.41.28   Young, Edward J. *The Book of Isaiah: The English Text, with Introduction, Exposition and Notes.* 3 vols. New International Commentary on the Old Testament. Grand Rapids: Eerdmans, 1965, 1969, 1972. 534/604/579pp.

2.42 Jeremiah

Highly Recommended

2.42.1   Allen, Leslie C. *Jeremiah.* Old Testament Library. Louisville: Westminster John Knox, 2009. 546pp.

Gives attention to both diachronic (development of the traditions within the book) and synchronic (the book as it stands) concerns, though with emphasis upon the synchronic. Sees the theme of grace and restoration as central to the message of the book. Attends to the theological message of the book. Interprets passages primarily within book context, but with some concern to make connections with other OT and even NT passages. Discussion of technical matters are brief and generally relegated to footnotes. Little interaction with the interpretation of others.

2.42.2   Brueggemann, Walter. *A Commentary on Jeremiah: Exile and Homecoming.* Grand Rapids: Eerdmans, 1998. 502pp.

Stimulating and engaging study. Breaks new ground in interpretive method. Rejects concern to reconstruct history of Jeremiah's prophetic ministry in favor of understanding the book as an ideological appeal to accept its new and daring framework of reality, i.e., to live and think differently in relation to God. By combining sociological insights, literary analysis, and perspectives from other OT passages with playful imagination, Brueggemann helps the reader to experience the power of this ideological transformation. Because his imagination sometimes leaps beyond the data of the text, the reader should critically evaluate Brueggemann's interpretations in light of pertinent evidence. But the reader will consistently find this volume richly suggestive of meaning for contemporary life.

2.42.3   Carroll, Robert P. *Jeremiah: A Commentary.* Old Testament Library. Philadelphia: Westminster, 1986. 874pp.

Massive commentary that has significantly influenced recent Jeremiah studies. Argues that the book is composed of a variety of responses to the fall of Jerusalem emerging from different groups in different settings throughout an extended period well into postexilic times. Each of these responses is concerned to press its own ideology. Carroll concludes that the book tells us little about the historical Jeremiah and that it lacks an overarching scheme and a coherent theology. The commentary focuses on the ideological appeal of these various voices, and as such it gives attention to the theological meaning of individual passages. Carroll relies on (reconstructed) historical background and close attention to the language of the text (especially meaning of metaphor and symbolic language) rather than broader-book context for interpretation. Although commentary is closely joined to Carroll's critical theories, its attention to language and its ideological analysis can illuminate the meaning of passages even for those who do not share Carroll's critical perspective.

2.42.4   Clements, Ronald E. *Jeremiah*. Interpretation: A Bible Commentary for Teaching and Preaching. Atlanta: John Knox, 1988. 276pp.

Focuses on the audience of the book rather than the audience of Jeremiah's own prophetic ministry. Probes how those who compiled this book in its final form addressed concerns of its original readers who needed a message of hope against a background of political disaster and tremendous suffering. Commentary consistently draws connections between this proclamation to the original audience and the ways it can speak to contemporary persons who experience much the same type of personal anxiety and challenge. Tends to speak to the existence of persons in general, with relatively little explicit mention of how the text witnesses to Jesus Christ and Christian faith.

2.42.5   Fretheim, Terence E. *Jeremiah*. Smyth & Helwys Bible Commentary. Macon, Ga.: Smith & Helwys, 2002. 684pp.

Written by one of the most distinguished OT scholars in the world today. Moves section by section, dealing with literary and theological matters. Commentary grows out of deep reservoir of scholarly research, which remains hidden beneath the surface. Highly accessible to the nonspecialist and very useful and reliable guide for preaching and teaching.

2.42.6   Holladay, William L. *Jeremiah*. 2 vols. Hermeneia: A Critical and Historical Commentary on the Bible. Philadelphia: Fortress, 1986, 1989. 682/543pp.

One of the most complete and detailed commentaries on Jeremiah. Addresses two crucial matters: chronology of Jeremiah's career, and the literary history of the book's formation. Tends toward historical reliability of the book and the view that Jeremiah had much to do with its production.

Gives special consideration to the structure of passages, linguistic analysis, historical background, and illumination from other OT texts. In spite of its technical interests, it is written in a lively style and attends to theological issues, at points reflecting briefly on matters of abiding theological significance for Christians.

2.42.7   Lundbom, Jack R. *Jeremiah 1–20; Jeremiah 21–36; Jeremiah 37–52.* Anchor Bible. New York: Doubleday, 1999, 2004, 2004. 934/649/624pp.

Massive, learned commentary that combines technical analysis of the Hebrew with accessible discussions of the meaning and message of passages throughout Jeremiah. In contrast to McKane (§2.42.8) insists that the key to the book's interpretation is not the development of oral traditions but the literary product as we have it in its final form. Employs a sophisticated and helpful form of rhetorical criticism that explores the structure and various rhetorical devices with a view toward grasping the impact upon the audience—both original ancient and modern readers. Gives considerable attention to theological significance and even contemporary connections and appropriation. Contains an extended and useful introduction to the book. Could do more to explore how individual passages function within the broader book.

2.42.8   McKane, William. *A Critical and Exegetical Commentary on the Book of Jeremiah.* 2 vols. International Critical Commentary. Edinburgh: T&T Clark, 1986, 1996. 1396pp.

On the basis of text-critical considerations concludes that the book developed as a "rolling corpus," i.e., an original core of Jeremiah traditions generated haphazard expansions from a variety of groups over a long period of time. McKane's purpose is not to reconstruct the life or words of Jeremiah, but to trace the history of the traditions around Jeremiah that found their way into this book. Gives meticulous attention to linguistic analysis and comparison of ancient versions, and engages in vigorous interaction with the history of interpretation. In the process, offers helpful and at times insightful illumination of the meaning of the final form of the text, with occasional profound theological insights.

2.42.9   Thompson, J. A. *The Book of Jeremiah.* New International Commentary on the Old Testament. Grand Rapids: Eerdmans, 1980. 819pp.

Writes from an evangelical perspective, and argues for the essential historical accuracy of the book. Largely ignores the significance of the final form of the book for the original intended readers in favor of focusing

178

interpretive attention on the historical ministry of Jeremiah. Gives attention to language and historical background, including insights from other OT passages, so as to arrive at biographical reflections on Jeremiah's experience, historical reflections on Israel's moral and spiritual failure, and theological reflections on God's relationship with and actions toward his people, all with a view toward noting ongoing significance for the people of God, the church.

Also Significant

2.42.10   Bright, John. *Jeremiah*. Anchor Bible. Garden City, N.Y.: Doubleday, 1965. 372pp.

2.42.11   Brueggemann, Walter. *Like Fire in the Bones: Listening for the Prophetic Word in Jeremiah*. Edited by Patrick D. Miller. Minneapolis: Fortress, 2006. 255pp.

2.42.12   Craigie, Peter C., Page H. Kelly, and Joel F. Drinkard Jr. *Jeremiah 1–25*. Word Biblical Commentary. Waco, Tex.: Word, 1991. 388pp.

2.42.13   Curtis, A. H. W., and T. Römer, eds. *The Book of Jeremiah and Its Reception*. Louvain: Louvain University Press, 1997. 331pp.

2.42.14   Keown, Gerald L., Pamela J. Sclaise, and Thomas G. Smothers. *Jeremiah 26–52*. Word Biblical Commentary. Dallas: Word, 1995. 402pp.

2.42.15   King, Philip J. *Jeremiah: An Archaeological Companion*. Philadelphia: Westminster, 1993. 204pp.

2.42.16   McConville, J. G. *Judgment and Promise: An Interpretation of the Book of Jeremiah*. Winona Lake, Ind.: Eisenbrauns, 1994. 208pp.

2.42.17   Nicholson, E. W. *Preaching to the Exiles*. Oxford: Oxford University Press, 1970. 154pp.

2.42.18   Overholt, Thomas W. *The Threat of Falsehood: A Study in the Theology of the Book of Jeremiah*. Studies in Biblical Theology, Second Series 16. Naperville, Ill.: Allenson, 1970. 110pp.

2.42.19   Thompson, Henry O. *The Book of Jeremiah: An Annotated Bibliography.* ATLA Bibliography Series. Lanham, Md.: Scarecrow, 1996. 745pp.

2.42.20   Welch, Adam C. *Jeremiah: His Time and His Work.* Oxford: Basil Black- well, 1951. 263pp.

2.43   Lamentations

See also JEREMIAH (§2.42) and SONG OF SOLOMON (§2.39)

Highly Recommended

2.43.1   Berlin, Adele. *Lamentations.* Old Testament Library. Louisville: Westmin- ster John Knox, 2002. 135pp.

Fills a significant gap in the study of Lamentations by approaching Lam- entations as a literary product, examining its images, metaphors, and poetic discourse. Berlin pursues the meaning of these literary features in order to identify and understand the religious worldview that gave rise to them. In this worldview she focuses on such concepts as purity, mourn- ing, repentance, and the Davidic covenant. In the process she engages in constant comparison with other biblical and ANE materials. She considers the historical-critical reconstruction of events referenced in Lamentations or sources lying behind the final form to be speculative and, in any case, not necessary to experience the literary impact of the book. Draws heavily on the Hebrew Masoretic text, but one can easily use this volume with- out knowledge of Hebrew. Although Berlin constantly references religious ideas and themes that lie behind the language of Lamentations, she does little to provide a constructive presentation of the book's theology or its contribution to the theological vision of the OT.

2.43.2   Dobbs-Allsopp, F. W. *Lamentations.* Interpretation: A Bible Commentary for Teaching and Preaching. Louisville: John Knox, 2002. 159pp.

An incisive analysis of the thought of Lamentations that masterfully relates the original message of the book to the theology of the OT as a whole and to contemporary reflection on the perduring problems broached by Lam- entations, e.g., suffering, violence, the hidden/mysterious plan of God, and hope. Gives some (limited) attention to significance of Lamentations for Christian theology and faith. Dobbs-Allsopp's ideological emphasis nicely complements Berlin's (§2.43.1) literary study and Renkema's (§2.43.4) historical examination.

2.43.3   Hillers, Delbert R. *Lamentations.* Rev. ed. Anchor Bible. New York: Doubleday, 1992. 116pp.

Argues that Lamentations was not written by Jeremiah but is a unity produced by an eyewitness to the events described. Gives special attention to the writer's adoption of biblical language, motifs, and rhythmic patterns so as to bind the laments together, to give voice to feelings of deep despair, and to communicate theological questions and affirmations. Depth of treatment is compromised somewhat by commentary's brevity. Contains no specific discussion of the book's theology, and thus should be supplemented with Westermann (§2.43.6).

2.43.4   Renkema, Johan. *Lamentations.* Historical Commentary on the Old Testament. Leuven: Peeters, 1998. 641pp.

Recently translated from the Dutch, the most comprehensive commentary on Lamentations presently available in English. Introduction addresses literary structure, authorship, date, provenance, and theology. Insists on the unity of the book, and holds that it was produced by temple singers left behind after the fall of Jerusalem. Exhaustive commentary provides technical but relevant discussions of structural and linguistic analysis, historical background, and history of interpretation.

2.43.5   Salters, R. B. *A Critical and Exegetical Commentary on Lamentations.* International Critical Commentary. London: T&T Clark, 2010. 375pp.

Considers that the book was composed of five originally separate poems (for the most part of equal length) written by different persons. Attends to the structure of the individual poems, but gives by far the greatest attention to minute analysis of the Hebrew text. Interacts with history of interpretation, both ancient and modern. And discusses in a limited way the theological claims of the various passages.

2.43.6   Westermann, Claus. *Lamentations: Issues and Interpretation.* Minneapolis: Fortress, 1994. 252pp.

Carefully surveys history of research into Lamentations and concludes that the book's message has been largely missed because of certain invalid presuppositions, chiefly that laments have no theological significance. Sets Lamentations within the broader context of laments in the ANE, presents an overview of the book as a whole, pursues a close reading of each of the five lamentations in the book, paying special attention to literary structure and meaning of key elements in each, and concludes with an insightful summary of the theology of Lamentations.

Also Significant

2.43.7 Baumgartner, Walter. *Jeremiah's Poems of Lament*. Historic Texts and Interpreters 7. Sheffield: Almond, 1988. 114pp.

2.43.8 Gottwald, Norman K. *Studies in the Book of Lamentations*. Rev. ed. London: SCM, 1962. 126pp.

2.43.9 Joyce, Paul M., and Diana Lipton. *Lamentations through the Centuries*. Malden, Mass: Wiley-Blackwell, 2013. 232pp.

2.43.10 Neusner, Jacob. *Israel after Calamity: The Book of Lamentations*. The Bible of Judaism Library. Valley Forge, Pa.: Trinity Press International, 1995. 117pp.

2.43.11 Provan, Iain. *Lamentations*. New Century Bible Commentary. Grand Rapids: Eerdmans, 1991. 142pp.

2.44   Ezekiel

See also HOSEA (§2.47)

Highly Recommended

2.44.1 Allen, Leslie C. *Ezekiel*. 2 vols. Word Biblical Commentary. Dallas: Word, 1994, 1990. 306/301pp.

This evangelical scholar adopts a moderating position that affirms authentic Ezekiel tradition in the book, but gives full weight to the redactional process that led to the production of the final form of the book. Insists that Ezekiel himself initiated the literary production of the book soon after the conclusion of his ministry, and that his disciples, who knew Ezekiel well and shared his aims, completed the editorial process. Allen focuses on the final canonical text, but explores how the redactional process as he reconstructs it illumines the final form. He attends to the theological meaning for the original exilic audience and relates passages to other biblical texts (including NT ones), but gives no direct attention to contemporary appropriation. A significant contribution is the original and detailed discussion of text-critical matters.

2.44.2 Blenkinsopp, Joseph. *Ezekiel.* Interpretation: A Bible Commentary for Teaching and Preaching. Louisville: Westminster John Knox, 1990. 242pp.

Lucid and engaging interpretation of this difficult book according to a twofold focus: (1) meaning of the ministry and oracles of the prophet Ezekiel in relation to his original audience; and (2) meaning intended by the later compilers of this book to the generation of Jews they wished to address. As such, Blenkinsopp interprets Ezekiel by examining both the historical background of Ezekiel's ministry and the literary structure and method of composition of the book itself. In the course of commenting on original meaning, Blenkinsopp deftly weaves in suggestions pertaining to continuing relevance.

2.44.3 Block, Daniel I. *The Book of Ezekiel.* New International Commentary on the Old Testament. Grand Rapids: Eerdmans, 1997, 1998. 887/826pp.

Detailed, yet readable and engaging commentary by prominent evangelical OT scholar. Commentary on each passage is clearly organized around textual notes, structure of passage, verse-by-verse interpretation, and theological significance (where Block lists theological lessons derived from the passage). Considers it most likely that Ezekiel was responsible for the book. Commentary emphasizes structure, linguistic analysis, historical background, and broader-book context, but contains little interaction with history of interpretation.

2.44.4 Eichrodt, Walther. *Ezekiel.* Old Testament Library. Philadelphia: Westminster, 1970. 594pp.

This great OT scholar maintains that Ezekiel himself was the basic compiler of the book, though it was revised by editors who expanded or modified his message. The introduction, treating the "Prophet Ezekiel and His Book," is the most authoritative, lucid, and succinct description of Ezekiel to be found anywhere. The commentary attempts to capture the perspective of the prophet, employing careful exegesis based on language and literary and historical context to probe the thinking, emotions, and experience of Ezekiel. In the process, Eichrodt deftly shows how theological insights pertaining to NT faith arise out of this close, prophet-oriented reading of the text.

2.44.5 Zimmerli, Walther. *Ezekiel.* 2 vols. Hermeneia: A Critical and Historical Commentary on the Bible. Philadelphia: Fortress, 1979, 1983. 509/606pp.

Highly technical, detailed, and authoritative. Maintains that the present book was not produced by Ezekiel, but by a "school" that edited the prophet's oracles, with some additions and modifications. Commentary emphasizes text-critical considerations, form-critical analysis (probing how the form of the passage points to original setting, function, and significance), and tradition-critical analysis (evaluating the historicity of passages and their relationship to other OT traditions). Interacts extensively with other interpreters. Contains brief, but profound reflection on theological significance, with some suggestions as to how the theological message of Ezekiel bears witness to Jesus Christ.

Also Significant

2.44.6 Brownlee, William H. *Ezekiel 1–19.* Word Biblical Commentary. Waco, Tex.: Word, 1986. 321pp.

2.44.7 Cooke, George A. *A Critical and Exegetical Commentary on the Book of Ezekiel.* International Critical Commentary. Edinburgh: T&T Clark, 1936. 558pp.

2.44.8 Fairbairn, Patrick. *Ezekiel and the Book of His Prophecy.* Edinburgh: T&T Clark, 1851. 504pp.

2.44.9 Greenberg, Moshe. *Ezekiel.* 2 vols. Anchor Bible. New York: Doubleday, 1983, 1997. 760pp.

2.44.10 Hals, Ronald M. *Ezekiel.* Forms of the Old Testament Literature 19. Grand Rapids: Eerdmans, 1989. 363pp.

2.44.11 Joyce, Paul M. *Ezekiel: A Commentary.* Library of Hebrew Bible/Old Testament Studies, no. 482. London: T&T Clark, 2007. 307pp.

2.44.12 Kutsko, John F. *Between Heaven and Earth: Divine Presence and Absence in the Book of Ezekiel.* Biblical and Judaic Studies 7. Winona Lake, Ind.: Eisenbrauns, 2000. 185pp.

2.44.13   Odell, Margaret S., and John T. Strong, eds. *The Book of Ezekiel: Theo-logical and Anthropological Perspectives.* Society of Biblical Literature Symposium Series 9. Atlanta: Society of Biblical Literature, 2000. 270pp.

2.44.14   Renz, Thomas. *The Rhetorical Function of the Book of Ezekiel.* Supplements to Vetus Testamentum 76. Leiden: Brill, 1999. 298pp.

2.44.15   Taylor, John B. *Ezekiel: An Introduction and Commentary.* Tyndale Old Testament Commentaries. Downers Grove, Ill.: InterVarsity, 1969. 285pp.

2.44.16   Tuell, Steven. *Ezekiel.* New International Biblical Commentary. Peabody, Mass.: Hendrickson, 2009. 368pp.

2.45   Daniel

Highly Recommended

2.45.1   Baldwin, Joyce G. *Daniel.* Tyndale Old Testament Commentaries. Downers Grove, Ill.: InterVarsity, 1979. 210pp.

Unlike most other modern interpreters, this prominent British evangelical scholar argues that the book was likely composed around the turn of the fifth century BCE. Yet the commentary does not focus on historical reconstruction but on the development of the story and visions throughout the book and on details of the story and visions with a view toward ascertaining their theological significance. Gives some attention to historical background and evidence from other OT passages.

2.45.2   Collins, John J. *Daniel.* Hermeneia: A Critical and Historical Commentary on the Bible. Minneapolis: Fortress, 1993. 499pp.

The most complete and detailed commentary available in English. Considers the stories of the book to be legendary, and maintains that Daniel never existed. Thus, the book is a work of religious fiction that has no historical value in relation to events described. The extensive introduction provides a wealth of information; most helpful is a discussion by Adela Yarbro Collins on the influence of Daniel on the NT. The commentary itself (a) discusses the literary structure of the passage; (b) gives a verse-by-verse interpretation that is rich in linguistic analysis, historical background, and the author's use of traditional material; (c) identifies the passage's genre and discusses significance of form for the construal of the passage; and (d) treats the setting and function of the passage, summarizing the religious and social significance for the original readers (with some suggestions regarding theology), and discussing its function within the book.

2.45.3   Goldingay, John E. *Daniel.* Word Biblical Commentary. Waco, Tex.: Word, 1989. 351pp.

Like Collins (§2.45.2), offers a detailed interpretation of Daniel, emphasizing text-critical, form-critical, linguistic, and historical analysis. Introduction is briefer and more general than Collins, and Goldingay insists on the possibility of some historical value to the book's stories, although maintains that the purpose is not historiography but religious instruction to Jews in the late Persian period. Emphasizes dynamic interplay between stories (chs. 1–6) and visions (chs. 7–12). Discusses at length the theological significance of passages for original readers and explicitly explores continuing theological and religious significance for Christians. Overall one of the most useful commentary on Daniel for preaching and teaching.

2.45.4   Lucas, Ernest C. *Daniel.* Apollos Old Testament Commentary. Downers Grove, Ill.: InterVarsity, 2002. 359pp.

One of the most original and illuminating volumes in the Apollos commentary series. Reserves discussion of introductory issues (e.g., date and authorship) to the end of the book, so as to draw conclusions from the movement through the text of Daniel. For each passage progresses from a discussion of form and structure, to verse-by-verse comment, to explanation of theological themes and implications. Although acknowledging the likelihood of the development of the tradition behind the text, focuses upon the final form of the text as the basis for the church's preaching and teaching.

2.45.5   Porteous, Norman W. *Daniel: A Commentary.* 2d ed. Old Testament Library. Philadelphia: Westminster, 1979. 196pp.

Dates the book just before 164 BCE. Virtually ignores text-critical or linguistic matters so as to concentrate on the meaning of the book for the religious experience of Jews during the Maccabean period and to explore the book's theological witness. Interprets passages primarily in terms of (a) their function within the book and (b) significance of historical setting of Israel during the Maccabean period. Focuses on the theological witness of the book of Daniel itself, but does discuss how passages in the book were used subsequently, including their use in the NT.

Also Significant

2.45.6   Buber, Martin. *Daniel: Dialogues on Realization*. New York: Holt, Rinehart, and Winston, 1964. 144pp

2.45.7   Charles, R. H. *A Critical and Exegetical Commentary on the Book of Daniel*. Oxford: Oxford University Press, 1929. 408pp.

2.45.8   Collins, John J. *The Apocalyptic Vision of the Book of Daniel*. Harvard Semitic Monographs. Missoula, Mont.: Scholars, 1977. 239pp.

2.45.9   Collins, John J., and Peter W. Flint, eds. *The Book of Daniel: Composition and Reception*. 2 vols. Supplements to Vetus Testamentum 83. Leiden: Brill, 2001. 292/482pp.

2.45.10   Driver, S. R. *The Book of Daniel*. Cambridge Bible for Schools and Colleges. Cambridge: Cambridge University Press, 1900. 215pp.

2.45.11   Hartman, Louis F., and Alexander A. DiLella. *The Book of Daniel*. Anchor Bible. Garden City, N.Y.: Doubleday, 1978. 345pp.

2.45.12   Montgomery, James A. *A Critical and Exegetical Commentary on the Book of Daniel*. International Critical Commentary. Edinburgh: T&T Clark, 1927. 488pp.

2.45.13   Redditt, Paul L. *Daniel*. New Century Bible Commentary. Sheffield: Sheffield Academic Press, 1999. 211pp.

2.45.14   Russell, D. S. Daniel. *Daily Study Bible*. Philadelphia: Westminster, 1981. 234pp.

2.45.15   Thompson, Henry O. *The Book of Daniel: An Annotated Bibliography*. Garland Reference Library of the Humanities: Books of the Bible 1. New York: Garland, 1992. 547pp.

2.45.16   Towner, W. Sibley. *Daniel*. Interpretation: A Bible Commentary for Teaching and Preaching. Atlanta: John Knox, 1984. 186pp.

2.45.17 Woude, A. S. van der, ed. *The Book of Daniel in the Light of New Findings*. Bibliotheca Ephemeridum Theologicarum Lovaniensium 106. Leuven: Leuven University Press, 1993. 574pp.

2.46 The Twelve (Minor) Prophets: General Works

Highly Recommended

2.46.1 Achtemeier, Elizabeth. *Nahum–Malachi*. Interpretation: A Bible Commentary for Teaching and Preaching. Atlanta: John Knox, 1986. 201pp.

Solid discussion of the message of the text for the original audience based on careful but concise treatment of historical background, genre, literary structure, and the meaning of key words, leading to insightful reflections on the theology of the passage and its contribution to biblical revelation as a whole. Theological reflection leads in turn to helpful suggestions for present Christian application. Gives some attention to relation between the various Minor Prophets discussed, but for the most part deals with them as distinct and separate books.

2.46.2 ———. *Preaching from the Minor Prophets: Texts and Sermon Suggestions*. Grand Rapids: Eerdmans, 1998. 143pp.

Eminently practical guide to assist ministers in preaching from the Minor Prophets. Treatment of each of the Minor Prophets includes recommended commentaries, historical context, theological context, and studies of selected passages, which provides a discussion of linguistic and literary features, sermon possibilities, and homiletical exposition. These studies of selected passages serve as models that can be applied to other portions of the Minor Prophets.

2.46.3 Limburg, James. *Hosea–Micah*. Interpretation: A Bible Commentary for Teaching and Preaching. Atlanta: John Knox, 1988. 201pp.

Like the companion volume by Achtemeier (§2.46.1), moves from careful examination of the message of passage based on solid interpretive work to theological significance and contemporary Christian application. Tends to present theology of passages in terms of major themes, to trace these themes throughout the whole of Scripture (including the NT), and to show how these themes can be used as the basis for Christian proclamation.

2.46.4   McComiskey, Thomas Edward, ed. *The Minor Prophets: An Exegetical and Expository Commentary.* 3 vols. Grand Rapids: Baker, 1998. 1412pp.

Consistently evangelical commentary, with contributions by Douglas Stuart, J. Alec Motyer, Joyce Baldwin, F. F. Bruce, and Raymond Dillard, among others. Notes on the Hebrew text (lexical, syntactical, and text-critical) appear at the top of each page (typically occupying about forty percent of the page), with exposition below, where there is virtually no reference to technical matters pertaining to the Hebrew. Exposition focuses on historical background, connections with other OT passages, theological reflection, and appropriation to contemporary Christian life. Solid and reliable, but rarely groundbreaking or original.

2.46.5   Smith, Ralph L. *Micah–Malachi.* Word Biblical Commentary. Waco, Tex.: Word, 1984. 358pp.

Adopts generally conservative conclusions on questions of the unity and authorship of the various books considered. Emphasizes ways in which the different audiences and circumstances addressed by the prophets determine the message of the several books discussed, while affirming also a fundamental unity lying behind all these books, viz., judgment and hope based on an understanding of the character of Yahweh. Somewhat less technical than most of the volumes in this series, but a major strength is Smith's practice of presenting clearly the major interpretive options from the history of exegesis, giving arguments for and against each. Employs principal of analogy in moving from original meaning to contemporary Christian application, noting how contemporary Christians experience the same kinds of questions, struggles, and challenges as the original audiences of the prophets.

2.46.6   Stuart, Douglas. *Hosea–Jonah.* Word Biblical Commentary. Waco, Tex.: Word, 1987. 537pp.

Like Smith, adopts conservative perspective on questions such as unity, authorship, and date of the various books. Emphasizes prophets' dependence on earlier biblical tradition, and argues that all of these prophets attempted to call the people back to obedience to the Mosaic covenant. Commentary is more technical than the volume by Smith (§2.46.5), but gives less attention to the history of interpretation. Concentrates on meaning of significant theological issues in the text, and attends to the ways in which contemporary Christians can apply the prophet's insights to these issues.

2.46.7   Sweeney, Marvin A. *The Twelve Prophets.* Berit Olam: Studies in Hebrew Narrative and Poetry. Collegeville, Minn.: Liturgical Press, 2000. 802pp.

189

Adopts a twofold interpretive perspective: treats the Minor Prophets as a coherent literary work with its own structures, themes, and theology ("The Book of the Twelve"), but also deals with each of these books as a distinct literary work. Thus, commentary is concerned to identify the message of each book, and also to note how the message of that book is informed by its relationship to the other Minor Prophets and contributes to the overall impact of the Book of the Twelve. Concentrates on the canonical text, with little attention to the history of traditions or the process of editing lying behind the final form. Attends to literary structure, linguistic analysis, and historical, social, religious, and cultural background. Since his emphasis is on the final text, Sweeney attends to theological meaning, but provides no explicit reflection on broad theological implications or significance for contemporary Christians.

Also Significant

2.46.8   Albertz, Rainer, James D. Nogalski, and Jakob Wörle, eds. *Perspectives on the Formation of the Book of the Twelve: Methodological Foundations, Redactional Processes, Historical Insights*. Beihefte zur Zeitschrift für die alttestamentliche Wissenschaft, Bd. 433. Berlin: de Gruyter, 2012. 414pp.

2.46.9   Allen, Leslie C. *The Books of Joel, Obadiah, Jonah and Micah*. New International Commentary on the Old Testament. Grand Rapids: Eerdmans, 1976. 427pp.

2.46.10   Coggins, Richard, and Jin H. Han. *Six Minor Prophets through the Centuries: Nahum, Habakkuk, Zephaniah, Haggai, Zechariah, and Malachi*. Blackwell Bible Commentaries. Malden, Mass.: Wiley-Blackwell, 2011. 274pp.

2.46.11   Craigie, Peter C. *Twelve Prophets*. 2 vols. Daily Study Bible. Philadelphia: Westminster, 1984, 1985. 239/248pp.

2.46.12   House, Paul R. *The Unity of the Twelve*. Journal for the Study of the Old Testament Supplement Series 97. Sheffield: Almond, 1990. 262pp.

2.46.13   King, Philip J. *Amos, Hosea, Micah: An Archaeological Commentary*. Philadelphia: Westminster, 1988. 176pp.

2.46.14   Mitchell, Hinckley G., John Merlin Powis Smith, and Julius A. Bewer. *A Critical and Exegetical Commentary on Haggai, Zechariah, Malachi, and Jonah.* International Critical Commentary. Edinburgh: T&T Clark, 1912. 362 + 88 + 65pp.

2.46.15   Nogalski, James D. *The Book of the Twelve.* 2 vols. Smyth & Helwys Commentary. Macon, Ga.: Smyth & Helwys, 2011. 1112pp.

2.46.16   Nogalski, James D., and Marvin A. Sweeney, eds. *Reading and Hearing the Book of the Twelve.* Society of Biblical Literature Symposium Series 15. Atlanta: Society of Biblical Literature, 2000. 235pp.

2.46.17   Orelli, Conrad von. *The Twelve Minor Prophets.* Edinburgh: T&T Clark, 1897. 405pp.

2.46.18   Reddit, Paul L., and Aaron Schart. *Thematic Threads in the Book of the Twelve.* Beihefte zur Zeitschrift für die alttestamentliche Wissenschaft, Bd. 325. Berlin: de Gruyter, 2003. 376pp.

2.46.19   Smith, John Merlin Powis, William Hayes Ward, and Julius A. Bewer. *A Critical and Exegetical Commentary on Micah, Zephaniah, Nahum, Habakkuk, Obadiah, and Joel.* International Critical Commentary. Edinburgh: T&T Clark, 1911. 360 + 28 + 146pp.

2.47   Hosea

Highly Recommended

2.47.1   Andersen, Francis I., and David Noel Freedman. *Hosea.* Anchor Bible. Garden City, N.Y.: Doubleday, 1980. 699pp.

Massive, detailed commentary that emphasizes cultural background, linguistic analysis (especially Hebrew vocabulary, syntax, and poetic language), and literary structure in its careful interpretation of virtually every word of Hosea. Focuses on technical matters of language and history, and gives little specific attention to theological issues. Considers it likely that the book was compiled in the seventh century BCE by reformers in Judah during the reign of Manasseh, and thus gives attention both to the significance of passages for audience of the historical Hosea and to the impact of the book on the later seventh-century audience.

2.47.2   Dearman, J. Andrew. *The Book of Hosea.* New International Commentary on the Old Testament. Grand Rapids: Eerdmans, 2010. 408pp.

Solid, informed commentary. Believes that Hosea was likely responsible for the composition of most of the present book, although acknowledges the tentativeness of any conclusion. Most helpful are the discussions on simile and metaphor and on the theology of Hosea found in the introduction, as well as several "excurses" throughout the volume that develop significant elements within the text. The latter are complemented by ten appendices that discuss a variety of elements in Hosea (e.g., Baal in Hosea). Focuses upon the final form of the text, with emphasis upon insights from the Hebrew, historical background, and other OT passages.

2.47.3   Macintosh, A. A. *A Critical and Exegetical Commentary on Hosea.* International Critical Commentary. Edinburgh: T&T Clark, 1997. 600pp.

Focuses on ways in which Hosea's personal experience of his cultural, religious, and political environment shaped his message. Includes both comments accessible to the general reader and more technical discussions of linguistic and text-critical issues of interest to the specialist. Maintains that Hosea was himself responsible for the compilation of the book; the emphasis is therefore on the impact of this book as a literary product on Hosea's audience. Of special value are the constant allusions to the history of interpretation, and especially to ancient rabbinic interpreters. Introduction contains helpful discussion of the essence of Hosea's thought, and commentary necessarily deals with theological issues raised in the text; but Macintosh gives little explicit attention to theological reflection, and (as one would expect in the ICC) no attention to contemporary appropriation.

2.47.4   Mays, James Luther. *Hosea: A Commentary.* Old Testament Library. Philadelphia: Westminster, 1969. 190pp.

Produced by a most perceptive interpreter and lucid writer, this brief commentary focuses on the most significant interpretive issues of passages in Hosea and their theological meaning. Deals primarily with the distinctive theological witness of Hosea, and therefore does not attempt to relate Hosea's theology to other parts of the OT canon or explicitly to the Christian faith.

2.47.5   Wolff, Hans Walter. *Hosea: A Commentary on the Book of the Prophet Hosea.* Hermeneia: A Critical and Historical Commentary on the Bible. Philadelphia: Fortress, 1974. 259pp.

Authoritative, judicious commentary by one of the most prominent German OT scholars. Argues that the original prophecy of Hosea forms the core of the book, which was subsequently compiled over a long process, reaching its present stage in the postexilic period. Deals with each passage in terms of its form (genre and literary structure), its setting (historical examination as to whether it belongs to the ministry of the historical Hosea or to a later editorial stage and function within the final book), its interpretation (careful exploration of technical linguistic and historical issues), and the theological aim of the passage, in which Wolff typically relates the message to NT faith.

Also Significant

2.47.6   Brueggemann, Walter. *Tradition for Crisis: A Study in Hosea.* Richmond, Va.: John Knox, 1968. 164pp.

2.47.7   Davies, Graham I. *Hosea.* New Century Bible Commentary. Grand Rapids: Eerdmans, 1992. 315pp.

2.47.8   Doorly, William J. *Prophet of Love: Understanding the Book of Hosea.* New York: Paulist, 1991. 138pp.

2.47.9   Emmerson, Grace I. *Hosea: An Israelite Prophet in Judean Perspective.* Journal for the Study of the Old Testament Supplement Series 28. Sheffield: JSOT, 1984. 224pp.

2.47.10   Hubbard, David A. *Hosea: An Introduction and Commentary.* Tyndale Old Testament Commentaries. Downers Grove, Ill.: InterVarsity, 1990. 234pp.

2.47.11   Ward, James M. *Hosea: A Theological Commentary.* New York: Harper & Row, 1966. 264pp.

2.48   Joel

Highly Recommended

2.48.1   Barton, John. *Joel and Obadiah.* Old Testament Library. Louisville: Westminster John Knox, 2001. 168pp.

Although produced at beginning of the twenty-first century, this solid commentary stands closer in method (and to some extent in conclusions) to those written at end of the nineteenth. Identifies sources lying behind the text, and insists on the literary disunity of both Joel and Obadiah. Accepts Duhm's theory that Joel is composed of two originally separate prophecies, and argues similarly that the end of Obadiah is a later addition. While emphasizing the interpretation of earlier stages of tradition, Barton gives some attention to the theological meaning of the final composition of the book. Employs linguistic analysis of the Hebrew, history of (modern) interpretation, and insights from other OT prophecies, an important consideration given significant role of earlier prophecies in both Joel and Obadiah. Develops theological meaning and contemporary relevance.

2.48.2   Crenshaw, James L. *Joel.* Anchor Bible. New York: Doubleday, 1995. 251pp.

Careful, sensitive interpretation, with original and compelling insights. Interpretation focuses on historical background, literary structure, and especially linguistic analysis (Hebrew terms and syntax), but commentary is accessible to those who do not know Hebrew. Maintains that the prophet Joel was "a learned scribe, a teacher of preserved religious tradition" around the turn of the fifth century BCE, and thus emphasizes the ways in which Joel has adopted and reinterpreted earlier prophetic material. Gives serious attention to Joel's religious views, but does little to address theological significance for NT faith.

2.48.3   Wolff, Hans Walter. *A Commentary on the Books of the Prophets Joel and Amos.* Hermeneia: A Critical and Historical Commentary on the Bible. Philadelphia: Fortress, 1977. 392pp.

Similar in quality and approach to Wolff's commentary on Hosea (§2.47.5). Seriously considers the setting of the passage in the ministry of the prophet and in the book, the genre and literary structure of the passage, the language and historical background, and theological claims. In Joel, Wolff gives somewhat more attention to the way in which the structure of the whole book affects meaning than he does in most of his other commentaries. In Amos, he posits an extended process of the growth of the book and emphasizes not only the final text but the interpretive significance of the history of tradition lying behind it. The theological discussions reflect a Lutheran perspective. This volume represents two commentaries, originally published separately, with an interval of several years between.

Also Significant

2.48.4   Assis, Elie. *Book of Joel: A Prophet between Calamity and Hope.* New York: T&T Clark, 2013. 304pp.

2.48.5   Coggins, Richard James. *Joel and Amos.* New Century Bible Commentary. Sheffield: Sheffield Academic Press, 2000. 170pp.

2.48.6   Driver, S. R. *The Books of Joel and Amos.* Cambridge Bible for Schools and Colleges. Cambridge: Cambridge University Press, 1915. 251pp.

2.48.7   Hubbard, David A. *Joel and Amos.* Tyndale Old Testament Commentaries. Downers Grove, Ill.: InterVarsity, 1989. 245pp.

2.48.8   Kapelrud, Arvid Schou. *Joel Studies.* Uppsala: Lundequistska, 1948. 211pp.

2.48.9   Prinsloo, Willem S. *The Theology of the Book of Joel.* Berlin: Walter De Gruyter, 1985. 136pp.

2.48.10   Strazicich, John. *Joel's Use of Scripture and the Scripture's Use of Joel: Appropriation and Resignification in Second Temple Judaism and Early Christianity.* Biblical Interpretation Series, no. 82. Leiden: Brill, 2007. 441pp.

2.49   Amos

See also JOEL (§2.48)

Highly Recommended

2.49.1   Andersen, Francis I., and David Noel Freedman. *Amos.* Anchor Bible. New York: Doubleday, 1989. 979pp.

Massive, encyclopedic commentary. Introduction alone is almost two hundred pages in length. Considers that Amos, or someone close to the prophet, is responsible for the book's composition. Interprets the book as it stands over against concern with earlier traditions or forms, and emphasizes the role of book context for meaning of individual passages. Employs historical background, archaeological insights, analysis of literary structure and rhetorical devices, linguistic analysis of the Hebrew, comparative philology of cognate Semitic languages, relationship to other prophets, and history of interpretation. Gives attention to Amos's message, but the commentary tends not to develop the theological aspects of passages.

2.49.2   Hasel, Gerhard F. *Understanding the Book of Amos: Basic Issues in the Current Interpretations.* Grand Rapids: Baker, 1991. 171pp.

An introduction to the book of Amos in the form of a survey of scholarly work on Amos between 1960 and 1990. Describes the development of modern interpretation of the book and devotes a separate chapter to each of the major issues of Amos. Review of literature is informed, balanced (with opposing views represented), and given with little of the author's own evaluations, but Hasel does discuss questions and issues derived from the review. Includes a bibliography of more than eight hundred works.

2.49.3   Jeremias, Jörg. *The Book of Amos.* Old Testament Library. Louisville: Westminster John Knox, 1998. 177pp.

Contends that the book of Amos can tell us little about the ministry or oracles of Amos himself, since it is the product of an extended process of compilation that reached its final form in the postexilic period. Thus, Jeremias employs redaction criticism to identify the various stages of compilation and to interpret individual passages in terms of the intention of the editors responsible for their inclusion. Yet Jeremias gives primary attention to the message of the book in its final form, carefully interpreting passages in terms of their function within the book and their impact on the intended reader. Hence the commentary offers insights helpful even to students who do not share the author's critical views.

2.49.4   Mays, James Luther. *Amos: A Commentary.* Old Testament Library. Philadelphia: Westminster, 1969. 169pp.

Like Mays's commentary on Hosea (§2.47.4), this volume offers a concise and clearly written interpretation focusing on the theological message of the text. Asserts that the book contains authentic material from Amos but also includes later additions, and owes its arrangement to the intentions of later editors. Commentary deals with the meaning of passages both in the context of Amos's ministry and in the role they play within the setting of the book. Gives special attention to the interpretive significance of various forms of prophetic speech. Offers rich theological reflection from Christian perspective.

2.49.5   Paul, Shalom. *Amos.* Hermeneia: A Critical and Historical Commentary on the Bible. Minneapolis: Fortress, 1991. 409pp.

Learned, technical commentary by prominent Jewish scholar carefully differentiates elements that belong to the ministry of the historical Amos (and where they fit in his ministry) and those that were introduced by later editors, in an effort to identify as precisely as possible the meaning of passages in their original contexts. Employs historical background and especially meticulous linguistic analysis (including the meaning and background of Hebrew terms, syntactical analysis, and comparison with cognates from other Semitic languages). Interacts significantly with the history of interpretation, especially on higher-critical questions. Excellent for serious grappling with technical issues, but gives little attention to theological matters.

Also Significant

2.49.6   Barton, John. *The Theology of the Book of Amos.* Cambridge: Cambridge University Press, 2012. 216pp.

2.49.7   Carroll R., M. Daniel. *Amos: The Prophet & His Oracles.* Louisville: Westminster John Knox, 2002. 224pp.

2.49.8   Coote, Robert B. *Amos among the Prophets: Composition and Theology.* Philadelphia: Fortress, 1981. 138pp.

2.49.9   Harper, William Rainey. *A Critical and Exegetical Commentary on Amos and Hosea.* International Critical Commentary. Edinburgh: T&T Clark, 1905. 424pp.

2.49.10   Hayes, John H. *Amos, the Eighth Century Prophet: His Times and His Preaching.* Nashville: Abingdon, 1988. 240pp.

2.49.11   Kapelrud, Arvid Schou. *Central Ideas in Amos.* Oslo: Universitets-forlaget, 1971. 86pp.

2.49.12   Polley, Max E. *Amos and the Davidic Empire: A Socio-Historical Approach.* New York: Oxford University Press, 1989. 243pp.

2.49.13   Smith, Gary V. *Amos: A Commentary.* Library of Biblical Interpretation. Grand Rapids: Zondervan, 1989. 307pp.

2.49.14   Watts, John D. W. *Vision and Prophecy in Amos.* Expanded ed. Macon, Ga.: Mercer University Press, 1997. 144pp.

2.50   Obadiah

Highly Recommended

2.50.1   Rabbe, Paul R. *Obadiah.* Anchor Bible. New York: Doubleday, 1996. 310pp.

Most current and complete commentary on Obadiah presently available. Engages in a sympathetic interpretation, attempting to read the book on its own terms and according to the concerns of its original writer and readers. To this end gives careful attention to grammatical and lexical issues, poetic forms, rhetorical strategies and goals, historical background pertaining to Edom, allusions to the Jacob-Esau narratives of Genesis, and theological claims. Claims that Obadiah summarizes many of the great prophetic themes, and thus explores Obadiah's contribution to the OT understanding of divine judgment against Israel's enemies, the day of Yahweh, the principle of retaliation, Zion theology, Israel's possession of the land, and the kingship of Yahweh.

2.50.2   Watts, John D. W. *Obadiah: A Critical and Exegetical Commentary.* Grand Rapids: Eerdmans, 1967. 78pp.

Packs a remarkable amount of relevant and helpful information in a very small compass. Includes discussion of history of interpretation, history of Edom, Obadiah's position in biblical prophecy, Obadiah's role in Israel's worship, theological background, and theology of the book itself, along with commentary that gives attention to text-critical, grammatical, and historical issues. Especially valuable for moving from careful historical and grammatical analysis to insightful theological reflection.

2.50.3   Wolff, Hans Walter. *Obadiah and Jonah: A Commentary.* Minneapolis: Augsburg, 1986. 191pp.

Employs technical linguistic and literary analysis and careful attention to historical background to ascertain the theological message of the text and to explore its contemporary significance. Asserts that both Obadiah and Jonah explore God's intention toward Gentiles and the relationship between Israel and the Gentile world, but answer these questions in quite different ways; this leads the Christian reader to draw insights regarding the relationship between the church as the people of God and the wider world of humanity. Stresses Obadiah's role as a "cult prophet" who reinterprets earlier traditions for his own day. Emphasizes the role of "comedy" in the book of Jonah, and the ways in which that book employs various literary forms to achieve its intended didactic impact on the reader.

Also Significant

2.50.4   Baker, David W. *Obadiah, Jonah, Micah*. Tyndale Old Testament Commentaries. Downers Grove, Ill.: InterVarsity, 1989. 207pp.

2.50.5   Ben Zvi, Ehud. *A Historical-Critical Study of the Book of Obadiah*. Beihefte zur Zeitschrift für die alttestamentliche Wissenschaft 242. Berlin: Walter De Gruyter, 1996. 309pp.

2.50.6   Lanchester, H. C. O. *Obadiah and Jonah*. Rev. ed. Cambridge: Cambridge University Press, 1918. 76pp.

2.51   Jonah

See also OBADIAH (§2.50)

Highly Recommended

2.51.1   Fretheim, Terence E.. *The Message of Jonah: A Theological Commentary*. Minneapolis: Augsburg, 1977. 142pp.

Highly illuminating and engaging close reading of Jonah, emphasizing especially literary features of the book, leading to acute theological insights and suggestions regarding contemporary Christian appropriation. The most helpful volume available for preaching and teaching on Jonah.

2.51.2   Limburg, James. *Jonah: A Commentary*. Old Testament Library. Louisville: Westminster John Knox, 1993. 123pp.

Solid, reliable commentary dealing with the origin of the story, its place and function within the Bible, the theological claims of the text, and possibilities for contemporary (Christian) application. Interpretation gives primary attention to structure of the book, historical background, meaning of the Hebrew, and relation to other OT texts. A unique feature is insight from the use of Jonah by artists, musicians, painters, and sculptors to illuminate the meaning of the text. Includes extensive appendix dealing with the understanding of Jonah in Judaism, Islam, and Christianity.

2.51.3   Sasson, Jack M. *Jonah*. Anchor Bible. New York: Doubleday, 1990. 368pp.

Most comprehensive and detailed commentary on Jonah available. Involves a meticulous interpretation of each verse, with particular attention to Hebrew grammar and vocabulary, comparative analysis with other Semitic languages, literary forms and structures, historical background, and illumination from other OT passages. Although technical, commentary is readable and largely accessible to those who do not know Hebrew. Gives less explicit attention to theological matters than does Fretheim (§2.51.1) or Limburg (§2.51.2).

Also Significant

2.51.4   Bolin, Thomas M. *Freedom beyond Forgiveness: The Book of Jonah Re-Examined*. Journal for the Study of the Old Testament Supplement Series 236; Copenhagen International Seminar 3. Sheffield: Sheffield Academic Press, 1997. 217pp.

2.51.5   Ellul, Jacques. *The Judgment of Jonah*. Grand Rapids: Eerdmans, 1971. 103pp.

2.51.6   Fairbairn, Patrick. *Jonah: His Life, Character, and Mission*. Edinburgh: John Johnstone, 1849. 237pp.

2.51.7   Hasel, Gerhard F. *Jonah: Messenger of the Eleventh Hour*. Mt. View, Calif.: Pacific, 1976. 112pp.

2.51.8   Kamp, Albert. *Inner Worlds: A Cognitive-Linguistic Approach to the Book of Jonah*. Biblical Interpretation Series, no. 68. Leiden: Brill, 2004. 280pp.

2.51.9   Magonet, Jonathan. *Form and Meaning: Studies in the Literary Techniques in the Book of Jonah*. Bible and Literature Series 8. Sheffield: Almond, 1983. 184pp.

2.51.10   Simon, Uriel. *Jonah*. JPS Bible Commentary. Philadelphia: Jewish Publication Society, 1999. 52pp.

See also Phyllis Trible's *Rhetorical Criticism: Context, Method, and the Book of Jonah* (§2.13.40).

2.52 Micah

See also OBADIAH (§2.50)

Highly Recommended

2.52.1   Andersen, Francis I., and David Noel Freedman. *Micah*. Anchor Bible. New York: Doubleday, 2000. 637pp.

Considers reconstruction of stages of the book's compilation hopelessly speculative and therefore treats the book in its final form as a literary unity, thus giving almost exclusive attention to literary and linguistic analysis. Emphasizes the structure of passages, their role within the broader book context, employment of poetic artistry and literary devices, and careful analysis of poetic Hebrew (which they consider to be decisively distinct from prose). Gives little attention to historical or theological matters.

2.52.2   Mays, James Luther. *Micah: A Commentary*. Old Testament Library. Philadelphia: Westminster, 1976. 169pp.

Argues that the book exhibits an extended process of transmission, from the prophet Micah himself to its final form in the postexilic period. Interprets individual sayings according to their literary form, historical setting, and function in the ministry of the prophets from whom they derived, as they were understood and used in the developing composition, and as they function in the final canonical book. Mays draws out the theological meaning of passages at each of these stages. Concerned only with the theological witness of this book; gives no serious attention to its contribution to OT theology or to NT faith.

2.52.3   McKane, William. *Micah: Introduction and Commentary.* Edinburgh: T&T Clark, 1998. 242pp.

Argues that chs. 1–3 contain the prophecy of Micah himself, but that the book was developed after the fall of Jerusalem by a "school" that adapted Micah's message to later contexts, at times underscoring Micah's proclamation of judgment and at other times emphasizing hope. Contains detailed textual and linguistic analysis, extended discussion of ancient versions, and careful description of history of interpretation (medieval and modern). Excellent for full discussion of technical matters of text and language, but gives little attention to the meaning of the final form of passages, to the message of the book, or to theological implications.

2.52.4   Waltke, Bruce K. *A Commentary on Micah.* Grand Rapids: Eerdmans, 2007. 490pp.

In contrast to the judgment of most recent scholars, argues that Micah wrote and edited nineteen sermons that comprise the present book. Commentary gives attention to both technical matters (especially text-critical considerations, Hebrew syntax, and ANE background), to rhetorical devices employed for the sake of persuasion, and to the theological meaning of the text for the church, including suggestions pertaining to contemporary appropriation. Thus it is useful to the scholar as well as the preacher or teacher. Overall, the most helpful commentary on Micah for Christian proclamation and instruction.

2.52.5   Wolff, Hans Walter. *Micah: A Commentary.* Minneapolis: Augsburg, 1990. 258pp.

Like Mays (§2.52.2), argues for an extended process of development from the prophet Micah to the early Persian period, and examines with more precision than Mays how each passage fits within this long process. Quite technical in his linguistic analysis and discussion of literary forms and historical background. Gives relatively little attention to the meaning of passages within the final canonical book, but does consider the theological message of passages and briefly discusses Christian appropriation. Contains extensive bibliographies of works in German, French, and English.

Also Significant

2.52.6   Ben Zvi, Ehud. *Micah.* Forms of the Old Testament Literature 21B. Grand Rapids: Eerdmans, 2000. 189pp.

2.52.7   Hagstrom, David Gerald. *The Coherence of the Book of Micah: A Literary Analysis*. Society of Biblical Literature Dissertation Series 89. Atlanta: Scholars, 1988. 152pp.

2.52.8   Hillers, Delbert R. *Micah*. Hermeneia: A Critical and Historical Commentary on the Bible. Philadelphia: Fortress, 1984. 116pp.

2.52.9   Jacobs, Mignon R. *The Conceptual Coherence of the Book of Micah*. Journal for the Study of the Old Testament Supplement Series 322. Sheffield: JSOT, 2001. 288pp.

2.52.10   Wal, Adri van der. *Micah: A Classified Bibliography*. Applicatio 8. Amsterdam: Free University Press, 1990. 207pp.

2.52.11   Wolff, Hans Walter. *Micah the Prophet*. Philadelphia: Fortress, 1981. 223pp.

2.53   Nahum, Habakkuk, and Zephaniah

Highly Recommended

2.53.1   Andersen, Francis I. *Habakkuk*. Anchor Bible. New York: Doubleday, 2001. 387pp.

Most comprehensive and authoritative commentary on Habakkuk presently available in English. Attends seriously to literary structure of entire book and interprets individual passages in relation to the whole. Emphasizes, in addition, linguistic phenomena of the Hebrew (with special attention to the history of development of the Hebrew language), historical background (especially social, economic, religious, and political issues), Ancient Near Eastern culture, connections with other OT passages, and personal/existential experience of the prophet himself. All of this Andersen pursues in order to grasp fully the theological meaning of the final form of the text.

2.53.2   Berlin, Adele. *Zephaniah*. Anchor Bible. New York: Doubleday, 1994. 165pp.

Adopts a literary approach, but gives attention also to historical setting and relationship to other OT passages. Attends to rhetorical features, literary forms, structure of passage, and role within whole book. A valuable feature is repeated reference to traditional Jewish exegesis, especially medieval and early modern. Makes no attempt to be exhaustive, but focuses on issues significant for understanding the message of the prophet and aspects of the text of foremost concern to readers. Little explicit attention to theological significance.

2.53.3   Gowan, Donald E. *The Triumph of Faith in Habakkuk.* Atlanta: John Knox, 1976. 94pp.

A most informative and stimulating book. Explores the original meaning of Habakkuk by attending to issues of text, literary form, structure, and historical setting, but all for the sake of theological reflection surrounding the perennial issues of human life and suffering as addressed by Habakkuk. Carries on a successful dialogue between original meaning and specific contemporary concerns. Extremely helpful for preaching and teaching.

2.53.4   Maier, Walter A. *The Book of Nahum: A Commentary.* St. Louis, Mo.: Concordia, 1959. 386pp.

Serious, informed commentary from a conservative perspective. Examines historical background, relationship to other OT passages, Hebrew language, and literary structure in an attempt to ascertain the original message of Nahum and to probe its continuing relevance for Christians. Sees contemporary significance in the thrust of Nahum's message, which Maier takes to be Yahweh's active concern in the face of a powerful nation's abuse of its power by promoting its own selfish aims to oppress weak nations.

2.53.5   Roberts, J. J. M. *Nahum, Habakkuk, and Zephaniah: A Commentary.* Old Testament Library. Louisville: Westminster John Knox, 1991. 223pp.

Technical yet readable commentary employing textual criticism, philology, historical background, Ancient Near Eastern parallels, and literary conventions employed by prophets. Focuses on individual prophetic oracles in an attempt to interpret them in their original setting; correspondingly, has little interest in the overall scheme of the final canonical book or the role of individual oracles within the book as a whole. An exception is Habakkuk, which Roberts considers to be (unlike most prophetic books) a coherent literary unity. Concerned to relate the message of passages to other OT and even NT passages, and to develop briefly the theological meaning, with some suggestions regarding contemporary significance.

2.53.6   Robertson, O. Palmer. *The Books of Nahum, Habakkuk, and Zephaniah.* New International Commentary on the Old Testament. Grand Rapids: Eerdmans, 1989. 357pp.

Written from a conservative perspective. Emphasizes historical context, literary structure, role within the canon of OT and NT (with little concern for technical textual and linguistic issues), all in the pursuit of the theological message. Moves quickly from original message to specific contemporary Christian application. Suggestive for preaching and teaching, but should be used critically, since there is a tendency to interpret passages in light of Christian theological categories and the concerns of modern American evangelicals.

2.53.7   Spronk, Klaas. *Nahum*. Historical Commentary on the Old Testament. Kampen: Kok Pharos, 1997. 153pp.

Maintains that Nahum was written in Jerusalem around 660 BCE by a royal scribe, using Nahum as a pseudonym pointing to his purpose: to encourage people of Judah living under Assyrian oppression. This purpose he accomplished by adapting earlier traditions from Isaiah and the Psalms, and by borrowing from the motifs of Assyrian literature, which he used against Assyria. Interprets final form of text by emphasizing its relationship to other OT passages, examining ancient versions and texts, linguistic analysis, discussion of literary forms and structure, and interaction with history of interpretation. Somewhat technical, but accessible to the nonspecialist while also illuminating for the scholar. Gives little explicit attention to theological reflection.

2.53.8   Sweeney, Marvin A. *Zephaniah*. Hermeneia: A Critical and Historical Commentary on the Bible. Minneapolis: Fortress, 2003. 227pp.

Interprets the book from the perspective that the purpose of Zephaniah is to exhort the readers to prepare for God's judgment and salvation upon both Israel and the nations by aligning with Yahweh and submitting to Yahweh's demands. This highly technical commentary attempts to address the multiple interpretive issues pertaining to Zephaniah, including the socio-religious and historical matters relating to its original production during the Josianic reforms, the hermeneutical considerations arising from its placement within the Book of the Twelve, and the theological differences between the Masoretic and LXX forms of the book. Emphasizes relation to the religion of the OT and to later Jewish concerns but gives practically no attention to Christian use and appropriation.

2.53.9   Vlaardingerbroek, Johannes. *Zephaniah*. Historical Commentary on the Old Testament. Leuven: Peeters, 1999. 222pp.

Interprets Zephaniah in its historical setting in relation to the Josianic Reform and thus emphasizes its relationship to Deuteronomic theology.

Attends to linguistic analysis, ancient versions, history of interpretation, and the role of passages in the arrangement of the final form of book. Offers significant theological discussion of the original message of Zephaniah, with particular attention to the theology of the Day of Yahweh.

Also Significant

2.53.10   Baker, David W. *Nahum, Habakkuk, Zephaniah.* Tyndale Old Testament Commentaries. Downers Grove, Ill.: InterVarsity, 1989. 121pp.

2.53.11   Ben Zvi, Ehud. *A Historical-Critical Study of the Book of Zephaniah.* Beihefte zur Zeitschrift für die Alttestamentliche Wissenschaft 198. Berlin: Walter De Gruyter, 1991. 390pp.

2.53.12   Bennett, T. Miles. *The Books of Nahum and Zephaniah.* Grand Rapids: Baker, 1968. 102pp.

2.53.13   Haak, Robert D. *Habakkuk.* Supplements to Vetus Testamentum 44. Leiden: Brill, 1992. 180pp.

2.53.14   House, Paul R. *Zephaniah: A Prophetic Drama.* Bible and Literature Series 16. Sheffield: Almond, 1988. 146pp.

2.53.15   Kapelrud, Arvid S. *The Message of the Prophet Zephaniah: Morphology and Ideas.* Oslo: Universitatesfolaget, 1975. 116pp.

2.53.16   Patterson, Richard D. *Nahum, Habakkuk, Zephaniah.* Wycliffe Exegetical Commentary. Chicago: Moody, 1991. 416pp.

2.53.17   Wal, Adri van der. *Nahum, Habakkuk: A Classified Bibliography.* Applicatio 6. Amsterdam: Free University Press, 1988. 208pp.

2.54 Haggai, Zechariah, and Malachi

Highly Recommended

2.54.1   Hill, Andrew E. *Malachi.* Anchor Bible. New York: Doubleday, 1998. 436pp.

Most thorough and current commentary on Malachi available in English. This evangelical scholar assumes the Masoretic text, avoids speculation regarding redactions and interpolations, and favors the authenticity and unity of Malachi. Emphasizes historical and sociopolitical background, language (lexical, philological, syntactic), history of interpretation (ancient and modern, Jewish and Christian), and literary structure. Analyzes Malachi's message within context of OT (and often NT) canon. Technical and detailed, treating every phrase or clause exhaustively. Gives relatively little attention to theological issues.

2.54.2   Meyers, Carol L., and Eric M. Meyers. *Haggai, Zechariah 1–8*. Anchor Bible. New York: Doubleday, 1987. 478pp.

Probably the most complete and detailed commentary on this material in English. Argues that Haggai and Zechariah 1–8 form a composite work, the product probably of redaction by Zechariah himself shortly after the conclusion of his and Haggai's prophetic activity around 518 BCE. Thus the authors see little difference between the work of the historical Haggai and Zechariah and the witness of the final book. Considers the literary impact of the book, emphasizing how the message is conveyed through literary artistry. Attends especially to sociopolitical issues and to the religious message, but (as is the case with most volumes in this series) does little with theological implications.

2.54.3   ———. *Zechariah 9–14*. Anchor Bible. New York: Doubleday, 1993. 552pp.

Similar in scope and method to their volume on Haggai and Zechariah 1–8 (§2.54.2). Argues that Zechariah 9–14 postdates Haggai and Zechariah 1–8 by more than fifty years, and thus has a distinct sociopolitical and religious setting. Views the period not as one of religious and political decline, but as a creative and dynamic time in which the people maintained their identity in the midst of a changing world. Attends also to the canonical process according to which this material was combined with Zechariah 1–8, and considers the significance of this process for both the formation of the canon and transmission of tradition. Emphasizes ways this material adopts and adapts earlier Scriptures so as to communicate its own religious message.

2.54.4   Petersen, David L. *Haggai and Zechariah 1–8: A Commentary*. Old Testament Library. Philadelphia: Westminster, 1984. 320pp.

In contrast to Meyers and Meyers (§2.54.2), emphasizes differences between Haggai and Zechariah. Sees Haggai as an activist and Zechariah as a contemplative theologian, a difference that points to a kind of "prophetic pluralism" that exists in the OT as a whole. Employs linguistic analysis, historical criticism, historical background, and literary analysis selectively so as to illuminate the most significant interpretive issues. Concentrates on the historical ministry and oracles of Haggai and Zechariah over against the literary impact of the final form of the text. Discusses in detail the religious issues of the text, but does not address contemporary Christian appropriation.

2.54.5 ———. *Zechariah 9–14 and Malachi.* Old Testament Library. Louisville: Westminster John Knox, 1995. 233pp.

Similar in scope and method to Petersen's volume on Haggai and Zechariah 1–8 (§2.54.4). Treats Zechariah 9–11, Zechariah 12–14, and Malachi as three separate collections that were bound together in the process of compiling the canonical Minor Prophets. Emphasizes the historical, political, social, and religious background of the Persian period in the interpretation of this material, with a view to how this material presents Israel's God in relation to the Persian Empire on the one hand and the community of faith on the other.

2.54.6 Verhoef, Pieter A. *The Books of Haggai and Malachi.* New International Commentary on the Old Testament. Grand Rapids: Eerdmans, 1987. 364pp.

Argues from a conservative evangelical perspective for the historical authenticity and authorial and literary unity of both books. Employs insights from the ANE, other OT passages and traditions, linguistic considerations (analysis of Hebrew and of comparative Semitic languages), and literary structure of passages and of entire books for an interpretation that is fully informed and useful for the specialist, but readable and accessible to the nonspecialist. Concentrates on the theological message and relates it critically to NT faith, noting both points of continuity and discontinuity. Extremely useful for preaching and teaching.

2.54.7 Wolff, Hans Walter. *Haggai.* Minneapolis: Augsburg, 1988. 128pp.

Insists on the importance of Haggai as one of the most influential figures in postexilic community. Considers the book a "model of effective proclamation," leading the audience from "soreness of failure to hope of glory" in five scenes, based on Haggai's oracles, but developed and expanded to address the book's own readership. Commentary thus adopts twofold concern: (1) to reconstruct the ministry and oracles of Haggai and to consider their significance for his original hearers, and (2) to explore the function of passages in the final book context. Includes technical discussions of text, form-critical categories, redaction, linguistic analysis, and historical background, but with concern for the theological message and to some extent the relevance of this theology for Christian fulfillment.

Also Significant

2.54.8   Baldwin, Joyce G. *Haggai, Zechariah, Malachi: An Introduction and Commentary*. Tyndale Old Testament Commentaries. Downers Grove, Ill.: InterVarsity, 1972. 253pp.

2.54.9   Boda, Mark J. *Haggai & Zechariah Research: A Bibliographic Survey*. Leiden: Deo, 2003. 267pp

2.54.10   Hill, Andrew E. *Haggai, Zechariah, Malachi*. Tyndale Old Testament Commentaries. Downers Grove, Ill.: InterVarsity, 2012. 368pp.

2.54.11   Kaiser, Walter C., Jr. *God's Unchanging Love*. Grand Rapids: Baker, 1984. 171pp.

2.54.12   Mason, R. A. *The Books of Haggai, Zechariah and Malachi*. Cambridge Bible Commentary. Cambridge: Cambridge University Press, 1977. 168pp.

2.54.13   McDonald, Beth Glazier. *Malachi: The Divine Messenger*. Society of Biblical Literature Dissertation Series 98. Atlanta: Scholars, 1987. 288pp.

2.54.14   Oswalt, John N. *Where Are You, God?* Wheaton, Ill.: Victor, 1982. 156pp.

2.54.15   Redditt, Paul L. *Haggai, Zechariah, Malachi*. New Century Bible Commentary. Grand Rapids: Eerdmans, 1995. 196pp.

2.54.16   Tuckett, Christopher, ed. *The Book of Zechariah and Its Influence*. Burlington, Vt.: Ashgate, 2003. 208pp.

3

Early Judaism

3.1 Judaism and Jewish Culture: Primary Sources

See also APOCRYPHA AND PSEUDEPIGRAPHA OF THE OLD TESTAMENT (§3.3)

Highly Recommended

3.1.1 Cathcart, Kevin, Michael Maher, and Martin McNamara, eds. *The Aramaic Bible: The Targums.* Collegeville, Minn.: Liturgical Press, 1987–. Volumes average 270pp. (19 vols. out of 22 available).

The only readily accessible English edition of these Aramaic translations of the Hebrew Bible from the early Christian era. Includes all traditionally known Targums, translated into modern English idiom. Produced by a variety of scholars, but with consistent quality and generally uniform translation style. Translators consulted both critical editions and manuscripts. Includes textual apparatus and notes, which primarily clarify the translation. Begins each Targum with an introduction containing necessary background information. Each volume concludes with select bibliography and index of biblical, Qumranic, rabbinic, early Jewish, and early Christian (including NT) references.

3.1.2 Danby, Herbert. *The Mishnah: Translated from the Hebrew with Introduction and Brief Explanatory Notes.* London: Oxford University Press, 1933. 844pp.

Offers a translation of the entire Mishnah that is literal and easily accessible to the average reader. Contains brief annotations that explain allusions and clarify difficulties, but no commentary. Follows traditional Jewish interpretation in translation and notes. Includes full index of biblical passages, persons, and subjects.

3.1.3   Epstein, Isidore, ed. *The Babylonian Talmud.* 18 vols. London: Soncino, 1961. Volumes average 700pp.

The most complete and current translation of this material until Neusner (§3.1.11). Translations were produced by various scholars, and thus style or mode of translations vary somewhat. Yet translations are consistently accurate and readable. Includes brief annotations consisting of basic explanations and cross-references to other Talmudic and biblical passages. Epstein revised and supplemented these translations and interpretations, and added footnotes in brackets containing alternative explanations and discussions of matters pertaining to history and geography. Each volume contains a glossary and index of persons, subjects, and biblical passages. Final volume consists of general index.

3.1.4   ———, ed. *The Midrash Rabbah.* 10 vols. London: Soncino, 1977. Volumes average 500pp.

Similar in approach to Epstein's Talmud (§3.1.3). The midrashim are translated by a variety of scholars, with a generally high level of accuracy and readability. Contains brief notes, mostly explaining meaning or clarifying the translation. Text includes frequent citation of terms from original language (in transliteration). Final volume contains index of persons, subjects, and biblical passages.

3.1.5   Whiston, William. *The Works of Josephus: Complete and Unabridged.* New updated ed. Peabody, Mass.: Hendrickson, 1985. 782pp.

Although produced in the eighteenth century, probably still the standard translation of the works of this significant Jewish historian. Includes only the English (as opposed to the Loeb edition, which includes the original Greek). Offers a new numbering system that corresponds to the one used in the Loeb edition, as well as citations, cross-references, and indexes to biblical passages, persons, and subjects. Contains a few very brief explanatory annotations.

3.1.6   Yonge, C. D. *The Works of Philo: Complete and Unabridged.* New updated ed. Peabody, Mass.: Hendrickson, 1993. 918pp.

Produced by C. D. Yonge, an eminent classicist of the mid-nineteenth century, this volume is virtually the only affordable and easily accessible translation of Philo presently available. Yonge's translation was based on Mangey's text, which is different in sequence and completeness from the superior Cohn-Wendland text that appeared about forty years after Yonge. This edition updates Yonge's work: it conforms to the sequence of the Cohn-Wendland text and contains newly translated passages from Cohn-Wendland. Includes informative foreword by David M. Scholer, describing the life and significance of Philo and the editions of his writings, and offering a select bibliography. Unlike the Loeb edition, contains only English translation.

Also Significant

3.1.7   Blackman, Philip. *Mishnayot: Pointed Hebrew Text: English Translation, Introductions.* 7 vols. Rev. ed. New York: Judaica, 1963–1964.

3.1.8   Colson, F. H., G. H. Whitaker, J. W. Earp, and Ralph Marcus. *Philo.* 12 vols. Loeb Classical Library. Cambridge: Harvard University Press, 1929–1953.

3.1.9   Gianotti, Charles R. *The New Testament and the Mishnah: A Cross-Reference Index.* Grand Rapids: Baker, 1983. 63pp.

3.1.10   Glatzer, Norman, ed. *The Essential Philo.* New York: Schocken, 1971. 360pp.

3.1.11   Neusner, Jacob. *The Babylonian Talmud.* 22 vols. Peabody, Mass.: Hendrickson, 2005.

3.1.12   ———. *The Talmud of the Land of Israel: Preliminary Translation and Explanation.* 35 vols. Chicago: University of Chicago Press, 1982–1993.

3.1.13   ———. *The Tosefta: Translated from the Hebrew with a New Introduction.* 6 vols. in 2. Peabody, Mass.: Hendrickson, 2002.

3.1.14   Nickelsburg, George W. E., and Michael E. Stone. *Faith and Piety in Early Judaism: Texts and Documents.* Philadelphia: Fortress, 1983. 243pp.

3.1.15   Thackeray, H. St. J., Ralph Marcus, Allen Wikgren, and L. H. Feldman. *Josephus.* 10 vols. Loeb Classical Library. Cambridge: Harvard University Press, 1926–1965.

3.2   Judaism and Jewish Culture: Secondary Sources

See also NEW TESTAMENT: HISTORY AND GEOGRAPHY (§4.5) and EZRA AND NEHEMIAH (§2.32)

Highly Recommended

3.2.1   Boccaccini, Gabriele. *Middle Judaism: Jewish Thought, 300 B.C.E.– 200 C.E.* Minneapolis: Fortress, 1991. 289pp.

Seeks to establish a "non-biased" reconstruction of Jewish thought (primarily religious, but also philosophical and social), employing a method that is free from the confessional constraints of either Judaism or Christianity. This method involves a commitment to examine all relevant material and to recognize not only unity but also diversity in an authoritative account of the intellectual history of the period. Includes extensive bibliography.

3.2.2   Collins, John J, and Daniel C. Harlow, eds. *The Eerdmans Dictionary of Early Judaism.* Grand Rapids: Eerdmans, 2010. 1360pp.

The most broadly recognized authorities in early Judaism contributed to this volume, which is the only reference work dealing exclusively with Second Temple Judaism. The volume begins with thirteen lengthy essays addressing significant aspects of Judaistic study that are especially relevant for Christian biblical interpretation (including "Early Judaism in Modern Scholarship" and "Early Judaism and Early Christianity") before presenting over five hundred articles dealing in some detail with every important topic pertaining to this history. Each article concludes with a bibliography. Essential for anyone who wishes to delve into this area as background for biblical interpretation.

3.2.3   Davies, W. D., Louis Finkelstein, William Horbury, and John Sturdy, eds. *The Cambridge History of Judaism.* 4 vols. Cambridge: Cambridge University Press, 1984–2008. 1254pp.

Articles by most prominent Jewish and Gentile scholars on both sides of the Atlantic deal with every major issue pertaining to the history of the

Jews from the exile in 587 BCE to the codification of the Mishnah around 250 CE, with special attention to interaction with Persian, Hellenistic, and Roman cultures. Articles consider all relevant literary and archaeological evidence. Volumes deal in succession with the Persian, Hellenistic, and Roman periods. The final and forthcoming volume will deal with the period between 70 and 250 CE. Authoritative, complete, and extremely helpful in providing historical background for biblical interpretation.

3.2.4   Grabbe, Lester L. *A History of the Jews and Judaism in the Second Temple Period.* 4 vols. (Vols. 1 and 2 presently available). London: T&T Clark, 2004, 2008. 471/434pp.

When completed will be perhaps the most comprehensive and meticulous study of Second Temple Judaism. Argues that most formative for Second Temple Judaism was the Persian period, and accordingly gives over the first volume to that era. The second volume treats the Early Hellenistic Period (335–175 BCE). The final volumes will explore Jewish history to the Bar Kochba rebellion. Each volume begins with a discussion of methodological issues, then discusses successive stages of Jewish history and some of the major issues pertaining to that history. These discussions include examination of original sources, a survey of scholarly research, and a synthetic description of that stage in the history of the Jews and Judaism. Each volume concludes with a massive bibliography. More complete and current than Grabbe's *Judaism from Cyrus to Hadrian* (§3.2.5), but the latter will continue to be useful until this project is completed.

3.2.5   ———. *Judaism from Cyrus to Hadrian: Sources, History, Synthesis.* 2 vols. Philadelphia: Fortress, 1992. 792pp.

A guide to early Judaism, from the latter stages of the OT into the time of the NT. Grabbe divides his study into historical segments; in each he moves from critical evaluation of primary extant sources to a survey of major interpretive issues, where he presents a range of scholarly opinions, to a synthesis of that historical period. He concludes each segment with a bibliography of modern works.

3.2.6   Kraft, Robert A., and George W. E. Nickelsburg, eds. *Early Judaism and Its Modern Interpreters.* The Bible and Its Modern Interpreters. Atlanta: Scholars, 1986. 494pp.

Describes major developments in the study of "early Judaism" (330 BCE to 138 CE) from about 1945 through 1980, when most of the essays in this volume were written. Includes a lengthy and helpful introductory chapter discussing the field, new tools and methods, major issues, and

215

prospects for the future. Deals with the major approaches to the political, social, and religious history of the period, recent discoveries pertaining to early Judaism, and discussions of different types of literature, primarily the Apocrypha, Pseudepigrapha, Philo, and Josephus. Each article contains critical survey of scholarship, with focus on trends, emphases, and prospects for future study, and includes a bibliography.

3.2.7 Neusner, Jacob. *Introduction to Rabbinic Literature.* Anchor Bible Reference Library. New York: Doubleday, 1994. 720pp.

Written for the nonspecialist, this is a fine introduction to Neusner's views on rabbinic literature, which are developed in the several books he has produced on more specific aspects of this literature. Here he describes the major writings, where they can be found, how they should be read, and how they bear on the OT and Christianity.

3.2.8 Neusner, Jacob, and William Scott Green, eds. *Dictionary of Judaism in the Biblical Period.* Peabody, Mass.: Hendrickson, 1996. 693pp.

This dictionary seeks to define concepts, religious practices, theological terms, persons, places, and vocabulary that are found in the writings of Judaism or in those that are related to Judaism (including Jewish elements in early Christianity) from 450 BCE through CE 600. Is in fact a dictionary, not an encyclopedia, in that it gives lexical definitions and basic descriptions rather than full-length discussions. Contains more than thirty-three hundred entries written by seventy scholars of global recognition. Most current and reliable repository of essential information concerning Judaism in this period to be found in a single volume.

3.2.9 Sanders, E. P. *Judaism: Practice and Belief, 63 B.C.E.–66 C.E.* Philadelphia: Trinity Press International, 1992. 580pp.

This lucid, comprehensive, and groundbreaking work argues that the dominant portrait of Palestinian Judaism derived from such classic works as Schürer's *History of the Jewish People in the Age of Jesus Christ* (§4.5.7) or Jeremias's *Jerusalem in the Time of Jesus* (§4.5.22) is seriously skewed in that the Pharisees are presented as determinative for Judaism prior to the destruction of the temple and the Mishnah is assumed to describe general practice. Sanders insists on a recovery of "common Judaism," the daily observance of the people as a whole, and argues that early rabbinic material should be understood as reflecting debates within the context of the life of the people. Offers detailed examination of various common aspects of religious life of the people.

Periodical

3.2.10   *Journal for the Study of Judaism in the Persian, Hellenistic, & Roman Periods.* Leiden: Brill, 1969–.

Also Significant

3.2.11   Cohen, Shaye J. D. *From the Maccabees to the Mishnah.* 2d ed. Louisville: Westminster John Knox, 2006. 250pp.

3.2.12   Collins, John J. *Between Athens and Jerusalem: Jewish Identity in the Hellenistic Diaspora.* 2d ed. Biblical Resource Series. Grand Rapids: Eerdmans, 2000. 327pp.

3.2.13   Elliott, Mark Adam. *The Survivors of Judaism: A Reconsideration of the Theology of Pre-Christian Judaism.* Grand Rapids: Eerdmans, 2000. 760pp.

3.2.14   Foerster, Werner. *From the Exile to Christ: Historical Introduction to Palestinian Judaism.* Philadelphia: Fortress, 1964. 247pp.

3.2.15   Hayes, John H., and Sara R. Mandell. *The Jewish People in Classical Antiquity: From Alexander to Bar Kochba.* Louisville: Westminster John Knox, 1998. 246pp.

3.2.16   Hengel, Martin. *Jews, Greeks and Barbarians.* Philadelphia: Fortress, 1980. 174pp.

3.2.17   ———. *Judaism and Hellenism: Studies in Their Encounter in Palestine during the Early Hellenistic Period.* 2 vols. in 1. Philadelphia: Fortress, 1974. 314/335pp.

3.2.18   Jastrow, Marcus. *A Dictionary of the Targumim, the Talmud Babli and Yerushalmi, and the Midrashic Literature.* London: Luzac & Co., 1903. 1760pp. Repr. Peabody, Mass.: Hendrickson, 2003.

3.2.19   Mason, Steve. *Josephus and the New Testament.* 2d ed. Peabody, Mass.: Hendrickson, 2003. 256pp.

217

3.2.20   Murphy, Frederick. *Early Judaism: The Exile to the Time of Jesus.* Peabody, Mass.: Hendrickson, 2002. 474pp.

3.2.21   Neusner, Jacob. *The Mishnah: Introduction and Reader.* Philadelphia: Trinity Press International, 1992. 226pp.

3.2.22   ———. *The Talmud: Introduction and Reader.* South Florida Studies in the History of Judaism. Atlanta: Scholars, 1995. 155pp.

3.2.23   ———. *The Tosefta: Translated from the Hebrew, with a New Introduction.* 2 vols. Peabody, Mass.: Hendrickson, 2002. 1984pp.

3.2.24   ———. *What Is Midrash? Guides to Biblical Scholarship.* Philadelphia: Fortress, 1987. 114pp.

3.2.25   Nickelsburg, George W. E. *Jewish Literature between the Bible and the Mishnah: A Historical and Literary Introduction.* 2d ed. Minneapolis: Fortress, 2005. 445pp.

3.2.26   Peters, F. E. *The Harvest of Hellenism: A History of the Near East from Alexander the Great to the Triumph of Christianity.* New York: Simon & Schuster, 1970. 800pp.

3.2.27   Runia, David T. *Philo of Alexandria: An Annotated Bibliography.* Leiden: Brill, 2000. 412pp.

3.2.28   Russell, D. S. *The Jews from Alexander to Herod.* London: Oxford, 1967. 329pp.

3.2.29   Sandmel, Samuel. *Judaism and Christian Beginnings.* New York: Oxford University Press, 1978. 510pp.

3.2.30   Schechter, Solomon. *Aspects of Rabbinic Theology: Major Concepts of the Talmud.* New York: Macmillan, 1909. Repr. Peabody, Mass.: Hendrickson, 1998. 384pp.

3.2.31   Strack, Hermann L., and Gunter Stemberger. *Introduction to the Talmud and Midrash*. Minneapolis: Fortress, 1992. 472pp.

3.2.32   Tcherikover, Victor. *Hellenistic Civilization and the Jews*. New York: Atheneum, 1975. 563pp.

3.2.33   VanderKam, James C. *An Introduction to Early Judaism*. Grand Rapids: Eerdmans, 2001. 234pp.

Note also the series Compendia Rerum Iudaicarum ad Novum Testamentum (CRINT). Section 2 is titled The Literature of the Jewish People in the Period of the Second Temple and the Talmud. Section 3 is titled Jewish Traditions in Early Christian Literature.

3.2.34   Mulder, Martin Jan, ed. *Mikra: Text, Translation, Reading and Interpretation of the Hebrew Bible in Ancient Judaism and Early Christianity*. CRINT 2.1. Philadelphia: Fortress, 1988. 327pp.

3.2.35   Runia, David T., ed. *Philo in Early Christian Literature: A Survey*. CRINT 3.3. Minneapolis: Fortress, 1993. 418pp.

3.2.36   Safrai, Shemuel. *The Literature of the Sages: Oral Tora, Halakha, Mishna, Tosefta, Talmud, External Tractates*. CRINT 2.3A. Philadelphia: Fortress, 1988. 418pp.

3.2.37   Schreckenberg, Heinz, and Kurt Schubert. *Jewish Historiography and Iconography in Early and Medieval Christianity*. CRINT 3.2. Philadelphia: Fortress, 1991. 307pp.

3.2.38   Stone, Michael E. *Jewish Writings of the Second Temple Period: Apocrypha, Pseudepigrapha, Qumran, Sectarian Writings, Philo, Josephus*. CRINT 2.2. Philadelphia: Fortress, 1984. 307pp.

3.2.39   Tomson, Peter J. *Paul and the Jewish Law: Halakha in the Letters of the Apostle to the Gentiles*. CRINT 3.1. Philadelphia: Fortress, 1990. 327pp.

3.3 Apocrypha and Pseudepigrapha of the Old Testament

Highly Recommended

3.3.1   Charles, R. H., ed. *The Apocrypha and Pseudepigrapha of the Old Testament in English: With Introductions and Critical and Explanatory Notes.* 2 vols. Oxford: Clarendon, 1913. 657/871pp.

Edited by arguably the foremost authority on this material in his generation, and including introductions and explanatory notes by the most prominent authorities of Jewish intertestamental literature, this work is a solid and reliable classic. Each contribution includes an introduction (discussing the book's contents, title, manuscripts, versions, date, unity, authorship, influence on later Jewish or Christian literature, and theology, with bibliography). The notes are brief but technical, and assume a significant amount of linguistic and historical background. Should be supplemented at points by more recent treatments, especially the two volumes edited by Charlesworth (§§3.3.2, 3.3.3).

3.3.2   Charlesworth, James H., ed. *The Old Testament Pseudepigrapha.* 2 vols. Garden City, N.J.: Doubleday, 1983, 1985. 996/1006pp.

Similar to Charles's second volume (§3.3.1), dealing with the Pseudepigrapha, which it attempts to replace. Differs from Charles in that it gives no consideration to the Apocrypha, but includes under Pseudepigrapha a number of later works and fragments not found in Charles. Naturally, it also brings to bear more recent discoveries and scholarly discussion. Each contribution was written by a recognized authority on the book, and includes a synopsis of the book's contents, and discussion of text, original language, date, provenance, historical background, theology, relationship to canonical material, relationship to apocryphal material, and cultural importance. The translations are literal, and the brief interpretive notes are informed and technical.

3.3.3   ———. *The Old Testament Pseudepigrapha and the New Testament: Prolegomena for the Study of Christian Origins.* New ed. Cambridge: Cambridge University Press, 1998. 145pp.

This clearly written volume deals with the study of the Pseudepigrapha as a whole; there is no attempt here to treat introductory matters pertaining to the individual books (for such treatment one should consult Charlesworth's *The Old Testament Pseudepigrapha* [§3.3.2]). Argues here for the significance of the Pseudepigrapha for understanding early Judaism and especially the NT. In the process, explores history of research into the Pseudepigrapha and shows how social history and ideology of scholars influenced that research, demonstrates sophistication and erudition of this literature, polemicizes against easy dismissal of religious value of these writings, provides historical context in which the writings can be appreciated and assessed, demonstrates the wide range of accepted views in early Judaism, and discusses proper method for studying these documents and comparing them with Christian and other Jewish materials.

3.3.4   deSilva, David. *Introducing the Apocrypha: Message, Context, and Significance.* Grand Rapids: Baker, 2002. 428pp.

Designed to be an aid in the reading of the Apocrypha. Begins with a general introduction to the entire Apocrypha, discussing the value of the Apocrypha for Christians, the issue of canonicity, followed by a description of the historical context of the writings. Proceeds to present a discussion of each book in turn: its structure and contents; textual transmission; author, date, and setting; genre and purpose; theology; and influence (including influence upon the NT). Accessible, yet comprehensive. Especially illuminating for the use of the Apocrypha in the study of the Bible—both OT and NT.

3.3.5   Kohlenberger, John R., III, ed. *The Parallel Apocrypha.* New York: Oxford University Press, 1997. 1188pp.

Only parallel Apocrypha readily available. Contains Greek, KJV, Douay, Ronald Knox, NRSV, NAB, and NJB. Includes also six introductory essays dealing with the significance of the Apocrypha for Jewish, Orthodox, Anglican, Protestant, and evangelical communities, written by leading representatives of these groups.

Periodical

3.3.6   *Journal for the Study of the Pseudepigrapha.* Sheffield: Sheffield Academic Press, 1987–.

Also Significant

3.3.7   DiTommoso, Lorenzo. *A Bibliography of Pseudepigrapha Research 1850–1999.* Journal for the Study of the Pseudepigrapha Supplement Series 39. Sheffield: Sheffield Academic Press, 2001. 650pp.

3.3.8   Harrington, Daniel J. *Invitation to the Apocrypha*. Grand Rapids: Eerd-
         mans, 1999. 222pp.

3.3.9   Kaiser, Otto. *The Old Testament Apocrypha: An Introduction*. Peabody,
         Mass.: Hendrickson, 2004. 125pp.

3.3.10   Lightfoot, J. B., M. R. James, and H. B. Swete, trans. *Excluded Books of
         the New Testament*. London: E. Nash & Grayson, 1927. 403pp.

3.3.11   Metzger, Bruce M. *An Introduction to the Apocrypha: Based on the Revised
         Standard Version*. New York: Oxford University Press, 1957. 274pp

3.3.12   Russell, D. S. *The Old Testament Pseudepigrapha: Patriarchs and Prophets
         in Early Judaism*. Philadelphia: Fortress, 1987. 144pp.

3.3.13   Sparks, H. F. D. *The Apocryphal Old Testament*. Oxford: Clarendon,
         1985. 990pp.

See also the introductions to the several books of the Apocrypha and Pseudepigrapha published in the series Guides to the Apocrypha and Pseudepigrapha (Bloomsbury Publishing).

3.4   Qumran and the Dead Sea Scrolls

Highly Recommended

3.4.1   Charlesworth, James H., ed. *The Bible and the Dead Sea Scrolls: The
         Princeton Symposium on the Dead Sea Scrolls*. 3 vols. Waco, Tex.: Baylor
         University Press, 2006. 319/491/734pp.

         Authoritative, current articles by some of the most notable scrolls scholars
         on a host of specific yet relevant topics pertaining to the scrolls' signifi-
         cance for the study of the Bible. The first volume focuses upon the scrolls
         and the OT; the second treats the theology of the scrolls; and the third
         deals with the significance of the scrolls for the NT. Nowhere else can such
         detailed studies of such a wide range of issues be found.

3.4.2   ———, ed. *The Dead Sea Scrolls: Hebrew, Aramaic, and Greek Texts with English Translations*. 10 vols. Princeton Theological Seminary Dead Sea Scrolls Project. Louisville: Westminster John Knox, 1994–. Vols. 1, 2, and 4 are available. Volumes average 160pp.

Reliable, comprehensive, critical edition of the Dead Sea Scrolls. Much more accessible and user friendly, more consistent in style and method, more interested in theology of the text, and more reasonably priced than *Discoveries in the Judean Desert* (§3.4.7). Gives less attention to linguistic matters and contains somewhat fewer notes than does DJD. Includes texts, English translation, and introductions. In contrast to DJD, excludes biblical materials, but devotes one volume to Qumran documents that are part of the Apocrypha and Pseudepigrapha. Introduction to each scroll includes discussion of text, language, provenance, history or historical events reflected in the scroll, major theological ideas, relation to other writings, especially Hebrew Bible, other Jewish literature, and the NT.

3.4.3   García Martínez, Florentino, and Eibert J. C. Tigchelaar, eds. *The Dead Sea Scrolls: Study Edition*. 2 vols. Leiden: Brill, 1997. 1361pp.

Overall the most usable and accessible edition of the Dead Sea Scrolls for regular reading or study. Contains Hebrew and Aramaic transcription and literal English translation on facing pages. Each Q-number contains a brief heading with information on the text and very select bibliography. Omits unidentified and unclassified fragments, and omits also biblical materials among the scrolls.

3.4.4   Ringgren, Helmer. *The Faith of Qumran: Theology of the Dead Sea Scrolls*. Enl. ed. New York: Crossroad, 1995. 330pp.

Begins with a brief introduction to the history and literature of the community, but gives bulk of attention to analysis of the major theological concepts represented in the scrolls. Deals extensively with God, humanity, and eschatology, but gives some attention to other categories, including angels, sin, forgiveness, ethics, and Messianism. Systematic presentation of beliefs of the Qumran community as a whole could lead to enforcement of alien ideological unity on diverse material, but Ringgren acknowledges and generally allows for theological differences and tensions within the scrolls. Volume concludes with discussions on religious organization and practices of the community and relationship to other forms of religion, especially Christianity.

3.4.5   Schiffman, Lawrence H., and James C. VanderKam, eds. *Encyclopedia of the Dead Sea Scrolls*. 2 vols. Oxford: Oxford University Press, 2000. 1132pp.

Only reference work to bring all relevant information on Qumran and the Dead Sea Scrolls together in one place. Presents lucid current discussion of every significant aspect of the scrolls. Treats all Judean desert texts, including those found at Wadi ed-Daliyeh and Masada. Each article emphasizes relevance for biblical scholarship, and each entry concludes with highly selective bibliography (sometimes with brief annotations).

3.4.6   VanderKam, James C. *The Dead Sea Scrolls Today.* 2d ed. Grand Rapids: Eerdmans, 2010. 260pp.

Eminently readable introduction to Qumran and the Dead Sea Scrolls. Covers all major aspects of the community and the scrolls on the basis of the most current findings and scholarly investigation. Describes the history and physical setting of the Qumran discoveries; provides brief surveys of the manuscripts; discusses the theology, practices, and history of the Qumran community (which VanderKam believes to be Essene); and relates the scrolls to the OT and NT. At several points develops major elements of the theology of the scrolls. Concludes each chapter with select annotated bibliography. Remarkable amount of useful information packed into this small volume.

3.4.7   Vaux, Roland de et al., eds. *Discoveries in the Judean Desert.* 36 vols. thus far. Oxford: Clarendon, 1955–. Volumes average 200pp.

The most authoritative and complete edition of the Dead Sea Scrolls ever published. Individual volumes edited by the most prominent international authorities on the scrolls. Treatment of each portion of the scrolls includes (1) introduction describing condition and contents of the manuscripts, paleography, and orthography; (2) transcription of the original text; (3) translation (of nonbiblical materials); (4) textual notes; (5) commentary (mostly orthographical, grammatical, and lexical, or references to related biblical passages; some commentators clarify or explicate the meaning of the text); and (6) plates showing the actual fragments. Highly technical, with portions of each volume accessible only to those who are competent in Hebrew and Aramaic. Most of the volumes are in English; a few are in French.

Periodical

3.4.8   *Dead Sea Discoveries.* Leiden: Brill Academic Publishing, 1994–.

Also Significant

3.4.9   Charlesworth, James H. *Graphic Concordance to the Dead Sea Scrolls.*
Princeton Theological Seminary Dead Sea Scrolls Project. Louisville:
Westminster John Knox, 1991. 529pp.

3.4.10   ———, ed. *Jesus and the Dead Sea Scrolls.* Anchor Bible Reference
Library. New York: Doubleday, 1992. 370pp.

3.4.11   Collins, John J., and Craig A. Evans, eds. *Christian Beginnings and the
Dead Sea Scrolls.* Grand Rapids: Baker, 2006. 144pp.

3.4.12   Collins, John J., and Robert A. Kugler, eds. *Religion in the Dead Sea
Scrolls.* Studies in the Dead Sea Scrolls and Related Literature. Grand
Rapids: Eerdmans, 2000. 167pp.

3.4.13   Cross, Frank Moore. *Ancient Library of Qumran and Modern Biblical
Studies.* 3d ed. Minneapolis: Fortress, 1995. 204pp.

3.4.14   Fields, Weston W. *The Dead Sea Scrolls: A Full History.* 2 vols. (Vol. 1
presently available.) Leiden: Brill, 2009. 592pp.

3.4.15   Fitzmyer, Joseph A. *The Dead Sea Scrolls and Christian Origins.* Studies in
the Dead Sea Scrolls and Related Literature. Grand Rapids: Eerdmans,
2000. 290pp.

3.4.16   ———. *A Guide to the Dead Sea Scrolls and Related Literature.* Rev. ed.
Grand Rapids: Eerdmans, 2008. 302pp.

3.4.17   Flint, Peter W., ed. *The Bible at Qumran: Text, Shape, and Interpretation.*
Studies in the Dead Sea Scrolls and Related Literature. Grand Rapids:
Eerdmans, 2001. 266pp.

3.4.18   García Martínez, Florentino. *A Bibliography of the Finds in the Desert of
Judah 1970–1995.* Studies on the Texts of Judah 19. Leiden: Brill, 1996.
561pp.

3.4.19   García Martínez, Florentino, and Julio Trebolle Barrera. *The People of
the Dead Sea Scrolls: Their Literature, Social Organization and Religious
Beliefs.* Leiden: Brill, 1994. 269pp.

3.4.20   Magness, Jodi. *The Archaeology of Qumran and the Dead Sea Scrolls.*
Studies in the Dead Sea Scrolls and Related Literature. Grand Rapids:
Eerdmans, 2002. 256pp.

3.4.21   Pate, C. Marvin. *Communities of the Last Days: The Dead Sea Scrolls, the
New Testament, and the Story of Israel.* Downers Grove, Ill.: InterVarsity,
2000. 303pp.

3.4.22   Schiffman, Lawrence H. *Reclaiming the Dead Sea Scrolls: Their True
Meaning for Judaism and* Christianity. Anchor Bible Reference Library.
New York: Doubleday, 1995. 529pp.

3.4.23   Shanks, Hershel. *The Mystery and Meaning of the Dead Sea Scrolls.* New
York: Random House, 1998. 246pp.

3.4.24   Stegemann, Hartmut. *The Library of Qumran: On the Essenes, Qumran,
John the Baptist, and Jesus.* Grand Rapids: Eerdmans, 1998. 299pp.

3.4.25   Ulrich, Eugene. *The Dead Sea Scrolls and the Origins of the Bible.* Studies
in the Dead Sea Scrolls and Related Literature. Grand Rapids: Eerdmans,
1999. 309pp.

3.4.26   Vermes, Geza. *The Complete Dead Sea Scrolls in English.* 7th ed. New
York: Penguin, 2012. 720pp.

3.4.27   ———. *An Introduction to the Complete Dead Sea Scrolls.* Minneapolis:
Fortress, 1999. 256pp.

3.4.28   Wise, Michael, Martin Abegg Jr., and Edward Cook. *The Dead Sea
Scrolls: A New Translation.* San Francisco: HarperSanFrancisco, 1996.
513pp.

3.5   Apocalyptic and Apocalypticism

Highly Recommended

3.5.1   Collins, John J. *The Apocalyptic Imagination: An Introduction to Jewish
Apocalyptic Literatu*re. 2d ed. Biblical Resources Series. Grand Rapids:
Eerdmans, 1998. 337pp.

Current and engaging introduction to apocalyptic literature. Argues that the essence of apocalypticism involved responding to crises not by offering reasonable solutions but by appealing to imagination and faith. Whereas Russell (§3.5.7) deals with apocalyptic literature as a whole, Collins gives separate treatment to each significant apocalyptic writing, including apocalyptic passages in the NT. In each case he discusses unity and structure, content, historical background (especially socioreligious factors), history of interpretation, and message. In the process, notes connections between the individual writings.

3.5.2   Collins, John J., Bernard McGinn, and Stephen J. Stein, eds. *The Encyclopedia of Apocalypticism*. 3 vols. New York: Continuum, 1998. 494/524/498pp.

Volume 1 deals with apocalypticism as a religious worldview or system involving belief "that God has revealed the imminent end of the ongoing struggle between good and evil in history." Understands this to be the central tenet of Judaism, Christianity, and Islam, and examines the origins of this belief system and the initial manifestations of it in the OT, intertestamental Judaism, and the NT. This is an encyclopedia, not a dictionary, in that it contains not brief articles identifying every person or document pertaining to apocalypticism, but rather a series of full-length articles detailing essential aspects of this belief system. Volumes 2 and 3 are not oriented to biblical data, but treat "Apocalypticism in Western History and Culture" and "Apocalypticism in the Modern Period and the Contemporary Age."

3.5.3   Hanson, Paul D. *The Dawn of Apocalyptic*. 2d ed. Philadelphia: Fortress, 1979. 444pp.

Focuses on the religious influences that gave rise to the apocalyptic movement. In contrast to prevailing scholarly opinion, argues that the forces behind the emergence of apocalypticism are to be found not in Persian or Greek circles but deep within the religious tradition (especially prophetic) of Israel. In the process, deals carefully with a number of OT prophetic books and passages so as to demonstrate their contribution to the development of apocalypticism. Shows how such an understanding of the development of apocalypticism within the OT illuminates the eschatological message of this vast and significant literature.

3.5.4   ———. *Old Testament Apocalyptic*. Interpreting Biblical Texts. Nashville: Abingdon, 1987. 144pp.

Basic guide to apocalyptic material in the OT, written for the nonspecialist, and helpful for reflection on the use of this material for preaching and teaching within the church. Describes significance, identification and character, original theological message, and proper versus improper process of applying apocalyptic texts. Argues against "illegitimate and improper" applications (e.g., Hal Lindsey's *Late Great Planet Earth*). Treats several specific OT apocalyptic passages to show how they should be interpreted and how their proper interpretation can be creatively and compellingly applied to specific contemporary issues.

3.5.5   Minear, Paul S. *New Testament Apocalyptic.* Interpreting Biblical Texts. Nashville: Abingdon, 1981. 157pp.

Similar to Hanson's *Old Testament Apocalyptic* (§3.5.4) in that there is a concern to identify NT apocalyptic, discuss its character, and present examples of appropriate interpretation and contemporary application of key NT passages (in contrast to "illegitimate" use of these texts by some contemporary American movements, especially certain forms of the charismatic movement). But whereas Hanson focuses on the apocalyptic genre, Minear understands apocalyptic more broadly as constituting not only a type of literature but also a religious movement and a type of religious thinking. Consequently, Minear treats passages that represent apocalyptic thinking or themes, but are not apocalyptic in genre.

3.5.6   Murphy, Frederick J. *Apocalypticism in the Bible and Its World: A Comprehensive Introduction.* Grand Rapids: Baker, 2012. 416pp.

No other book offers such a sustained and detailed exploration of the significance of apocalypticism for the interpretation of the Bible. The volume begins with a helpful discussion of the definitions and origins of apocalyptic, and then explores the forerunners of apocalyptic and the presence and influence of apocalypticism in the OT, intertestamental Jewish literature, and various portions of the NT. Emphasizes the dynamic development of apocalypticism.

3.5.7   Russell, D. S. *The Method and Message of Jewish Apocalyptic: 200 BC–AD 100.* Old Testament Library. Philadelphia: Westminster, 1964. 464pp.

Remains the standard text for reliable, comprehensive treatment of Jewish apocalyptic literature. Limited to Jewish literature, and thus excludes Christian apocalyptic (yet constantly refers to NT passages). Gives no attention to the apocalyptic movement as a socioreligious phenomenon. Especially helpful is the discussion of the literary characteristics of apocalyptic and the analysis of apocalyptic theology. Explores theological categories that are of particular significance for Christianity and examines the influence of apocalyptic thought on subsequent Judaism and Christianity.

Also Significant

3.5.8   Carey, Greg. *Ultimate Things: An Introduction to Jewish and Christian Apocalyptic Literature.* St. Louis: Chalice, 2005. 280pp.

3.5.9   Carey, Greg, and Gregory L. Bloomquist, eds. *Vision and Persuasion: Rhetorical Dimensions of Apocalyptic Discourse.* St. Louis, Mo.: Chalice, 1999. 203pp.

3.5.10   Collins, John J., ed. *Oxford Handbook of Apocalyptic Literature.* New York: Oxford University Press, 2014. 528pp.

3.5.11   Cook, Stephen L. *The Apocalyptic Literature.* Interpreting Biblical Texts. Nashville: Abingdon, 2003. 233pp.

3.5.12   ———. *Prophecy and Apocalypticism: The Postexilic Social Setting.* Minneapolis: Fortress, 1995. 246pp.

3.5.13   Frost, S. B. *Old Testament Apocalyptic: Its Origins and Growth.* London: Epworth, 1952. 270pp.

3.5.14   Lewis, Scott M. *What Are They Saying about New Testament Apocalyptic?* New York: Paulist, 2004. 115pp.

3.5.15   Reddish, Mitchell G., ed. *Apocalyptic Literature: A Reader.* Peabody, Mass.: Hendrickson, 1995. 352pp.

3.5.16   Rowland, C. *The Open Heaven: A Study of Apocalyptic in Judaism and Early Christianity.* New York: Crossroad, 1982. 562pp.

3.5.17   Schmithals, Walter. *The Apocalyptic Movement: Introduction and Interpretation.* Nashville: Abingdon, 1975. 255pp.

3.5.18   VanderKam, James C., and William Adler, eds. *The Jewish Apocalyptic Heritage in Early Christianity.* Compendia Rerum Iudaicarum ad Novum Testamentum 3.4. Minneapolis: Fortress, 1996. 286pp.

3.5.19   Watson, Duane F., ed. *The Intertexture of Apocalyptic Discourse in the New Testament.* Society of Biblical Literature Symposium Series. Leiden: Brill, 2002. 299pp.

229

4

The New Testament

4.1   Bibliographic Helps

See also PERIODICALS (§4.2)

Highly Recommended

4.1.1   Carson, D. A. *New Testament Commentary Survey*. 7th ed. Grand Rapids: Baker, 2013. 176pp.

Annotated bibliography of significant NT resources, especially commentaries. Treats commentary sets as well as individual volumes. Limited almost exclusively to English titles, and to exegetical works over against homiletical resources. Although written by a leading conservative evangelical scholar, works cited represent a variety of theological traditions. Brief but trenchant, specific, and frank comments presented in a lively narrative style discuss reliability, methodological approach, theological slant, and price.

4.1.2   Harrington, Daniel J. *The New Testament: A Bibliography*. Wilmington, Del.: Michael Glazier, 1985. 242pp.

Produced by a significant Catholic NT scholar and editor of New Testament Abstracts, represents what he considers to be those works that are most authoritative and useful for students, Christian educators, theologians, clergy, and interested laity. Includes both books and articles, almost entirely in English. Identifies especially recommended works. List is theologically ecumenical, but evangelical titles are not well represented. Includes a wide range of topics, not only concordances and commentaries, but also categories (e.g., Eucharist, marriage and divorce, politics). Consequently, each section contains only a few titles, and there are no annotations.

4.1.3   Mills, Watson E., ed. *Bibliographies for Biblical Research: New Testament Series.* 21 vols. Lewiston, N.Y.: Mellen Biblical Press, 1993–2002. Volumes average 250pp., but vary greatly in length.

Includes citations of twentieth-century works that make important contributions to understanding the text and its backgrounds. Each volume has its own compiler, who assesses works to be included. Although this selection is necessarily subjective, the choices are judicious, reasonable, and fair, and few scholars would have serious problems with the majority of selections. Each volume includes three divisions: scriptural passages, subjects, and commentaries. There is some duplication between the first two categories. Lists works in all European languages, without annotations.

4.1.4   ———, ed. *Bibliographies for Biblical Research: Periodical Literature for the Study of the New Testament.* 11 vols. Lewiston, N.Y.: Mellen, 2002. Volumes average 175pp.

Similar in format to *Bibliographies for Biblical Research: New Testament Series* (§4.1.3), citing works published in periodical literature throughout the twentieth century, but limited to journal articles (arranged by chapter and verse citation). Many of the same articles appear in these two works, but without complete overlap in that some articles are cited in only one of these resources. Contains English, French, German, and Italian titles, with slightly more than half in English. The final volume is given over to an author index.

4.1.5   Wagner, Günter. *An Exegetical Bibliography of the New Testament.* 4 vols. Macon, Ga.: Mercer University Press, 1983–1996. 667/550/350/379pp.

Presumably this work will eventually cover the entire NT, but as yet only four volumes are available, covering Matthew–Mark (1983), Luke–Acts (1985), the Johannine Writings (1987), and Romans and Galatians (1996). Includes books and articles in major journals, in all the European languages. Moves through each biblical book passage by passage, giving rather complete bibliography for each. Gives little attention to works dealing with an entire biblical book or corpus.

232

Also Significant

4.1.6   France, R. T. *A Bibliographic Guide to New Testament Research*. Sheffield: JSOT, 1979. 56pp.

4.1.7   Martin, Ralph P. *New Testament Books for Pastor and Teacher*. Philadelphia: Westminster, 1984. 152pp.

4.1.8   Mills, Watson E., ed. *Bibliographies for Biblical Research Supplemental Series, Volume I: New Testament Commentaries*. Lewiston, N.Y.: Mellen, 2001. 260pp.

4.1.9   ———. *Critical Tools for the Study of the New Testament*. Mellen Biblical Press Series 27. Lewiston, N.Y.: Mellen, 1995. 142pp.

4.2 Periodicals

4.2.1   *Journal for the Study of the New Testament*. 1978–. Quarterly.

Published by Department of Biblical Studies, Sheffield, UK. Consistently high-quality articles directed toward scholars and serious students, but written in lucid style and largely accessible to the nonspecialist. Represents balance between treatment of broad NT issues and specific interpretation of individual passages; in both cases, inclined to deal with issues that are relevant for theological understanding of the text. Articles tend to employ the more traditional historical-critical methods, with forays into literary or narrative criticism. Language: English. Book reviews: few and brief.

4.2.2   *New Testament Abstracts*. 1956–. 3 issues/year.

Like *Old Testament Abstracts* (§2.2.2), published by Boston College School of Theology and Ministry. Abstracts more than two thousand articles per year from more than five hundred periodicals, and summarizes more than 850 books; these works represent all European languages. Makes no attempt to evaluate, but simply describes works in terms of content, argument, and method. Language: English.

4.2.3   *New Testament Studies*. 1954–. Quarterly.

Produced by Studiorum Novi Testamenti Societas (Society for the Study of the New Testament) and published by Cambridge University Press,

Cambridge, UK, this is the preeminent scholarly journal for NT studies. Articles from mostly European and North American scholars employing predominantly traditional higher-critical methods, with some of the
newer literary approaches, but avoids especially political approaches, e.g.,
feminist and liberationist readings. Articles are technical, but often accessible to nonspecialists, and frequently deal with issues that are relevant for
understanding the message of the text. Some articles focus on theological
or hermeneutical issues. Language: English, German, and French. Book
reviews: recent issues contain none.

4.2.4   *Novum Testamentum.* 1956–. Quarterly.

Published by Brill Academic Publishers in Leiden, the Netherlands, a premier scholarly journal. Articles are consistently technical and somewhat
less accessible to nonspecialists than articles in *JSNT* or even *NTS*, tend-
ing to treat historical-critical, text-critical, and grammatical issues, with
relatively little attention to specifically theological concerns. Language:
English, German, and French. Book reviews: many, but brief.

4.3   History of the Canon and History of Interpretation

Highly Recommended

4.3.1   Baird, William. *History of New Testament Research.* 3 vols. Minneapolis:
Fortress, 1992, 2003, 2013. 450/565/688pp.

Baird's primary scholarly field is NT history, and he brings his habits of
meticulous historical research to bear on the history of NT interpretation in the modern period. Accessible to the nonspecialist, yet informative to the scholar. The first volume treats the period from Deism to the
emergence of the Tübingen School in the mid-nineteenth century, while
the second volume explores NT interpretation to the beginning of the
Second World War. The third volume deals with the subject to the end of
the twentieth century and includes also the history of biblical theology.
Chapters deal with various areas of NT research, tracing the developments
in terms of significant critical scholars and major movements. Deals with
all areas of NT studies, with an emphasis upon the higher critical method.
Little attention to emerging newer methods; evangelicals may feel somewhat excluded. Each volume concludes with an extensive bibliography.
Should be used in combination with McKnight and Osborne (§4.3.4) for
exposure to more recent trends and scholars and for those outside of the
mainline higher critical tradition.

4.3.2   Epp, Eldon Jay, and George W. MacRae, eds. *The New Testament and Its Modern Interpreters.* The Bible and Its Modern Interpreters. Philadelphia: Fortress, 1989. 601pp.

Examines and evaluates the state of scholarly research in each major area of NT study, with a view toward suggesting how developments since the Second World War point to directions for future study. Groups individual chapters according to three broad areas: the world of the NT, methods (mostly traditional ones, e.g., textual criticism, form criticism, redaction criticism, and linguistics, but attends also to literary criticism), and NT literature. This last section includes the NT Apocrypha and Apostolic Fathers. Devotes considerable space to the Synoptic Problem and gospel genre but only a couple of pages to Matthew and Mark. Comprehensive in categories covered, but that means several categories are treated in very cursory fashion, ameliorated in part by an extensive bibliography concluding each chapter.

4.3.3   Kümmel, Werner Georg. *The New Testament: The History of the Investigation of Its Problems.* Nashville: Abingdon, 1972. 510pp.

A most authoritative text, virtually a standard for the history of NT interpretation up to 1970. Because of the emphases of the period in which it was written and the convictions of its author, this volume treats the whole of the history of NT interpretation from the perspective of the rise of the historical-critical method. Considers everything prior to the eighteenth century as "prehistory." Emphasizes Continental, and especially German, scholarship. Gives scant attention to British and American scholars, and should therefore be supplemented with Neill-Wright (§4.3.6) or Epp-McCrae (§4.3.2), both of which give prominence to British and American scholarship (and are more current).

4.3.4   McKnight, Scot, and Grant R. Osborne, eds. *The Face of New Testament Studies: A Survey of Recent Research.* Grand Rapids: Baker Academic, 2004. 544pp.

A companion to Baker and Arnold, *The Face of Old Testament Studies* (§2.3.1), offers an overview of recent scholarship that is serviceable as an introduction to the novice while also informative for seasoned scholars who desire a sense of developing research in areas outside their narrow specialization. Deals with research into the context (i.e., historical background) of the NT, NT hermeneutics, Jesus studies, and "earliest Christianity," which involves research into various books or portions of the NT (here the whole of the NT is discussed, with the exception of Jude and the Johannine epistles). Although written by evangelicals who give appropriate attention to evangelical scholarship, discussions are quite broad and

235

focus on "mainstream" NT scholarship. Centers on research since 1900, with emphasis upon the last twenty years.

4.3.5   Metzger, Bruce M. *The Canon of the New Testament: Its Origin, Development, and Significance.* Oxford: Clarendon, 1987. 326pp.

Volume is divided into three parts: Part 1 surveys the literature on the canon, discussing almost every work that deals directly with the NT canon from 1650 to the present. Part 2 tracks the development of the NT canon in the church, dealing with the Apostolic Fathers, the various influences that led to the canon, the emergence of the canon in the East and West, and Christian apocryphal literature. This is the most careful, complete, and balanced presentation of the NT canon to be found anywhere. Part 3 explores the various problems the church confronted in the canonizing process, e.g., the criteria for canonicity, relationship between inspiration and canon, and the problem of four different Gospels. Here also are addressed several theological questions the canon raises for the church today. Metzger's discussion of these theological questions is helpful, but he is stronger when working with historical matters.

4.3.6   Neill, Stephen, and Tom Wright. *The Interpretation of the New Testament 1861–1986.* 2d ed. London: Oxford, 1988. 464pp.

Original edition written by Stephen Neill, covering 1861 through 1961, has been revised and updated by N. T. Wright to include developments through 1986. Written in engaging narrative style with personal touches, especially descriptions of the scholars discussed. Gives detailed treatment of selected scholars and works rather than a broad survey of all literature. Attends to British and American scholarship without diminishing the German contribution. Provides an understanding of the history of scholarship and points out key problems of NT interpretation.

Also Significant

4.3.7   Gamble, Harry Y. *The New Testament Canon: Its Making and Meaning.* Guides to Biblical Scholarship. Philadelphia: Fortress, 1985. 95pp.

4.3.8   Grant, Robert M. *The Formation of the New Testament.* New York: Harper & Row, 1965. 194pp.

4.3.9   Harris, Horton. *The Tübingen School: A Historical and Theological Investigation of the School of F. C. Baur.* Grand Rapids: Baker, 1990. 288pp.

4.3.10   Riches, John K. *A Century of New Testament Study.* Valley Forge, Pa.: Trinity Press International, 1993. 246pp.

4.3.11   Westcott, Brooke Foss. *A General Survey of the History of the Canon of the New Testament.* 7th ed. Cambridge: Macmillan, 1896. 605pp.

4.4   History and Geography: Primary Sources

Highly Recommended

4.4.1   Barrett, C. K., ed. *The New Testament Background: Selected Documents.* Rev. ed. San Francisco: HarperSanFrancisco, 1989. 361pp.

Selection of passages from Roman imperial sources, the papyri, various inscriptions, philosophers, poets, gnostics, mystery religions, works of Jewish history, rabbinic literature, Qumran, Philo, Josephus, the Septuagint, Targums, apocalyptic literature, and mysticism. Intended to give the nonspecialist a sense of the world (Roman, Greek, Jewish) in which the NT was produced. Begins with a helpful bibliography of each of these areas, listing both primary and secondary sources. Introduces each area with a short paragraph, describing its history and significance, while brief annotations explain translation and historical significance. Selections are not chosen by reference to specific NT passages but because of their ability to provide a sense of the world that surrounded the NT.

4.4.2   Cartlidge, David R., and David L. Dungan, eds. *Documents for the Study of the Gospels.* Rev. ed. Minneapolis: Fortress, 1993. 298pp.

Passages chosen to demonstrate the diversity of the religious world that surrounded the NT. Selections from Jewish, Greek, Roman, Egyptian, Syrian, and early Christian sources are intended to illuminate the Christian acknowledgment of Jesus as Savior and God. Shows how the Gospels both reflected and differed from the worship of other savior gods, and provides insight as to how the Gospels arose and how their original readers understood them. Contains a brief but informative introductory chapter on savior gods in the Mediterranean world. Each subsequent chapter begins with a brief introduction, placing the work in its historical context and describing its significance for the NT, followed by a fresh translation produced by the authors, with a few concise explanatory annotations.

237

4.4.3   Kee, Howard Clark, ed. *The Origins of Christianity: Sources and Documents*. Englewood Cliffs, N.J.: Prentice-Hall, 1973. 270pp.

Careful selection of documents meant to illustrate how persons in the first and second centuries before and after Christ thought about and related to key aspects of life, e.g., religion, the gods, life and death, the future, and anxieties of everyday life. Represents a vast range of material, including literary works, letters, magical texts, and documents from rabbinic and sectarian Judaism. The purpose is to provide depth and clarity for understanding the NT as a whole and broad themes or issues within it; excerpts were not chosen in reference to specific NT passages. Introductions provide historical background to the documents, while notes offer helpful explanation to historical references and allusions.

Also Significant

4.4.4   Layton, Bentley. *Gnostic Scriptures: A New Translation with Introduction and Notes*. New York: Doubleday, 1995. 576pp.

4.4.5   Robinson, James M., ed. *The Nag Hammadi Library*. 4th ed. Leiden: Brill, 1996. 549pp.

4.5   History and Geography: Secondary Sources

See also JUDAISM AND JEWISH CULTURE: SECONDARY SOURCES (§3.2)

Highly Recommended

4.5.1   Boring, M. Eugene, Klaus Berger, and Carsten Colpe, eds. *Hellenistic Commentary to the New Testament*. Nashville: Abingdon, 1995. 633pp.

Passage-by-passage commentary cites Hellenistic texts that provide relevant background for the passage. The most complete collection of Hellenistic texts correlated to the NT available in English. Contains 976 relatively extensive citations, each one annotated to describe ways in which the citation illuminates the passage. Introductory chapter describes the use and potential misuse of this information. Helpful supplement to Keener (§4.5.5), who gives prominence to Jewish background and does not explicitly cite sources when he does refer to Hellenistic material.

238

4.5.2   Evans, Craig A. *Ancient Texts for New Testament Studies: A Guide to the Background Literature.* Grand Rapids: Baker Academic, 2005. 539pp.

Recognizing the magnitude and diversity of the background material relevant for the interpretation of the NT, Evans provides an overview of these writings in general, including discussion of their relevance and of methodological issues surrounding their use for interpretation. He then deals in turn with the major bodies of this material, including the OT Apocrypha, the Dead Sea Scrolls, Philo and Josephus, the rabbinic literature, and gnostic writings (to mention only a few). In each case he provides a summary listing of the relevant documents (primary sources) and a bibliography (secondary literature). In many of these categories he includes a description of major themes found therein. A fine introduction to the literature pertaining to this vast material.

4.5.3   Evans, Craig A., and Stanley E. Porter, eds. *Dictionary of New Testament Background.* Downers Grove, Ill.: InterVarsity, 2000. 1328pp.

Articles deal with virtually every imaginable aspect of Jewish and Greco-Roman background to the NT. Articles are written by recognized experts in the field and are of consistently high quality. Reflects generally conservative perspective. All entries were selected and written with a view toward assisting in the interpretation of the NT. Each article concludes with extensive bibliography.

4.5.4   Ferguson, Everett. *Backgrounds of Early Christianity.* 2d ed. Grand Rapids: Eerdmans, 1993. 611pp.

Overall the best introduction to NT background. Deals with political, social, literary, and religious backgrounds of the Roman, Greek, and Jewish worlds. Gives somewhat more attention to Jewish background, reflecting the author's conviction that it is most significant. Written for college and seminary students, it will prove valuable also to pastors and even interested laypersons. Current, comprehensive, and informed, but written in clear, straightforward style. Frequently refers to NT texts to show relevance for NT interpretation. Of special value are the bibliographies to general works at the beginning of each chapter and to specialized works at the end of each subsection.

4.5.5   Keener, Craig S. *The IVP Bible Background Commentary: New Testament.* Downers Grove, Ill.: InterVarsity, 1994. 831pp.

Background information is essential for NT interpretation, but is diffuse and often difficult to find. Keener's verse-by-verse commentary focuses exclusively on cultural, social, and historical background. Concentrates on

OT and Jewish background, providing explicit citations of the OT and OT Apocrypha and Pseudepigrapha, but notes also Greek and Roman background (which Keener tends to present in a general way, without citing references). Written in clear, nontechnical language. Includes a glossary of cultural terms and important figures, maps and charts, introductory essay on importance of cultural background, and bibliographies for each biblical book listing commentaries and other works that emphasize background.

4.5.6   Martin, Ralph P., and Peter H. Davids, eds. *Dictionary of the Later New Testament and Its Developments.* Downers Grove, Ill.: InterVarsity, 1997. 1289pp.

Covers all NT literature outside the Gospels and Paul (companion volumes treat these areas; see "The Gospels: Studies in the Gospels" [§4.20] and "Paul" [§ 4.30]). Offers comprehensive discussion of apostolic fathers and early Christianity through middle of the second century. Discusses topics specific to this portion of NT and thus in many cases missing from even the most comprehensive Bible dictionaries. Narrow focus of this dictionary permits relatively full treatment of the topics included. Contributors include prominent evangelical scholars who make responsible use of critical methods, and who represent North America, Europe, Australia, New Zealand, and Asia.

4.5.7   Schürer, Emil. *The History of the Jewish People in the Age of Jesus Christ.* 3 vols. Revised and edited by Geza Vermes, Fergus Millar, and Matthew Black. Edinburgh: T&T Clark, 1973–1987. 611/606/1014pp.

By far the most thorough and authoritative study of Jewish history, institutions, and literature between 175 BCE and 135 CE ever produced. Originally published in 1874, with a fourth edition in 1909. This new English edition is based on the German fourth. Retains the structure and information that continues to be valid from the original work but provides a fresh English translation with full revision of the material reflecting recent discoveries and the most current scholarly judgments. Highly technical, but most material accessible to nonspecialists.

Also Significant

4.5.8   Brown, Raymond E. *The Churches the Apostles Left Behind.* New York: Paulist, 1984. 156pp.

4.5.9   Brown, Raymond E., and Paul Meier. *Antioch and Rome: New Testament Cradles of Catholic Christianity.* New York: Paulist, 1983. 242pp.

4.5.10   Bruce, F. F. *New Testament History*. 4th ed. London: Pickering & Inglis, 1982. 434pp.

4.5.11   Charlesworth, James H., ed. *The Messiah: Developments in Earliest Judaism and Christianity*. First Princeton Symposium on Judaism and Christian Origins. Minneapolis: Fortress, 1992. 597pp.

4.5.12   Collins, Adela Yarbro, and John J. Collins. *King and Messiah as Son of God: Divine, Human, and Angelic Messianic Figures in Biblical and Related Literature*. Grand Rapids: Eerdmans, 2008. 261pp.

4.5.13   Collins, John J. *The Scepter and the Star: The Messiahs of the Dead Sea Scrolls and Other Ancient Literature*. Anchor Bible Reference Library. New York: Doubleday, 1995. 270pp.

4.5.14   Deissmann, Adolf. *Light from the Ancient East: The New Testament Illustrated by Recently Discovered Texts of the Graeco-Roman World*. New York: Doran, 1927. 535pp. (Originally published in German in 1909.)

4.5.15   Evans, Craig A. *Noncanonical Writings and New Testament Interpretation*. Peabody, Mass.: Hendrickson, 1992. 281pp.

4.5.16   Green, Joel B., and Lee Martin McDonald, eds. *The World of the New Testament: Cultural, Social, and Historical Contexts*. Grand Rapids: Baker Academic, 2013. 672pp.

4.5.17   Hedrick, Charles, ed. *Nag Hammadi, Gnosticism and Early Christianity*. Peabody, Mass.: Hendrickson, 1983. 232pp.

4.5.18   Horbury, William. *Messianism among Jews and Christians: Twelve Biblical and Historical Studies*. London: T&T. Clark, 2003. 417pp.

4.5.19   Horsley, Richard A. *Archaeology, History, and Society in Galilee: The Social Context of Jesus and the Rabbis*. Harrisburg, Pa.: Trinity Press International, 1996. 240pp.

4.5.20   Horsley, Richard A., and John S. Hanson. *Bandits, Prophets, and Messiahs: Popular Movements at the Time of Jesus*. San Francisco: Harper, 1985. 271pp.

4.5.21   Jeffers, James S. *The Greco-Roman World of the New Testament Era: Exploring the Background of Early Christianity.* Downers Grove, Ill.: InterVarsity, 1999. 352pp.

4.5.22   Jeremias, Joachim. *Jerusalem in the Time of Jesus: An Investigation into Economic and Social Conditions during the New Testament Period.* Philadelphia: Fortress, 1969. 405pp.

4.5.23   Jonas, Hans. *The Gnostic Religions: The Message of the Alien God at the Beginnings of Christianity.* 3d ed. Boston: Beacon, 2001. 359pp.

4.5.24   Magness, Jodi. *Stone and Dung, Oil and Spit: Jewish Daily Life in the Time of Jesus.* Grand Rapids: Eerdmans, 2011. 335pp.

4.5.25   Mowinkel, Sigmund. *He That Cometh.* New York: Abingdon, 1954. 528pp.

4.5.26   Perkins, Pheme. *Gnosticism and the New Testament.* Minneapolis: Fortress, 1993. 261pp.

4.5.27   Pierson, Birger A. *Ancient Gnosticism: Traditions and Literature.* Minneapolis: Fortress, 2007. 362pp.

4.5.28   Reicke, Bo. *The New Testament Era: The World of the Bible from 500 B.C. to A.D. 100.* Philadelphia: Fortress, 1974. 336pp.

4.5.29   Roetzel, Calvin J. *The World That Shaped the New Testament.* Rev. ed. Louisville: Westminster John Knox, 2002. 168pp.

4.5.30   Rudolph, Kurt. *Gnosis: The Nature and History of Gnosticism.* San Francisco: Harper & Row, 1984. 411pp.

4.5.31   Sherwin-White, A. N. *Roman Society and Roman Law in the New Testament.* London: Oxford, 1963. 204pp.

4.5.32   Simon, Marcel. *Jewish Sects at the Time of Jesus.* Philadelphia: Fortress, 1967. 180pp.

4.5.33   Witherington, Ben, III. *New Testament History: A Narrative Account.*
          Grand Rapids: Baker, 2001. 430pp.

See also the series The Library of Early Christianity, edited by Wayne A.
Meeks:

4.5.34   Aune, David E. *The New Testament in Its Literary Environment.* Philadel-
          phia: Westminster, 1987. 260pp.

4.5.35   Cohen, Shaye J. D. *From the Maccabees to the Mishnah.* Philadelphia:
          Westminster, 1987. 251pp.

4.5.36   Grant, Robert M. *Gods and the One God.* Philadelphia: Westminster,
          1986. 211pp.

4.5.37   Kugel, James L., and Rowan A. Greer. *Early Biblical Interpretation.* Phila-
          delphia: Westminster, 1986. 214pp.

4.5.38   Malherbe, Abraham J. *Moral Exhortation: A Greco-Roman Sourcebook.*
          Philadelphia: Westminster, 1986. 178pp.

4.5.39   Meeks, Wayne A. *The Moral World of the First Christians.* Philadelphia:
          Westminster, 1986. 182pp.

4.5.40   Stambaugh, John E., and David L. Balch. *The New Testament in Its Social
          Environment.* Philadelphia: Westminster, 1986. 194pp.

4.5.41   Stowers, Stanley K. *Letter Writing in Greco-Roman Antiquity.* Philadel-
          phia: Westminster, 1986. 188pp.

For historical background (and history of interpretation) dealing with major
NT characters, see the series, published originally by University of South
Carolina Press and reprinted in paperback by Fortress Press, Studies on Per-
sonalities of the New Testament, ed. by D. Moody Smith:

4.5.42   Black, C. Clifton. *Mark: Images of an Apostolic Interpreter.* Minneapolis:
          Fortress, 2001. 400pp.

243

4.5.43   Culpepper, R. Alan. *John, the Son of Zebedee: The Life of a Legend.* Minneapolis: Fortress, 2000. 367pp.

4.5.44   Gaventa, Beverly Roberts. *Mary: Glimpses of the Mother of Jesus.* Minneapolis: Fortress, 1999. 164pp.

4.5.45   Painter, John. *Just James: The Brother of Jesus in History and Tradition.* Minneapolis: Fortress, 1999. 326pp.

4.5.46   Perkins, Pheme. *Peter: Apostle for the Whole Church.* Minneapolis: Fortress, 2000. 209pp.

4.5.47   Reinhartz, Adele. *Caiaphas the High Priest.* Minneapolis: Fortress, 2013. 264pp.

4.5.48   Richardson, Peter. *Herod: King of the Jews and Friend of the Romans.* Minneapolis: Fortress, 1999. 360pp.

4.5.49   Roetzel, Calvin J. *Paul: The Man and the Myth.* Minneapolis: Fortress, 1999. 269pp.

4.6   Editions of the New Testament

4.6.1   Holmes, Michael W., ed. *The Greek New Testament. SBL Edition.* Atlanta: Society of Biblical Literature. 2010. 516pp.

Compares the Greek texts adopted by Tregelles, the NIV, Robinson and Pierpont with the critical text of Westcott and Hort, with a view toward making a judgment about the original reading of each passage on the basis of this comparison. The text, then, does not reflect a judgment on the manuscript tradition directly, but rather a preference from among some of the leading editions of the Greek NT. The "textual apparatus" at the bottom of the page thus lists alternative readings among these versions of the Greek NT. Helpful in presenting a comparison of readings by these major editions. Is made available free in electronic form (http://sblgnt.com)

4.6.2   Nestle, Eberhard, Barbara and Kurt Aland, Johannes Karavidopoulos, Carlo M. Martini, and Bruce M. Metzger, eds. *The Greek New Testament.* 4th rev. ed. New York: United Bible Societies, 1998. 918pp.

This volume represents the printed text of the Nestle-Aland 27th ed., which was generally regarded as the most reliable available until the publication of the Nestle-Aland 28th ed., described later in this section. *Novum Testamentum Graece* has a more extensive and detailed text-critical apparatus, while the textual apparatus in *The Greek New Testament* is limited to those textual variants about which there is some controversy and over which translators differ. The 5th revised edition, whose text will presumably be identical to the Nestle-Aland 28th edition, is awaited. The textual variants appearing in *The Greek New Testament* are discussed in Bruce M. Metzger, *A Textual Commentary on the Greek New Testament* (§4.11.3). See Kurt and Barbara Aland, *The Text of the New Testament* (§4.11.1), for discussion of other editions of the Greek NT.

4.6.3 ———. *Novum Testamentum Graece*. 28th ed. Stuttgart: Deutsche Bibelgesellschaft, 2012. 878pp.

Presents what is considered by the majority of scholars to be the most reliable text of the Greek NT. The critical apparatus has been revised from the 27th edition and made easier to use and includes citations from the recently discovered papyri 117–127. In addition, the Catholic Epistles incorporate some of the readings from the Editio Critica Maior, a major project of the Institute für neutestamentliche Textforschung, which will eventually produce a multiple-volume compilation of early manuscripts, translations, and quotations of the NT (only the volume on the Catholic Epistles has yet appeared).

4.7 Greek Grammars

Highly Recommended

4.7.1 Blass, F., and A. Debrunner. *A Greek Grammar of the New Testament and Other Early Christian Literature*. Edited by Robert W. Funk. Chicago: University of Chicago Press, 1961. 325pp.

"Blass and Debrunner" was a standard grammar in Germany, which Robert Funk translated, revised, and edited. Emphasizes the relationship of NT Greek to classical Greek, and explains the Greek of the NT by comparison and contrast with the classical models. Especially helpful are subsections that explore difficulties, rare or irregular features, and disputed points. In that it represents the German tradition of grammars, deals with grammatical issues somewhat differently (and at times more satisfactorily) than British and American counterparts. Somewhat more technical (and in some cases more arcane) than Robertson (§4.7.3), and its format and arrangement render it more difficult to use.

4.7.2   Moulton, James Hope, Wilbert Francis Howard, and Nigel Turner. *A Grammar of New Testament Greek*. 4 vols. Edinburgh: T&T Clark, 1976. 293/543/417/174pp.

Begun in 1906 by Moulton but, due to the unexpected deaths of both Moulton and Howard, brought to completion only in 1976 by Turner. The most comprehensive study of NT Greek ever produced by British scholars. Intended as a learned assessment that would be of value for scholars but would serve also as a practical guide for students and pastors in their work of NT exegesis. Discussion of syntax emphasizes relationship of NT Greek to the common Greek of the period ("Koine") and that of the Septuagint, over against classical Greek and in comparison with other Indo-European languages (which are stressed by Robertson [§4.7.3] and Blass-Debrunner [§4.7.1]). Unlike most other grammars offers valuable analysis of differences in construction and style between the various NT writers.

4.7.3   Robertson, A. T. *A Grammar of the Greek New Testament in the Light of Historical Research*. Nashville: Broadman, 1934. 1454pp.

Often called Robertson's "large grammar," this is the most comprehensive and detailed NT grammar available in English. Deals with every significant aspect of the language, including its relationship to other Indo-European tongues, its role within the history of the Greek language, accidence, and virtually every imaginable dimension of syntax. Emphasis is on the function of syntax for communicating exact and precise meaning, and thus the grammar is eminently useful for accurate and insightful interpretation. Although discussions often reflect views of linguistics and the nature of the development of the NT that are now considered outdated, this volume remains indispensable for serious work in NT Greek.

4.7.4   Smyth, Herbert Weir. *Greek Grammar*. Revised by Gordon M. Messing. Cambridge, Mass.: Harvard University Press, 1956. 784pp.

Most authoritative, comprehensive, and detailed reference grammar on ancient Greek available. Brief explanations of forms and other grammatical features are extremely useful to readers of the Greek NT in that they serve to place the grammatical phenomena of the Greek NT within the setting of the Greek language of antiquity in general. This volume thus complements grammars that deal specifically with the Greek NT, but does not replace them, since the latter deal with grammatical features of the Greek language that were prevalent specifically at the time of the writing of the Greek NT.

4.7.5   Wallace, Daniel B. *Greek beyond the Basics: An Exegetical Syntax of the New Testament.* Grand Rapids: Zondervan, 1996. 827pp.

An "exegetical grammar," intended for those who have a solid foundation in the essentials of NT Greek and who wish to make serious use of syntactical analysis in the exegesis of the NT. The most comprehensive of the exegetical grammars presently available. Makes use of the most current linguistic theory. Extremely detailed, analytical, and exact. Provides numerous illuminating examples from NT passages. Indeed, there is so much information that it is possible to become lost in the sheer mass of material. Wallace has therefore produced an abridged version (*The Basics of New Testament Syntax* [§4.7.23]) that omits minor categories, some theoretical discussions, and many scriptural examples, and is thus better adapted to regular readers of the Greek NT.

4.7.6   Zerwick, Maximilian. *Biblical Greek.* Scripta Pontificii Instititi Biblici 114. Rome: Pontifical Biblical Institute Press, 1963. 185pp.

Reliable and straightforward reference grammar. Selective, in that it makes no attempt to deal with all of the grammatical phenomena of the Greek NT but seeks rather to discuss briefly only those grammatical features that tend to be of most significance for precise understanding of the Greek and for exegesis.

4.7.7   Zerwick, Maximilian, and Mary Grosvenor. *A Grammatical Analysis of the Greek New Testament.* 5th ed. Rome: Pontifical Biblical Institute, 1996. 778pp.

Moves through the text of the Greek NT, parsing and defining each word. Occasionally provides extremely brief (one sentence) description of background or significance of the terms. Constantly refers the reader to the appropriate paragraph in Zerwick's *Biblical Greek* (§4.7.6) for fuller discussions of inflections or other grammatical points.

Also Significant

4.7.8   Black, David Alan. *It's Still Greek to Me: An Easy-to-Understand Guide to Intermediate Greek.* Grand Rapids: Baker, 1998. 191pp.

4.7.9   ———. *Linguistics for Students of New Testament Greek: A Survey of Basic Concepts and Applications.* 2d ed. Grand Rapids: Baker, 1995. 216pp.

4.7.10 ———. *Using New Testament Greek in Ministry: A Practical Guide for Students and Pastors*. Grand Rapids: Baker, 1993. 128pp.

4.7.11 Brooks, James A., and Carlton L. Winbery. *A Morphology of New Testament Greek: A Review and Reference Grammar*. Lanham, Md.: University Press of America, 1994. 468pp.

4.7.12 ———. *Syntax of New Testament Greek*. Lanham, Md.: University Press of America, 1979. 204pp.

4.7.13 Burton, Ernest De Witt. *Syntax of the Moods and Tenses in New Testament Greek*. Chicago: University of Chicago Press, 1900. 215pp.

4.7.14 Caragounis, Chrys C. *The Development of Greek and the New Testament: Morphology, Syntax, Phonology, and Textual Transmission*. Grand Rapids: Baker Academic, 2004. 732pp.

4.7.15 Dana, H. E., and Julius R. Mantey. *A Manual Grammar of the Greek New Testament*. New York: Macmillan, 1927. 356pp.

4.7.16 Greenlee, J. Harold. *A Concise Exegetical Grammar of New Testament Greek*. 4th ed. Grand Rapids: Eerdmans, 1986. 79pp.

4.7.17 Harris, Murray J. *Prepositions and Theology in the Greek New Testament: An Essential Reference Resource for Exegesis*. Grand Rapids: Zondervan, 2012. 293pp.

4.7.18 Moule, C. F. D. *An Idiom Book of New Testament Greek*. 2d ed. Cambridge: Cambridge University Press, 1959. 246pp.

4.7.19 Owings, Timothy. *A Cumulative Index to New Testament Greek Grammars*. Grand Rapids: Baker, 1983. 204pp.

4.7.20 Porter, Stanley E. *Idioms of the Greek New Testament. Biblical Languages: Greek 2*. Sheffield: JSOT, 1992. 339pp.

4.7.21   ———. *Verbal Aspect in the Greek of the New Testament, with Reference to Tense and Mood.* Studies in Biblical Greek, vol. 1. New York: Peter Lang, 1989. 582pp.

4.7.22   Porter, Stanley E., and D. A. Carson, eds. *Biblical Greek Language and Linguistics: Open Questions in Current Research.* Journal for the Study of the New Testament Supplement Series 80. Sheffield: JSOT, 1993. 217pp.

4.7.23   Robertson, A. T. *The Minister and His Greek New Testament.* New York: Doran, 1923. 139pp.

4.7.24   Wallace, Daniel B. *The Basics of New Testament Syntax: An Intermediate Greek Grammar.* Grand Rapids: Zondervan, 2000. 334pp.

4.7.25   Waugh, R. M. L. *The Preacher and His Greek Testament.* London: Epworth, 1953. 104pp.

4.7.26   Young, Richard A. *Intermediate New Testament Greek: A Linguistic and Exegetical Approach.* Nashville: Broadman & Holman, 1994. 307pp.

Popular Beginning Grammars

4.7.27   Adam, A. K. M. *A Grammar for New Testament Greek.* Nashville: Abingdon, 1999. 227pp.

4.7.28   Black, David Alan. *Learn to Read New Testament Greek.* Expanded ed. Nashville: Broadman & Holman, 1994. 236pp.

4.7.29   Duff, Jeremy. *The Elements of New Testament Greek.* 3d ed. Cambridge: Cambridge University Press, 2005. 340pp.

4.7.30   Hewett, James Allen. *New Testament Greek: A Beginning and Intermediate Grammar.* Rev. ed. Peabody, Mass.: Hendrickson, 2009. 324pp.

4.7.31   Jay, Eric. *New Testament Greek: An Introductory Grammar.* London: SPCK, 1958. 350pp.

4.7.32   Kubo, Sakae. *A Beginner's New Testament Greek Grammar*. Rev. ed. Washington, D.C.: University Press of America, 1995. 235pp.

4.7.33   LaSor, William Sanford. *Handbook of New Testament Greek: An Inductive Approach Based on the Greek Text of Acts*. 2 vols. Grand Rapids: Eerdmans, 1973. 260/231pp.

4.7.34   Machen, J. Gresham. *New Testament Greek for Beginners*. New York: Macmillan, 1923. 287pp.

4.7.35   McLean, B. H. *New Testament Greek: An Introduction*. Cambridge: Cambridge University Press, 2011. 266pp.

4.7.36   Mounce, William D. *Basics of Biblical Greek*. 2d ed. Grand Rapids: Zondervan, 2003. 448pp.

4.8   Greek Lexicons

Highly Recommended

4.8.1   Danker, Frederick W. *A Greek-English Lexicon of the New Testament and Other Early Christian Literature*. 3d ed. Revised and edited by Frederick William Danker. Based on Walter Bauer's *Griechisch-deutsches Wörterbuch zu den Schriften des Neuen Testaments und der frühchristlichen Literatur*, 6th edition, edited by Kurt Aland and Barbara Aland, with Viktor Reichmann, and on previous English editions by W. F. Arndt, F. W. Gingrich, and F. W. Danker. Chicago: University of Chicago Press, 2000. 1108pp.

The most current, complete, and authoritative NT lexicon available in English. Contains detailed definitions of each word found in the Greek NT and in much of other early Christian literature. Gives basic definition and, where applicable, groups occurrences of the term around the more specific ways it is used. Entries frequently list not only occurrences in early Christian literature, but also cite the term in Jewish writings (especially the Septuagint, Apocrypha, Pseudepigrapha, Philo, and Josephus). In keeping with most recent linguistic and translation theory, this new edition avoids simple one-word equivalents in favor of extended and specific definitions that provide a fuller explanation of the meaning. This third edition is often cited as "BDAG"; the second edition was "BAGD" (see §4.8.9).

4.8.2   Kubo, Sakae. *A Reader's Greek-English Lexicon of the New Testament.* Grand Rapids: Zondervan, 1975. 327pp.

Moves through the NT book by book, and within books passage by passage, giving the lexical form and basic definition of every word occurring fewer than fifty times in the NT. Each entry indicates the number of times the word appears in the particular book and in the NT as a whole. Words that occur fewer than fifty times in the NT but more than five times in a particular book are placed alphabetically at the beginning of that book in a special vocabulary, thus helping the student to identify the key themes and concerns of the book. Contains an appendix that lists words occurring more than fifty times in the NT, and a second appendix that lists unusual or irregular forms. Helpful for rapid reading of the NT.

4.8.3   Liddell, Henry George, and Robert Scott. *A Greek-English Lexicon.* Revised and augmented by Henry Stuart Jones and Roderick McKenzie. Oxford: Clarendon, 1940. 2111pp.

A massive work that treats the meaning of Greek terms appearing in literary texts from the beginning of literary Greek to 600 CE. It is thus not a lexicon of NT Greek, but of ancient Greek language in general, although it does include many references to the Septuagint and the NT. Useful for identifying the original meaning of terms, the wide range of their use and their historical development in Greek literature, and their etymology (i.e., the history of the formation of the word as a means of discovering its essential meaning). Functions virtually as a concordance to literary Greek, with specific citations of passages. Very helpful in placing the meaning of NT words in broader semantic perspective and thereby providing depth and nuance to the significance of these terms.

4.8.4   Louw, Johannes P., and Eugene A. Nida. *Greek-English Lexicon of the New Testament Based on Semantic Domains.* 2 vols. New York: United Bible Societies, 1988. 843/375pp.

The first lexicon to make consistent, thoroughgoing use of the most recent developments in linguistic theory. Arranged according to "semantic domains," i.e., types or spheres of meaning, with various NT Greek terms of a particular domain listed and described so that the reader can ascertain how each of these Greek terms communicates and develops its own specific emphases within the larger area. For example, lists "Elevated Land Formations" as a semantic domain, and discusses five separate Greek terms that pertain to that concept. Avoids single-word definitions in favor of fuller, more expansive explanations of meaning. This approach provides a rich and precise understanding of terms and their relationship to associated words.

251

4.8.5   Moulton, James Hope, and George Millian. *The Vocabulary of the Greek Testament Illustrated from the Papyri and Other Non-Literary Sources*. Grand Rapids: Eerdmans, 1930. 705pp.

The work of Adolf Deissmann (e.g., *Light from the Ancient East* [§4.5.14]), who pioneered the study of everyday (Koine) Greek as represented in Egyptian papyri for understanding the Greek of the NT, was the impetus for this lexicon that explores the use of Greek terms in the papyri (and to a lesser extent in inscriptions) that were essentially contemporary with the NT. When one remembers that the Greek of the NT was in fact everyday spoken Greek, one recognizes the value of this volume, which is the only resource to make accessible this highly relevant information.

4.8.6   Perschbacher, Wesley J., ed. *The New Analytical Greek Lexicon*. Peabody, Mass.: Hendrickson, 1990. 449pp.

Represents the most thorough and accurate revision of George V. Wigram's *Analytical Greek Lexicon of the New Testament,* originally published in 1852. Lexicon gives basic definition of each word in its lexical form, but the real value of this volume is its function as a parsing guide, which offers complete parsing of every word that appears in the Greek NT (including variant readings). Includes paradigms of Greek declensions and conjugations, with explanatory grammatical remarks. Unusual or irregular forms in the lexicon are cross-referenced to explanatory grammatical remarks. Inclusion of Strong's numbers renders this volume accessible to those who do not know Greek well.

4.8.7   Thayer, Joseph Henry. *Greek-English Lexicon of the New Testament: Coded with the Numbering System from Strong's Exhaustive Concordance of the Bible*. Peabody, Mass.: Hendrickson, 1996.

For many years this lexicon, based on the earlier German work by C. G. Wilke and C. L. W. Grimm, was the standard NT Greek lexicon in the English-speaking world. This volume is a reprint of the fourth edition, originally published in 1896. In spite of its age and the fact that it has been superseded by the magisterial volume by BDAG (§4.8.1), it remains a basically reliable work and is often suggestive in its definitions. At points it offers nuances beyond even what can be found in BDAG. It often discusses the etymology of a term (i.e., the history of the formation of the term as providing insight into its essential meaning), which can be helpful, but one must remember that the original meaning of a term is not necessarily carried over into every occurrence, and significance must be determined by context. The inclusion of Strong's numbers makes this lexicon accessible to those who do not know Greek.

Also Significant

4.8.8   Abbott-Smith, G. A. *A Manual Greek Lexicon and Supplement.* 3d ed. Edinburgh: T&T Clark, 1937. 512pp.

4.8.9   Arndt, William F., and F. Wilbur Gingrich. *A Greek-English Lexicon of the New Testament and Other Early Christian Literature: A Translation and Adaptation of the fourth revised and augmented edition of Walter Bauer's Griechisch-Deutsches Wörterbuch zu den Schriften des Neuen Testaments und der übrigen urchristlichen Literatur.* 2d ed. rev. and augmented by F. Wilbur Gingrich and Frederick W. Danker from Walter Bauer's 5th ed., 1958. Chicago: University of Chicago Press, 1979. 900pp.

4.8.10   Bullinger, Ethelbert W. *A Critical Lexicon and Concordance to the English and Greek New Testament.* London: Longmans, Green, 1877. 999pp.

4.8.11   Friberg, Timothy, Barbara Friberg, and Neva F. M. Miller, eds. *Analytical Lexicon to the Greek New Testament.* Grand Rapids: Baker, 2000. 439pp.

4.8.12   Hickie, W. J. *Greek-English Lexicon to the New Testament.* Grand Rapids: Baker, 1977. 213pp.

4.8.13   Mounce, William D. *An Analytical Lexicon to the Greek New Testament.* Grand Rapids: Zondervan, 1993. 542pp.

4.8.14   Newman, Barclay. *A Concise Greek-English Dictionary of the New Testament.* Stuttgart: United Bible Societies, 1993. 203pp.

4.8.15   Nida, Eugene A., and Johannes P. Louw. *Lexical Semantics of the Greek New Testament: A Supplement to the Greek-English Lexicon of the New Testament Based on Semantic Domains.* Society of Biblical Literature Resources for Biblical Study 25. Atlanta: Scholars, 1992. 155pp.

4.8.16   Taylor, Bernard, John A. L. Lee, Peter R. Burton, and Richard E. Whitaker, eds. *Biblical Greek Language and Lexicography: Essays in Honor of Frederick W. Danker.* Grand Rapids: Eerdmans, 2004. 266pp.

4.8.17   Whiton, James M. *A Lexicon Abridged from Liddell and Scott's Greek-English Lexicon.* New York: American Book Co., 1906. 831pp.

4.9 Theological Dictionaries (Wordbooks)

Highly Recommended

4.9.1   Balz, Horst, and Gerhard Schneider, eds. *Exegetical Dictionary of the New Testament*. 3 vols. Grand Rapids: Eerdmans, 1990. 463/555/566pp.

Provides basic meaning and explores usage of every NT word in its various contexts for the purposes of providing insight into the exegesis of specific passages and of contributing to the theological understanding of the NT. Each entry includes transliteration, discussion of (usually) all NT occurrences, and bibliography (reference works, articles, monographs) that discusses the word and passages where the word plays a significant role. Most significant words are treated in longer articles that contain more extended bibliographies; fuller discussions of meanings and occurrences; background in classical Greek, the Septuagint, Judaism, and Hellenistic literature; exegetical problems that involve the word; and contribution to NT theology. More current than Kittel's *Theological Dictionary of the New Testament* (§4.9.3) in that it takes into account recent discoveries and newer trends in scholarly investigation and emerging insights into linguistic theory, without adopting any particular linguistic model. Contributors represent the most prominent critical NT scholars in German-speaking countries.

4.9.2   Brown, Colin, ed. *The New International Dictionary of New Testament Theology*. 4 vols. Grand Rapids: Zondervan, 1975–1979. 747/944/1223/592pp.

Based on *Theologisches Begriffslexikon zum Neuen Testament*, translated, revised, and enlarged by Brown, with additional articles by (primarily) evangelicals from Britain and North America. Concise discussions of major NT theological terms are arranged in English alphabetical order. Discusses the use of each word in classical Greek, the OT, rabbinic literature, and the NT. Contains relatively extensive bibliographies of works in English, French, and German. More concise, more conservative in critical, historical, and theological outlook, and more accessible to the nonspecialist (i.e., less technical) than Kittel's *Theological Dictionary of the New Testament* (§4.9.3).

4.9.3   Kittel, Gerhard, and Gerhard Friedrich. *Theological Dictionary of the New Testament*. 10 vols. Grand Rapids: Eerdmans, 1964–1976. Volumes average 1000pp.

Translated by Geoffrey Bromiley from *Theologisches Wörterbuch zum Neuen Testament*, this set is without peer among works in this category, although articles vary significantly in quality. The most authoritative, comprehensive, and detailed discussion of major NT terms ever published. Treats every significant NT term by discussing its secular Greek background, its use in the OT (both the Hebrew Bible and the Septuagint), in Jewish sources (especially Philo, Josephus, the Pseudepigrapha, and rabbinic material), and in the NT, often discussing differences among the various NT writers. The final volume comprises comprehensive indexes. The inclusion of discussion of coordinate Hebrew terms enables this set to be used for exploring the meaning of Hebrew terms for OT exegesis. Students should heed the warning of James Barr (*The Semantics of Biblical Language* [London: Oxford University Press, 1961]) that this set could encourage the false conclusion that the meaning of a term in one passage necessarily determines its sense in another passage. But if students are aware of this danger and give primary consideration to the way the word is used in the context of the passage they are interpreting, they will find this resource reliable. Recent printings include Strong's numbers.

Also Significant

4.9.4   Barclay, William. *New Testament Words*. Philadelphia: Westminster, 1964. 301pp.

4.9.5   Cremer, H. *Biblico-Theological Lexicon of New Testament Greek*. 4th ed. New York: Scribner's, 1895. 943pp.

4.9.6   Earle, Ralph. *Word Meanings in the New Testament*. Kansas City, Mo.: Beacon Hill, 1986. 487pp.

4.9.7   Kittel, Gerhard, and Gerhard Friedrich. *Theological Dictionary of the New Testament: Abridged in One Volume by Geoffrey W. Bromiley*. Grand Rapids: Eerdmans, 1985. 1356pp.

4.9.8   Richards, Larry. *Expository Dictionary of Bible Words*. Grand Rapids: Zondervan, 1985. 720pp.

4.9.9   Spicq, Ceslas. *Theological Lexicon of the New Testament*. 3 vols. Peabody, Mass.: Hendrickson, 1994. 492/603/691pp.

4.9.10   Trench, Richard C. *Synonyms of the New Testament.* 9th ed. Grand Rapids: Eerdmans, 1953. (Originally published in 1880.) 405pp.

4.9.11   Turner, Nigel. *Christian Words.* Nashville: Thomas Nelson, 1981. 513pp.

4.9.12   Verbrugge, Verlyn. *The NIV Theological Dictionary of New Testament Words: An Abridgment of The New International Dictionary of New Testament Theology.* Grand Rapids: Zondervan, 2000. 1544pp.

4.9.13   Zodhiates, Spiros, ed. *The Complete Word Study Dictionary: New Testament.* Chattanooga, Tenn.: AMG, 1994. 1505pp.

4.10   Concordances to the Greek New Testament

Highly Recommended

4.10.1   Aland, Kurt, ed. *Vollständige Konkordanz zum Griechischen Neuen Testament.* 2 vols. Berlin: Walter De Gruyter, 1975. 1352/557pp.

Despite the German title, use of this work does not require knowledge of German; terms are listed in Greek, and the introductory material appears in both German and English. Based on Nestle-Aland 26th edition. The work's distinctive value is its extremely detailed presentation of textual variants. Subdivides the occurrences of a word according to the major ways it is used in the NT. Citations are slightly longer than in Moulton-Geden (§4.10.3), thus providing more of the sense of context. Very accurate and complete, but expensive.

4.10.2   Bachmann, H., and W. A. Slaby, eds. *Concordance to the Novum Testamentum Graece of Nestle-Aland, 26th Edition, and to the Greek New Testament, 3rd Edition.* Edited by the Institute for New Testament Textual Research and the Computer Center of Münster University. Berlin: Walter De Gruyter, 1987. 1014pp.

Produced with the aid of electronic data processing, this concordance benefits from the accuracy and reliability of such technological assistance, while careful and competent work on the part of the editors has guarded against some of the unfortunate byproducts that accompany this kind of electronic searching. Employs Nestle-Aland 26th edition, and any variants appearing in the apparatus in the Nestle-Aland text are simply listed and identified with an asterisk (*), over against the comprehensive and complex identification of variants found in Aland's concordance (§4.10.1). Like Aland, gives more extensive citations than Moulton-Geden, but unlike Moulton-Geden, and especially Aland, does not subdivide occurrences according to the term's use in the NT.

4.10.3   Moulton, W. F., and A. S. Geden. *A Concordance to the Greek Testament.* 6th ed. Edited by I. Howard Marshall. New York: Continuum, 2002. 1120pp.

For many years the standard concordance to the Greek NT in the English-speaking world, it continues to be a valuable resource. The first five editions were based on the Westcott-Hort text, but the new sixth edition is based on the Nestle-Aland 27th edition, lists important variants, and frequently subdivides occurrences on the basis of the various ways the term is used in the NT or on the basis of the various phrases in which it is found. Gives brief citations, usually long enough to give some basic sense of the immediate context. Recent printings are coded to Strong's numbers.

Also Significant

4.10.4   Clapp, Philip S., Barbara Friberg, and Timothy Friberg. *Analytical Concordance of the Greek New Testament.* Grand Rapids: Baker, 1991. 2619pp.

4.10.5   Hoffmann, Paul, Thomas Hieke, and Ulrich Bauer, eds. *Synoptic Concordance: A Greek Concordance to the First Three Gospels in Synoptic Arrangement, Statistically Evaluated, Including Occurrences in Acts.* 4 vols. Berlin: Walter de Gruyter, 1999–2000. 1034/957/997/1066pp.

4.10.6   Kohlenberger, John R., III, Edward W. Goodrick, and James A. Swanson, eds. *The Exhaustive Concordance to the Greek New Testament.* Grand Rapids: Zondervan, 1995. 1055pp.

4.10.7   ———. *The Greek-English Concordance to the New Testament: With the New International Version.* Grand Rapids: Zondervan, 1997. 1131pp.

4.10.8   Smith, J. B. *Greek-English Concordance to the New Testament: A Tabular and Statistical Greek-English Concordance Based on the King James Version with an English-to-Greek Index.* Scottsdale, Pa.: Herald, 1955. 430pp.

4.10.9   Wigram, George V. *The Englishman's Greek Concordance of the New Testament: Coded with Numbering System from Strong's Exhaustive Concordance of the Bible.* 9th ed. Peabody, Mass.: Hendrickson, 1998. (Concordance itself originally published in 1903.) 1020pp.

4.11   Textual Criticism

Highly Recommended

4.11.1   Aland, Kurt, and Barbara Aland. *The Text of the New Testament: An Introduction to the Critical Editions and to the Theory and Practice of Modern Textual Criticism.* 2d ed. Grand Rapids: Eerdmans, 1989. 366pp.

Thorough, current, and lucid introduction to all major aspects of textual criticism. Produced by two of Germany's most prominent authorities in the field. Enables beginning students to make practical use of the textual apparatus in modern editions of the Greek NT so as to form independent judgments regarding text-critical matters. Especially valuable are the overview of editions of the Greek NT from Erasmus to Nestle-Aland 26th ed., extensive explanation of the textual apparatus in modern editions, discussions of the major criteria for making text-critical decisions, and examples of text-critical analysis from specific NT passages. Gives basic but limited attention to most significant ancient versions and Greek manuscripts. Argues against practice among many NT text critics to make decisions largely on the basis of the "text-type" or "family" of texts to which a manuscript belongs; insists on a more dynamic approach that examines each reading on its own terms without primary attention to the quality of the "family" to which the manuscript belongs.

4.11.2   Comfort, Philip W. *New Testament Text and Translation Commentary: Commentary on the Variant Readings of the Ancient New Testament Manuscripts and How They Relate to Major English Translations.* Carol Stream, Ill.: Tyndale House, 2008. 899pp.

Like Metzger (§4.11.3) discusses the major variant readings in the manuscript tradition, making judgments about the most probable original readings on the basis of broadly accepted criteria of textual criticism, e.g., the quality and age of the manuscripts, scribal tendencies; and gives comments on the variants that illumine the interpretive significance of the competing readings. Discusses about 30 percent more textual variants than does Metzger. Lists the critical editions of the Greek NT and the major English translations that adopt the various readings; and in an introductory chapter describes briefly the text-critical philosophies and tendencies of these critical editions and English versions.

4.11.3   Metzger, Bruce M., ed. *A Textual Commentary on the Greek New Testament*. 2d ed. Stuttgart: United Bible Societies, 1994. 696pp.

Designed to serve as companion to the fourth edition of the Greek NT, published by the United Bible Societies, but is of value to those who use other modern editions of the Greek NT. Discusses briefly the most significant textual variants listed in the apparatus of the fourth edition by describing the text-critical bases of the UBS committee's decision to adopt a particular reading and by exploring the interpretive (and sometimes theological) significance of the text-critical issues of the passage. Indeed, sometimes the discussion regarding the reasons why scribes attempted to "correct" the text can bring to light theological issues in passages that modern readers might tend to overlook.

4.11.4   Metzger, Bruce M., and Bart D. Ehrman. *The Text of the New Testament: Its Transmission, Corruption, and Restoration*. 4th ed. Oxford: Oxford University Press, 2005. 310pp.

Like the Alands' *Text of the New Testament* (§4.11.1), intended as an introduction to NT textual criticism. Covers virtually all areas of the field, but gives special attention to ways in which ancient manuscripts were produced and transmitted, the major witnesses (versions and manuscripts) to the NT text, the various causes of errors in the transmission of the text, and the basic criteria for evaluating variant treadings. Gives examples of textual analysis from selected NT passages. In contrast to the Alands', gives significant role to "text-type" or "family" of manuscripts in the process of making decisions between variant readings.

4.11.5   Westcott, Brooke Foss, and Fenton John Anthony Hort. *Introduction to the New Testament in the Original Greek*. New York: Harper & Row, 1882. 324pp. + appendix.

Probably the most significant volume ever produced in the history of the field of textual criticism. Westcott and Hort produced the critical edition of the NT text that was the standard for almost a century, at least in the English-speaking world. In this volume they set forth the principles that remain the fundamental framework for the method of textual criticism. Here also they present their views (adopted by almost all subsequent text-critics) of the "genealogical" relationship between manuscripts, i.e., that virtually all ancient manuscripts and versions belong to a "text-type" or "family," and that judgments between variant manuscript readings should be based in large part on the general reliability or unreliability of the family to which the manuscript belongs. Concludes with a lengthy appendix discussing significant textual variants in specific NT passages.

Also Significant

4.11.6   Aland, Barbara, and Joël Delobel, eds. *New Testament Textual Criticism, Exegesis, and Early Church History: A Discussion of Methods.* Kampen: Pharos, 1994, 152pp.

4.11.7   Comfort, Philip W. *Encountering the Manuscripts: An Introduction to New Testament Paleography & Textual Criticism.* Nashville: Broadman, 2005. 420pp.

4.11.8   Comfort, Philip W. *The Quest for the Original Text of the New Testament.* Grand Rapids: Baker, 1992. 200pp.

4.11.9   Ehrman, Bart D., and Michael W. Holmes, eds. *The Text of the New Testament in Contemporary Research: Essays on the Status Quaestionis.* Grand Rapids: Eerdmans, 1995. 401pp.

4.11.10   Elliott, J. K. *A Bibliography of Greek New Testament Manuscripts.* 2d ed. Society for New Testament Studies Monograph Series 109. Cambridge: Cambridge University Press, 2000. 314pp.

4.11.11   Elliott, Keith, and Ian Moir. *Manuscripts and the Text of the New Testament: An Introduction for English Readers.* Edinburgh: T&T Clark, 1995. 111pp.

4.11.12   Epp, Eldon Jay, and Gordon D. Fee. *Studies in the Theory and Method of New Testament Textual Criticism.* Studies and Documents 45. Grand Rapids: Eerdmans, 1993. 414pp.

4.11.13   Finegan, Jack. *Encountering New Testament Manuscripts: A Working Introduction to Textual Criticism.* Grand Rapids: Eerdmans, 1974. 203pp.

4.11.14   Greenlee, J. Harold. *Introduction to New Testament Textual Criticism.* Rev. ed. Peabody, Mass.: Hendrickson, 1995. 100pp.

4.11.15   Hull, Robert F., Jr. *The Story of the New Testament Text: Materials, Methods, and Models.* Atlanta: Society of Biblical Literature, 2010. 229pp.

4.11.16   McKendrick, Scot, and Orlaith A. O'Sullivan. *The Bible as Book: The Transmission of the Greek Text.* Grand Haven, Mich.: Oak Knoll, 2003. 260pp.

4.11.17   Metzger, Bruce M. *The Early Versions of the New Testament: Their Origin, Transmission, and Limitations.* Oxford: Clarendon, 1977. 498pp.

4.11.18   ———. *Manuscripts of the Greek Bible: An Introduction to Paleography.* New York: Oxford, 1991. 150pp.

4.11.19   Parker, D. C. *An Introduction to the New Testament Manuscripts and Their Texts.* Cambridge: Cambridge University Press, 2008. 368pp.

4.11.20   Vaganay, Léon, and Christian-Bernard Amphoux. *An Introduction to New Testament Textual Criticism.* 2d ed. Cambridge: Cambridge University Press, 1991. 227pp.

4.12   Exegetical Method/Hermeneutics

Highly Recommended

4.12.1   Black, David Alan, and David S. Dockery, eds. *Interpreting the New Testament: Essays on Methods and Issues.* Nashville: Broadman & Holman, 2001. 565pp.

Contains twenty-two essays by leading scholars, all evangelical, mostly younger, and almost all North American. Represents various theological traditions within evangelicalism, though Baptists are in the majority. Includes two fine introductory articles that place critical study of the NT in theological and historical perspective. Peter Davids's "Authority, Hermeneutics, and Criticism" is especially helpful in explaining how critical methods can be employed by those who adopt an evangelical view of the Bible's inspiration. The body of the book is divided into two sections. The first discusses each major critical method, including the newer literary and sociological ones, noting strengths and weaknesses. The second discusses major issues, e.g., the use of the OT in the NT, and the problem of pseudonymity, and describes significant issues for interpretation in various portions of the NT. Practical, reliable, and fair. Comprehensive in the scope of issues treated, but individual discussions are often quite brief.

4.12.2   Croy, N. Clayton. *Prima Scriptura: In Introduction to New Testament Interpretation.* Grand Rapids: Baker Academic, 2011. 240pp.

A most helpful introduction to the practice of NT exegesis, in that it discusses theoretical issues and explicitly and clearly relates these foundational considerations to a suggested process for the interpretation and contemporary appropriation of passages within the NT. Insofar as this volume sets forth a specific program for doing NT exegesis it is similar to Fee (described immediately below), but differs in that it gives much more consideration to hermeneutical matters and to the process of contemporary application. It also addresses at length the significant issue of the relationship between theological commitments and an inductive study of the NT text.

4.12.3   Fee, Gordon D. *New Testament Exegesis: A Handbook for Students and Pastors.* 3d ed. Louisville: Westminster John Knox, 2002. 195pp.

Leading evangelical scholar offers straightforward step-by-step guidance for beginning students to move from initial encounter with a NT passage to the final stages of writing an exegesis paper or preparing a sermon. Discusses use of original language, but makes allowance for readers who do not know Greek. Describes most individual steps very briefly, but gives fuller treatment to the role of literary genre and analysis of grammatical structure of sentences. Gives almost no attention to critical methods, e.g., form criticism or redaction criticism, or to emerging literary approaches. Should be supplemented with volumes edited by Black-Dockery (§4.12.1), Green (§4.12.4), or Marshall (§4.12.5) that explain the use of these critical approaches in the overall exegetical process.

4.12.4   Green, Joel B., ed. *Hearing the New Testament: Strategies for Interpretation.* Grand Rapids: Eerdmans, 1995. 444pp.

The nineteen contributors represent a variety of theological traditions, including but not limited to the evangelical. Contains lucid and nontechnical discussion of a series of hermeneutical issues and modern approaches to NT interpretation. Five NT passages are used as examples throughout, illustrating how each approach can illuminate the meaning of the text. Articles reflect diversity among the various approaches, a diversity that generally characterizes contemporary NT scholarship; an introductory article by Anthony Thiselton helpfully places this present methodological diversity in historical perspective. Each approach is set out by a practitioner (and therefore an advocate) of that approach, who gives little attention to weaknesses or shortcomings. The best introduction to the newer emerging methods and to the most current debates in NT hermeneutics.

4.12.5   Marshall, I. Howard, ed. *New Testament Interpretation: Essays on Principles and Methods.* Grand Rapids: Eerdmans, 1977. 406pp.

Similar to the more recent volume edited by Black-Dockery (§4.12.1) in that it covers many of the same topics and represents an evangelical perspective. The contributors to this volume, however, are mostly British. Articles assume a slightly more sophisticated audience, tend to be generally more supportive of the major critical approaches and less inclined to probe their weaknesses, and give greater attention to specific examples from the NT that illustrate the employment of these methods than is the case with Black-Dockery. Of course, this volume, produced in 1977, does not discuss the newer, emerging methods; for such discussions one should consult the volumes edited by Black-Dockery, and Green (§4.12.4).

4.12.6   Thiselton, Anthony C. *The Two Horizons: New Testament Hermeneutics and Philosophical Description.* Grand Rapids: Eerdmans, 1980. 484pp.

Written by a scholar who reveres the text as Scripture, this groundbreaking work has significantly affected subsequent discussions on NT hermeneutics. Explores how philosophical assumptions affect the way NT scholars (and general readers) interpret and apply the text. Surveys modern philosophical thought pertaining to the nature of knowledge and of language and examines how this philosophical reflection can inform the hermeneutical process and illuminate the meaning of NT passages. Includes a number of examples from the study of specific NT passages. Argues that an informed, creative, and complex fusion of the world of the NT with the world of the interpreter is necessary. Highly technical, and assumes at least basic background in nineteenth- and twentieth-century philosophy. Written in heavy, turbid style. Still, the quality of the discussion and its importance make the effort to digest this book worthwhile.

Also Significant

4.12.7   Adam, A. K. M. *What Is Postmodern Biblical Criticism? Guides to Biblical Scholarship.* Minneapolis: Fortress, 1995. 81pp.

4.12.8   Bailey, James L., and Lyle D. Vander Broek. *Literary Forms in the New Testament: A Handbook*. Louisville: Westminster John Knox, 1992. 219pp.

4.12.9   Bockmuehl, Markus. *Seeing the Word: Refocusing New Testament Study*. Grand Rapids: Baker Academic, 2006. 297pp.

4.12.10   Conzelmann, Hans, and Andreas Lindemann. *Interpreting the New Testament: An Introduction to the Principles and Methods of New Testament Exegesis*. Peabody, Mass.: Hendrickson, 1988. 389pp.

4.12.11   Doty, W. G. *Letters in Primitive Christianity*. Guides to Biblical Scholarship. Philadelphia: Fortress, 1973. 84pp.

4.12.12   Duvall, J. Scott, and Daniel J. Hays. *Grasping God's Word: A Hands-On Approach to Reading, Interpreting, and Applying the Bible*. 2d ed. Grand Rapids: Zondervan, 2005. 462pp.

4.12.13   Elliott, John H. *What Is Social-Scientific Criticism? Guides to Biblical Scholarship*. Minneapolis: Fortress, 1993. 174pp.

4.12.14   Green, Joel B., and Max Turner, eds. *Between Two Horizons: Spanning New Testament Studies and Systematic Theology*. Grand Rapids: Eerdmans, 2000. 246pp.

4.12.15   Holmberg, Bengt. *Sociology and the New Testament: An Appraisal*. Minneapolis: Fortress, 1990. 173pp.

4.12.16   Horrell, David G., ed. *Social-Scientific Approaches to New Testament Interpretation*. Edinburgh: T&T Clark, 1999. 426pp.

4.12.17   Ladd, George Eldon. *The New Testament and Criticism*. Grand Rapids: Eerdmans, 1967. 222pp.

4.12.18   Malina, Bruce J. *Christian Origins and Cultural Anthropology: Practical Models for Biblical Interpretation*. Atlanta: John Knox, 1986. 230pp.

4.12.19 ———. *The New Testament World: Insights from Cultural Anthropology.* 3d ed. Louisville: Westminster John Knox, 2001. 256pp.

4.12.20 McKnight, Edgar V. *What Is Form Criticism? Guides to Biblical Scholarship.* Philadelphia: Fortress, 1969. 86pp.

4.12.21 McKnight, Edgar V., and Elizabeth Struthers Malbon, eds. *The New Literary Criticism and the New Testament.* Valley Forge, Pa.: Trinity Press International, 1994. 399pp.

4.12.22 Meyer, Ben F. *Reality and Illusion in New Testament Scholarship: A Primer in Critical Realist Hermeneutics.* Collegeville, Minn.: Liturgical Press, 1994. 244pp.

4.12.23 Neyrey, Jerome H., and Eric C. Steward, eds. *The Social World of the New Testament: Insights and Models.* Peabody, Mass.: Hendrickson, 2008. 295pp.

4.12.24 Patte, Daniel. *Structural Exegesis for New Testament Critics. Guides to Biblical Scholarship.* Minneapolis: Fortress, 1989. 134pp.

4.12.25 Perrin, Norman. *What Is Redaction Criticism? Guides to Biblical Scholarship.* Philadelphia: Fortress, 1969. 86pp.

4.12.26 Petersen, Norman R. *Literary Criticism for New Testament Critics.* Guides to Biblical Scholarship. Philadelphia: Fortress, 1978. 92pp.

4.12.27 Porter, Stanley E., ed. *Handbook to Exegesis of the New Testament.* New Testament Tools and Studies 25. Leiden: Brill, 1997. 638pp.

4.12.28 Powell, Mark Allan. *What Is Narrative Criticism? Guides to Biblical Scholarship.* Minneapolis: Fortress, 1990. 125pp.

4.12.29 Resseguie, James L. *Narrative Criticism of the New Testament: An Introduction.* Grand Rapids: Baker Academic, 2005. 288pp.

4.12.30 Rohrbaugh, Richard L., ed. *The Social Sciences and New Testament Interpretation.* Peabody, Mass.: Hendrickson, 1996. 240pp.

4.12.31 Wilder, Amon N. *Early Christian Rhetoric: The Language of the Gospel.* Cambridge, Mass.: Harvard University Press, 1971. 135pp.

Students should be aware also of the emerging interest in the employment of insights from rhetorical studies for NT interpretation. "Rhetorical" refers to devices writers use in order to persuade their audiences. Most rhetorical studies focus upon the ways in which NT writers make use of communicative devices or strategies that were employed in the first-century Greco-Roman world. But some wish to include modern rhetorical models as well. The following are representative titles:

4.12.32 Classen, Carl Joachim, *Rhetorical Criticism of the New Testament.* Boston: Brill, 2002. 194pp.

4.12.33 Kennedy, George A. *New Testament Interpretation through Rhetorical Criticism.* Chapel Hill: University of North Carolina Press, 1984. 171pp.

4.12.34 Mack, Burton L. *Rhetoric and the New Testament.* Guides to Biblical Scholarship. Minneapolis: Fortress, 1989. 110pp.

4.12.35 Porter, Stanley E., ed., *Handbook of Classical Rhetoric in the Hellenistic Period 330 B.C.–A.D. 400.* Leiden: Brill, 1997. 901pp.

4.12.36 Porter, Stanley E., and Dennis L. Stamps. *Rhetorical Criticism and the Bible.* London: Sheffield Academic, 2007. 571pp.

4.12.37 Robbins, Vernon K. *Exploring the Texture of Texts: A Guide to Socio-Rhetorical Interpretation.* Valley Forge, Pa.: Trinity Press International, 1996. 148pp.

4.12.38 Watson, Duane F. *The Rhetoric of the New Testament: A Bibliographic Survey.* Tools for Biblical Study, no. 8. Blandford Forum, U.K.: Deo, 2006. 182pp.

4.12.39 Witherington, Ben, III. *New Testament Rhetoric: An Introductory Guide to the Art of Persuasion in and of the New Testament.* Eugene, Ore.: Cascade, 2009. 274pp.

4.13 New Testament Introductions

Highly Recommended

4.13.1   Achtemeier, Paul J., Joel B. Green, and Marianne Meye Thompson. *The New Testament: Its Literature and Theology.* Grand Rapids: Eerdmans, 2001. 544pp.

Synthesizes historical, sociological, cultural, literary, and theological considerations so as to address the most significant issues that arise in the minds of modern readers of the NT. Reflects the most recent conclusions of the best scholarship in a readable, nontechnical fashion. Describes at points the history of interpretation, but mentions only the most significant figures. Analyzes the content and message of each book and discusses critical issues, e.g., author and date of writing, only insofar as they inform the message of the book. Usually accepts traditional views on date and authorship. Probes significant questions that emerge from the book, e.g., historicity, and examines the book's overall theological message. Provides very selective bibliographies. Probably the most accessible and engaging introduction for persons beginning NT studies.

4.13.2   Brown, Raymond E. *An Introduction to the New Testament.* Anchor Bible Reference Library. New York: Doubleday, 1997. 878pp.

Written by arguably the most prominent Roman Catholic NT scholar of the twentieth century. Produced for students rather than scholars, though scholars will take note of Brown's arguments and conclusions. Focuses on the final form of NT books rather than sources that lie behind the text (which Brown considers too speculative to be of much value, especially for beginning students). Carefully analyzes the content and development of thought within each book, discusses critical issues (e.g., authorship and date), explores theological issues, and offers extensive bibliography of works in English. Although a Roman Catholic, writes for an ecumenical audience. Tends toward moderate positions in critical issues, typically accepting the general critical consensus, but with sensitivity to and appreciation for conservative sentiment and arguments.

4.13.3   Dunn, James D. G. *Christianity in the Making.* 3 vols. (Vols. 1 and 2 currently available.) Grand Rapids: Eerdmans, 2003, 2008. 1019/1347pp.

Like Wright's *The New Testament and the People of God* (§4.13.7), it is difficult to know how to categorize this work. It is at the same time a history, an introduction, and a theology of the NT. But since NT introductions address both historical context and theology it seems appropriate to include it here. This massive three-volume work traces the history of the beginnings of Christianity into the middle of the second century, with overwhelming attention to the NT. The first volume, entitled *Jesus Remembered*, addresses the quest for the historical Jesus, but also traces the memory of Jesus in the early church. It is thus as much a study of the Jesus tradition as it is of the historical Jesus. In short, Dunn argues that the memory of Jesus was modified and developed, and yet the church's memory was largely congruent with the history of Jesus. The second volume, entitled *Beginning from Jerusalem*, addresses the quest for the historical church and deals with Luke–Acts and most of the NT epistles, with special attention to Paul. Dunn emphasizes that faith cannot be separated from this history nor from critical study of this history. Dunn is an evangelical whose theological commitments are reflected in his reverence for the text and his high regard for the Christian faith; but many evangelicals may not be comfortable with some of his arguments. Dunn is highly creative in terms both of method and conclusions; readers will find some of his conclusions more compelling than others.

4.13.4   Guthrie, Donald. *New Testament Introduction*. 4th ed. Downers Grove, Ill.: InterVarsity, 1990. 1161pp.

Represents the best of British conservative scholarship. Discusses major critical issues for each NT writing, but focuses on authorship and date. Although consistently arrives at conservative conclusions, presents competing positions with clarity, detail, and fairness. Argues especially against pseudepigraphical writings in the NT. At points seems to move in the direction of conservative apologetics, as when he gives more than fifty pages to discussion of the Pastoral Epistles, almost twice the space given to Romans. Yet even those who disagree with certain conclusions will benefit from almost encyclopedic citations and rigorous reasoning.

4.13.5   Hagner, Donald A. *The New Testament: A Historical and Theological Introduction*. Grand Rapids: Baker Academic, 2012. 872pp.

Written by a leading evangelical scholar who adopts a moderately critical approach. Is remarkably successful in synthesizing historical, literary, and theological issues. Is much more theologically oriented than most introductions, making use of the framework of salvation history as the basis for unity of the NT. Although Hagner presents his own conclusions clearly, he represents other perspectives fairly and respectfully. Written from the perspective of the church's faith. Helpful extensive bibliographies conclude each chapter.

4.13.6   Johnson, Luke Timothy. *The Writings of the New Testament: An Interpretation*. 3d ed. Minneapolis: Fortress, 2010. 544pp.

Prominent Roman Catholic scholar explores the origin and shape of the NT in this comprehensive study that is at once both nontechnical and insightful. Written for students rather than scholars, discusses the most important critical issues for an understanding of the message of the NT texts. Presents his own informed conclusions, without referring to other scholars by name in the text, and without footnotes. Concludes each chapter with annotated bibliography of works almost exclusively in English. Incorporates the newest insights into NT origins and hermeneutics, dealing with introductory issues by a model that attends to anthropological, historical, literary, and religious aspects. Concludes with two helpful appendices on the new methods and on the historical Jesus.

4.13.7   Wright, N. T. *The New Testament and the People of God*. Vol. 1 of *Christian Origins and the Question of God*. Minneapolis: Fortress, 1992. 535pp.

So sweeping are the concerns of this book that it is difficult to know under which category to classify it. It deals seriously with hermeneutical and methodological matters by discussing the challenge of NT interpretation in the current epistemological climate, and sets forth a hermeneutic that meets the tests provided by the nature of the text on the one hand and the intellectual demands of the modern (or postmodern) world on the other. It seeks to set the world of the NT within the context of Judaism and its interactions with the broader Greco-Roman world. And it shows how an appreciation of this setting, applied to the reading of the NT with methodological rigor and integrity, illuminates the theology of the NT. A truly groundbreaking work, and one that will expand the vision for the study and interpretation of the NT on the part of everyone who reads it, both student and scholar.

Also Significant

4.13.8   Carson, D. A., Douglas J. Moo, and Leon Morris. *An Introduction to the New Testament*. Grand Rapids: Zondervan, 1992. 537pp.

4.13.9   Childs, Brevard S. *The New Testament as Canon: An Introduction*. Philadelphia: Fortress, 1985. 572pp.

4.13.10   Drane, John. *Introducing the New Testament*. 3d ed. Minneapolis: Fortress, 2011. 478pp.

4.13.11   Ehrman, Bart D. *The New Testament: A Historical Introduction to the Early Christian Writings.* 4th ed. New York: Oxford University Press, 2008. 527pp.

4.13.12   Ellis, E. Earle. *The Making of the New Testament Documents.* Biblical Interpretation Series 39. Leiden: Brill, 1999. 517pp.

4.13.13   Koester, Helmut. *Introduction to the New Testament.* 2d ed. 2 vols. New York: Walter de Gruyter, 1995. 416/364pp.

4.13.14   Kümmel, Werner Georg. *Introduction to the New Testament.* Rev. ed. Nashville: Abingdon, 1975. 629pp.

4.13.15   Martin, Ralph P. *New Testament Foundations.* Rev. ed. 2 vols. Grand Rapids: Eerdmans, 1986. 326/470pp.

4.13.16   McDonald, Lee Martin, and Stanley E. Porter. *Early Christianity and Its Sacred Literature.* Peabody, Mass.: Hendrickson, 2000. 708pp.

4.13.17   Moule, C. F. D. *The Birth of the New Testament.* 3d ed. Black's New Testament Commentaries. London: Adam & Charles Black, 1981. 382pp.

4.13.18   Porter, Stanley E., and Lee Martin McDonald. *New Testament Introduction.* IBR Bibliographies 12. Grand Rapids: Baker, 1995. 234pp.

4.13.19   Powell, Mark Allan. *Introducing the New Testament: A Historical, Literary, and Theological Survey.* Grand Rapids: Baker Academic, 2009. 560pp.

4.13.20   Pregeant, Russell. *Encounter with the New Testament: An Interdisciplinary Approach.* Minneapolis: Fortress, 2009. 369pp.

4.13.21   Robinson, John A. T. *Redating the New Testament.* Philadelphia: Westminster, 1976. 369pp.

4.13.22   Schnelle, Udo. *The History and Theology of the New Testament Writings.* Minneapolis: Fortress, 1998. 573pp.

4.13.23   Schweizer, Eduard. *A Theological Introduction to the New Testament.* Nashville: Abingdon, 1991. 191pp.

4.13.24   Spivey, Robert A., and D. Moody Smith. *Anatomy of the New Testament: A Guide to Its Structure and Meaning.* 5th ed. Englewood Cliffs, N.J.: Prentice Hall, 1995. 513pp.

4.13.25   Strecker, Georg. *History of New Testament Literature.* Harrisburg, Pa.: Trinity Press International, 1997. 238pp.

4.13.26   Weiss, Bernhard. *A Manual of Introduction to the New Testament.* 2 vols. Foreign Biblical Library. London: Hodder & Stoughton, 1888. 420/426pp.

4.13.27   Wikenhauser, Alfred. *New Testament Introduction.* New York: Herder & Herder, 1958. 579pp.

4.13.28   Witherington, Ben, III. *Invitation to the New Testament: First Things.* New York: Oxford University Press, 2012. 480pp.

4.13.29   Zahn, Theodor. *Introduction to the New Testament.* 3 vols. Edinburgh: T&T Clark, 1909. 564/617/539pp.

4.14   New Testament Theology

Highly Recommended

4.14.1   Bultmann, Rudolf. *Theology of the New Testament.* 2 vols. in 1. Scribner Studies in Contemporary Theology. New York: Scribner's, 1955. 366/278pp.

Although many scholars consider Bultmann's method and conclusions to be questionable, this book commands attention because of its great influence on the study of NT theology in the twentieth century. Rejects the notion that the teaching of Jesus is the center of NT theology, since the theology of the NT focuses on christological claims made for Jesus, and (according to Bultmann) Jesus did not consider himself to be the Messiah. Thus, "the teaching of Jesus is the presupposition for NT theology but not part of that theology itself." New Testament theology is actually expressed in the major documents of the NT: the Pauline and Johannine materials. Bultmann attempts to understand NT theology in terms of its original cultural setting on the one hand, and its contemporary significance (i.e., its enduring significance for the human condition) on the other. Emphasizes the variety of theological views in the NT over against a coherent theology in the NT as a whole. Interprets NT theology according to the existentialism of Martin Heidegger, and inasmuch as Bultmann emphasizes the significance of NT theology for the human condition he insists that it should be understood in terms of anthropology. Contains numerous profound insights, but weakened by its wholesale dependence on a particular philosophical model and on questionable historical-critical reconstructions.

4.14.2   Caird, G. B. *New Testament Theology*. Edited by L. D. Hurst. Oxford: Clarendon, 1994. 498pp.

Characterized by the comprehensive knowledge, balanced judgment, and critical reverence for the text that one associates with Caird. Edited and completed by Caird's student, L. D. Hurst, after Caird's untimely death in 1984. Hurst completed the unfinished portions of the book from Caird's lecture notes, articles Caird left behind, and informed conjectures. Yet there are no evident seams or disjunctions of thought; Hurst has presented the thinking of his teacher with great reliability. Adopts a dialogical model that sets forth the theological claims of the various NT authors in the form of an imaginary roundtable discussion. Caird concludes with a discussion of the theology of Jesus. This roundtable approach has the advantage of recognizing both unity and diversity among the theologies of the NT writers (though Caird emphasizes the unity) and provides a dynamic interplay between their views that illuminates the theologies of the various NT writers and their relationship to one another.

4.14.3   Cullmann, Oscar. *The Christology of the New Testament*. New Testament Library. Rev. ed. Philadelphia: Westminster, 1963. 346pp.

Despite its age remains probably the most authoritative treatment of NT Christology, a central issue in NT theology. Examines the major titles used of Jesus in the NT in terms of their history in the OT and Judaism, in the general history of religion, and especially in the various NT writings. This emphasis on titles has limitations in that the NT presents its Christology in a variety of ways, not simply through titles. But Cullmann recognizes that the broader narrative descriptions of Jesus can in large part be understood in terms of one or more of these major titles. Acknowledges differences but emphasizes continuity and coherence in the employment of these titles among the various NT writers.

4.14.4 Guthrie, Donald. *New Testament Theology.* Downers Grove, Ill.: InterVarsity, 1981. 1064pp.

Written from a clearly evangelical perspective, seeks to present the theology of the NT in such a way as to stress its unity against the prevailing emphasis on the diversity and even incoherence of NT theology, and thus to serve as a "handbook to Christian doctrine." The volume is therefore arranged topically, according to major theological categories, e.g., "God," "Christology," "The Mission of Christ," and "The Future." Discusses the treatment of the theme by individual NT writers and concludes each category with a synthesis or summary. The introductory discussions of the major issues pertaining to NT theology are especially helpful, including such issues as the development of NT theology, the relationship between history and theology, and the tension between variety and unity within the NT.

4.14.5 Ladd, George Eldon. *A Theology of the New Testament.* Revised and edited by Donald A. Hagner. Grand Rapids: Eerdmans, 1993. 764pp.

The original 1974 edition of this comprehensive introduction to NT theology, something of a standard in evangelical circles, has been revised by Hagner, Ladd's student and successor at Fuller Theological Seminary. The value of the book is not limited to evangelicals, for it does not attempt to be novel but seeks to make the NT understandable and to show how the theology of the NT developed and coheres, and how it is distinctive in relation to its environment. An excellent introduction to NT theology: lucid, coherent, concentrating on the final form of the text, informed by critical discussion but not dependent on the more highly speculative critical theories. Argues that NT theology coheres around the concept of "salvation history." Revised edition includes two helpful new chapters dealing with the theology of each of the synoptic evangelists (by R. T. France) and with the issue of unity and diversity in the NT (by David Wenham).

4.14.6 Marshall, I. Howard. *New Testament Theology: Many Witnesses, One Gospel.* Downers Grove, Ill.: InterVarsity, 2004. 765pp.

Marshall is perhaps the most respected evangelical NT scholar alive, and this volume forms something of a capstone to a lifetime of serious scholarship on virtually every portion of the NT. It is written primarily for the nonspecialist, but Marshall's deep reservoir of knowledge and wisdom regarding the NT makes it useful for the seasoned scholar. Assumes an underlying theological unity amidst the diversity of the NT witnesses. Because Marshall accepts the reliability of the Gospel accounts he does not explore the theology of Jesus separately from the Gospels. Moves book

273

by book through the NT, presenting the "theological story" (essentially a theologically oriented rehearsal of the contents of the book), a discussion of major theological themes, a summary conclusion, and a brief bibliography. The conclusion to the volume is intended to offer a theological synthesis of the the individual books, providing something of a general NT theology; but its brevity prevents it from fulfilling this role in a very complete way.

4.14.7   Strecker, Georg. *Theology of the New Testament*. Edited by Friedrich Wilhelm Horn. Louisville: Westminster John Knox, 2000. 758pp.

Offers an alternative perspective and method to most of the other NT theologies recommended here. Emphasizes the diversity of the theology of the various NT witnesses virtually to the point of rejecting a unified or coherent "NT theology." Attempts to incorporate into the study of NT theology insights from a critical reconstruction of the development of the traditions within the NT. Volume is thus arranged historically, beginning with Paul, moving then to the synoptic tradition, then to the Johannine school, and concluding with Jude and James. Moreover, the study of the theology of each of these writers is based in part on the ways in which the NT writer has adapted and interpreted earlier traditions he inherited. Helpful in terms of understanding the distinctive theology of each NT writer, but insofar as Strecker sees continuity within NT theology only in terms of historical development rather than in terms of conceptual coherence, his presentation of NT theology as a whole will be of limited value for those readers who do not share his critical reconstruction of the NT.

4.14.8   Witherington, Ben, III. *The Indelible Image: The Theological and Ethical Thought World of the New Testament*. 2 vols. Downers Grove, Ill.: InterVarsity, 2009, 2010. 856/838pp.

Having written commentaries on every book of the NT (a highly unusual achievement), Witherington has drawn upon this extensive study to produce a massive work that presents the theology of the NT. Witherington recognizes that the study of the theology of the NT emerges from its exegesis and is inevitably linked to its ethics; and thus this work discusses exegetical and historical issues as a basis for the presentation of NT theology. Witherington employs higher-critical method, and rather consistently arrives at conservative positions. While acknowledging some theological diversity throughout the NT, Witherington emphasizes its unity. The first volume deals with the theological and ethical witness of individual NT books, while the second volume offers a synthetic description for the whole of the NT.

Also Significant

4.14.9   Adam, A. K. M. *Making Sense of New Testament Theology: "Modern" Problems and Prospects.* Studies in American Biblical Hermeneutics 11. Macon, Ga.: Mercer University Press, 1995. 238pp.

4.14.10   Balla, Peter. *Challenges to New Testament Theology: An Attempt to Justify the Enterprise.* Peabody, Mass.: Hendrickson, 1997. 279pp.

4.14.11   Bauckham, Richard. *Jesus and the God of Israel: God Crucified and Other Studies on the New Testament's Christology of Divine Identity.* Grand Rapids: Eerdmans, 2008. 285pp.

4.14.12   Bauer, Walter. *Orthodoxy and Heresy in Earliest Christianity.* Philadelphia: Fortress, 1971. 326pp.

4.14.13   Beale, G. K. *A New Testament Biblical Theology: The Unfolding of the Old Testament in the New.* Grand Rapids: Baker Academic, 2011. 1047pp.

4.14.14   Cullmann, Oscar. *Christ and Time: The Primitive Christian Conception of Time and History.* Rev. ed. Philadelphia: Westminster, 1964. 253pp.

4.14.15   Dodd, C. H. *The Apostolic Preaching and Its Developments.* London: Hodder & Stoughton, 1936. 240pp.

4.14.16   Dunn, James D. G. *Unity and Diversity in the New Testament: An Inquiry into the Character of Earliest Christianity.* Philadelphia: Westminster, 1977. 470pp.

4.14.17   Esler, Philip F. *New Testament Theology: Communion and Community.* Minneapolis: Fortress, 2005. 353pp.

4.14.18   Goppelt, Leonhard. *Theology of the New Testament.* 2 vols. Grand Rapids: Eerdmans, 1981. 292/348pp.

4.14.19   Hasel, Gerhard F. *New Testament Theology: Basic Issues in the Current Debate.* Grand Rapids: Eerdmans, 1978. 254pp.

4.14.20   Jeremias, Joachim. *New Testament Theology*. Part 1. *The Proclamation of Jesus*. New Testament Library. London: SCM, 1971. 330pp.

4.14.21   Kümmel, Werner Georg. *The Theology of the New Testament according to Its Major Witnesses, Jesus—Paul—John*. Nashville: Abingdon, 1973. 350pp.

4.14.22   Matera, Frank J. *New Testament Theology: Exploring Diversity and Unity*. Louisville: Westminster John Knox, 2007. 485pp.

4.14.23   Räisänen, Heikki. *Beyond New Testament Theology: A Story and a Programme*. Philadelphia: Trinity Press International, 1990. 206pp.

4.14.24   Reumann, John. *Variety and Unity in New Testament Thought*. Oxford Biblical Series. Oxford: Oxford University Press, 1991. 330pp.

4.14.25   Schlatter, Adolf. *The History of the Christ: The Foundation of New Testament Theology*. Grand Rapids: Baker, 1997. (Originally published in German in 1923.) 426pp.

4.14.26   ———. *The Theology of the Apostles: The Development of New Testament Theology*. Grand Rapids: Baker, 1988. (Originally published in German in 1922.) 452pp.

4.14.27   Schmithals, Walter. *The Theology of the First Christians*. Louisville: Westminster John Knox, 1997. 396pp.

4.14.28   Schnelle, Udo. *Theology of the New Testament*. Grand Rapids: Baker Academic, 2007. 910pp.

4.14.29   Schreiner, Thomas R. *New Testament Theology: Magnifying God in Christ*. Grand Rapids: Baker Academic, 2008. 990pp.

4.14.30   Thielman, Frank. *Theology of the New Testament: A Canonical and Synthetic Approach*. Grand Rapids: Zondervan, 2005. 798pp.

4.14.31   Vanhoozer, Kevin J., ed. *Theological Interpretation of the New Testament: A Book-by-Book Survey.* Grand Rapids: Baker Academic, 2005. 270pp.

4.14.32   Via, Dan O. *What Is New Testament Theology?* Guides to Biblical Scholarship New Testament Series. Minneapolis: Fortress, 2002. 160pp.

4.14.33   Weiss, Bernhard. *Biblical Theology of the New Testament.* 2 vols. Clark's Foreign Theological Library, new series, vols. 12–13. Edinburgh: T&T Clark, 1889–1892. 489/450pp.

4.15   New Testament Ethics

Highly Recommended

4.15.1   Hays, Richard B. *The Moral Vision of the New Testament: A Contemporary Introduction to New Testament Ethics.* San Francisco: HarperSanFrancisco, 1996. 508pp.

Probably the most important book on NT ethics to appear in a generation. Argues that the NT presents a unified ethical vision around the concepts of community, cross, and new creation. Discusses this ethical vision around four "tasks": (1) the "descriptive task" examines the moral vision presented by each of the NT writers; (2) the "synthetic task" attempts to identify the coherence of the NT's moral vision; (3) the "hermeneutical task" explores the method of appropriation of NT ethics to the contemporary scene and assesses the attempts of major theologians and biblical scholars to relate the NT to contemporary ethics; and (4) the "pragmatic task" illustrates the application of NT moral vision to the current issues of violence, divorce, homosexuality, ethnic conflict, and abortion. Valuable for its descriptions of the ethical teachings of the NT writers, although more incisive on the writings of Paul and John than on the other NT materials. Especially helpful in putting forth a comprehensive and coherent method for ethical appropriation.

4.15.2   Matera, Frank J. *New Testament Ethics: The Legacies of Jesus and Paul.* Louisville: Westminster John Knox, 1996. 325pp.

Lucid, nontechnical description of the ethical vision of Jesus and Paul as they are presented in the NT literature itself. Pursues literary analysis of the Gospels (in their final form) and the Pauline Epistles (both authentic and deuteropauline) to explore the ethical visions of Jesus and Paul. Recognizes that the ethics of Jesus and Paul must be linked to the message and experience of salvation that they both proclaim. While acknowledging diversity in these presentations, finds also a core of unity that gives coherence to the ethics of both Jesus and Paul. In contrast to Hays (§4.15.1) and Verhey (§4.15.4), gives no attention to the method of contemporary ethical appropriation.

4.15.3   Pregeant, Russell. *Knowing Truth, Doing Good: Engaging New Testament Ethics.* Minneapolis: Fortress, 2008. 388pp.

Is concerned primarily with the hermeneutical process involved in using NT passages as the basis for ethical reflection. After a helpful introduction describing the major ways in which scholars have used the NT for Christian ethics, Pregeant moves through the NT book by book, exploring significant ethical issues prompted by the text. Pregeant's own process in working with these passages ethically (which involves a combination of exegesis, biblical theology, and modern scientific knowledge) serves as a model for the hermeneutic of ethical decision-making. Not all readers will agree with the details of his process or with his conclusions, but all will benefit from the methodological insights and stimulation prompted by his careful work.

4.15.4   Verhey, Allen. *The Great Reversal: Ethics and the New Testament.* Grand Rapids: Eerdmans, 1984. 246pp.

Examines how the material of the NT bears on the church today as a community of moral discernment. Describes the moral teachings of the NT: the ethics of Jesus, of the developing Jesus traditions, and of the final form of the NT books. A survey of literature concerned with the method of using the NT for ethics is followed by a final section in which the author proposes a methodological model for the use of the NT in the church's task of moral discernment. Characterized by careful and informed analysis. Insightful judgment takes fully into account the complexities of the NT data and the process of appropriating them.

Also Significant

4.15.5   Brawley, Robert L., ed. *Character Ethics and the New Testament: Moral Dimensions of Scripture.* Louisville: Westminster John Knox, 2007. 269pp.

4.15.6   Dodd, C. H. *Gospel and Law: The Relation of Faith and Ethics in Early Christianity.* New York: Columbia University Press, 1951. 83pp.

4.15.7   Furnish, Victor Paul. *The Love Commandment in the New Testament.* Nashville: Abingdon, 1972. 240pp.

4.15.8   Houlden, J. L. *Ethics and the New Testament.* New York: Oxford University Press, 1977. 133pp.

4.15.9   Lohse, Eduard. *Theological Ethics of the New Testament.* Minneapolis: Fortress, 1991. 236pp.

4.15.10   Longenecker, Richard N. *New Testament Social Ethics for Today.* Grand Rapids, Eerdmans, 1984. 108pp.

4.15.11   Marxsen, Willi. *New Testament Foundations for Christian Ethics.* Minneapolis: Fortress, 1989. 319pp.

4.15.12   Sanders, Jack T. *Ethics in the New Testament: Change and Development.* London: SCM, 1986. 144pp.

4.15.13   Schnackenburg, Rudolf. *The Moral Teaching of the New Testament.* Rev. ed. New York: Herder & Herder, 1969. 387pp.

4.15.14   Schrage, Wolfgang. *The Ethics of the New Testament.* Minneapolis: Fortress, 1988. 369pp.

4.15.15   Yoder, John Howard. *The Politics of Jesus: Vicit Agnus Noster.* Rev. ed. Grand Rapids: Eerdmans, 1993. 252pp.

4.16   Use of the Old Testament in the New Testament

Highly Recommended

4.16.1   Beale, G. K. *Handbook on the New Testament Use of the Old Testament: Exegesis and Interpretation.* Grand Rapids: Baker Academic, 2012. 173pp.

Beale has focused his academic energies on the use of the OT within the NT and has become perhaps the leading authority in the field. Here he discusses the methodological issues and offers a specific (but not rigid) process for determining and interpreting the OT quotations and allusions within the NT, with multiple examples. The volume provides a methodological foundation for the commentary by Beale and Carson described immediately below. Accessible to the nonspecialist, but helpful for seasoned scholars.

4.16.2   Beale, G. K., and D. A. Carson, eds. *Commentary on the New Testament Use of the Old Testament.* Grand Rapids: Baker Academic, 2007. 1239pp.

Produced by a team of globally recognized evangelical NT scholars. Is meant to illumine how the several NT writers use the OT, and to present the multiple and varied intertextual connections between OT and NT. For each significant OT quotation or allusion, they discuss the NT book context, the immediate (or book-level) OT context, the use of the OT passage in Jewish sources, textual background (LXX, MT, etc.), the hermeneutic employed by the NT writer, concluding with theological use, which brings together findings in the aforementioned discussion to illumine the theological significance of the quotation or allusion. Contributors are committed to the unity of Scripture; and they thus tend to emphasize agreement or at least correlation between the NT quotation or allusion and the OT passage in its context, but not in a forced or simplistic way. An extremely thorough, responsible, and helpful resource.

4.16.3   Ellis, E. Earle. *The Old Testament in Early Christianity: Canon and Interpretation in the Light of Modern Research.* Grand Rapids: Baker, 1992. 188pp.

Writes from the conviction that "the use of the OT by the NT writers is the primary key to their theology." Divides volume essentially into two parts. The first addresses the OT canon in the early church, its contents (virtually identical with the OT as Protestants acknowledge it), its authority (normative Scripture), and its growth (adaptation of earlier traditions to meet contemporary needs). All of this discussion is foundational for the second part, dealing specifically with the use of the OT in the NT: OT quotations in the NT, exegetical methods employed by NT writers (and their relationship to Jewish exegetical practices), and perspectives and presuppositions relating to the NT writers' use of the OT. Informed and incisive analysis, illuminating the message of the NT and guiding contemporary exegetical practices, though tilted toward an evangelical Protestant perspective. Suggests that the NT's use of the OT is in continuity with the dynamics found within the OT itself and offers a model for Christians' contemporary use of Scripture.

4.16.4   Hays, Richard B. *Echoes of Scripture in the Letters of Paul.* New Haven, Conn.: Yale University Press, 1989. 240pp.

Although limited to Paul's use of the OT, this volume has significance for the broader question of the use of the OT by NT writers. Employs current literary insights concerning textuality to identify scriptural quotations or allusions ("echoes"), to determine their function (e.g., does the writer intend that the reader should consider the original context of the OT passage in question?), and to discern their significance for the meaning of the Pauline text. Analyzes selected passages in Paul's undisputed letters, and concludes that Paul's approach is more church-centered than Christ-centered. Specifically, Paul employs Scripture not as fulfillment of prophecy pointing to Jesus as the Messiah, but as prefigurement of the church, a model for the way the church is to live. Concludes with practical discussion as to whether the modern church should read Scripture in the same way. Especially helpful are the seven tests for determining when OT echoes are present in NT texts.

4.16.5   Longenecker, Richard N., *Biblical Exegesis in the Apostolic Period*. 2d ed. Grand Rapids: Eerdmans, 1999. 238pp.

Engaging and lucid examination of the "exegetical procedures" of the NT writers toward the OT, i.e., explores the major ways in which the NT writers understood the OT, based on their quotations of OT Scripture, and in comparison with the exegetical practices represented in Jewish documents from the same period (especially Talmud, Apocrypha, Dead Sea Scrolls, Targums, and Philo). Concludes with a brief but suggestive discussion on the normative character of these NT exegetical practices, i.e., considering whether NT exegetical practices obligate modern Christians to use the OT in the same way.

Also Significant

4.16.6   Bruce, F. F. *New Testament Development of Old Testament Themes*. Grand Rapids: Eerdmans, 1968. 122pp.

4.16.7   Dodd, C. H. *According to the Scriptures: The Substructure of New Testament Theology*. London: Nisbet, 1952. 145pp.

4.16.8   Ellis, E. Earle. *Paul's Use of the Old Testament*. Grand Rapids: Eerdmans, 1957. 204pp.

4.16.9   France, R. T. *Jesus and the Old Testament*. Downers Grove, Ill.: Inter-Varsity, 1971. 286pp.

4.16.10   Goppelt, Leonhard. *Typos: The Typological Interpretation of the Old Testament in the New.* Grand Rapids: Eerdmans, 1981. 264pp.

4.16.11   Juel, Donald. *Messianic Exegesis: Christological Interpretation of the Old Testament in Early Christianity.* Philadelphia: Fortress, 1988. 193pp.

4.16.12   Kaiser, Walter C., Jr., Darrell L. Bock, and Peter Enns. *Three Views on the New Testament Use of the Old Testament.* Grand Rapids: Zondervan, 2007. 256pp.

4.16.13   Lindars, Barnabas. *New Testament Apologetic: The Doctrinal Significance of the Old Testament Quotations.* London: SCM, 1961. 302pp.

4.16.14   Moyise, Steve. *The Old Testament in the New: An Introduction.* New York: Continuum, 2001. 160pp.

4.17   New Testament Apocrypha

See also HISTORY AND GEOGRAPHY: PRIMARY SOURCES (§4.4)

Highly Recommended

4.17.1   Ehrman, Bart D., and Zlatko Pleše, eds. *The Apocryphal Gospels: Texts and Translations.* Oxford: Oxford University Press, 2011. 608pp.

While Elliot (§4.17.2) and Hennecke (§4.17.4) include a broad range of apocryphal material, this volume contains only the apocryphal gospels; and in contrast to almost all other resources it contains both original text and translation (on facing pages). No attempt was made to provide a critical edition of the texts. All the apocryphal gospels from the early centuries of Christianity are included, with the exception of certain documents from the Nag Hammadi Library that are otherwise accessible in both original text and translation. The editors have provided a brief introduction to each gospel, and in the footnotes they have indicated connections with the canonical gospels.

4.17.2   Elliott, J. K., ed. *The Apocryphal New Testament: A Collection of Apocryphal Christian Literature in an English Translation.* Oxford: Oxford University Press, 1994. 747pp.

Complete revision of the classic work by Montague Rhodes James, originally published in 1924 and used for years as a reliable handbook for the most pertinent NT apocryphal literature. Does not attempt to be exhaustive, but includes those texts deemed to be the oldest, most important, influential, and popular. Yet unlike most other modern editions, is not limited to early texts but includes certain medieval texts considered to be significant for the history of Christian piety and devotion. Offers smooth, elegant, modern translations, along with formal introductions to each text that include fairly extensive bibliography of works in all European languages. Translations and especially introductions are more current than in Hennecke (§4.17.4).

4.17.3   Finegan, Jack. *Hidden Records of the Life of Jesus: An Introduction to the New Testament Apocrypha.* Philadelphia: Pilgrim, 1969. 320pp.

Introduction to the NT Apocrypha and the communities through which these apocryphal writings were transmitted. Does not attempt to deal with all apocryphal writings, but selects material considered most likely to contain fragments of early, extra-canonical tradition regarding Jesus. Begins with the most comprehensive description available of the communities responsible for the origin and transmission of apocryphal materials, then proceeds to the citation of texts (including both English translation and original Greek and Latin), with explanations pertaining to meaning of difficult elements and relationship to canonical passages.

4.17.4   Hennecke, Edgar. *New Testament Apocrypha.* Edited by Wilhelm Schneemelcher. 2 vols. Philadelphia: Westminster, 1963. 531/951pp.

The standard work on the NT Apocrypha. Most comprehensive and authoritative collection of NT apocryphal texts available. Originally produced by Hennecke in 1904, revised by Schneemelcher, and further revised and translated by R. McL. Wilson. First volume contains translations of apocryphal gospels and related writings, while the second contains writings related to the apostles, apocalypses, and related subjects. Each volume includes introductory articles surveying the entire field, followed by brief introductions to and translations of specific apocryphal books or texts. Does not include original language, nor does it offer commentary on the text.

Also Significant

4.17.5   Cameron, Ron, ed. *The Other Gospels: Non-Canonical Gospel Texts.* Philadelphia: Westminster, 1982. 191pp.

4.17.6   Charlesworth, James H., and James R. Mueller, eds. *The New Testament Apocrypha and Pseudepigrapha: A Guide to Publications, with Excurses on Apocalypses.* ATLA Bibliography Series 17. Metuchen, N.J.: Scarecrow, 1987. 450pp.

4.17.7   Elliott, J. K., ed. *The Apocryphal Jesus: Legends of the Early Church.* Oxford: Oxford University Press, 1996. 214pp.

4.17.8   Foster, Paul, ed. *The Non-Canonical Gospels.* London: T&T Clark, 2008. 201pp.

4.17.9   Grant, Robert M. *The Secret Sayings of Jesus.* Garden City, NY: Doubleday, 1960. 206pp.

4.17.10   Klauck, Hans-Josef. *Apocryphal Gospels: An Introduction.* London: T&T Clark, 2003. 236pp.

4.17.11   Lapham, Fred. *An Introduction to the New Testament Apocrypha.* London: T&T Clark, 2003. 193pp.

4.17.12   Pagels, Elaine. *The Gnostic Gospels.* New York: Random House, 1979. 182pp.

4.18   New Testament Commentaries: Multivolume

4.18.1   Alford, Henry. *The Greek Testament.* 7th ed. 4 vols. London: Rivingtons, 1875. Volumes average 400pp.

Produced by an Anglican clergyman of erudition and piety. Commentary is generally conservative on matters of authenticity and historical accuracy. Assumes some unusual positions, e.g., that the Synoptic Gospels were written independently of each other. Includes lengthy introductions dealing with critical matters, with extensive attention to textual criticism. Places Greek text at top of page, with text-critical notes and commentary on the Greek text below. Comments focus on linguistic matters (both lexical and syntactical), historical background, connections with other biblical passages (especially OT), and history of interpretation, especially the Fathers whom Alford often quotes in the original Greek or Latin. Attends seriously to theological implications.

4.18.2   Bengel, John Albert. *Gnomon of the New Testament*. Revised and translated by Charlton T. Lewis and Marvin R. Vincent. 2 vols. Philadelphia: Perkinpine & Higgins, 1864. 925/980pp.

A true classic in the history of interpretation. Bengel (1687–1752) was a towering pietistic scholar, a professor at the renowned Tübingen University, a pioneer in NT textual criticism, and the greatest commentator of his generation. Provides a brief introduction to each NT book, discussing its history and significance and offering a detailed outline of its contents. Comments themselves are terse, but they give careful attention to the original Greek, to immediate context, to connections with other biblical materials, and to theological insights.

4.18.3   Lenski, R. C. H. *Commentary on the New Testament*. 12 vols. Peabody, Mass.: Hendrickson, 1998. Volumes average 1000pp.

Frequently insightful commentary on the final form of the text, making use of context, lexical and syntactical analysis of original Greek, and canonical connections to determine theological meaning, with some attention to modern significance. Represents strongly Lutheran orthodox position. Originally published in the 1930s and 1940s and now somewhat dated. Written particularly for pastors to aid in preaching and teaching.

4.18.4   Nicoll, W. Robertson, ed. *The Expositor's Greek Testament*. 5 vols. London: Hodder & Stoughton, 1897–1910. Volumes average 500pp.

Intended to be a successor to Alford's *Greek Testament* (§4.18.1), in that it presents commentary on the whole Greek NT accessible to educated English-speaking readers. Prints the text of the Greek NT at the top of the page and fills the remainder of the page with brief comments on each verse. Contributors represent the most erudite British (especially Scottish) scholars of the period, all of them churchmen who revered the text as scripture. The commentary therefore frequently offers theological and even pastoral and devotional insights. In spite of its brevity and age, continues to have value but, like Alford (§4.18.1) and Bengel (§4.18.2), should be supplemented with more recent resources.

4.18.5   Wesley, John. *Explanatory Notes upon the New Testament*. London: W. Bowyer, 1755. 1054pp.

Written for "plain, unlettered men" who possess no knowledge of the original language. Suggests alterations at points to the Authorized Version. Attempts to make notes as short and plain as possible, avoiding interpretive or critical difficulties. Based on Bengel (§4.18.2), as Wesley acknowledges, which he translated, abbreviated, and modified. Attempts a "reasonable interpretation" of the text, by construing individual verses in light of the flow of the book or of the broader passage. Although helpful and engaging, one learns more about Wesley's theology, his understanding of the NT bases for his distinct beliefs, and his hermeneutic than about the text itself.

4.19   New Testament Commentaries: Series

Highly Recommended

4.19.1   Abingdon New Testament Commentaries. Edited by Victor Paul Furnish. 20 vols. Nashville: Abingdon, 1996–2011. Volumes average 275pp.

Like its corollary, the Abingdon Old Testament Commentaries (2.18.1), this series offers straightforward and informed explanation of the final form of the text, with attention to the text's theology. Includes often significant, though brief, interaction with both primary and secondary sources. Typically interprets passages according to their literary structure, their role within the biblical book, and their function within the canon, while attending also to matters of historical background that illumine the message of the text. No explicit attention to contemporary appropriation.

4.19.2   Augsburg Commentary on the New Testament. Edited by Roy A. Harrisville, Jack Dean Kingsbury, and Gerhard A. Krodel. 15 vols. Minneapolis: Augsburg, 1980–1990. Volumes average 300pp.

Concise and readable, purpose is to set forth the basic meaning of the text for laypersons, pastors, and teachers. Introductions include brief discussions of background issues. Commentary moves section by section, giving thoughtful attention to contemporary significance as well as to original meaning. Written by Lutheran seminary and university professors.

4.19.3   The IVP New Testament Commentary Series. Edited by Grant R. Osborne. 20 vols. currently available. Downers Grove, Ill.: InterVarsity, 1992–. Volumes average 175pp.

This series, written from an evangelical perspective and intended for pastors and teachers within the church, attempts to join sound exposition based on solid exegesis of the text with implications for theological reflection and Christian devotion relevant for the contemporary church. Contributors include important NT scholars as well as prominent clergy with a reputation for serious biblical exposition. Concentrates on the primary message of larger passages, but at points attends to specific significant exegetical problems.

4.19.4 Paideia Commentaries on the New Testament. Edited by Mikeal C. Parsons and Charles H. Talbert. 7 vols. currently available. Grand Rapids: Baker Academic, 2008. Volumes average 350pp.

Highly reputable NT scholars contribute to this series that represents a moderately critical perspective. Produced for pastors, college and university students, it is accessible to the nonspecialist. Emphasizes the ways in which ancient narrative and rhetoric inform the meaning of the text, as well as the role of the literary structure of the final form of the text. Attends also to matters of historical and cultural background. Is intentional in drawing out the theological meaning of the text. Is helpful for preaching and teaching, but one will seldom find profound or original insights.

4.19.5 The Pillar New Testament Commentary Series. Edited by D. A. Carson. 14 vols. currently available. Grand Rapids: Eerdmans, 1990–. Volumes average 350pp.

Offers solid and informed interpretation of the final form of the text from a conservative evangelical perspective, with some interaction with alternative perspectives. Attends to both original meaning and contemporary significance for the church. While based upon careful scholarship, is accessible to the nonspecialist. Volumes vary greatly in quality.

Series Whose Individual Volumes Are Frequently Included in Lists on Specific Books

4.19.6 Baker Exegetical Commentary on the New Testament. Edited by Robert W. Yarbrough and Robert H. Stein. Grand Rapids: Baker, 1996–.

4.19.7 Black's New Testament Commentary. Edited by Henry Chadwick. Peabody, Mass.: Hendrickson, 1960–.

4.19.8 Harper's New Testament Commentaries. Edited by Henry Chadwick. New York: Harper & Row, 1957–1973.

4.19.9 New International Commentary on the New Testament. Edited by Ned B. Stonehouse (1946–1962), F. F. Bruce (1962–1990), Gordon D. Fee (1990–2011), and Joel B. Green (2012–). Grand Rapids: Eerdmans, 1951–.

4.19.10 New International Greek Testament Commentary. Edited by I. Howard Marshall, W. Ward Gasque, and Donald A. Hagner. Grand Rapids: Eerdmans, 1978–.

4.19.11   Tyndale New Testament Commentaries. Edited by Leon Morris. Grand
Rapids: Eerdmans, 1958–1989.

4.20   The Gospels: Studies in the Gospels

Highly Recommended

4.20.1   Burridge, Richard A. *What Are the Gospels? A Comparison with Graeco-
Roman Biography.* Cambridge: Cambridge University Press, 1992.
292pp.

The issue of the genre of the Gospels (i.e., the nature of their literary form,
and whether it was common in the first-century Mediterranean world or
unique to these four NT books) has been disputed for hundreds of years.
This volume is the most current, comprehensive, and compelling study of
this key issue presently available. Traces the history of the debate, and carefully argues that the genre of our Gospels is not unique but that they share
the form of Greco-Roman biographies. Concludes with brief discussion of
the hermeneutical implications of this finding.

4.20.2   Green, Joel B., Jeannine K. Brown, and Nicholas Perrin, eds. *Dictionary
of Jesus and the Gospels: A Compendium of Contemporary Biblical Scholarship.* 2d ed. Downers Grove, Ill.: InterVarsity, 2013. 996pp.

Worthy successor to the monumental *Dictionary of Christ and the Gospels*
(§4.20.13). Attempts to make the most current Gospel scholarship accessible to students and pastors; but many of these articles also contribute to
the scholarly discussion. Represents generally conservative perspective, but
committed to responsible employment of critical tools and largely supportive of general critical consensus (e.g., two-source hypothesis for the
relationship between Synoptic Gospels). Complements more general Bible
dictionaries by offering in-depth treatment of subjects that pertain specifically to the Gospels. Deals with theological topics (e.g., Holy Spirit, Son of
David, Son of God), methods of interpretation, events (e.g., birth, temp-
tation), each of the four Gospels, background (e.g., Pharisees, revolutionary movements), and items of general interest (e.g., historical reliability of
the Gospels, preaching from the Gospels). Each entry concludes with brief
bibliography of works mostly in English, but also in German and French.

4.20.3   Kingsbury, Jack Dean. *Jesus Christ in Matthew, Mark, and Luke.* Proclamation Commentaries. Philadelphia: Fortress, 1981. 134pp.

Lucid and concise presentation of the major aspects of the theology of the Synoptic Gospels and the hypothetical sayings-source Q. Deals with each Gospel in turn, discussing the "accomplishment" of the evangelist; i.e., what he set out to do and how he shaped his Gospel in such a way as to fulfill his theological and pastoral purposes in writing; the figure of Jesus; the mission of Jesus; discipleship; and soteriology. Emphasizes final composition of the Gospel, giving little attention to sources lying behind the Gospels or to the evangelists' redaction of these sources. Contains extensive footnotes.

4.20.4 Streeter, Burnett Hillman. *The Four Gospels: A Study in Origins*. London: Macmillan, 1926. 624pp.

A classic work, still considered the standard in its discussion of the Synoptic Problem (i.e., the literary and historical relationships between the first three Gospels) and synoptic origins (i.e., the date and place of origin of the Gospels). Although Streeter's text-critical discussion of the manuscript tradition is somewhat dated, his arguments for the two-source hypothesis for the Synoptic Problem (still by far the predominant scholarly position) have become the basis for all subsequent debate on this central issue.

Also Significant

4.20.5 Bauckham, Richard. *The Gospels for All Christians: Rethinking the Gospel Audiences*. Grand Rapids: Eerdmans, 1998. 220pp.

4.20.6 ———. *Jesus and the Eyewitnesses: The Gospels as Eyewitness Testimony*. Grand Rapids: Eerdmans, 2006. 538pp.

4.20.7 Blomberg, Craig L. *The Historical Reliability of the Gospels*. 2d ed. Downers Grove, Ill.: InterVarsity, 2007. 416pp.

4.20.8 Bultmann, Rudolf. *The History of the Synoptic Tradition*. Rev. ed. New York: Harper & Row, 1963. 462pp.

4.20.9 Dibelius, Martin. *From Tradition to Gospel*. Cambridge: James Clarke, 1971. 311pp.

4.20.10 Farmer, William R. *The Synoptic Problem: A Critical Analysis*. New York: Macmillan, 1964. 308pp.

4.20.11   Foster, P., A. Gregory, J. S. Kloppenborg, and J. Verheyden, eds. *New Studies in the Synoptic Problem*. Bibliotheca Ephemeridum theologicarum Lovaniensium, no. 239. Louvain: Peeters, 2011. 961pp.

4.20.12   Gerhardsson, Birger. *The Reliability of the Gospel Tradition*. Peabody, Mass.: Hendrickson, 2001. 143pp.

4.20.13   Hastings, James, ed. *A Dictionary of Christ and the Gospels*. 2 vols. Edinburgh: T&T Clark, 1906. 936/912pp.

4.20.14   Hengel, Martin. *The Four Gospels and the One Gospel of Jesus Christ*. Harrisburg, Pa.: Trinity Press International, 2000. 354pp.

4.20.15   Kingsbury, Jack Dean, ed. *Gospel Interpretation: Narrative-Critical and Social-Scientific Approaches*. Harrisburg, Pa.: Trinity Press International, 1997. 307pp.

4.20.16   Lightfoot, Robert Henry. *History and Interpretation in the Gospels*. London: Hodder & Stoughton, 1935. 236pp.

4.20.17   Malina, Bruce J. *The Social World of Jesus and the Gospels*. London: Routledge, 1996. 255pp.

4.20.18   Malina, Bruce J., and Richard L. Rohrbaugh. *Social Science Commentary on the Synoptic Gospels*. 2d ed. Minneapolis: Fortress, 2003. 439pp.

4.20.19   Mays, James Luther, ed. *Interpreting the Gospels*. Philadelphia: Fortress, 1981. 307pp.

4.20.20   McKnight, Scot, and Matthew C. Williams. *The Synoptic Gospels: An Annotated Bibliography*. IBR Bibliographies 6. Grand Rapids: Baker, 2000. 126pp.

4.20.21   Mills, Watson E. *Index to Periodical Literature on Christ and the Gospels*. New Testament Tools and Studies 27. Leiden: Brill, 1998. 959pp.

4.20.22   Pennington, Jonathan T. *Reading the Gospels Wisely: A Narrative and Theological Introduction.* Grand Rapids: Baker Academic, 2012. 268pp.

4.20.23   Rohde, Joachim. *Rediscovering the Teaching of the Evangelists.* New Testament Library. London: SCM, 1968. 278pp.

4.20.24   Stein, Robert H. *Studying the Synoptic Gospels: Origin and Interpretation.* 2d ed. Grand Rapids: Baker, 2001. 302pp.

4.20.25   ————. *The Synoptic Problem: An Introduction.* Grand Rapids: Baker, 1987. 292pp.

4.20.26   Stonehouse, Ned B. *The Witness of the Synoptic Gospels to Christ.* Grand Rapids: Baker, 1979. Reprint of *The Witness of Matthew and Mark to Christ* (Philadelphia: Presbyterian Guardian, 1944, 269pp.) and *The Witness of Luke to Christ* (Grand Rapids: Eerdmans, 1951, 184pp.).

4.20.27   Taylor, Vincent. *The Formation of the Gospel Tradition.* London: Macmillan, 1960. 217pp.

4.20.28   Theissen, Gerd. *The Gospels in Context: Social and Political History in the Synoptic Tradition.* Minneapolis: Fortress, 1991. 320pp.

4.21   Studies in Specific Aspects of the Gospels

Highly Recommended

4.21.1   Blomberg, Craig L. *Interpreting the Parables.* 2d ed. Downers Grove, Ill.: InterVarsity, 2012. 463pp.

Offers a two hundred-page critical description of modern parable interpretation, then presents his own approach to parable interpretation, which involves a limited allegorical approach, taking Jesus' explanations as a guide to the interpretation of the parables. Accessible to the nonspecialist but written out of the deep resources of an expert on the parables. Complements the many contributions on the parables written from the mainline critical "consensus" that rejects significant use of the canonical explanations for parable interpretation.

4.21.2   Brown, Raymond E. *The Birth of the Messiah: A Commentary on the Infancy Narratives in the Gospels of Matthew and Luke.* Rev. ed. Anchor Bible Reference Library. New York: Doubleday, 1993. 752pp.

Written by a leading Roman Catholic scholar, the most complete study ever produced on the infancy narratives in Matthew and Luke. Deals thoroughly with virtually every aspect of these passages, with encyclopedic citation of both ancient and modern sources. Focuses on the distinctive emphases of Matthew and Luke. Combines meticulous critical analysis with reverence for the text as the church's Scripture. Gives significant attention to theological (and at points pastoral) issues. Although it deals only with the first two chapters of each of these Gospels, it sheds light on the theological purpose and message of the two Gospels as a whole.

4.21.3   ———. *The Death of the Messiah: A Commentary on the Passion Narratives.* 2 vols. Anchor Bible Reference Library. New York: Doubleday, 1994. 1608pp.

Companion to Brown's *Birth of the Messiah* (§4.21.2). Again, probably the most complete examination of the passion narratives ever compiled. Focuses on the final form of the text, and analyzes each of the four accounts in terms of the distinctive theological and pastoral concerns of each of the evangelists. Also attends to the historical events that lie behind the accounts and to the development of traditions in the sources that were used by the final Gospel writers. Historical conclusions are informed by critical analysis of the texts, but are generally supportive of the historical reliability of the accounts. Since the passion narrative climaxes each of the Gospels, this study provides insight into the theology of the Gospels as a whole.

4.21.4   Dodd, C. H. *The Parables of the Kingdom.* New York: Scribner's, 1961. 176pp.

Extremely significant book in the history of parable interpretation, by a towering British NT scholar. Follows Jülicher (*Die Gleichnisreden Jesu,* 1899–1910) in his insistence that the parables, as Jesus spoke them, had one point only, and that the details of the story had no spiritual counterpoint but existed simply to give "color" to the story, with the consequence that Jesus' "explanations" to the parables (e.g., Matt 13:18-23) were later creations by the church or the evangelists. Dodd thus concentrates on the meaning the parables had for Jesus, and gives no attention to their function within their final Gospel contexts. Argues that the parables consistently proclaimed "realized eschatology," i.e., announced that the end-time kingdom of God was already coming to earth in the ministry of Jesus. While somewhat dated, Dodd's book reflects massive learning and continues to provide helpful insights from historical background and the analysis of the language of the parables.

4.21.5   Hultgren, Arland J. *The Parables of Jesus: A Commentary.* Grand Rapids: Eerdmans, 2000. 522pp.

Of the many books that have appeared recently offering commentary on all or most of the NT parables, this is the most comprehensive in scope, current in its employment of the most recent insights, interactive with both older and more recent scholarship, inclusive in target audience (scholars, students, and pastors), and insightful into the theological implications of the exegesis. Holistic in method, giving attention to historical background and development of the parables in the tradition. Introduction describes the methods for identifying and classifying parables, the distinguishing features of parables, and various interpretive approaches. Examines the thirty-eight NT parables in depth. Line-by-line exegesis attends to the original form of each parable as Jesus spoke it, but concentrates on its meaning in its final Gospel context. In each case offers a fresh translation, notes on the text and translation, exegetical commentary, (brief) theological exposition, and select bibliography. Adopts critical methods, but conclusions are generally conservative.

4.21.6   Jeremias, Joachim. *Rediscovering the Parables.* New York: Scribner's, 1966. 191pp.

Like Dodd (§4.21.4), Jeremias is concerned to interpret the parables as Jesus understood them, and likewise follows Jülicher in insisting that these parables had one point only and contained no allegorical tendencies such as we find in the explanations to the parables the evangelists allegedly put into Jesus' mouth. Jeremias's academic focus was intertestamental and first-century Jewish background, and therefore he emphasized this setting much more than Dodd in his interpretation of the parables. He rejected as one-sided Dodd's insistence on "realized eschatology," and argued instead that we should interpret each parable in terms of the specific situation in Jesus' life that called it forth. Jeremias believed this almost always involved conflict, with the result that he saw the parables as "weapons of controversy." The continuing value of this work is its careful attention to the Jewish background of the details of each of Jesus' parables.

4.21.7   Scott, Bernard Brandon. *Hear Then the Parable: A Commentary on the Parables of Jesus.* Minneapolis: Fortress, 1989. 464pp.

Commentary on twenty-five parables of Jesus in the NT. This volume is set off from the many other commentaries on Jesus' parables by its creative synthesis of recent insights from the emerging literary, sociological, and cultural anthropological approaches with more traditional concerns for historical background, the authenticity of the parable, and the role of the parable within its final Gospel context. Characterized by original interpretations and fresh insights, especially from social history and from rabbinic and other Jewish sources. Even when the reader disagrees with the interpretation, it will often cause the reader to think in new ways about the parable and thus to obtain useful insights.

Also Significant

4.21.8   Bailey, Kenneth Ewing. *Poet and Peasant: A Literary Cultural Approach to the Parables in Luke.* Grand Rapids: Eerdmans, 1976. 238pp.

4.21.9   ———. *Through Peasant Eyes: More Lucan Parables, Their Culture and Style.* Grand Rapids: Eerdmans, 1980. 187pp.

4.21.10   Carter, Warren, and Heil, John Paul. *Matthew's Parables: Audience-Oriented Perspectives.* Catholic Biblical Quarterly Monograph Series 30. Washington, D.C.: Catholic Biblical Association of America, 1998. 255pp.

4.21.11   Gowler, David B. *What Are They Saying about the Parables?* New York: Paulist, 2000. 150pp.

4.21.12   Jones, Ivor Harold. *The Matthean Parables: A Literary and Historical Commentary.* Supplements to Novum Testamentum 80. Leiden: Brill, 1995. 602pp.

4.21.13   Kingsbury, Jack Dean. *The Parables of Jesus in Matthew 13: A Study in Redaction Criticism.* London: SCM, 1969. 180pp.

4.21.14   Kissinger, Warren S. *The Parables of Jesus: A History of Interpretation and Bibliography.* Metuchen, N.J.: Scarecrow, 1979. 439pp.

4.21.15   Lambrecht, Jan. *Once More Astonished: The Parables of Jesus.* New York: Crossroad, 1983. 245pp.

4.21.16 ———. *Out of the Treasure: The Parables in the Gospel of Matthew.* Louvain Theological and Pastoral Monographs 10. Louvain: Peeters, 1991. 299pp.

4.21.17 Longenecker, Richard N., ed. *The Challenge of Jesus' Parables.* Grand Rapids: Eerdmans, 2000. 324pp.

4.21.18 Manson, T. W. *The Sayings of Jesus: As Recorded in the Gospels according to St. Matthew and St. Luke Arranged with Introduction and Commentary.* London: SCM, 1949. 347pp.

4.21.19 Sider, John W. *Interpreting the Parables: A Hermeneutical Guide to Their Meaning.* Studies in Contemporary Interpretation. Grand Rapids: Zondervan, 1995. 283pp.

4.21.20 Theissen, Gerd. *The Miracle Stories of the Early Christian Tradition.* Philadelphia: Fortress, 1983. 322pp.

4.21.21 Tolbert, Mary Ann. *Perspectives on the Parables: An Approach to Multiple Interpretations.* Philadelphia: Fortress, 1979. 141pp.

4.21.22 Westermann, Claus. *The Parables of Jesus in Light of the Old Testament.* Edinburgh: T&T Clark, 1990. 211pp.

4.21.23 Young, Brad H. *The Parables: Jewish Tradition and Christian Interpretation.* Peabody, Mass.: Hendrickson, 1998. 332pp.

4.22   Studies in the Life of Christ

Highly Recommended

4.22.1 Crossan, John Dominic. *The Historical Jesus: The Life of a Mediterranean Jewish Peasant.* San Francisco: Harper, 1991. 507pp.

Written by the cochair of the Jesus Seminar, this volume reflects in general the perspective of that group. Crossan contends that the basic problem with life-of-Jesus research lies with method. Crossan seeks to remedy this situation by presenting a complex process of historical reconstruction, employing cultural anthropology, history of first-century Mediterranean culture, and literary criticism (i.e., the procedure separating the actual words and deeds of Jesus from later expansions). The Jesus that emerges represents a social and political response on the part of the peasantry to economic, religious, and political exploitation of the ruling classes. Though not a revolutionary, he sought to relieve the plight of the peasant class by proclaiming that God reigns on behalf of the oppressed, even in the most brutal circumstances. Jesus challenged the ruling authorities in indirect as well as direct ways, such as providing healing to the people through the use of magic, thereby diverting the sick away from the usual channels of healing that came through temple rituals and authorities. This view rejects the notion that Jesus thought of himself in any way as the Jewish Messiah and repudiates the notion that one can speak historically of a bodily resurrection. This volume is included under "highly recommended" not because it offers significant help in our understanding of the historical Jesus (since many scholars consider it to be tendentious and extremely conjectural), but because it represents a major stream of recent history-of-Jesus research.

4.22.2   Evans, Craig A., ed. *Encyclopedia of the Historical Jesus*. New York: Routledge, 2008. 728pp.

The 227 articles in this encyclopedia deal with major scholars, methods, themes, issues, institutions, figures, places, and groups related to the study of the historical Jesus. The contributors write from a moderately critical and generally moderately conservative perspective. The term "encyclopedia," is a bit misleading; the articles are quite short and thus it may be better to think of this work as a dictionary.

4.22.3   Keener, Craig S. *The Historical Jesus of the Gospels*. Grand Rapids: Eerdmans, 2009. 831pp.

Argues that the fundamental issue in Jesus-research involves the selection and assessment of sources. Seeks to demonstrate that the canonical Gospels provide the most reliable and accurate information regarding Jesus. Examines carefully the genre of the Gospels as ancient biography that incorporates eyewitness testimony. Includes a helpful critical review of modern Jesus studies. Detailed, informed, meticulous, and judicious, and constantly interacting with primary and secondary sources; footnotes and bibliography constitute about half the book. Explores "samples" of themes, sayings, and deeds that can be attributed to Jesus with a high degree of probability, showing how socioreligious context illumines Jesus' teachings and actions, and thus adds richness and depth to the historical reportage of the Gospels.

4.22.4   Meier, John P. *A Marginal Jew: Rethinking the Historical Jesus.* 4 vols. Anchor Bible Reference Library. New York: Doubleday, 1987, 1994, 2001, 2009. 496/1232/720/735pp.

The most massive, detailed, meticulous, and careful study available. Written by a leading American Roman Catholic scholar. Approach involves imagining an ecumenical group of historical critics (Catholic, Protestant, Jewish, Muslim) who were called upon to develop a reconstructed Jesus on whom they could all agree. Meier acknowledges that this reconstructed "historical Jesus" is not identical with the real Jesus, but a "scientific construct, a theoretical abstraction of modern scholars that coincides only partially with the real Jesus of Nazareth." Yet, according to Meier, this is the best scholarship can do. This "historical Jesus" is a prophet of the last days, which he proclaims as imminent and yet in some sense present in his own ministry; in recognition of that fact he called twelve disciples as a symbolic expression of the gathering of the twelve tribes of Israel, gave instruction regarding the true meaning of the Mosaic law, and performed exorcisms and healings.

4.22.5   Powell, Mark Allan. *Jesus as a Figure in History: How Modern Historians View the Man from Galilee.* 2d ed. Louisville: Westminster John Knox, 2013. 288pp.

The most comprehensive and balanced of all surveys of current Jesus research. Places the current interest in recovering the historical Jesus ("the third quest") in historical context by describing earlier attempts (beginning with Reimarus in 1774) and in methodological context by exploring the sources and criteria scholars employ in this task. Discusses in turn each of the major scholars or team of scholars involved in the current quest, describing their approach, summarizing their results (i.e., the portrait of Jesus they present), and identifying criticisms leveled by other historians. Concluding chapter identifies major issues that have emerged and presents likely future directions. Powell is descriptive throughout, and refuses to offer his own assessments; even evaluations of the various scholars are presented as reports of criticism leveled by others in the guild.

4.22.6   Sanders, E. P. *Jesus and Judaism.* Philadelphia: Fortress, 1985. 444pp.

Written by a leading authority on first-century Judaism. Adopts an approach that emphasizes critical reliance on canonical traditions (especially synoptic) and that depends heavily on the "social world" of first-century Judaism. Argues that Jesus adopted a restoration theology that insisted that God was about to restore Israel in fulfillment of covenant promises, and that Jesus considered himself the eschatological prophet who announced this restoration and who, along with his disciples, would be central to it. Jesus announced this restoration through his proclamation of the kingdom and his healings (a sign that God was already beginning to usher in his kingdom), and especially through the choosing of the twelve and the cleansing of the temple, which was the direct cause of his crucifixion. A highly regarded study, and one that significantly illumines the Jewish setting for Jesus' life and ministry. See also the author's abridged but more current study, *The Historical Figure of Jesus* (§4.22.33).

4.22.7   Schweitzer, Albert. *The Quest of the Historical Jesus: The First Complete Edition.* Edited by John Bowden. Minneapolis: Fortress, 2001. 608pp. (Originally published in German in 1906.)

A brilliant, groundbreaking work. Presents in engaging and elegant style a survey of the massive literature on the historical Jesus from Reimarus (1774) through Wrede (1901), who wrote just five years before the original German edition of Schweitzer's book. Schweitzer concluded that these scholars had not discovered the historical Jesus at all, but rather had created a Jesus in their own modern European image. Schweitzer himself insisted that the historical Jesus was committed to a "thoroughgoing eschatology," i.e., convinced that God was about to inaugurate the end-time kingdom and that his death would play a central role in that inauguration. This volume is of supreme importance in history-of-Jesus research, and in spite of its age it continues to have much to teach all subsequent Jesus research.

4.22.8   Wright, N. T. *Jesus and the Victory of God.* Vol. 2 of *Christian Origins and the Question of God.* Minneapolis: Fortress, 1996. 741pp.

This second volume in a projected six-volume project rests on the fundamental methodological and historical discussions of the first volume, *The New Testament and the People of God* (§4.13.7). Writes as a historian and a committed Christian, and insists that history and faith need not be separated in this search for Jesus; correspondingly, argues against Kähler's (*The So-Called Historical Jesus and the Historic Biblical Christ* [§4.22.26]) distinction (that often resurfaces) between the Jesus of history and the Christ of faith whom the church confesses. Insists that historians must take seriously the oldest traditions we have, i.e., those found within the Synoptic Gospels, and arrive at a portrait of the historical Jesus that best explains these data in light of what we know about first-century Judaism and the development of the Jesus movement into the second century. Moves from a reconstruction of Jesus' acts (deeds and speech) to conclusions regarding his beliefs and mindset. Sees Jesus as an eschatological prophet who declared the inauguration of God's kingdom and who believed that he, as the Messiah, was the embodiment of this coming kingdom. Although his portrait of Jesus generally follows the synoptic framework, Wright frequently offers bold and original insights on Jesus' life, words, and deeds.

4.22.9 ———. *The Resurrection of the Son of God.* Vol. 3 of *Christian Origins and the Question of God.* Minneapolis: Fortress, 2003. 817pp.

The most comprehensive and detailed examination of the resurrection of Jesus available, dealing carefully with primary sources from Judaism and early Christianity to show that the earliest Christians believed, with good reason, in Jesus' bodily resurrection and that the Christian understanding of Jesus' resurrection is in continuity with the resurrection hope of many in Judaism, with some mutations. Explicates the character of the resurrection and of Easter faith.

Also Significant

4.22.10 Allison, Dale C., Jr. *Constructing Jesus: Memory, Imagination, and History.* Grand Rapids: Baker Academic, 2010. 588pp.

4.22.11 Beilby, James K., and Paul Rhodes Eddy, eds. *The Historical Jesus: Five Views.* Downers Grove, Ill.: InterVarsity, 2009. 312pp.

4.22.12 Bock, Darrell L. *Studying the Historical Jesus: A Guide to Sources and Methods.* Grand Rapids: Baker, 2002. 224pp.

4.22.13 Borg, Marcus J. *Jesus: A New Vision.* San Francisco: Harper & Row, 1987. 216pp.

4.22.14 ———. *Meeting Jesus Again for the First Time: The Historical Jesus and the Heart of Contemporary Faith.* San Francisco: HarperSanFrancisco, 1994. 150pp.

4.22.15 Borg, Marcus J., and N. T. Wright. *The Meaning of Jesus: Two Visions.* London: SPCK, 1999. 290pp.

4.22.16 Bornkamm, Günther. *Jesus of Nazareth.* New York: Harper & Bros., 1960. 239pp.

4.22.17 Conzelmann, Hans. *Jesus.* Philadelphia: Fortress, 1973. 116pp.

4.22.18   Dalman, Gustaf. *The Words of Jesus: Considered in the Light of Post-Biblical Jewish Writings and the Aramaic Language.* Edinburgh: T&T Clark, 1902. 350pp.

4.22.19   DeJonge, Marinus. *Jesus: The Servant-Messiah.* New Haven, Conn.: Yale University Press, 1991. 115pp.

4.22.20   Dodd, C. H. *The Founder of Christianity.* New York: Macmillan, 1970. 181pp.

4.22.21   Dunn, James D. G. *The Evidence for Jesus.* Atlanta: John Knox, 1985. 113pp.

4.22.22   Evans, C. Stephen. *The Historical Christ and the Jesus of Faith: The Incarnational Narrative as History.* Oxford: Clarendon, 1996. 386pp.

4.22.23   Evans, Craig A., ed. *The Historical Jesus: Critical Concepts in Religious Studies.* 4 vols. New York: Routledge, 2004. 1600pp.

4.22.24   ———. *Jesus.* IBR Bibliographies 5. Grand Rapids: Baker, 1992. 152pp.

4.22.25   Johnson, Luke Timothy. *The Real Jesus: The Misguided Quest for the Historical Jesus and the Truth of the Traditional Gospels.* San Francisco: HarperSanFrancisco, 1996. 182pp.

4.22.26   Kähler, Martin. *The So-Called Historical Jesus and the Historic Biblical Christ.* Philadelphia: Fortress, 1964. 153pp. (Originally published in German in 1896.)

4.22.27   Keck, Leander E. *A Future for the Historical Jesus: The Place of Jesus in Preaching and Theology.* Nashville: Abingdon, 1971. 271pp.

4.22.28   ———. *Who Is Jesus? History in Perfect Tense.* Personalities of the New Testament. Minneapolis: Fortress, 2001. 207pp.

4.22.29   Kissinger, Warren S. *The Lives of Jesus: A History and Bibliography.* New York: Garland, 1985. 230pp.

4.22.30   Mack, Burton L. *A Myth of Innocence: Mark and Christian Origins.* Philadelphia: Fortress, 1988. 432pp

4.22.31   Marshall, I. Howard. *I Believe in the Historical Jesus.* Grand Rapids: Eerdmans, 1977. 253pp.

4.22.32   Robinson, James M. *A New Quest of the Historical Jesus.* Studies in Biblical Theology 25. London: SCM, 1959. 128pp.

4.22.33   Sanders, E. P. *The Historical Figure of Jesus.* New York: Penguin, 1994. 337pp.

4.22.34   Strauss, David Friedrich. *The Life of Jesus Critically Examined.* Lives of Jesus Series. Philadelphia: Fortress, 1972. 812pp. (Originally published in German 1835.)

4.22.35   Stuhlmacher, Peter. *Jesus of Nazareth, Christ of Faith.* Peabody, Mass.: Hendrickson, 1993. 109pp.

4.22.36   Vermes, Geza. *Jesus in the Jewish World.* London: SCM, 2010. 268pp.

4.22.37   Weiss, Johannes. *Jesus' Proclamation of the Kingdom of God.* Philadelphia: Fortress, 1971. 148pp. (Originally published in German in 1892.)

4.22.38   Witherington, Ben, III. *The Christology of Jesus.* Minneapolis: Fortress, 1990. 310pp.

4.22.39   ———. *The Jesus Quest: The Third Search for the Jew of Nazareth.* Downers Grove, Ill.: InterVarsity, 1995. 304pp.

4.23   Gospel Harmonies/Synopses

Highly Recommended

4.23.1   Aland, Kurt, ed. *Synopsis of the Four Gospels: Completely Revised on the Basis of the Greek Text of Nestle-Aland 26th Edition and the Greek New Testament 3d edition.* New York: United Bible Societies, 1985. 361pp.

Now generally considered the standard, it is the most complete and accurate Gospel synopsis, employing the best and most current Greek text. Greek and English (RSV) appear on opposite pages. Substantial text-critical notes (from Nestle-Aland, 26th ed.) are supplied under the Greek text with comparisons with readings of other major English translations under the English text. Presents parallel passages in columns, and (unlike Throckmorton [§4.23.3]) includes John along with the Synoptics.

4.23.2   Huck, Albert. *A Synopsis of the First Three Gospels with the Addition of the Johannine Parallels.* 13th ed. Revised by Heinrich Greeven. Grand Rapids: Eerdmans, 1982. 298pp.

Huck's Synopsis appeared first in 1892. This most recent edition is based on Greeven's own recension of the Greek text. Includes extensive textual apparatus. Refers to parallels in apocryphal gospels and similar noncanonical sources. Notes are in German and English, but (unlike Aland [§4.23.1]) the NT text is entirely in Greek. Has some helpful features absent in Aland, but the use of Greeven's own Greek text and textual apparatus renders it less useful than Aland.

4.23.3   Throckmorton, Burton H. *Gospel Parallels: A Comparison of the Synoptic Gospels.* 5th ed. Nashville: Thomas Nelson, 1992. 212pp.

Arranges Synoptic Gospels in parallel columns, employing the New Revised Standard Version. Does not include John, except in footnotes. Scriptural cross-references and selective current information on textual variants are helpful for those who know Greek. Notes all parallels with the Gospel of Thomas and other noncanonical writings, especially papyri, church fathers, and NT Apocrypha. Includes index of Gospel and noncanonical parallels. The most complete and current synopsis based on the English Bible.

Also Significant

4.23.4   Crook, Zeba A. *Parallel Gospels: A Synopsis of Early Christian Writing.* New York: Oxford University Press, 2012. 320pp.

4.23.5   Funk, Robert W., ed. *New Gospel Parallels.* 2 vols. Foundations and Facets: New Testament. Philadelphia: Fortress, 1985. 492/396pp.

4.23.6   ———, ed. *New Gospel Parallels.* Vol. 1.2. Mark. Rev. ed. Sonoma, Calif.: Polebridge, 1990. 271pp.

4.23.7   Green, Joel B., and Gil Shin, eds. *Common English Bible Gospel Parallels.*
Nashville: Common English Bible, 2012. 264pp.

4.23.8   Orchard, John Bernard, ed. *A Synopsis of the Four Gospels: Arranged
according to the Two-Gospel Hypothesis.* Macon, Ga.: Mercer University
Press, 1982. 294pp.

4.23.9   Sparks, H. F. D. *The Johannine Synopsis of the Gospels.* New York: Harper
& Row, 1974. 96pp.

4.23.10   ———. *A Synopsis of the Gospels: The Synoptic Gospels with the Johannine
Parallels.* Philadelphia: Fortress, 1964. 248pp.

4.23.11   Stevens, William Arnold, and Ernest De Witt Burton. *A Harmony of the
Gospels for Historical Study.* New York: Scribner's, 1932. 283pp.

4.23.12   Swanson, Reuben J. *The Horizontal Line Synopsis of the Gospels.* Dillsboro:
Western North Carolina Press, 1975. 597pp.

4.23.13   Thomas, Robert L., and Stanley N. Gundry, eds. *The NIV Harmony of
the Gospels: With Explanations and Essays.* San Francisco: Harper & Row,
1988. 341pp.

4.24 Matthew

See also STUDIES ON THE SERMON ON THE MOUNT (§4.25)

Highly Recommended

4.24.1   Davies, W. D., and Dale C. Allison. *A Critical and Exegetical Commentary on the Gospel according to Saint Matthew.* 3 vols. International Critical Commentary. Edinburgh: T&T Clark, 1988–1997. 731/807/789pp.

Produced by two mature scholars who have written widely in NT studies, with particular attention to Matthew. The most detailed commentary
available; the massive first volume covers only the introduction and chs.
1–7. The authors claim to opt for a holistic approach that takes seriously

the traditional historical-critical analysis while also employing insights from the emerging literary- and canonical-critical methods. In fact, however, they typically focus attention on historical parallels (mostly Jewish) and the details of Matthew's redaction of his sources, with little notice of the flow of the narrative or the function of passages within the broader literary program of the canonical Gospel. Nevertheless, contains a wealth of background information, exhaustive citations of rabbinic and other Jewish parallels, and clear presentation of the history of interpretation.

4.24.2   France, R. T. *The Gospel of Matthew.* New International Commentary on the New Testament. Grand Rapids: Eerdmans, 2007. 1169pp.

Produced by a prominent British evangelical scholar who is globally recognized as an authority on Matthew's Gospel. Includes a relatively brief introduction, inviting readers to consult the fuller presentation of introductory matters in his earlier book, *Matthew: Evangelist and Teacher*, listed immediately below. Wishes to avoid dependence upon uncertain historical claims (e.g., exactly when and where the Gospel was produced, and detailed reconstructions of the relationship between Matthew's church and the synagogue) in favor of basing exegesis upon the final form of the text and the historical considerations about which there can be little disagreement. A careful, judicious commentary, whose primary advantage is the constant attempt to situate and interpret smaller passages or details within the broader framework of larger sections and the Gospel in the large.

4.24.3   ———. *Matthew: Evangelist and Teacher.* Grand Rapids: Zondervan, 1989. 345pp.

This volume is probably the most complete and helpful introduction to Matthew's Gospel. Deals with a range of introductory issues (including some theological ones) that France believes are most interesting to modern readers who approach the Gospel as the church's Scripture and most significant for its interpretation. At certain points argues against easy acceptance of "critical orthodoxy," i.e., the tendency on the part of critical scholars to consider certain conclusions axiomatic. Even if one does not always agree with France (e.g., he thinks it likely, though not certain, that the Apostle Matthew wrote this Gospel), one will encounter informed and carefully reasoned arguments and a healthy reminder of the tentative character of many generally accepted critical conclusions.

4.24.4   Hagner, Donald A. *Matthew.* 2 vols. Word Biblical Commentary. Dallas: Word, 1993. 935pp.

Overall the most helpful commentary on Matthew presently available in English. Carefully considers Matthew's redaction of the traditions he inherited, especially Mark and Q, but gives greater attention to the final composition of the text. Consistently presents the major exegetical options and through lively interaction with the history of interpretation arrives at judicious and informed conclusions. In contrast to most volumes in this series, the "explanation" section develops theological issues that are of concern to contemporary Christians. Embraces critical methods, but conclusions are generally conservative, especially in regard to historical authenticity.

4.24.5   Kingsbury, Jack Dean. *Matthew: Structure, Christology, Kingdom.* New preface. Minneapolis: Fortress, 1989. 178pp.

Overall the most compelling presentation of Matthew's theology. Employs "composition criticism," an approach that considers Matthew's redaction of his sources but gives primary attention to the final composition of the Gospel. Argues for a tripartite structure to the Gospel (1:1–4:16; 4:17–16:20; 16:21–28:20), in which each major division reaches its climax in the declaration that Jesus is Son of God. On this and other grounds argues that Son of God is the major christological category in Matthew. Discusses all christological titles and develops their meaning and role. Insists also that Matthew has a bipartite view of salvation history, dividing this history into the time of preparation (prophets) and the time of fulfillment in Christ earthly and exalted, thus linking closely the ministry of the earthly Jesus to the present period of the church.

4.24.6   Luz, Ulrich. *Matthew 1–7: A Commentary.* Minneapolis: Augsburg, 1989. 460pp. *Matthew 8–20: A Commentary.* Hermeneia: A Critical and Historical Commentary on the Bible. Minneapolis: Fortress, 2001. 607pp. *Matthew 21–28: A Commentary.* Hermeneia: A Critical and Historical Commentary on the Bible. Minneapolis: Fortress, 2005. 681pp.

Originally published in German as part of the series, Evangelish-Katholischer Kommentar zum Neuen Testament, which adopts the interpretive method of *Wirkungsgeschichte*, usually translated "history of influence," and involves interpreting passages in light of the "history, reception, and actualizing of a text in media other than the commentary, e.g., in sermons, canonical law, hymnody, art, and in the actions and sufferings of the church." Thus, all the ways in which a passage has been appropriated can serve the heuristic function of helping readers discover meaning in the text that might otherwise be missed. Luz also attends to historical background (especially intertestamental and first-century Jewish writings) and history of the tradition towards its final form in Matthew, with special attention to Matthew's redaction of his sources. Luz masterfully integrates all these aspects into a holistic theological interpretation of the text.

4.24.7   Nolland, John. *The Gospel of Matthew: A Commentary on the Greek Text.* New International Greek Testament Commentary. Grand Rapids: Eerdmans, 2005. 1481pp.

Like France, Nolland is a prominent British evangelical NT scholar. But unlike France, Nolland rejects the notion of Matthean authorship of the First Gospel and adopts the view that the author of Matthew's Gospel engaged in consistant and deliberate editing of his Markan source. Nolland adopts an eclectic method, employing primarily redaction criticism, but combining it with narrative criticism and considerations of ancient rhetoric. Is strong in discussion of technical textual matters, description of editorial processes or historical background, and interaction with (mostly modern) history of interpretation, but weaker in probing the depths of the theology of the text. Includes helpful bibliographies preceding each section and on occasion preceding the discussion of significant verses.

Also Significant

4.24.8   Aune, David E., ed. *The Gospel of Matthew in Current Study: Studies in Memory of William G. Thompson.* Grand Rapids: Eerdmans, 2001. 191pp.

4.24.9   Bacon, Benjamin W. *Studies in Matthew.* New York: Henry Holt, 1930. 533pp.

4.24.10   Balch, David L., ed. *Social History of the Matthean Community: Cross-Disciplinary Approaches.* Minneapolis: Fortress, 1991. 286pp.

4.24.11   Bauer, David R. *The Structure of Matthew's Gospel: A Study in Literary Design.* Journal for the Study of the New Testament Supplement Series 31. Sheffield: Almond, 1988. 182pp.

4.24.12   Bauer, David R., and Mark Allan Powell, eds. *Treasures New and Old: Contributions to Matthean Studies.* Society of Biblical Literature Symposium Series 1. Atlanta: Scholars, 1996. 454pp.

4.24.13   Beare, Francis Wright. *The Gospel according to Matthew.* San Francisco: Harper & Row, 1981. 550pp.

4.24.14   Bornkamm, Günther, Gerhard Barth, and Heinz Joachim Held. *Tradition and Interpretation in Matthew.* New Testament Library. Philadelphia: Westminster, 1963. 307pp.

4.24.15   Carter, Warren. *Matthew and Empire: Initial Explorations.* Harrisburg, Pa.: Trinity Press International, 2001. 249pp.

4.24.16   ———. *Matthew and the Margins: A Sociopolitical and Religious Reading.* Maryknoll, NY: Orbis, 2000. 636pp.

4.24.17   ———. *Matthew: Storyteller, Interpreter, Evangelist.* Rev. ed. Peabody, Mass.: Hendrickson, 2004. 287pp.

4.24.18   Duling, Dennis C. *A Marginal Scribe: Studies in the Gospel of Matthew in a Social Scientific Perspective.* Eugene, Ore.: Cascade, 2012. 385pp.

4.24.19   Garland, David E. *Reading Matthew: A Literary and Theological Commentary on the First Gospel.* New York: Crossroad, 1993. 269pp.

4.24.20   Gundry, Robert H. *Matthew: A Commentary on His Handbook for a Mixed Church under Persecution.* Grand Rapids: Eerdmans, 1994. 685pp.

4.24.21   Harrington, Daniel J. *The Gospel of Matthew.* Sacra Pagina. Collegeville, Minn.: Michael Glazier, 1991. 429pp.

4.24.22   Hill, David. *The Gospel of Matthew.* New Century Bible Commentary. Grand Rapids: Eerdmans, 1972. 367pp.

4.24.23   Keener, Craig S. *A Commentary on the Gospel of Matthew.* Grand Rapids: Eerdmans, 1999. 1040pp.

4.24.24   Kilpatrick, G. D. *The Origins of the Gospel according to St. Matthew.* Oxford: Clarendon, 1946. 150pp.

4.24.25   Kingsbury, Jack Dean. *Matthew*. 3d ed. Nappanee, Ind.: Evangel, 1998. 134pp.

4.24.26   ———. *Matthew as Story*. Rev. ed. Philadelphia: Fortress, 1988. 181pp.

4.24.27   Luz, Ulrich. *Matthew in History: Interpretation, Influence, and Effects*. Minneapolis: Fortress, 1994. 108pp.

4.24.28   ———. *The Theology of the Gospel of Matthew*. New Testament Theology. Cambridge: Cambridge University Press, 1995. 166pp.

4.24.29   McNeile, Alan Hugh. *The Gospel according to St. Matthew: The Greek Text with Introduction, Notes, and Indices*. London: Macmillan, 1938. 448pp.

4.24.30   Powell, Mark Allan. *God with Us: A Pastoral Theology of Matthew's Gospel*. Minneapolis: Fortress, 1995. 156pp.

4.24.31   ———, ed. *Methods for Matthew*. Cambridge: Cambridge University Press, 2009. 261pp.

4.24.32   Schnackenburg, Rudolf. *The Gospel of Matthew*. Grand Rapids: Eerdmans, 2002. 329pp.

4.24.33   Senior, Donald. *What Are They Saying about Matthew?* Rev. ed. New York: Paulist, 1996. 136pp.

4.24.34   Stanton, Graham N. *A Gospel for a New People: Studies in Matthew*. Edinburgh: T&T Clark, 1992. 424pp.

4.25   Studies on the Sermon on the Mount

Highly Recommended

4.25.1   Allison, Dale C. *The Sermon on the Mount: Inspiring the Moral Imagination*. New York: Crossroad, 1999. 188pp.

Although relatively short, this commentary packs a great deal of useful insight. Insists on interpreting the Sermon in light of its function within the whole narrative of Matthew's Gospel rather than in virtual isolation from its context. Gives significant attention also to Jewish background and the history of interpretation throughout the Christian era: premodern and modern. Theologically oriented, it addresses moral questions in light of perduring realities of Christian discipleship and not simply in terms of postmodern Western Christianity.

4.25.2   Baumen, Clarence. *The Sermon on the Mount: The Modern Quest for Its Meanings*. Macon, Ga.: Mercer University Press, 1985. 440pp.

Detailed examination of the work of nineteen prominent thinkers who have shaped modern views regarding the Sermon, beginning with Tolstoy. Each entry includes a biographical sketch of the scholar so as to illuminate the role played by background, experience, and culture in that scholar's interpretation. Gives special attention to the role of presuppositions in determining the scholar's method and conclusions. Includes extended quotations from primary sources. Final synthetic chapters focus on major theological aspects. Illuminates the character of the Sermon and its contemporary significance for Christians.

4.25.3   Betz, Hans Dieter. *The Sermon on the Mount: A Commentary on the Sermon on the Mount, Including the Sermon on the Plain* (Matthew 5:3–7:27 and Luke 6:20–49). Hermeneia: A Critical and Historical Commentary on the Bible. Minneapolis: Fortress, 1995. 695pp.

One of the most massive studies of the Sermon ever produced. After presenting an introductory survey of the Sermon on the Mount and Sermon on the Plain, which includes discussion of the history of interpretation (beginning with the Fathers), source and tradition history, and genre of the Sermon, Betz offers a detailed commentary on each verse, giving more attention to Matthew's Sermon on the Mount than to Luke's Sermon on the Plain. Adopts the unusual source theory that the Sermon arose as a summary of Jesus' teachings in the hypothetical sayings source Q in conversation with Hellenistic philosophy, and that this summary developed in two directions: for Jewish Christians (adopted by Matthew), and for Gentile Christians (adopted by Luke). Consequently, Betz tends to ignore the broader context of Matthew's (and Luke's) Gospel for the interpretation of the Sermon and to emphasize the Hellenistic rather than Jewish background. The resultant portrait of Jesus in the Sermon is at odds with that of Matthew's Gospel. Most scholars have rejected this source theory. The value of the commentary lies in its minute attention to every detail of the text, its in-depth exploration of exegetical problems, and its presentation of Jewish, and especially Greco-Roman, parallels.

4.25.4   Davies, W. D. *The Setting of the Sermon on the Mount.* Cambridge: Cambridge University Press, 1966. 546pp.

Explores four contexts of the Sermon: (1) the world of Matthew's Gospel and of Matthew's church (including the role of Jamnia and the rise of formative Judaism for Matthew's community); (2) Jewish messianic expectations and hopes of a messianic teacher and lawgiver (including the relationship of Qumran's "Teacher of Righteousness" to the Jesus of the Sermon); (3) the first-century church, especially Paul, the hypothetical sayings source Q, and M (Matthew's "special source"); and (4) the life of Jesus, i.e., the extent to which the Sermon presents the actual teaching of Jesus. Somewhat dated in terms of issues pursed, methods employed, and sources emphasized, but remains a helpful analysis of pertinent background and an astute interpretation of the Sermon.

4.25.5   Guelich, Robert A. *The Sermon on the Mount: A Foundation for Understanding.* Waco, Tex.: Word, 1982. 451pp.

One of the few full-scale commentaries on the Sermon, and the most helpful for the use of the Sermon in preaching and teaching within the church. Unlike Betz (§4.25.3), emphasizes the Sermon's role in Matthew's Gospel in terms both of its literary development and its meaning, especially its theological message. Introduction offers a brief history of interpretation and discussions of Sermon's role in Matthew, its sources, and its structure. Verse-by-verse commentary makes use of critical tools (e.g., text, source, form, and redaction criticism), historical background (especially Jewish, and particularly rabbinic), and history of interpretation. Focuses on the final form of the text to determine what the Sermon meant for the evangelist and his original audience. Full of rich theological discussion. Scholars will find it illuminating, and students and pastors will find it accessible and engaging.

Also Significant

4.25.6   Bonhoeffer, Dietrich. *The Cost of Discipleship.* Rev. ed. New York: Macmillan, 1963. 352pp. (Originally published in German in 1937.)

4.25.7   Carson, D. A. *The Sermon on the Mount: An Evangelical Exposition of Matthew 5–7.* Grand Rapids: Baker, 1978. 157pp.

4.25.8   Greenman, Jeffrey P., Timothy Larsen, and Stephen R. Spencer, eds. *The Sermon on the Mount through the Centuries: From the Early Church to John Paul II.* Grand Rapids: Brazos, 2007. 280pp.

4.25.9   Kissinger, Warren S. *The Sermon on the Mount: A History of Interpretation and Bibliography.* ATLA Bibliography Series 3. Metuchen, N.J.: Scarecrow, 1975. 296pp.

4.25.10   Patte, Daniel. *The Challenge of Discipleship: A Critical Study of the Sermon on the Mount as Scripture.* Harrisburg, Penn.: Trinity Press International, 1999. 265pp.

4.25.11   ———. *Discipleship according to the Sermon on the Mount: Four Legitimate Readings, Four Plausible Views of Discipleship and Their Relative Values.* Valley Forge, Pa.: Trinity Press International, 1996. 416pp.

4.25.12   Strecker, Georg. *The Sermon on the Mount: An Exegetical Commentary.* Nashville: Abingdon, 1988. 223pp.

4.25.13   Talbert, Charles H. *Reading the Sermon on the Mount: Character Formation and Ethical Decision Making in Matthew 5–7.* Grand Rapids: Baker, 2004. 181pp.

4.26 Mark

Highly Recommended

4.26.1   Collins, Adela Yarbro. *Mark.* Hermeneia: A Critical and Historical Commentary on the Bible. Minneapolis: Fortress, 2007. 894pp.

Scholars have long believed that Mark is a Roman Gospel, but no commentary has explored in such detail the Roman and especially Hellenistic connections in Mark. Collins considers Mark to be "an eschatological counterpart of foundational sacred history," written as an eschatological historical monograph in analogy to the great OT Mosaic narratives in order to proclaim "God's activity in Jesus to reform the people and bring in the new age." Thus Mark is written against the backdrop of both the OT and Greek and Hellenistic heroes. This emphasis upon Greek and Hellenistic analogies is both a strength and a weakness, since many will be unpersuaded by some of the Greco-Roman connections and may consider that Collins has pursued parallels ("parallelomania") to the neglect of some of the narrative, structural, and rhetorical features in the text. Commentary is written from a historical-critical perspective, with only slight use of newer methods. Interacts much with recent interpreters but does very little with premodern ones.

4.26.2   Evans, Craig A. *Mark 8:27–16:20*. Word Biblical Commentary. Nashville: Thomas Nelson, 2001. 594pp.

This volume completes the Word Biblical Commentary on Mark, which began with Guelich's volume on 1:1–8:26 (§4.26.4). Evans is in essential agreement with Guelich's positions (especially regarding historical reliability of Mark's account), and his commentary is of the same character and high quality as the first volume. Emphasizes more than does Guelich the Greco-Roman cultural background—and insists that the theological purpose of Mark is to challenge the claims of that culture and especially to repudiate the emperor cult by affirming that Jesus is king precisely in his role as crucified one, his royalty validated by God through the resurrection. Gives virtually no attention to contemporary application.

4.26.3   France, R. T. *The Gospel of Mark: A Commentary on the Greek Text.* New International Greek Testament Commentary. Grand Rapids: Eerdmans, 2002. 719pp.

Careful and detailed commentary by noted British evangelical scholar. Focuses on final form of the text, giving little attention to sources lying behind Mark's Gospel or the provenance or the original audience of Mark. Attends instead to the structure of the Gospel, ways in which individual passages contribute to the whole, and how intertextuality (especially OT passages) illumines the text. Draws heavily on historical and cultural context. Concerned to explain passages according to how a "Christian reader" would construe the text, but does little to develop the theology of passages or of the Gospel as a whole. Assumes knowledge of Greek.

4.26.4   Guelich, Robert A. *Mark 1–8:26.* Word Biblical Commentary. Waco, Tex.: Word, 1989. 454pp.

Because of Guelich's untimely death, only the first volume of his anticipated two-volume commentary is available (Craig Evans prepared the second volume [§4.26.2]). Gives meticulous attention to every detail of every verse, with special regard to linguistic analysis (both lexical and syntactic), Mark's sources, Mark's redaction of earlier traditions, the social and religious setting of the Gospel, the logical flow of the immediate context and the broader narrative context of the Gospel, and ways in which individual passages contribute to and are illuminated by Mark's purpose. Although he acknowledges growth of the tradition and Mark's creative hand, Guelich affirms the general reliability of Mark's Gospel as a report of Jesus' ministry. Highly technical commentary, and although there is concern for theological claims within the text, gives little attention to developing theological implications or continuing relevance for Christians.

4.26.5   Gundry, Robert H. *Mark: A Commentary on His Apology for the Cross.* Grand Rapids: Eerdmans, 1993. 1069pp.

Since Gundry believes that Mark was the first Gospel written and that we do not possess the earlier traditions that Mark used, concludes that a redaction-critical examination that seeks to analyze Mark's editing of earlier sources is inapplicable. Thus he pursues a close reading of the final form of the text, giving detailed attention to the literary structure of passages, linguistic analysis, and historical background. Follows each passage with thorough history of interpretation. Treats introductory matters (e.g., place and date of writing) at the end of the commentary, suggesting that these issues should be decided on the basis of the exegesis of individual passages. Concludes that the Gospel contains the recollections of Peter compiled by Mark (as Papias reported) before the trial of Paul (i.e., before 62 CE) for the evangelistic purpose of presenting to the population of Rome a defense of the Christian proclamation of Jesus' crucifixion. Since Gundry presents all this as a conclusion to his interpretation, setting and purpose play no role in his exegesis. Learned, judicious, and comprehensive.

4.26.6   Kingsbury, Jack Dean. *The Christology of Mark's Gospel.* Philadelphia: Fortress, 1983. 203pp.

Lucid, engaging, and illuminating study of the Christology of Mark, the major theological issue of the Gospel. Begins with the clearest survey of twentieth-century investigation into Mark's Christology available. Critically engages the two dominant scholarly perspectives on Mark's Christology. Corrects the contention of Wrede (§4.26.37) that Mark has shaped his Gospel so as to present Jesus as one who wishes to keep his messiahship a secret by pointing out that the secret in Mark is not that Jesus is the Christ but that he is Son of God. Corrects the contention of Weeden (§4.26.36) that Mark "corrected" an inappropriate understanding of Jesus' divine Sonship by de-emphasizing the title "Son of God" in favor of "Son of Man" by pointing out, on narrative grounds, that God himself affirms the appropriateness and centrality of "Son of God" in this Gospel. The remainder of the volume is devoted to an exegetically informed tracing of the narrative of the Gospel in order to provide specific content to both "Son of God," "Son of Man," and the other christological titles.

313

4.26.7   Lane, William L. *Commentary on the Gospel of Mark*. New International
Commentary on the New Testament. Grand Rapids: Eerdmans, 1974.
652pp.

In contrast to Gundry (§4.26.5), Lane, who shares Gundry's evangelical
perspective, embraces a redaction-critical approach to this Gospel, analyzing how Mark's editing of earlier tradition provides an understanding of
Mark's theological message and pastoral concerns. Also gives serious attention to the literary structure of passages, broader narrative of the Gospel,
and historical background (especially Jewish). Gives less attention to details of the Greek language than does Guelich (§4.26.4) or Gundry, but
more attention to theological reflection on the text. Much less technical
than Guelich or Gundry.

4.26.8   Marcus, Joel. *Mark 1–8*. Anchor Bible. New York: Doubleday, 2000.
Mark 8–16. Yale Anchor Bible. New Haven, Conn.: Yale University
Press, 2009. 1182pp.

While Collins (§4.26.1) interprets Mark's Gospel against the backdrop
of the Greco-Roman world, Marcus sees this Gospel as emerging at the
time of the Jewish rebellion of BCE 66–70 and insists that Mark adopts
an apocalyptic framework in order to offer a Christian alternative to the
apocalypticism at work among the Jews in the years leading up to the
Jewish War. A detailed, meticulous, and informative commentary. But its
value may be compromised to some extent by its heavy reliance upon a
theory regarding specific historical and ideological background to which
some readers may be reluctant to grant such a dominant role.

4.26.9   Telford, W. R. *The Theology of the Gospel of Mark*. New Testament Theology. Cambridge: Cambridge University Press, 1999. 275pp.

Presents Mark's theology in its several historical contexts. First, sets Mark's
theology in the context of his community and the broader Greco-Roman
world of which it was a part. Second, places Mark's theology in the context
of the first-century church, noting points of continuity and discontinuity with other writings and theologies of the church as reflected in the
various traditions and documents included in the NT. Third, discusses his
own view of Mark's theology in dialogue with the history of interpretation
(especially twentieth century). Fourth, probes the significance of Mark's
theology for contemporary Christians in their own historical context.
Written in technical style, with constant reference to details of history of
interpretation, specific citations of Jewish and Greco-Roman sources, and
reconstructions of earlier tradition and of Mark's redaction of this earlier
tradition. In contrast to Kingsbury (§4.26.6), who works exclusively with

the final form of the text, Telford derives Mark's theological purposes both from the final composition and from Mark's shaping of earlier traditions.

4.26.10   Witherington, Ben, III. *The Gospel of Mark: A Socio-Rhetorical Commentary*. Grand Rapids: Eerdmans, 2001. 463pp.

Interprets Mark's Gospel by examining the dynamic interplay of the two "worlds" of Mark's Gospel: (1) The literary world involves the genre of Mark's Gospel (ancient biography of Jesus along the lines of other Greco-Roman biographies) and Mark's use of ancient rhetoric. Draws on certain insights from emerging literary approaches (e.g., narrative criticism) but rejects a thoroughgoing narrative approach as inappropriately ahistorical, i.e., contrary to Mark's theological purpose to report events he was convinced had actually occurred, and contrary to Mark's pastoral purpose to address challenges facing his church in its historical setting. (2) The social world involves the structure of social life in the first-century Mediterranean world in general and Mark's church in particular, but Witherington emphasizes the Jewish and Greco-Roman religious background. Of special value are the frequent excurses discussing specific exegetical, historical, and theological issues, and the applicable sections that explore points of continuing relevance for contemporary Christians.

Also Significant

4.26.11   Achtemeier, Paul J. *Mark*. 2d ed. Proclamation Commentaries. Philadelphia: Fortress, 1986. 138pp.

4.26.12   Anderson, Hugh. *The Gospel of Mark*. New Century Bible Commentary. Grand Rapids: Eerdmans, 1976. 366pp.

4.26.13   Anderson, Janice Capel, and Stephen D. Moore. *Mark and Method: New Approaches in Biblical Studies*. 2d ed. Minneapolis: Fortress, 2008. 288pp.

4.26.14   Boring, M. Eugene. *Mark: A Commentary*. New Testament Library. Louisville: Westminster John Knox, 2006. 482pp.

4.26.15   Bryan, Christopher. *A Preface to Mark: Notes on the Gospel in Its Literary and Cultural Settings*. New York: Oxford, 1993. 220pp.

4.26.16   Cranfield, C. E. B. *The Gospel according to St. Mark.* Cambridge Greek Testament Commentary. Cambridge: Cambridge University Press, 1977. 503pp.

4.26.17   Donahue, John R., and Daniel J. Harrington. *The Gospel of Mark.* Sacra Pagina. Collegeville, Minn.: Michael Glazier, 2002. 496pp.

4.26.18   Fowler, Robert M. *Let The Reader Understand: Reader-Response Criticism and the Gospel of Mark.* Minneapolis: Fortress, 1991. 279pp.

4.26.19   Harrington, Daniel J. *What Are They Saying about Mark?* New York: Paulist, 2004. 94pp.

4.26.20   Hengel, Martin. *Studies in the Gospel of Mark.* Philadelphia: Fortress, 1985. 206pp.

4.26.21   Hooker, Morna D. *The Gospel according to St. Mark.* Black's New Testament Commentary. Peabody, Mass.: Hendrickson, 1991. 424pp.

4.26.22   Iersel, Bastiaan Martinius Franciscus van. *Mark: A Reader-Response Commentary.* Sheffield: Sheffield Academic Press, 1998. 556pp.

4.26.23   Kingsbury, Jack Dean. *Conflict in Mark: Jesus, Authorities, Disciples.* Minneapolis: Fortress, 1989. 150pp.

4.26.24   Lightfoot, Robert Henry. *The Gospel Message of St. Mark.* Oxford: Clarendon, 1950. 116pp.

4.26.25   Malbon, Elizabeth Struthers. *Mark's Jesus: Characterization as Narrative Christology.* Waco, Tex.: Baylor University Press, 2009. 286pp.

4.26.26   Maloney, Francis J. *The Gospel of Mark: A Commentary.* Grand Rapids: Baker, 2002. 398pp.

4.26.27   ———. *Mark: Storyteller, Interpreter, Evangelist.* Peabody, Mass.: Hendrickson, 2004. 224pp.

4.26.28   Martin, Ralph P. *Mark: Evangelist and Theologian.* Contemporary Evangelical Perspectives. Grand Rapids: Zondervan, 1973. 240pp.

4.26.29   Rhoads, David. *Reading Mark, Engaging the Gospel.* Minneapolis: Fortress, 2004. 270pp.

4.26.30   Rhoads, David, Joanna Dewey, and Donald Michie. *Mark as Story: An Introduction to the Narrative of a Gospel.* 3d ed. Minneapolis: Fortress, 2012. 191pp.

4.26.31   Robbins, Vernon K. *Jesus the Teacher: A Socio-Rhetorical Interpretation of Mark.* New introduction. Minneapolis: Fortress, 1992. 249pp.

4.26.32   Samuel, Simon. *And They Crucified Him: A Postcolonial Reading of the Story of Jesus.* Dehradun, India: Saraswati, 2012. 247pp.

4.26.33   Taylor, Vincent. *The Gospel according to St. Mark: The Greek Text with Introduction, Notes, and Indexes.* London: Macmillan, 1952. 696pp.

4.26.34   Telford, William R., ed. *The Interpretation of Mark.* Rev. ed. Edinburgh: T&T Clark, 1994. 342pp.

4.26.35   Tolbert, Mary Ann. *Sowing the Gospel: Mark's World in Literary-Historical Perspective.* Minneapolis: Fortress, 1989. 336pp.

4.26.36   Weeden, Theodore J., Sr. *Mark: Traditions in Conflict.* Philadelphia: Fortress, 1971. 182pp.

4.26.37   Wrede, William. *The Messianic Secret.* Library of Theological Translations. Cambridge: James Clarke, 1971. 292pp. (Originally published in German in 1901.)

4.27   Luke and Luke–Acts

See also ACTS OF THE APOSTLES (§4.29)

Highly Recommended

4.27.1   Bovon, François. *Luke 1.* Hermeneia: A Critical and Historical Commentary on the Bible. Minneapolis: Fortress, 2002. 441pp. *Luke 2.*

Hermeneia: A Critical and Historical Commentary on the Bible. Minneapolis: Fortress, 2013. 560pp. *Luke 3*. Hermeneia: A Critical and Historical Commentary on the Bible. Minneapolis: Fortress, 2012. 492pp.

Commentary attempts to combine critical and historical considerations with the history of interpretation in order to arrive at a theological interpretation of Luke that will be of service to believers in the church. Bovon gives attention to all of these matters, but their interconnectedness is not always evident. Provides both a synchronic (function within immediate and broader-book context) and diachronic (redaction-critical considerations) analysis for each passage, with detailed comment on each verse. Originally produced for the Evangelisch-Katholischer series, which emphasizes the history of reception (*Wirkungsgeschichte*), i.e., the ways in which the text has been appropriated not only by scholars in commentaries but in art, literature, liturgy, etc. Accordingly, the commentary includes a section on "history of interpretation" for each passage, a section that receives more intentional treatment in the second and third volumes than in the first.

4.27.2   Fitzmyer, Joseph A. *The Gospel according to Luke.* 2 vols. Anchor Bible. Garden City, NY: Doubleday, 1981, 1985. 1642pp.

Employs a fully critical model, but often arrives at conservative conclusions (e.g., that the Gospel was probably written by Luke, the companion of Paul). Introduction includes discussion of historical and linguistic issues, and an illuminating and extensive presentation (130pp.) of Lucan theology. Commentary attends to Luke's redaction of his sources (Mark and Q), interpretive significance of forms or genres, linguistic analysis, and historical background for both the setting in the life of Jesus and the setting of the production of Luke's Gospel. All these considerations are employed to illuminate the final text. Thus gives most attention to the structure of passages and their role within the narrative of the whole of Luke–Acts, with a view toward identifying their theological theme and arriving at their essential message. A traditional commentary that makes no use of the emerging literary or sociological methods.

4.27.3   Franklin, Eric. *Christ the Lord: A Study in the Purpose and Theology of Luke–Acts.* Philadelphia: Westminster, 1975. 241pp.

Lucid, comprehensive, and (in the judgment of many) compelling discussion of Lucan theology and especially Christology. Argues that the purpose of Luke–Acts is to prompt readers to respond to the reality that is proclaimed in Jesus' ascension (according to Franklin, the central event in Luke's theology), viz., that Jesus is Lord and that the eschatological power of God was and is effective through him. Relates all the major aspects of

Luke's two-volume work to this central theme. Concludes by discussing implications of this theological program for Luke's pastoral concerns and for the identification of the evangelist himself, identified as a former God-fearer who embraced Christianity, possibly a companion of Paul.

4.27.4   Green, Joel B. *The Gospel of Luke*. New International Commentary on the New Testament. Grand Rapids: Eerdmans, 1997. 928pp.

Recognizing that no commentary can do everything, Green limits the scope of this volume by pursuing "discourse analysis," i.e., correlation of "culture-critical" and narratological concerns. This approach involves the dynamic interplay of cultural insights from the critical examination of historical background (with special attention to religious and cultural issues), illuminated by modern social and cultural-anthropological studies, with insights pertaining to the nature of narrative derived from the new literary approaches. This process gives rise to a narrative theology that speaks directly to contemporary readers. Adopts sophisticated understanding of the nature and function of historical narrative; insists that there is a concern to present historical events, but for the purpose of persuasion, and thus all available rhetorical resources are employed to fulfill this persuasive function. Emphasizes how each passage functions in the narrative development of the whole of Luke–Acts, and thus provides many fresh insights and original perspectives that are at once engaging and compelling.

4.27.5   Johnson, Luke Timothy. *The Gospel of Luke*. Sacra Pagina. Collegeville, Minn.: Michael Glazier, 1991. 466pp.

Written by a Catholic layperson who has emerged as a leading American NT scholar, this commentary focuses on the final form of the text. Attends carefully to the ways in which each passage fits into the whole of Luke–Acts. Exclusively a literary analysis, with no attention given to the historical Jesus or the history of the tradition behind the final form. This restricted scope allows for examination of literary comparisons from the ancient world (especially classical Greek and Hellenistic) and to literary and rhetorical devices commonly employed in the ancient Mediterranean world and appropriated by Luke. Both the more technical "notes" and the more expository "interpretation" are rather brief, and the discussion of each passage concludes with a very select bibliography. One often wishes Johnson would have developed his interpretation more fully, especially his suggestive remarks on the theological message of passages.

4.27.6   Marshall, I. Howard. *The Gospel of Luke: A Commentary on the Greek Text*. New International Greek Testament Commentary. Grand Rapids: Eerdmans, 1978. 928pp.

If Johnson's commentary (§4.27.5) is literary, Marshall's is linguistic. Meticulously analyzes virtually every phrase with lexical and syntactical thoroughness. In the process, examines Luke's redaction of his sources (Mark and Q) and notes how Luke's theology can be discerned both by what he takes over from these sources, and how he alters them, omits from them, or adds from his own hand. Gives significant attention also to historical background (especially Jewish) and to canonical connections (especially Septuagintal). Interprets passages in light of Luke's overall purpose and often refers to other passages in Luke–Acts, but gives relatively little attention to the flow of the narrative. Although written for students, many will find it overwhelming and quite technical, as it assumes a solid knowledge of Greek. Those who can master it will find the commentary extremely helpful, especially in its analysis of the Greek text.

4.27.7 ———. *Luke: Historian and Theologian.* Rev. ed. Downers Grove, Ill.: InterVarsity, 1988. 252pp.

Like Franklin, presents a comprehensive and coherent understanding of Luke's theology. In contrast to Franklin, however, considers the concept of salvation to be central to Luke's theology and consistently presents all aspects of Luke's theology within the framework of this concept (e.g., Marshall describes the doctrine of God under the heading "God my Savior"). Insists that no wedge should be drawn between history and theology. As a historian who sees theological significance in the events he records, Luke is concerned with the reliable reporting of events, and is thus conservative in dealing with his sources. Indeed, argues that Luke creatively developed his theology from ideas already present in the traditions he inherited, over against the view the Luke was an innovator whose thought stood in stark discontinuity with earlier Christian convictions.

Also Significant

4.27.8 Bartholomew, Craig G., Joel B. Green, and Anthony C. Thiselton, eds. *Reading Luke: Interpretation, Reflection, Formation.* Scripture and Hermeneutics, vol. 6. Grand Rapids: Zondervan, 2005. 484pp.

4.27.9 Bock, Darrell L. *Luke.* Baker Exegetical Commentary on the New Testament. 2 vols. Grand Rapids: Baker, 1994. 2148pp.

4.27.10 ———. *A Theology of Luke & Acts: God's Promised Program, Realized for All Nations.* Grand Rapids: Zondervan, 2012. 496pp.

4.27.11   Bovon, François. *Luke the Theologian.* 2d ed. Waco, Tex.: Baylor University Press, 2006. 681pp.

4.27.12   Carroll, John T. *Luke: A Commentary.* New Testament Library. Louisville: Westminster John Knox, 2012. 554pp.

4.27.13   Conzelmann, Hans. *The Theology of St. Luke.* New York: Harper & Row, 1960. 255pp.

4.27.14   Craddock, Fred B. *Luke.* Interpretation: A Bible Commentary for Teaching and Preaching. Louisville: John Knox, 1990. 298pp.

4.27.15   Darr, John A. *On Character Building: The Reader and the Rhetoric of Characterization in Luke–Acts.* Literary Currents in Biblical Interpretation. Louisville: Westminster John Knox, 1992. 208pp.

4.27.16   Fitzmyer, Joseph A. *Luke the Theologian: Aspects of His Teaching.* New York: Paulist, 1989. 250pp.

4.27.17   Green, Joel B., ed. *Methods for Luke.* Cambridge: Cambridge University Press, 2010. 157pp.

4.27.18   ———. *The Theology of the Gospel of Luke.* New Testament Theology. Cambridge: Cambridge University Press, 1995. 170pp.

4.27.19   Green, Joel B., and Michael C. McKeever. *Luke–Acts and New Testament Historiography.* IBR Bibliographies 8. Grand Rapids: Baker, 1994. 148pp.

4.27.20   Keck, Leander E., and J. Louis Martyn, eds. *Studies in Luke–Acts.* Philadelphia: Fortress, 1980. 316pp.

4.27.21   Kingsbury, Jack Dean. *Conflict in Luke.* Minneapolis: Fortress, 1991. 180pp.

4.27.22   Kurz, William S. *Reading Luke–Acts: Dynamics of Biblical Narrative.* Louisville: Westminster John Knox, 1993. 261pp.

4.27.23   Maddox, Robert. *The Purpose of Luke–Acts*. Studies of the New Testament and Its World. Edinburgh: T&T Clark, 1982. 218pp.

4.27.24   Neyrey, Jerome H., ed. *The Social World of Luke–Acts: Models for Interpretation*. Peabody, Mass.: Hendrickson, 1991. 436pp.

4.27.25   Nolland, John. *Luke*. 3 vols. Word Biblical Commentary. Dallas: Word, 1989–1993. 1293pp.

4.27.26   Parsons, Mikeal. *Luke: Storyteller, Interpreter, Evangelist*. Peabody, Mass.: Hendrickson, 2007. 230pp.

4.27.27   Plummer, Alfred. *A Critical and Exegetical Commentary on the Gospel according to St. Luke*. International Critical Commentary. Edinburgh: T&T Clark, 1910. 592pp.

4.27.28   Talbert, Charles H. *Reading Luke: A Literary and Theological Commentary on the Third Gospel*. New York: Crossroad, 1982. 246pp.

4.27.29   Tannehill, Robert. *The Gospel according to Luke*. Vol. 1 of *The Narrative Unity of Luke–Acts: A Literary Interpretation*. Foundations and Facets: New Testament. Philadelphia: Fortress, 1986. 334pp.

4.27.30   Tyson, Joseph B., ed. *Luke–Acts and the Jewish People: Eight Critical Perspectives*. Minneapolis: Augsburg, 1988. 160pp.

4.28   John and the Johannine School

See also JOHANNINE EPISTLES (§4.41)

Highly Recommended

4.28.1   Barrett, C. K. *The Gospel according to St. John: An Introduction with Commentary and Notes on the Greek Text*. 2d ed. Philadelphia: Westminster, 1978. 638pp.

Based on the Greek text, and not easily accessible to those who do not know Greek. Rejects much recent redaction criticism of the Gospel that posits several stages of editing in favor of treating it as a theological unity. Insists that John did not intend to supply historically verifiable information about the life and teaching of Jesus and that it is impossible to extract from the Gospel reliable historical traditions. Argues that John knew the Gospel of Mark and probably also Luke, and that he presents a creative theological interpretation based on these synoptic texts. Introduction contains helpful discussion of John's theology. Commentary focuses on linguistic analysis, textual variants, historical background (especially OT and Jewish), John's (supposed) development of synoptic passages and themes, and the theological meaning of the text.

4.28.2   Beasley-Murray, George R. *John*. Word Biblical Commentary. Waco, Tex.: Word, 1987. 441pp.

The word that best describes this commentary is "accessible." This British Baptist scholar who taught for several years in the United States writes for a varied audience (including scholars) but primarily for the average minister. Wishes to make available to nonspecialists the results of vast academic research into John along with the commentator's original insights. Like Barrett (§4.28.1), assumes the unity of the final form of the text. Refers to the Greek text, but gives primary attention to literary structure, historical background, and canonical connections. Relates each passage to broader book context and John's overall purpose. Develops theology of each passage, and relates this theology to NT faith as a whole and to concerns of modern Christians.

4.28.3   Brown, Raymond E. *The Gospel according to John*. 2 vols. Anchor Bible. Garden City, NY: Doubleday, 1966, 1970. 1208pp.

Discusses in depth major Johannine questions (e.g., authorship, composition, date, relationship to synoptics) in introduction, presenting major theories regarding these issues and assessing them in the light of the text itself and the historical setting of the book's production so as to arrive at a synthesis of relevant and reliable scholarly insights. Concludes that the Gospel originated in traditions of words and deeds of Jesus that were independent of the Synoptic Gospels and that these traditions developed into characteristic Johannine patterns through years of preaching and teaching. The evangelist organized this material into a Gospel, and later revised it to meet the current needs of his congregation. A final redactor later inserted additional material. Commentary draws on this hypothetical reconstruction at points, but focuses on the meaning of the final form. Gives some attention to linguistic issues and to literary structure, but commentary is

323

historically oriented, emphasizing historical background (mostly Jewish and first-century Christian), history of interpretation, and historical setting of original readers. Learned, detailed, and technical.

4.28.4   Keener, Craig S. *The Gospel of John: A Commentary.* 2 vols. Peabody, Mass.: Hendrickson, 2003. 1636pp.

No commentary can do everything; Keener has chosen to focus attention upon social-historical background, while also giving some limited attention to matters such as literary features and the relationship of John's Gospel to the historical Jesus. His immense and practically unparalleled knowledge of primary sources of the period allows him to offer profound insights into the way in which the intended original audience of John's Gospel would have understood the text. Keener focuses upon the final form of the text and the ways in which the reader was intended to have construed it. The commentary is thus a fine complement to others that emphasize other aspects of interpretation.

4.28.5   Michaels, J. Ramsey. *The Gospel of John.* New International Commentary on the New Testament. Grand Rapids: Eerdmans, 2010. 1094pp.

Focuses upon the final form of the text rather than pursuing matters of compositional history. Engages in a detailed and remarkably insightful analysis of the literary and narrative means the writer employed to convey his message, while giving attention also to the meaning of broad theological concepts in the Gospel. The stress upon literary/theological interpretation provides a fine complement to Keener's social-history emphasis (§4.28.4).

4.28.6   Schnackenburg, Rudolf. *The Gospel according to St. John.* 3 vols. New York: Crossroad, 1987. 638/556/510pp.

This German Roman Catholic NT scholar intends to present an "explanation" of the Johannine text understandable to modern persons, and to use "every available means" to do so. Thus, this incorporates a wide range of interpretive considerations, especially literary structure, linguistic analysis, historical background, and canonical connections. Focuses on the theological meaning of the final form of the text, but gives some limited attention to earlier sources and the evangelist's redaction of them. Maintains that the earliest traditions stem from John the son of Zebedee and that the evangelist was one of his disciples. Similar in scope and character to Brown's commentary (§4.28.3), but gives greater attention to evidence from Qumran and Coptic Gnostic materials, and is more theologically reflective. Profound theological insights repeatedly burst forth from his exegesis.

4.28.7   Smalley, Stephen S. *John: Evangelist and Interpreter*. 2d ed. Downers Grove, Ill.: InterVarsity, 1998. 340pp.

Intended primarily for theological students, but also provides many insights for the scholar. Critically discusses virtually all significant issues and problems in the study of John's Gospel, giving special attention to origin and background, composition and purpose, points of commonality with Christian tradition in general, and unique aspects where John's Gospel makes its own contribution to NT theology. Thus moves from historical discussion (where Smalley argues that John's Gospel was based on generally historically accurate tradition independent of the synoptists), to literary analysis (where Smalley emphasizes the literary development of the narrative, "analyzed as a sustained piece of dramatic writing"), to an examination of the rich theological vision of John. Focuses almost entirely on the Gospel, saying very little about the Johannine epistles or their relationship to the Gospel.

Also Significant

4.28.8   Ashton, John. *The Interpretation of John*. 2d ed. Edinburgh: T&T Clark, 1997. 329pp.

4.28.9   Bernard, J. H. *A Critical and Exegetical Commentary on the Gospel according to St. John*. 2 vols. International Critical Commentary. Edinburgh: T&T Clark, 1928. 739pp.

4.28.10   Blomberg, Craig L. *The Historical Reliability of John's Gospel: Issues and Commentary*. Downers Grove, Ill.: InterVarsity, 2002. 396pp.

4.28.11   Brodie, Thomas L. *The Gospel according to John: A Literary and Theological Commentary*. New York: Oxford University Press, 1993. 625pp.

4.28.12   Brown, Raymond E. *The Community of the Beloved Disciple: The Life, Loves, and Hates of an Individual Church in New Testament Times*. New York: Paulist, 1979. 204pp.

4.28.13   Bultmann, Rudolf. *The Gospel of John: A Commentary*. Philadelphia: Westminster, 1971. 744pp.

4.28.14 Carson, D. A. *The Gospel according to John.* Grand Rapids: Eerdmans, 1991. 715pp.

4.28.15 Carter, Warren. *John: Storyteller, Interpreter, Evangelist.* Peabody, Mass.: Hendrickson, 2006. 264pp.

4.28.16 Cullmann, Oscar. *The Johannine Circle.* Philadelphia: Westminster, 1976. 124pp.

4.28.17 Culpepper, R. Alan. *Anatomy of the Fourth Gospel: A Study in Literary Design.* Foundations and Facets: New Testament. Philadelphia: Fortress, 1983. 266pp.

4.28.18 Dodd, C. H. *The Interpretation of the Fourth Gospel.* Cambridge: Cambridge University Press, 1954. 477pp.

4.28.19 Fortna, Robert T., and Tony Thatcher, eds. *Jesus in the Johannine Tradition.* Louisville: Westminster John Knox, 2001. 384pp.

4.28.20 Haenchen, Ernst. *John.* 2 vols. Hermeneia: A Critical and Historical Commentary on the Bible. Philadelphia: Fortress, 1984. 308/366pp.

4.28.21 Hengel, Martin. *The Johannine Question.* Philadelphia: Trinity Press International, 1989. 240pp.

4.28.22 Hoskyns, Edwyn. *The Fourth Gospel.* Edited by Francis Noel Davey. Rev. ed. London: Faber and Faber, 1947. 604pp.

4.28.23 Koester, Craig R. *Symbolism in the Fourth Gospel: Meaning, Mystery, Community.* 2d ed. Minneapolis: Fortress, 2003.

4.28.24 ———. *The Word of Life: A Theology of John's Gospel.* Grand Rapids: Eerdmans, 2008. 245pp.

4.28.25 Köstenberger, Andreas J. *John.* Baker Exegetical Commentary on the New Testament. Grand Rapids: Baker Academic, 2004. 700pp.

4.28.26   ———. *A Theology of John's Gospel and Letters: The Word, the Christ, the Son of God.* Grand Rapids: Zondervan, 2009. 652pp.

4.28.27   Malina, Bruce J., and Richard L. Rohrbaugh. *Social-Science Commentary on the Gospel of John.* Minneapolis: Fortress, 1998. 326pp.

4.28.28   McHugh, John F. *John 1-4.* International Critical Commentary. London: T&T Clark, 2009. 323pp.

4.28.29   Morris, Leon. *The Gospel according to John.* New International Commentary on the New Testament. Rev. ed. Grand Rapids: Eerdmans, 1995. 824pp.

4.28.30   Painter, John. *The Quest for the Messiah: The History, Literature and Theology of the Johannine Community.* 2d ed. Nashville: Abingdon, 1993. 492pp.

4.28.31   Ridderbos, Herman. *The Gospel of John: A Theological Commentary.* Grand Rapids: Eerdmans, 1997. 719pp.

4.28.32   Segovia, Fernando F., ed. *What Is John?: Readers and Readings of the Fourth Gospel.* 2 vols. Society of Biblical Literature Symposium Series. Atlanta: Scholars, 1996–1998. 293/360pp.

4.28.33   Sloyan, Gerard. *What Are They Saying about John?* Rev. ed. New York: Paulist, 2006. 172pp.

4.28.34   Smith, D. Moody. *The Theology of the Gospel of John.* New Testament Theology. Cambridge: Cambridge University Press, 1995. 202pp.

4.28.35   Talbert, Charles H. *Reading John: A Literary and Theological Commentary on the Fourth Gospel and the Johannine Epistles.* New York: Crossroad, 1992. 284pp.

4.28.36   Thatcher, Tom, ed. *What We Have Heard from the Beginning: The Past, Present, and Future of Johannine Studies.* Waco, Tex.: Baylor University Press, 2007. 425pp.

327

4.28.37 Wahlde, Urban C. von. *The Gospel and Letters of John.* 3 vols. Eerdmans Critical Commentary. Grand Rapids: Eerdmans, 2010. 705/929/441pp.

4.28.38 Westcott, Brooke Foss. *The Gospel according to John: The Greek Text with Introduction and Notes.* 2 vols. London: J Murray, 1908. 282/394pp.

4.28.39 Witherington, Ben, III. *John's Wisdom: A Commentary on the Fourth Gospel.* Louisville: Westminster John Knox, 1995. 411pp.

4.29   Acts of the Apostles

Highly Recommended

4.29.1 Barrett, C. K. *A Critical and Exegetical Commentary on the Acts of the Apostles.* 2 vols. International Critical Commentary. Edinburgh: T&T Clark, 1994–1998. 1272pp.

Barrett had a well-deserved reputation for meticulous attention to detail, encyclopedic knowledge of almost everything pertaining to the text and world of the NT, sober judgment, and clear writing. This commentary only enhances this reputation. Introduction is postponed to the beginning of the second volume since such issues can be decided only on the basis of careful exegesis. Typically moves through a passage by setting forth the interpretive issue, identifying major possibilities, citing evidence (and sometimes quoting scholars, both ancient and modern, often in original Greek, Latin, German, or French), and analyzing evidence thus presented so as to arrive at a reasonable conclusion, frequently appending observations regarding its theological significance. Often relates passages to other parts of Luke–Acts or other NT texts. Gives little attention to role within the sustained dramatic narration of Acts and draws not at all from current narratological or sociological insights. This last is not necessarily a weakness, but it does mark this work as a traditional commentary, full of engaging and compelling, if not always boldly original, insights.

4.29.2 Bruce, F. F. *Commentary on the Book of Acts.* Rev. ed. New International Commentary on the New Testament. Grand Rapids: Eerdmans, 1988. 541pp.

Bruce was a classicist by training and a historian by temperament, and both these impulses are manifested in this commentary. Comments are replete with illuminating discussions of historical background with citations from ancient writers, both Jewish and Greco-Roman. Bruce gives some attention (mostly in footnotes) to nuances of the Greek. Treats Acts as essentially a history book whose purpose is to set forth the facts (with certain apologetic tendencies) of the emerging church. Consistently attempts to reconstruct and illuminate events herein recorded rather than attend to the narrative Luke has created and explore the theological message Luke thereby communicates. It is difficult to derive rich theological insights out of reconstructed historical events, explained without benefit of the theological purpose that the writer communicates by use of narrative strategies. Consequently, Bruce's commentary, though theologically suggestive in many ways, often lacks the theological depth it could have gained from attention to Luke's narrative and rhetorical strategies of persuasion.

4.29.3   Fitzmyer, Joseph A. *The Acts of the Apostles*. Anchor Bible. New York: Doubleday, 1998. 830pp.

Like Fitzmyer's commentary on Luke (§4.27.2), a traditional historical-critical commentary, giving no attention to newer narratological or sociological approaches, but rich in examination of the language and historical background. Allows for Lucan expansion and even free creation at points, and for nonhistorical accretions in the development of the tradition, but tends toward conservative conclusions on historical matters. Unlike his commentary on Luke, Fitzmyer was restricted here to a single volume, resulting in less attention to theological issues and the role of passages within the broader-book context. Apparently, Fitzmyer considered he had space to deal only with identification and illumination of events mentioned in the text, for he gives little attention to theological meaning, e.g., almost completely ignoring the often-noted literary and theological significance of money/possessions in Acts.

4.29.4   Johnson, Luke Timothy. *The Acts of the Apostles*. Sacra Pagina. Collegeville, Minn.: Michael Glazier, 1992. 568pp.

In some ways a continuation of Johnson's commentary on Luke (§4.27.5), to which he constantly refers in this commentary. Emphasizes continuity with the Gospel of Luke, taking seriously the literary unity of the two books. Treats both Luke's narrative artistry and his concern to present historical events, refusing to construe Acts as either a history book or as a work of fiction. Insists rather that all historical writing employs fictional techniques, and that Acts accords with standards and practices of ancient historiography. Thus Luke presents sustained narrative of events to communicate his theological message and purposes. Johnson traces these purposes through each passage of Acts.

4.29.5   Keener, Craig S. *Acts: An Exegetical Commentary.* 4 vols. (Vols. 1 and 2 currently available.) Grand Rapids: Baker Academic, 2012, 2013. 1038/1200pp.

This immense commentary is a model of methodological clarity and deep understanding of the world out of which the book of Acts emerged. Focuses on sociohistorical background (constantly citing ancient sources not generally known or previously not applied to Acts) and matters of genre, all with the purpose of illumining the theological message of the text. Although providing a wealth of new information for scholars, is clearly written and accessible to nonspecialists. In contrast to Pervo (§4.29.7), insists that Acts is a historical monograph that reports with essential accuracy the events it describes.

4.29.6   Marshall, I. Howard, ed. *Witness to the Gospel: The Theology of Acts.* Grand Rapids: Eerdmans, 1998. 610pp.

Comprehensive survey of virtually all the major theological themes in Acts, presented in twenty-five essays written by some of the most prominent contemporary scholars in Lucan studies, many of whom have written whole books or seminal articles on the topic of their essay. Essays vary in perspective and method. Some naturally deal with more central issues and are more insightful than others; the essays on "The Plan of God" (Squires), "Salvation to the Ends of the Earth: God as the Savior in the Acts of the Apostles" (Green), "The Role of the Apostles" (Clark), and "The Spirit of Prophecy" (Turner) are especially helpful, as is the final synthetic article by David Peterson, "Luke's Theological Enterprise: Integration and Intent."

4.29.7   Pervo, Richard I. *Acts.* Hermeneia: A Critical and Historical Commentary on the Bible. Minneapolis: Fortress, 2009. 811pp.

Adopts the rather unusual position that Acts was written between 110 and 120 CE by someone who was influenced by the Pauline and Deutero-Pauline epistles and the works of Josephus. Insists that Acts has no real historical value; indeed, it was written as a popular fiction, meant to entertain and at the same time to edify. Emphasizes the differences and the essential separation of Acts from the Gospel of Luke. Consequently, Pervo interprets the final form of the text with no attempt at historical reconstruction or compositional pre-history, giving almost exclusive attention to the ways in which the writer employed rhetorical and narrative devices (and the assumed sociocultural background knowledge and experience of his intended readers) to deliver his message (including the theological message) and to produce an impact upon the reader. In the process, carefully analyzes the Greek terms and syntax. Provides a very sensitive and illuminating reading of the text as a theological document.

4.29.8   Willimon, William. *Acts.* Interpretation: A Bible Commentary for Teaching and Preaching. Atlanta: John Knox, 1988. 197pp.

In the history of interpretation, few commentaries on Acts have given serious consideration to theological meaning of the text, preferring to focus almost entirely on historical issues. Only recently have some major commentaries attended noticeably to the theological dimension, and most of these have dealt with the theological meaning as only one aspect of their exposition. This commentary complements these other works in that it assumes the kind of careful exegesis presented in the standard commentaries, but focuses on the theological and pastoral significance of these exegetical insights. Willimon is not himself a NT scholar, but an authority on preaching and pastoral care. At points his lack of thorough technical knowledge becomes evident to the trained eye, but this lack of personal exegetical expertise is compensated by his engaging connections between the original meaning and its contemporary theological and pastoral impact.

Also Significant

4.29.9   Bauckham, Richard. *The Book of Acts in Its Palestinian Setting.* Vol. 4 of The Book of Acts in Its First Century Setting. Grand Rapids: Eerdmans, 1995. 526pp.

4.29.10   Bock, Darrell L. *Acts.* Baker Exegetical Commentary on the New Testament. Grand Rapids: Baker Academic, 2007. 848pp.

4.29.11   Conzelmann, Hans. *Acts of the Apostles.* Hermeneia: A Critical and Historical Commentary on the Bible. Philadelphia: Fortress, 1987. 287pp.

4.29.12   Foakes-Jackson, F. J., and Kirsopp Lake, eds. *The Acts of the Apostles.* 5 vols. London: Macmillan, 1920–1933. Volumes average 500pp.

4.29.13   Gasque, W. Ward. *A History of the Criticism of the Acts of the Apostles.* Rev. ed. Peabody, Mass.: Hendrickson, 1989. 359pp.

4.29.14   Gill, David W. J., and Conrad Gempf, eds. *The Book of Acts in its Graeco-Roman Setting.* Vol. 2 of The Book of Acts in Its First Century Setting. Grand Rapids: Eerdmans, 1994. 627pp.

4.29.15   Haenchen, Ernst. *The Acts of the Apostles: A Commentary.* Philadelphia: Westminster, 1971. 737pp.

4.29.16   Hemer, Colin J. *The Book of Acts in the Setting of Hellenistic History.* Winona Lake, Ind.: Eisenbrauns, 1990. 482pp.

4.29.17   Hengel, Martin. *Acts and the History of Earliest Christianity.* Philadelphia: Fortress, 1980. 149pp.

4.29.18   Jervell, Jacob. *The Theology of the Acts of the Apostles.* New Testament Theology. Cambridge: Cambridge University Press, 1996. 142pp.

4.29.19   Kee, Howard Clark. *Good News to the Ends of the Earth: The Theology of Acts.* Philadelphia: Trinity Press International, 1990. 122pp.

4.29.20   Kistemaker, Simon. *Exposition of the Acts of the Apostles.* New Testament Commentary. Grand Rapids: Baker, 1990. 1010pp.

4.29.21   Marguerat, Daniel. *The First Christian Historian: Writing "The Acts of the Apostles."* Cambridge: Cambridge University Press, 2002. 299pp.

4.29.22   Marshall, I. Howard. *The Acts of the Apostles.* Tyndale New Testament Commentaries. Grand Rapids: Eerdmans, 1980. 427pp.

4.29.23   Porter, Stanley E. *Paul in Acts.* Library of Pauline Studies. Peabody, Mass.: Hendrickson, 2001. 233pp.

4.29.24   Rapske, Brian. *The Book of Acts and Paul in Roman Custody.* Vol. 3 of The Book of Acts in Its First Century Setting. Grand Rapids: Eerdmans, 1994. 512pp.

4.29.25   Talbert, Charles H. *Reading Acts: A Literary and Theological Commentary on the Acts of the Apostles.* New York: Crossroad, 1997. 269pp.

4.29.26   Tannehill, Robert. *The Acts of the Apostles.* Vol. 2 of *The Narrative Unity of Luke–Acts: A Literary Interpretation.* Foundations and Facets: New Testament. Minneapolis: Fortress, 1986. 398pp.

4.29.27   Winter, Bruce W., and Andrew D. Clarke, eds. *The Book of Acts in Its Ancient Literary Setting.* Vol. 1 of The Book of Acts in Its First Century Setting. Grand Rapids: Eerdmans, 1993. 479pp.

4.29.28   Witherington, Ben, III. *The Acts of the Apostles: A Socio-Rhetorical Commentary.* Grand Rapids: Eerdmans, 1998. 874pp.

4.30 Paul

Highly Recommended

4.30.1   Beker, J. Christiaan. *Paul the Apostle: The Triumph of God in Life and Thought.* Philadelphia: Fortress, 1980. 452pp.

A groundbreaking work that has significantly influenced all subsequent studies of Pauline theology. Attempts to identify the basis of coherence of Paul's thought, and to explore how Paul has applied his theology to the churches under his care. Argues that the unifying theme of Paul's gospel is the apocalyptic concept of the triumph of God, i.e., "the hope in the dawning victory of God and in the imminent redemption of the created order, which he has inaugurated in Christ." In addition, claims that Paul adopted a hermeneutic that enabled him to apply this coherent theme to persons in a variety of conditions and circumstances (the "contingent particularities of the human situation"). Offers a learned, illuminating, and (in the judgment of many scholars) largely compelling portrait of the shape of Paul's thought.

4.30.2   Bruce, F. F. *Paul: Apostle of the Heart Set Free.* Grand Rapids: Eerdmans, 1977. 491pp.

Most comprehensive and informed account of Paul's life from a conservative evangelical perspective, lucidly written. Intended primarily for pastors and theological students, it nonetheless discusses issues of interest to the scholar. Takes Paul's undisputed letters as primary evidence, but has high regard for the historicity of Luke's presentation of Paul in Acts as strong secondary evidence. Deals with aspects of Paul's theology as they emerge from Paul's life.

4.30.3   Dunn, James D. G. *The Theology of Paul the Apostle.* Grand Rapids: Eerdmans, 1998. 808pp.

This prolific Pauline scholar presents the most complete and comprehensive theology of Paul since Ridderbos (§4.30.6), adopting recent insights from Sanders (§4.30.7) and Beker (§4.30.1). Offers lucid treatment of major themes (e.g., God, humankind, sin, Christian life and ethics), using Romans as a base but expanding on each theme with material from the other letters. Includes helpful discussion of methodological issues involved in developing a Pauline theology. Emphasizes the dynamic character of Paul's thought and the necessity to treat not only what Paul explicitly wrote but also Jewish and early Christian presuppositions of his thought, the role of transformative moments in Paul's life, and deeper issues involved in the situations Paul's letters attempt to address. This holistic approach gives the presentation breadth and depth.

4.30.4   Hawthorne, Gerald F., Ralph P. Martin, and Daniel G. Reid, eds. *Dictionary of Paul and His Letters: A Compendium of Contemporary Biblical Scholarship.* Downers Grove, Ill.: InterVarsity, 1993. 1038pp.

Most comprehensive reference work available for Pauline theology, literature, background, and scholarship. Contributors are prominent evangelical scholars from North America, Europe, Australia, and Asia. Clearly written, intended primarily for theological students and those engaged in preaching and teaching in the church, but authoritative, in-depth articles contribute to scholarly discussion. Articles pertain to Paul and all things associated with him, including theological themes (e.g., law, gifts of the Spirit, ethics, and Christology), hermeneutical methods (e.g., social scientific interpretation), and background (e.g., Greco-Roman religions). Devotes specific articles to each of the Pauline epistles, to hermeneutics, and to preaching Paul today. Articles conclude with extensive bibliographies.

4.30.5   Murphy-O'Connor, Jerome. *Paul: A Critical Life.* Oxford: Clarendon, 1996. 416pp.

Whereas Bruce (§4.30.2) presents a portrait of Paul based on a surface reading of the entire NT and accepting Acts as a witness almost on a par with the undisputed epistles, Murphy-O'Connor insists on a critical procedure that largely dismisses Luke's Paul as hopelessly tendentious. Reads the undisputed epistles through the lens of rhetorical and epistolary criticism, exploring how knowledge of rhetorical strategies current in Paul's day and insights into the epistolary genre reveal deeper aspects of Paul's circumstances, thought, and personality. Begins with early life and conversion and concludes with Paul's last years, but the bulk of the book is arranged according to the churches Paul addressed, and throughout the emphasis is on ways in which the letters reveal how Paul's relationship with his churches prompted him to change or modify formulations of his theology. Thus, offers more of a literary history than a full-fledged biography, but such a work has value, for it provides helpful discussion of the dynamic between Paul's pastoral circumstances and the theology presented in his epistles. Indeed, the chapters could serve as a kind of "introduction" to the several letters.

4.30.6 Ridderbos, Herman. *Paul: An Outline of His Theology*. Grand Rapids: Eerdmans, 1975. 587pp.

The Reformed perspective of this leading Dutch scholar necessarily affects his reading of Paul, yet he seeks above all to be fair to the witness of the text. Based on careful exegesis and presented in constant interaction with the history of Pauline scholarship. Argues that Paul's central message is that the eschatological time of salvation has been inaugurated in the advent, death, and resurrection of Christ. Similar in some respects to Beker (§4.30.1), but significantly broader. A major difference is that Ridderbos accepts the Pauline authorship of all canonical epistles attributed to him, including the Pastorals. The center of Paul's theology as set forth by Ridderbos is not as sharp or as focused as Beker's, but neither is it as narrow, and thus it is arguably better able to account for the vast range of Paul's theological interests. Volume is arranged according to theological topics, beginning with sin and concluding with the doctrine of the future. One might learn more about the center (and coherence) of Paul's theology from Beker, but more regarding its specific aspects from Ridderbos.

4.30.7 Sanders, E. P. *Paul and Palestinian Judaism: A Comparison of Patterns of Religion*. Philadelphia: Fortress, 1977. 627pp.

Paul often articulates his faith in relationship to Judaism, and thus an understanding of Judaism and of Paul's relationship to it is essential for the interpretation of Paul's thought. Sanders, himself a leading authority on Palestinian Judaism, has produced here a watershed study that has revolutionized scholarly discussion on Paul's theology. His familiar assertion is that Judaism was characterized by "covenantal nomism": "one's place in God's plan is established on the basis of the covenant and the covenant requires as proper response obedience to its commandments," i.e., one enters the covenant relationship by grace, but maintains the covenant relationship by obedience. In contrast to this view, Paul adopts "participationist eschatology," "one participates in salvation by becoming one person with Christ, dying with him and sharing the promise of his resurrection." Thus, Paul has much in common with covenantal nomism, but his Christology marks differences in the overall pattern of his faith. Paul's critique of Judaism did not involve accusations of a legalistic righteousness that repudiated grace, but rather stemmed from his insistence that salvation is in Christ, and in nothing else.

4.30.8   Schnelle, Udo. *Apostle Paul: His Life and Theology.* Grand Rapids: Baker, 2003. 695pp.

Perhaps the best overall introduction to Paul and his thought. After an introductory section exploring methodological issues pertaining to the exploration of both history and theology in relation to Paul, Schnelle offers a judicious account of Paul's life, with special attention to mission and the development of Paul's thought and examines each of the undisputed letters in terms of historical setting and theological claims, noting especially how the circumstances of each letter influenced the theology therein. The last section of the book offers a synthesis of Paul's theology (around the typical categories drawn from systematic theology, e.g., Christology, soteriology, eschatology, ethics) that grows out of the earlier discussion of the theology of the individual letters.

4.30.9   Witherington, Ben, III. *The Paul Quest: The Renewed Search for the Jew of Tarsus.* Downers Grove, Ill.: InterVarsity, 1998. 347pp.

Clearly written introduction to the major issues in contemporary Pauline research and the various ways scholars are addressing these issues. Gives special attention to social history and cultural anthropology for understanding Paul. Witherington evaluates these scholarly options and offers his own arguments and conclusions. Attempts to integrate careful and critical examination of the biblical and historical evidence with the perspectives of each scholar discussed so as to arrive at a balanced and compelling portrait of Paul and of his thought. Stresses the Jewish background of Paul. Considers Acts to be fully reliable and develops the relationship between the chronology of Paul derived from Acts and from the epistles.

4.30.10   Wright, N.T. *Paul and the Faithfulness of God.* 2 vols. Volume 4 of *Christian Origins and the Question of God.* Minneapolis: Fortress, 2013. 1700pp.

Seeks to understand Paul's theology by examining the intersection of his thought with the religion, politics, culture, and philosophy of the Jewish, Greek, and Roman worlds of his time. Engages in lively discussion of key exegetical issues in individual letters and passages. Insists on the fundamental unity of Paul's thought around the faithfulness of God to God's promises.

Also Significant

4.30.11   Ascough, Richard S. *What Are They Saying about the Formation of the Pauline Churches?* New York: Paulist, 1998. 133pp.

336

4.30.12   Ashton, John. *The Religion of Paul the Apostle*. New Haven, Conn.: Yale University Press, 2000. 261pp.

4.30.13   Barrett, C. K. *Paul: An Introduction to His Thought*. Louisville: Westminster John Knox, 1994. 180pp.

4.30.14   Bassler, Jouette M., ed. *Pauline Theology*. Vol. 1. *Thessalonians, Philippians, Galatians, Philemon*. Minneapolis: Fortress, 1991. 287pp.

4.30.15   Becker, Jürgen. *Paul: Apostle to the Gentiles*. Louisville: Westminster John Knox, 1993. 513pp.

4.30.16   Beilby, James K., and Paul Rhodes Eddy, eds. *Justification: Five Views*. Downers Grove, Ill.: InterVarsity, 2011. 319pp.

4.30.17   Bornkamm, Günther. *Paul*. New York: Harper & Row, 1971. 260pp.

4.30.18   Campbell, Douglas A. *The Deliverance of God: An Apocalyptic Rereading of Justification in Paul*. Grand Rapids: Eerdmans, 2009. 1218pp.

4.30.19   Childs, Brevard. *The Church's Guide for Reading Paul: The Canonical Shaping of the Pauline Corpus*. Grand Rapids: Eerdmans, 2008. 276pp.

4.30.20   Das, Andrew. *Paul, the Law, and the Covenant*. Peabody, Mass.: Hendrickson, 2001. 342pp.

4.30.21   Davies, W. D. *Paul and Rabbinic Judaism: Some Rabbinic Elements in Pauline Theology*. London: SPCK, 1948. 376pp.

4.30.22   Donfried, Karl P., and I. Howard Marshall. *The Theology of the Shorter Pauline Letters*. New Testament Theology. Cambridge: Cambridge University Press, 1993. 208pp.

4.30.23   Fee, Gordon D. *God's Empowering Presence: The Holy Spirit in the Letters of Paul*. Peabody, Mass.: Hendrickson, 1994. 967pp.

4.30.24 ———. *Pauline Christology: An Exegetical-Theological Study.* Peabody, Mass.: Hendrickson, 2007. 707pp.

4.30.25 Hays, Richard B. *The Conversion of the Imagination: Paul as Interpreter of Israel's Scripture.* Grand Rapids: Eerdmans, 2005. 213pp.

4.30.26 Johnson, E. Elizabeth, and David M. Hay, eds. *Pauline Theology, Volume 4: Looking Back, Pressing On.* Society of Biblical Literature Symposium Series 4. Atlanta: Scholars, 1997. 222pp.

4.30.27 Koperski, Veronica. *What Are They Saying about Paul and the Law?* New York: Paulist, 2001. 148pp.

4.30.28 Matera, Frank J. *Strategies for Preaching Paul.* Collegeville, Minn.: Liturgical Press, 2001. 186pp.

4.30.29 Meeks, Wayne A. *The First Urban Christians: The Social World of the Apostle Paul.* New Haven, Conn.: Yale University Press, 1983. 299pp.

4.30.30 Munck, Johannes. *Paul and the Salvation of Mankind.* Atlanta: John Knox, 1959. 351pp.

4.30.31 Neyrey, Jerome H. *Paul, In Other Words: A Cultural Reading of His Letters.* Louisville: Westminster John Knox, 1990. 263pp.

4.30.32 Plevnik, Joseph. *What Are They Saying about Paul and the Endtime?* New York: Paulist, 2009. 130pp.

4.30.33 Seifrid, Mark A., and Randall K. J. Tan. *The Pauline Writings.* IBR Bibliographies 9. Grand Rapids: Baker, 2002. 150pp.

4.30.34 Stewart, James S. *A Man in Christ: The Vital Elements of St. Paul's Religion.* Grand Rapids: Baker, 1975. 331pp.

4.30.35 Witherington, Ben, III. *Paul's Narrative Thought World: The Tapestry of Tragedy and Triumph.* Louisville: Westminster John Knox, 1994. 373pp.

4.30.36   Wright, N. T. *The Climax of the Covenant: Christ and the Law in Pauline Theology*. Minneapolis: Fortress, 1993. 316pp.

4.30.37   ———. *Paul*. Minneapolis: Fortress, 2005. 195pp.

4.30.38   ———. *Paul and His Recent Interpreters*. Minneapolis: Fortress, 2014. 384pp.

A major development in Pauline studies over the past twenty years has been the emergence of the "New Perspective on Paul," which is something of a reaction against certain aspects of the views concerning the Pauline doctrine of justification by faith and the relationship of Paul's gospel to Judaism that are commonly associated with the Protestant Reformation in the sixteenth century and accepted by most Protestants since. A helpful, if brief, explanation of the issues raised by the New Perspective, along with a basic bibliography (which includes some of the books listed above), is found in:

4.30.39   Thompson, Michael B. *The New Perspective on Paul*. Rev. ed. Cambridge: Grove Books, 2010. 28pp.

Those interested may consult also these major works dealing with the New Perspective:

4.30.40   Carson, D. A., Peter T. O'Brien, and Mark A. Seifrid, *Justification and Variegated Nomism: A Fresh Appraisal of Paul and Second Temple Judaism*. 2 vols. Grand Rapids: Baker Academic, 2001. 619/537pp.

4.30.41   Dunn, James D. G. *The New Perspective on Paul: Revised*. Grand Rapids: Eerdmans, 2007. 539pp.

4.30.42   Stuhlmacher, Peter. *Revisiting Paul's Doctrine of Justification: A Challenge to the New Perspective*. Downers Grove, Ill.: InterVarsity, 2001. 108pp.

4.30.43   Westerholm, Stephen. *Perspectives Old and New on Paul: The "Lutheran" Paul and His Critics*. Grand Rapids: Eerdmans, 2004. 488pp.

4.30.44   Wright, N. T. *Justification: God's Plan & Paul's Vision.* Downers Grove, Ill.: InterVarsity, 2009. 279pp.

4.30.45   ———. *What Saint Paul Really Said.* Oxford: Lion, 1997. 192pp.

4.31   Romans

Highly Recommended

4.31.1   Achtemeier, Paul J. *Romans.* Interpretation: A Bible Commentary for Teaching and Preaching. Atlanta: John Knox, 1985. 241pp.

Written by leading Presbyterian NT scholar, but his Reformed theological tradition does not determine his exposition (e.g., accepts a rather "Arminian" interpretation of ch. 7). Carefully examines Paul's theological argument, making use of "new avenues of investigation" from recent Pauline scholarship, especially the insight that Paul's thinking reflects his struggle over the role of the Jews as God's chosen people within God's whole plan for human salvation. Introduction provides helpful explanation of the structure of Paul's thought, particularly his Christian adaptation of Jewish apocalypticism. In view of this apocalyptic background, Achtemeier concludes that Paul is concerned not simply with the justification of the individual, but with the whole sweep of history and of creation. Relates this broad discussion of Paul's theology specifically to Romans, leading to a very helpful exposition of the shape of the theology of this epistle. Even more than is usually the case in this series, discusses specifically how passages (complex, and to the modern mind arcane) might be used for preaching and teaching.

4.31.2   Donfried, Karl P., ed. *The Romans Debate.* Rev. ed. Peabody, Mass.: Hendrickson, 1991. 372pp.

A standard work for exploring major issues pertaining to the study of Romans, especially the character, structure, historical setting, purpose, occasion, and theology of the book. Contains a series of essays, originally published elsewhere, by most prominent authorities in the field. Includes some classic older articles (e.g., by T. W. Manson, Günther Bornkamm, and F. F. Bruce), but primarily offers current discussion. Introductory essay by Donfried tracks major scholarly debates pertaining to Romans over the past half century. Includes extensive bibliography.

4.31.3 Dunn, James D. G. *Romans.* Word Biblical Commentary. 2 vols. Dallas: Word, 1988. 976pp.

Massive, detailed commentary that attempts to grasp the coherence of Paul's thought by carefully tracing the logic of the argument from the beginning of the letter to the end. Thus emphasizes the role of each passage within the flow of argument. Provides depth by exploring the lexical significance of Greek terms (does relatively little with grammatical analysis) and by considering Paul's broader theological program reflected in his other letters. Gives special attention to historical, cultural, and religious background, and is particularly concerned to explore the interaction in Paul's thought between his Jewish heritage and his Christian faith, considering this interface to be the primary religious and ideological background to the letter. By attending to the meaning of passages in the particularity of their original historical context Dunn is able to identify points of continuing relevance for contemporary Christians.

4.31.4 Fitzmyer, Joseph A. *Romans.* Anchor Bible. New York: Doubleday, 1993. 793pp.

First full-scale commentary on Romans written by an American Roman Catholic since 1934. Contains most complete bibliography of commentaries on Romans (from the Fathers to the present) available. In addition to usual treatment of authorship, date, occasion, and purpose, introduction includes illuminating sketch of the theology of this letter. Treatment of each passage begins with "comments," accessible to nonspecialists, with discussion of structure, main theological theme and the development of the theme in the passage, and role of passage within the letter's argument. "Notes" follow, offering detailed and technical discussions of exegetical issues, including linguistic evidence, relationship to the Pauline corpus, canonical connections, and historical background, some history of interpretation, and a bibliography of works on the passage or on matters pertaining to it. A model of fair, balanced, informed, and insightful interpretation.

4.31.5 Jewett, Robert. *Romans.* Hermeneia: A Critical and Historical Commentary on the Bible. Minneapolis: Fortress, 2007. 1140pp.

The most current, comprehensive and detailed commentary on Romans presently available. Combines traditional historical-critical method with the emerging emphases on ancient rhetoric and Roman imperial studies. Argues that the purpose of the epistle was to garner support for Paul's mission to the barbarians in Spain; and to that end Paul insisted that the gospel of free grace subverted the system of honor that both created divisions between Jew and Gentile within the Roman churches and promoted a cultural hubris that led to disdain of barbarians. Interprets each passage in light of this broad situational framework. Some will question whether all the major issues raised in the theological exposition of 1:18–11:36 can be easily subsumed under this situational umbrella. Nevertheless, Jewett's massive learning and his honed exegetical instincts render this commentary of immense value for every interpreter.

4.31.6   Moo, Douglas J. *The Epistle to the Romans*. New International Commentary on the New Testament. Grand Rapids: Eerdmans, 1996. 1012pp.

A detailed commentary from a leading American evangelical scholar. A fair and balanced commentary that is at points quite independent from Moo's Reformed tradition, although his manner of framing issues and his conclusions generally reflect a traditional Protestant (and more specifically Reformed) perspective. Based on the English text, but gives extensive attention to the Greek. Interacts extensively with the history of interpretation, and vigorously challenges some of the new scholarly perspectives on Paul. Attends seriously to ways in which practical issues facing the Roman Christians affected the shape of Paul's theological arguments. Considers both the meaning for the original readers and the significance for contemporary Christians.

4.31.7   Sanday, William, and Arthur Headlam. *A Critical and Exegetical Commentary on the Epistle to the Romans*. *International Critical Commentary*. Edinburgh: T&T Clark, 1898. 450pp.

In spite of its age, remains one of the most insightful commentaries on Romans. Offers clear, crisp comments that are to the point and almost entirely free of confessional or theological bias. Maintains careful balance between concern for general flow of the argument and attention to exegetical details. Well ahead of its time in its emphasis on critical consideration of Paul's Jewish religious background. Develops meaning of major theological themes, placing them in the context of broader biblical thought.

4.31.8   Witherington, Ben, III. *Paul's Letter to the Romans: A Socio-Rhetorical Commentary*. Grand Rapids: Eerdmans, 2004. 421pp.

Believing that Romans has typically been read through an Augustinian/Lutheran/Calvinistic lens this veteran commentator carefully and judiciously employs ancient rhetoric and considerations of the situation of the Roman churches to offer a fresh interpretation of the epistle. This commentary is valuable especially in explicitly relating the interpretation of each passage to the larger argument of the epistle. Preachers and teachers will particularly benefit from the discussions of contemporary relevance ("bridging the horizons") that conclude the discussion of each passage.

Also Significant

4.31.9   Barrett, C. K. *The Epistle to the Romans*. Rev. ed. Black's New Testament Commentary. Peabody, Mass.: Hendrickson, 1991. 278pp.

4.31.10   Barth, Karl. *The Epistle to the Romans*. London: Oxford, 1933. 547pp.

4.31.11   Byrne, Brendan. *Romans*. Sacra Pagina. Collegeville, Minn.: Liturgical Press, 1996. 503pp.

4.31.12   Cranfield, C. E. B. *A Critical and Exegetical Commentary on the Epistle to the Romans*. 2 vols. International Critical Commentary. Edinburgh: T&T Clark, 1975–1979. 927pp.

4.31.13   Esler, Philip F. *Conflict and Identity in Romans: The Social Setting of Paul's Letter*. Minneapolis: Fortress, 2003. 458pp.

4.31.14   Greenman, Jeffrey, and Timothy Larsen. *Reading Romans through the Centuries: From the Early Church to Karl Barth*. Grand Rapids: Brazos, 2005. 223pp.

4.31.15   Hay, David M., and E. Elizabeth Johnson, eds. *Pauline Theology, Volume 3: Romans*. Minneapolis: Fortress, 1995. 353pp.

4.31.16   Hultgren, Arland J. *Paul's Letter to the Romans: A Commentary*. Grand Rapids: Eerdmans, 2011. 804pp.

4.31.17   Käsemann, Ernst. *Commentary on Romans*. Grand Rapids: Eerdmans, 1980. 428pp.

4.31.18   Johnson, Luke Timothy. *Reading Romans: A Literary and Theological Commentary*. New York: Crossroad, 1996. 224pp.

4.31.19   Schlatter, Adolf. *Romans: The Righteousness of God.* Peabody, Mass.: Hendrickson, 1995. 287pp. (Originally published in German in 1935.)

4.31.20   Schreiner, Thomas R. *Romans.* Baker Exegetical Commentary on the New Testament. Grand Rapids: Baker, 1998. 919pp.

4.31.21   Stuhlmacher, Peter. *Paul's Letter to the Romans: A Commentary.* Louisville: Westminster John Knox, 1994. 269pp.

4.31.22   Tobin, Thomas H. *Paul's Rhetoric in its Contexts: The Argument of Romans.* Peabody, Mass.: Hendrickson, 2004. 69pp.

4.31.23   Wedderburn, A. J. M. *The Reasons for Romans.* Edinburgh: T&T Clark, 1991. 169pp.

4.32   Corinthian Epistles

Highly Recommended

4.32.1   Barnett, Paul. *The Second Epistle to the Corinthians.* New International Commentary on the New Testament. Grand Rapids: Eerdmans, 1997. 662pp.

Lucid and illuminating commentary. Based on the English text, but regularly refers to the Greek, both in the text and in footnotes bearing on text-critical and exegetical issues. Argues for the letter's unity and stresses the role of individual passages within the argument as a whole. Concludes that Paul responds to the triumphalism of the Corinthians by urging a theology of power-in-weakness, based on God's resurrection of the crucified one. Paul also addresses God's fulfillment of promise in Christ through the Spirit, and presents himself as a model of pastoral leadership. Concentrates on the meaning of text for the original audience, but gives specific (though brief) attention to contemporary significance. Accessible to nonspecialists, but stimulating for scholars.

4.32.2   Barrett, C. K. *The First Epistle to the Corinthians.* Black's New Testament Commentary. Peabody, Mass.: Hendrickson, 1968. 410pp.

Clear, concise, insightful, authoritative, and engaging. Introduction includes a helpful sketch of the Corinthian church and the history of the relationship between the Corinthians and Paul leading up to the production of this letter. (Even more illuminating is Barrett's explanation of the confusing history of that relationship through 2 Corinthinas, in his introduction to the commentary on that epistle, cited in next entry.) Barrett is the master of economy here, including just enough information and comment to bring the meaning of the passage into sharp focus. Manages even to offer significant theological reflection at points. Includes little explicit discussion of contemporary significance, but by exploring the connection between Paul's theological arguments and the practical problems Paul attempts to address, Barrett enables readers to make connections to contemporary situations.

4.32.3   ———. *The Second Epistle to the Corinthians.* Black's New Testament Commentary. Peabody, Mass.: Hendrickson, 1973. 353pp.

See Barrett's *First Epistle to the Corinthians* (§4.32.2).

4.32.4   Fee, Gordon D. *The First Epistle to the Corinthians.* New International Commentary on the New Testament. Grand Rapids: Eerdmans, 1987. 880pp.

Detailed and learned commentary, written primarily for theological students and those engaged in preaching and teaching in the church, but of value also for scholars. This evangelical and Pentecostal NT scholar gives meticulous attention to every word and phrase of the book, emphasizing (1) how every statement fits into the flow of its immediate context and every section fits into the development of the argument of the entire book; (2) ways in which the historical background of church, community, and culture illuminates each passage; (3) linguistic analysis of the Greek text; (4) interpretive significance of textual variants; and (5) contemporary significance, concluding each section with explicit suggestions for Christian application.

4.32.5   Fitzmyer, Joseph A. *First Corinthians.* Anchor Yale Bible. New Haven, Conn.: Yale University Press, 2008. 660pp.

Fitzmyer, perhaps the premier Catholic NT scholar today, brings the massive resources of a life of NT scholarship to bear upon this book. Employs the historical-critical method and gives little attention to the emerging studies in ancient rhetoric or the social sciences or Roman imperialism. Makes accessible the richness of technical historical and linguistic scholarship to the nonspecialist. Engages in constant interaction with other (mostly modern) interpreters. Gives serious attention to theological matters. Includes helpful current bibliographies for each passage.

4.32.6   Harris, Murray J. *The Second Epistle to the Corinthians*. New International Greek Testament Commentary. Grand Rapids: Eerdmans, 2005. 989pp.

This highly technical commentary focuses on the historical context of Paul's ministry and experience with the Corinthians, and attends especially to Greek grammar, lexicography, and matters of textual criticism. All this technical analysis leads explicitly to rich theological insight. Insists upon the unity of 2 Corinthians and is careful to relate individual passages to the argument of the book in the large.

4.32.7   Hays, Richard B. *First Corinthians*. Interpretation: A Bible Commentary for Teaching and Preaching. Louisville: Westminster John Knox, 1997. 299pp.

Offers more substantial and innovative exegetical insights into the original significance of the text than is typical of this series. Insists that only by attending to the specifics of the text can we direct our imagination in such a way as to discover analogies between our own situation and that of the original addressees. Argues that the letter presents Paul as a model pastor and urges the "conversion of the imagination," i.e., the adoption of a radical new perspective that challenges inherited sociocultural norms and practices. Explores the role of social and economic factors in the development of theological problems in the church. Paul's innovative employment of Israel's scriptures must be appreciated in order to understand Paul's argument. Paul's use of Scripture encourages us to emulate his model in our own appropriation of Scripture.

4.32.8   Martin, Ralph P. *2 Corinthians*. Word Biblical Commentary. Waco, Tex.: Word, 1986. 527pp.

Addresses the complex scholarly issues of 2 Corinthians as well as the theological meaning of the final form of the text. Argues for the unity of chapters 1–9, which he believes left Paul's hands and was on the way to Corinth when he was informed of additional problems, addressed in a subsequent letter that now comprises chapters 10–13. Emphasizes linguistic analysis of the Greek. Explores ways in which the historical and theological situation at this point when Paul's apostolic leadership was under attack illumines the text, while acknowledging the somewhat speculative character of this historical reconstruction. Carefully analyzes how Paul's response to various crises in the Corinthian church illuminates problems of Christian faith in a hedonistic and cosmopolitan setting. Insists that Paul consistently challenges the Corinthians' theology of glory with a theology of weakness manifested in servanthood and selfless ministry.

4.32.9   Matera, Frank J. *II Corinthians: A Commentary.* New Testament Library. Louisville: Westminster John Knox, 2003. 332pp.

This prominent Catholic scholar joins an increasing number of authorities who affirm the unity of 2 Corinthians. Argues that Paul deals with the crisis of his recent painful visit in chs. 1–9 and (related to the first problem) the crisis of false apostles in chs. 10–13. Employs grammatical, historical, and rhetorical considerations to illumine individual passages and the larger flow of the book. Among the most theologically oriented of all the commentaries on this book.

4.32.10   Thiselton, Anthony C. *The First Epistle to the Corinthians: A Commentary on the Greek Text.* New International Greek Testament Commentary. Grand Rapids: Eerdmans, 2000. 1446pp.

Most current, comprehensive, and definitive commentary on this book presently available. Attempts to answer every question readers might reasonably be expected to raise regarding the meaning of the text. Gives special attention to Greek syntax and lexicography, sociohistorical background, Paul's use of rhetorical strategies, and history of interpretation. Incorporates insights from emerging approaches, e.g., cultural anthropology, study of semantic domains, and *Wirkungsgeschichte* (i.e., "history of influence" of a passage reflected not just in commentaries, but in art, literature, liturgy, hymnody, etc.). Includes expanded discussions on such key historical and theological issues as apostleship, divorce and remarriage, and speaking in tongues. Technical, but accessible to those who do not know Greek.

4.32.11   Thrall, Margaret E. *A Critical and Exegetical Commentary on the Second Epistle to the Corinthians.* 2 vols. International Critical Commentary. Edinburgh: T&T Clark, 1994, 2000. 978pp.

Detailed and authoritative commentary characterized by highly technical discussion of the historical background and the linguistic evidence of the Greek. Includes the most extensive discussion of literary issues (i.e., unity or composite character of book) and chronology of Paul's relationship with the Corinthians to be found in any commentary, presenting both history of investigation into these questions and careful analysis of NT data. Concludes that 2 Corinthians includes three originally independent letters (chapters 1–8, 9, and 10–13). Recognizes that primary attention must be given to the emerging portrait of Paul and his theological thinking, but insists on the need to understand the viewpoint of the Corinthians as well. Almost exclusively historically oriented, with theological issues addressed only insofar as they are part of the exegesis of a text that has theological content and claims.

347

4.32.12   Witherington, Ben, III. *Conflict and Community in Corinth: A Socio-Rhetorical Commentary on 1 and 2 Corinthians.* Grand Rapids: Eerdmans, 1995. 492pp.

Presents in a lucid fashion the meaning of the final form of these two epistles primarily on the basis of a careful examination of sociological background and Paul's use of rhetorical devices that were frequently employed in his day. Takes seriously the flow of the argument, commenting on whole rhetorical sections over against the standard verse-by-verse approach. A significant advantage of this commentary over many others is that it deals in one volume with both Corinthian letters.

Also Significant

4.32.13   Adams, Edward, and David G. Horrell, eds. *Christianity at Corinth: The Quest for the Pauline Church.* Louisville: Westminster John Knox, 2004. 332pp.

4.32.14   Best, Ernest. *Second Corinthians.* Interpretation: A Bible Commentary for Teaching and Preaching. Atlanta: John Knox, 1987. 142pp.

4.32.15   Bieringer, R., ed. *The Corinthian Correspondence.* Bibliotheca Ephemeridum Theologicarum Lovaniensium 125. Leuven: Leuven University Press, 1996. 791pp.

4.32.16   Bieringer, R., and J. Lambrecht, eds. *Studies on 2 Corinthians.* Bibliotheca Ephemeridum Theologicarum Lovaniensium 112. Leuven: Leuven University Press, 1994. 632pp.

4.32.17   Collins, Raymond F. *First Corinthians.* Sacra Pagina. Collegeville, Minn.: Liturgical Press, 2000. 695pp.

4.32.18   Conzelmann, Hans. *1 Corinthians.* Hermeneia: A Critical and Historical Commentary on the Bible. Philadelphia: Fortress, 1975. 323pp.

4.32.19   Furnish, Victor Paul. *2 Corinthians.* Anchor Bible. Garden City, NY: Doubleday, 1984. 619pp.

4.32.20   Georgi, Dieter. *The Opponents of Paul in Second Corinthians.* Philadel-
           phia: Fortress, 1986. 463pp.

4.32.21   Grant, Robert M. *Paul in the Roman World: The Conflict at Corinth.* Louis-
           ville: Westminster John Knox, 2001. 200pp.

4.32.22   Harvey, A. E. *Renewal Through Suffering: A Study of 2 Corinthians.* Stud-
           ies of the New Testament and Its World. Edinburgh: T&T Clark, 1996.
           148pp.

4.32.23   Hay, David M. *Pauline Theology, Volume 2: 1 and 2 Corinthians.* Minne-
           apolis: Fortress, 1993. 300pp.

4.32.24   Hering, Jean. *The Second Epistle of St. Paul to the Corinthians.* London:
           Epworth, 1967. 111pp.

4.32.25   Hughes, Philip Edgcumbe. *Commentary on the Second Epistle to the Cor-
           inthians.* New International Commentary on the New Testament. Grand
           Rapids: Eerdmans, 1962. 508pp.

4.32.26   Kistemaker, Simon. *Exposition of the First Epistle to the Corinthians.* New
           Testament Commentary. Grand Rapids: Baker, 1993. 649pp.

4.32.27   ———. *Exposition of the Second Epistle to the Corinthians.* New Testa-
           ment Commentary. Grand Rapids: Baker, 1997. 495pp.

4.32.28   Lambrecht, Jan. *Second Corinthians.* Sacra Pagina. Collegeville, Minn.:
           Liturgical Press, 1999. 250pp.

4.32.29   Long, Fredrick. *Ancient Rhetoric and Paul's Apology: The Compositional
           Unity of 2 Corinthians.* Society for New Testament Studies Monograph
           Series. Cambridge: Cambridge University Press, 2008. 312pp.

4.32.30   Mitchell, Margaret M. *Paul and the Rhetoric of Reconciliation: An Exegeti-
           cal Investigation of the Language and Composition of 1 Corinthians.* Louis-
           ville: Westminster John Knox, 1991. 380pp.

4.32.31 Murphy-O'Connor, Jerome. *The Theology of the Second Letter to the Corinthians*. New Testament Theology. Cambridge: Cambridge University Press, 1991. 166pp.

4.32.32 Savage, Timothy B. *Power through Weakness: Paul's Understanding of the Christian Ministry in 2 Corinthians*. Society for New Testament Studies Monograph Series 86. Cambridge: Cambridge University Press, 1996. 251pp.

4.32.33 Talbert, Charles H. *Reading Corinthians: A Literary and Theological Commentary on 1 and 2 Corinthians*. Rev. ed. New York: Crossroads, 2002. 238pp.

4.32.34 Theissen, Gerd. *The Social Setting of Pauline Christianity: Essays on Corinth*. Philadelphia: Fortress, 1982. 214pp.

4.32.35 Winter, Bruce W. *After Paul Left Corinth: The Influence of Secular Ethics and Social Change*. Grand Rapids: Eerdmans, 2001. 344pp.

4.32.36 Young, Frances, and David F. Ford. *Meaning and Truth in 2 Corinthians*. Grand Rapids: Eerdmans, 1987. 289pp.

4.33 Galatians

Highly Recommended

4.33.1 Betz, Hans Dieter. *Galatians*. Hermeneia: A Critical and Historical Commentary on the Bible. Philadelphia: Fortress, 1979. 352pp.

Groundbreaking commentary on Galatians insofar as it introduced the significance of Greco-Roman rhetoric and epistolography (i.e., study of function, structure, and forms of ancient epistles) into the interpretation of Galatians. Argues that this book is an example of an apologetic letter ("forensic rhetoric"), and interprets the letter in light of that convention. The chief contribution of this volume is its careful tracing of the argument of the letter, understanding the letter primarily on the basis of its own internal dynamics and the historical situation that occasioned it. Possible weakness is the tendency to impose the concept of forensic rhetoric on the entire letter; many have argued that it is plausible for chapters 1–2, but less persuasive for the remainder of the letter.

4.33.2   De Boer, Martinus C. *Galatians: A Commentary.* New Testament Library. Louisville: Westminster John Knox, 2011. 461pp.

A most illuminating and balanced commentary. Interprets passages in light of their role within the thought development of the epistle and in terms of the ways in which the situation of the Galatians points to their understanding and reception of the letter. Insists that Galatians should be read on its own terms rather than in light of other Pauline epistles, since the Galatians would have had no access to these other epistles, including Romans. Lays out for each passage the major interpretive possibilities, carefully and fairly providing evidence for and against each, and judiciously making his own decisions. Includes excurses for the most controversial passages.

4.33.3   Longenecker, Richard N. *Galatians.* Word Biblical Commentary. Dallas: Word, 1990. 323pp.

Introduction offers the most detailed discussion available for the history of investigation into the key critical issues of destination and the relationship of Galatians to Acts 11 and 15. Also explores the problems Paul faced in the Galatian churches, the message of the opponents, and the impact of this letter on subsequent Christian thought and activity. Emphasizes the relationship between the doctrine of justification by faith and the vitality of Christian life empowered by God's Spirit. Methodology stresses Paul's employment of Hellenistic epistolary conventions, Greco-Roman rhetoric, and Jewish exegetical practices. Makes selective and eclectic use of recent approaches, especially epistolography (ancient letters in antiquity) and rhetorical analysis. Comments include detailed and technical discussions of language, historical background, and ancient rhetoric. "Explanation" sections synthesize main theological issues and offer occasional brief suggestions for contemporary relevance.

4.33.4   Martyn, J. Louis. *Galatians.* Anchor Bible. New York: Doubleday, 1997. 614pp.

Emphasizes the relationship between Paul and the Galatians implicit in this letter, including the roles played by Paul, the Galatians, and Paul's opponents ("the teachers"). Explores Paul's intentions by examining the understanding and reception of the letter by various segments of the Galatian church. Encourages interpreters to place themselves in the position of the original readers, who had one ear tuned to Paul's instructions here and the other to the sermons of "the teachers." In this way Martyn hopes to arrive at a scientific (i.e., historically accurate) and empathetic interpretation. Maintains that lack of attention to these dynamics have led some scholars to ascribe to Paul views that actually belonged to his opponents. The employment of historical imagination is innovative and illuminating, though somewhat speculative at points. Commentary is arranged as a series of "comments," extended discussions of the most significant historical and theological issues in each passage, set within a framework of "notes," brief, basic explanations of each verse.

4.33.5   Witherington, Ben, III. *Grace in Galatia: A Commentary on Paul's Letter to the Galatians.* Grand Rapids: Eerdmans, 1998. 475pp.

Like the commentary by Betz (§4.33.1), this volume gives serious attention to the flow of the argument, Paul's rhetorical devices, and the rhetorical macrostructure of the book. In contrast to Betz, Witherington identifies Galatians as "deliberative discourse," rather than "forensic" or "apologetic." Paul is not primarily concerned to defend himself or his apostolic authority, but offers robust explication of the gospel and its implications. Incorporates insights from discoveries and scholarly discussions developing over the quarter century since the appearance of Betz's commentary. Hence there is significant concern for sociological background, an area that was just emerging in the 1970s. Rhetorical and historical discussion is employed in service of the theological message of the book and its meaning for today. Witherington concludes each chapter by drawing out the significance for contemporary Christians.

Also Significant

4.33.6   Barclay, John M. G. *Obeying the Truth: Paul's Ethics in Galatians.* Minneapolis: Fortress, 1991. 298pp.

4.33.7   Barrett, C. K. *Freedom and Obligation: A Study of the Epistle to the Galatians.* Philadelphia: Westminster, 1985. 120pp.

4.33.8   Bruce, F. F. *The Epistle to the Galatians: A Commentary on the Greek Text.* New International Greek Testament Commentary. Grand Rapids: Eerdmans, 1982. 305pp.

4.33.9   Burton, Ernest De Witt. *A Critical and Exegetical Commentary on the Epistle to the Galatians.* International Critical Commentary. Edinburgh: T&T Clark, 1921. 541pp.

4.33.10   Cousar, Charles B. *Galatians*. Interpretation: A Bible Commentary for Teaching and Preaching. Atlanta: John Knox, 1982. 158pp.

4.33.11   Dunn, James D. G. *The Epistle to the Galatians*. Black's New Testament Commentary. Peabody, Mass.: Hendrickson, 1993. 375pp.

4.33.12   ———. *The Theology of Paul's Letter to the Galatians*. New Testament Theology. Cambridge: Cambridge University Press, 1993. 161pp.

4.33.13   Ebeling, Gerhard. *The Truth of the Gospel: An Exposition of Galatians*. Philadelphia: Fortress, 1985. 276pp.

4.33.14   Fung, Ronald Y. K. *The Epistle to the Galatians*. New International Commentary on the New Testament. Grand Rapids: Eerdmans, 1988. 342pp.

4.33.15   Hays, Richard B. *The Faith of Jesus Christ: The Narrative Substructure of Galatians 3:1–4:11*. 2d ed. Biblical Resource Series. Grand Rapids: Eerdmans, 2001. 304pp.

4.33.16   Howard, George. *Paul: Crisis in Galatia*. Society for New Testament Studies Monograph Series 35. Cambridge: Cambridge University Press, 1990. 113pp.

4.33.17   Lightfoot, J. B. *The Epistle of St. Paul to the Galatians*. London: Macmillan, 1865. 384pp.

4.33.18   Longenecker, Bruce W. *The Triumph of Abraham's God: The Transformation of Identity in Galatians*. Edinburgh: T&T Clark, 1998. 236pp.

4.33.19   Luther, Martin. *A Commentary on St. Paul's Epistle to the Galatians*. Grand Rapids: Zondervan, n.d. 252pp. (Originally published in German in 1539.)

4.33.20   Matera, Frank J. *Galatians*. Sacra Pagina. Collegeville, Minn.: Michael Glazier, 1992. 252pp.

353

4.33.21 Morris, Leon. *Galatians: Paul's Charter of Christian Freedom*. Downers Grove, Ill.: InterVarsity, 1996. 191pp.

4.33.22 Riches, John. *Galatians through the Centuries*. Oxford: Blackwell, 2008. 336pp.

4.33.23 Silva, Moisés. *Explorations in Exegetical Method: Galatians as a Test Case*. Grand Rapids: Baker Academic, 2001. 256pp.

4.33.24 Smiles, Vincent M. *The Gospel and the Law in Galatia: Paul's Response to Jewish-Christian Separatism and the Threat of Galatian Apostasy*. Collegeville, Minn.: Liturgical Press, 1998. 286pp.

4.34 Ephesians and Colossians

See also PHILIPPIANS AND PHILEMON (§4.35)

Highly Recommended

4.34.1 Barth, Markus. *Ephesians*. 2 vols. Anchor Bible. Garden City, N.Y.: Doubleday, 1974. 849pp.

Virtually all scholars regard this as one of the best commentaries on Ephesians ever produced, notable especially for its breadth of learning, meticulous attention to detail, careful citation of evidence, fair and balanced presentation, and theological depth. Barth (son of theologian Karl Barth) maintains, against the majority of contemporary critical scholars, that the letter was written by Paul to Gentile Christians living in Ephesus. The "notes" provide brief explanations of the sense of each verse, based primarily on detailed examination of the Greek, historical background (both Jewish and Greco-Roman), and canonical connections (especially Paul's letters). The "comments" are extended and insightful discussions on the most significant issues in each passage, focusing on the contribution of the passage to the presentation of the theme in the NT as a whole, its relationship to theological systems and the writings of theological thinkers in the history of the church, and significance for contemporary Christians.

4.34.2 Barth, Markus, and Helmut Blanke. *Colossians*. Anchor Bible. New York: Doubleday, 1994. 557pp.

Begun by Markus Barth and completed by his student Helmut Blanke as Barth's health failed. In spite of the dual authorship there are no evident seams and the volume flows evenly and coheres perfectly. Introduction contains extensive discussion of the nature of the Colossian "heresy," the relationship between Colossians and Ephesians, and the authorship of Colossians. Contends that Paul wrote this letter from Roman imprisonment around 60–61 to readers in acute danger of being led astray by a group largely outside the church. This group touted a religion involving Jewish and pagan elements synthesized in a remarkably complete, coherent, and therefore compelling system. Paul seeks to persuade readers of the ultimate and absolute sufficiency of Christ and the need to embrace a pattern of behavior that stems from affirmation of this ultimacy of Christ. Brief but specific notes explain the sense of each passage, with comments that expand on significant issues in each passage. The comments are eloquent even to the point of poetic, and offer rich theological insight and connections with historical and systematic theology.

4.34.3   Best, Ernest. *A Critical and Exegetical Commentary on Ephesians.* International Critical Commentary. Edinburgh: T&T Clark, 1998. 686pp.

Solid and detailed commentary, if not overly imaginative. Introduction includes lengthy discussion of authorship, concluding that Ephesians and Colossians were written by two separate representatives of a Pauline school; Ephesians was produced around 90 as a general letter addressed to churches throughout Asia Minor. Treatment of each passage includes select bibliography, general introduction (with description of the passage's structure, genre, and relationship to the book as a whole), and comments emphasizing linguistic analysis of the Greek, but with some attention to historical background and canonical connections, all with a view to clarification of the theological claims of the text.

4.34.4   Fowl, Stephen E. *Ephesians: A Commentary.* New Testament Library. Louisville: Westminster John Knox, 2012. 249pp.

Fowl is a prominent advocate of the theological interpretation of Scripture, which seeks to interpret the Bible in relation to the church's faith. This emphasis always carries the danger that the church's (or a particular church's) theological tradition will be imposed upon the text. This commentary does not succumb to that danger, but it is rather a model of interpretation that is done in conversation with (but not collapsed into) ecclesial theological issues. Attends to the function of Ephesians within the canon, and interacts selectively with both modern and premodern interpreters. Is unsure whether in fact Paul wrote Ephesians, but provides a lengthy discussion of authorship and of the relationship between the determination of Pauline authorship and the canonical status of the book.

4.34.5   Lightfoot, J. B. *Saint Paul's Epistles to the Colossians and to Philemon.* 6th ed. London: Macmillan, 1882. 430pp.

Lightfoot was one of the "Cambridge triumvirate," along with B. F. Westcott and F. J. A. Hort, who argued for the authenticity and early dating of NT documents over against the more radical positions of the "Tübingen school." All of Lightfoot's commentaries are erudite and insightful, but none has so influenced the history of interpretation as his commentary on Colossians. His analysis of the Colossian "heresy" is classic, and although his contention that the heresy arose out of the Essenes is generally rejected, his basic approach and many of his specific observations form the basis for all subsequent discussion. The Greek text appears at the top of the page, with notes below. Comments emphasize linguistic analysis of the Greek, contextual connections, ancient parallels, and history of interpretation (with quotes in the original Greek or Latin). Attends seriously to theological significance. In spite of its age remains extremely helpful.

4.34.6   Lincoln, Andrew T. *Ephesians.* Word Biblical Commentary. Dallas: Word, 1990. 494pp.

This evangelical scholar compares Ephesians with Colossians and other books in the Pauline corpus, concluding that Ephesians was written by a follower of Paul to a group of churches in Asia Minor after Paul's death. The author of Ephesians has redacted his sources (Colossians and other letters in the Pauline corpus) so as to apply the Pauline themes to the situation now facing his readers. Thus, explores the ways this redactional process illuminates the meaning of each passage. Also examines the lexical and syntactical significance of the Greek text, the employment of rhetorical strategies current at the time of writing, the structure of the passage, and the role of the passage in broader-book context. The purpose of the letter is to persuade readers to consider the role of the church (which includes the people of Israel) in the history of God's purposes, to embrace their Christian identity in a hostile socioreligious environment, and to recognize the ways in which this identity must be manifested in their behavior. Offers a more complete, coherent, and compelling portrait of the setting of this letter and of the letter's response to this setting than does Best (§4.34.3). Explanation sections synthesize the theology of each passage, but seldom address contemporary application.

4.34.7   O'Brien, Peter T. *Colossians, Philemon.* Word Biblical Commentary. Waco, Tex.: Word, 1982. 328pp.

Introduction provides illuminating history of interpretation into the Colossian "heresy," which O'Brien takes to be an admixture of Jewish and pagan elements, emphasizing mysticism and asceticism. To counter this teaching, Paul stresses realized eschatology, i.e., the aspects of salvation that Christians experience in the present, so as to insist that already Christ provides Christians with more than could possibly be offered by this competing religious system. Like Barth-Blanke (§4.34.2), contends that the letter was written by Paul during Roman imprisonment. But O'Brien's interpretation of individual passages often differs from Barth-Blanke, in some cases offering a more compelling interpretation. Emphasizes analysis of the Greek, religious and sociohistorical background, canonical connections, and history of interpretation. The "explanation" section synthesizes the theology of the passage and explores its significance for the religious experience of the original readers, but seldom addresses contemporary application.

4.34.8   Pokorný, Petr. *Colossians: A Commentary.* Peabody, Mass.: Hendrickson, 1991. 232pp.

Argues that Colossians is a pseudonymous letter written by a follower of Paul after the latter's death. Considers the theological significance of a pseudonymous canonical book, and concludes that the theological problems are manageable and that the letter "authentically renders apostolic witness." Reconstructs a plausible historical setting for the letter. Commentary focuses on the literary structure of whole book and of individual passages, and the structure of the theological argument. Gives secondary attention to linguistic analysis, historical background, and history of interpretation. Primarily concerned with theological exposition, and constantly relates the theological claims of specific passages in Colossians to the broader biblical witness. Gives no explicit attention to contemporary application.

4.34.9   Schnackenburg, Rudolf. *The Epistle to the Ephesians: A Commentary.* Edinburgh: T&T Clark, 1991. 356pp.

The author, a leading European Roman Catholic scholar, attempts to write for Protestants as well as Catholics. Considers Ephesians to be a post-Pauline pseudepigraphical work, a general letter addressed to a wide geographical area, whose author knew and used Colossians. Sees the focus of the letter as the church, and the purpose to persuade Christians in danger of conforming to their pagan environment to embrace decisively Christian commitment and behavior. Attends to the structure and form of each passage, its role within the argument of the whole work, linguistic analysis of the Greek, canonical connections, and contemporary significance.

357

4.34.10   Sumney, Jerry L. *Colossians: A Commentary.* New Testament Library. Louisville: Westminster John Knox, 2008. 305pp.

Insightful, theologically suggestive commentary. Draws upon technical grammatical and historical information while presenting conclusions in an eminently readable fashion. Interpretive decisions are consistently made carefully and judiciously. Believes that Colossians was written soon after Paul's death not to the church at Colossae but rather to a Christian community related to Philemon.

4.34.11   Wilson, R. McL. *Colossians and Philemon.* International Critical Commentary. London: T&T Clark, 2005. 380pp.

Highly technical commentary that attends carefully to Greek lexicography and syntax and to matters of historical background. Gives less attention to the development of argument in the epistles themselves and to the theology of the text. Believes that Colossians was written to the church at Colossae soon after Paul's death by a member of "the Pauline School" who had an original, creative, and independent theological mind.

Also Significant

4.34.12   Bruce, F. F. *The Epistle to the Colossians, to Philemon, and to the Ephesians.* New International Commentary on the New Testament. Grand Rapids: Eerdmans, 1984. 442pp.

4.34.13   Dahl, Nils Alstrup. *Studies in Ephesians: Introductory Questions, Text- and Edition-Critical Issues, Interpretation of Texts and Themes.* Edited by David Hellholm, Vemund Blomkvist, and Tord Fornberg. Tübingen: Mohr Siebeck, 2000. 548pp.

4.34.14   Dunn, James D. G. *The Epistles to the Colossians and to Philemon: A Commentary on the Greek Text.* New International Greek Testament Commentary. Grand Rapids: Eerdmans, 1996. 388pp.

4.34.15   Hoehner, Harold W. *Ephesians: An Exegetical Commentary.* Grand Rapids: Baker, 2002. 960pp.

4.34.16   Klein, William W. *The Book of Ephesians: An Annotated Bibliography.* New York: Garland, 1996. 312pp.

4.34.17　Lincoln, Andrew T., and A. J. M. Wedderburn. *The Theology of the Later Pauline Letters.* New Testament Theology. Cambridge: Cambridge University Press, 1993. 185pp.

4.34.18　Lohse, Eduard. *Colossians and Philemon.* Hermeneia: A Critical and Historical Commentary on the Bible. Philadelphia: Fortress, 1971. 233pp.

4.34.19　MacDonald, Margaret Y. *Colossians and Ephesians.* Sacra Pagina. Collegeville, Minn.: Liturgical Press, 2000. 390pp.

4.34.20　Mitton, C. Leslie. *Ephesians.* New Century Bible Commentary. London: Oliphants, 1976. 235pp.

4.34.21　Moule, C. F. D. *The Epistles of Paul the Apostle to the Colossians and to Philemon.* Cambridge Greek Testament Commentary. Cambridge: Cambridge University Press, 1957. 169pp.

4.34.22　Robinson, J. Armitage. *St. Paul's Epistle to the Ephesians.* London: Macmillan, 1922. 314pp.

4.34.23　Schweizer, Eduard. *The Letter to the Colossians: A Commentary.* Minneapolis: Augsburg, 1982. 319pp.

4.34.24　Thielman, Frank. *Ephesians.* Baker Exegetical Commentary on the New Testament. Grand Rapids: Baker Academic, 2010. 520pp.

4.34.25　Thurston, Bonnie. *Reading Colossians, Ephesians, and 2 Thessalonians: A Literary and Theological Commentary.* New York: Crossroad, 1995. 197pp.

4.34.26　Westcott, Brooke Foss. *Saint Paul's Epistle to the Ephesians.* London: Macmillan, 1906. 212pp.

4.34.27　Wright, N. T. *Colossians and Philemon.* Tyndale New Testament Commentaries. Grand Rapids: Eerdmans, 1986. 192pp.

4.35 Philippians and Philemon

See also EPHESIANS AND COLOSSIANS (§4.34)

Highly Recommended

4.35.1   Barth, Markus, and Helmut Blanke. *The Letter to Philemon*. Eerdmans
Critical Commentary. Grand Rapids: Eerdmans, 2000. 561pp.

Probably most comprehensive work on Philemon ever produced. Insists
that Philemon is significant for its unique insights into the social setting
of the NT and its creative and specific application of the central demand
of the gospel, brotherly love. Presents extensive analysis of aspects of the
ancient world relevant to Philemon, especially slavery, and compares references to slavery in Philemon with those in other Pauline letters. Verse-by-
verse commentary gives special attention to such major Pauline theological
themes as love, faith, Christian unity, and human responsibility. Surveys
history of interpretation from antiquity to the most recent discussions.
More detailed than Fitzmyer, especially in comments on individual passages, but bibliography is less thorough. Contains many excurses treating
significant historical and theological issues in relation to their role within
Philemon, Pauline theology, and biblical thought as a whole.

4.35.2   Bockmuehl, Markus. *The Epistle to the Philippians*. Black's New Testament Commentary. Peabody, Mass.: Hendrickson, 1998. 327pp.

One of the most methodologically reflective commentaries on Philippians
or any other NT book. Considers methodological issues involved in the
use of Acts for reconstructing the Philippian situation, concluding that
a cautious, critical, but sympathetic employment of Acts is appropriate.
Incorporates insights from sociological studies and investigations into ancient rhetoric, but rejects a heavy dependence on these recent approaches
in favor of a more general historical approach that makes use of all relevant
evidence for ascertaining the intended meaning of the text for its original
readers and that in turn leads to theological understanding. Packs a remarkable amount of relevant information and theological insight into a
small amount of space by focusing on those elements that are central to the
agenda of the text and are of greatest concern to modern readers.

4.35.3   Fee, Gordon D. *Paul's Letter to the Philippians*. New International Commentary on the New Testament. Grand Rapids: Eerdmans, 1995. 497pp.

Comprehensive and detailed commentary on the English text (NIV), but
with constant reference to the Greek. Writes primarily for pastors and

teachers, but with an eye also to the scholar. Argues for Pauline authorship and literary unity of the letter, which Fee takes to have been written from Roman imprisonment to a church facing opposition because of its commitment to Christ. Considers Philippians to have material and formal connections with two types of letters familiar to first-century readers: friendship, and moral exhortation. Introduction extensively discusses these two letter types, and commentary draws on literary and philosophical background of friendship and moral exhortation. Text of commentary is accessible to nonspecialist. Presents the theological meaning of the text, with references to original language, literary structure, and background of Paul's thought as discerned from his other letters all discussed more fully and technically in extensive footnotes.

4.35.4   Fitzmyer, Joseph A. *The Letter to Philemon.* Anchor Bible. New York: Doubleday, 2000. 138pp.

Deals in an informed and judicious manner with most significant issues in Philemon. The introduction, which comprises more than half of the volume, offers brief but illuminating discussions of slavery in antiquity, contemporary significance of this letter, theology, and complete bibliography. The "comments" on each passage, accessible to the nonspecialist, treat the literary structure of the passage, its function within the letter, and its basic meaning. The "notes" explore the meaning of each verse through linguistic analysis; social, political, economic, and religious background; and history of interpretation (both ancient and modern). Includes extensive bibliography on each passage.

4.35.5   Hawthorne, Gerald F. *Philippians.* Word Biblical Commentary. Waco, Tex.: Word, 1983. 232pp.

Solid and informed, though not particularly original, commentary written from an evangelical perspective. Argues that Philippians is a unity, written by Paul from Caesarean prison around 60. Comments are lucid and clearly organized, typically listing major interpretive possibilities along with arguments for and against each, concluding with Hawthorne's own considered judgment. Generally discusses major issues or aspects of a passage, developing the meaning of each and giving explicit citations of evidence, especially from structure, linguistic analysis, other Pauline passages, and parallels from Jewish and Greco-Roman writings. Explicates theological meaning of each passage and its pastoral significance for the original readers. Does little to address explicitly contemporary application.

361

4.35.6   O'Brien, Peter T. *Commentary on Philippians.* New International Greek
         Testament Commentary. Grand Rapids: Eerdmans, 1991. 597pp.

Traditional commentary, focused on historical-critical and linguistic exegesis of the Greek text and drawing little on the more recent literary, rhetorical, and sociological approaches. O'Brien interacts fully with history
of scholarship, but gives primary attention to his own engagement with
the text, often arriving at quite independent interpretive judgments. Deals
with each passage by exploring its structure, themes (overarching concerns
and their specific development within the paragraph), function within the
argument of the entire letter, and analysis of every phrase and word of
the Greek text. Gives particular attention to the background of the city
of Philippi, Paul's opponents, and the character and function within the
book of the christological hymn in 2:5-11. Focus is on the theological
meaning of the text and how it relates to other biblical passages and to
biblical theology as a whole.

4.35.7   Petersen, Norman R. *Rediscovering Paul: Philemon and the Sociology of
         Paul's Narrative World.* Philadelphia: Fortress, 1985. 308pp.

This pioneer in the new literary criticism of the Gospels here integrates
contemporary literary and sociological study with the traditional historical-
critical approach. Argues that letters have narrative substructures (i.e., that
they assume and present a story), and that the "narrative world" presented
in a letter has the same kinds of social arrangements ("social structures
underlying the social relations comprised of the actions of the actors in
Paul's letters and their stories") and symbolic forms ("systems of knowledge, belief, and value, that define these actors' identities and motivate
their actions") as does the real world. This volume is thus a groundbreaking work both in methodology and in the study of Philemon, arguing that
Paul relates the mundane experience of a slave and the dynamics between
this slave and his master to the story of the transcendent divine world,
in which God is Father, Christ is Lord, and love is ultimate reality. Paul
urges the church to submit this present temporal world to the kingdom of
God, which is already breaking in, and thus to function as "antistructure,"
replacing the old order with new order after the image of Christ. This vivid
portrait of the church as the manifestation of the new order makes Philemon central to understanding Paul's theology as a whole.

4.35.8   Reumann, John. *Philippians.* Anchor Yale Bible. New Haven, Conn.:
         Yale University Press, 2008. 805pp.

Massive, detailed, and highly technical commentary, the last major work
to be written by this prominent Lutheran scholar. Considers virtually

every possible aspect of the interpretation of this book: Greek grammar and lexicography, historical background, ancient rhetoric, and the role of "friendship" in the Greco-Roman world. Emphasizes that Paul maintains an ambiguous and dialectical attitude regarding the relationship between Christian discipleship and mission on the one hand and the virtues of the Greco-Roman world on the other. Written in a ponderous style, but is well worth the trouble to wade through. It is a bit surprising that Reumann, who was an astute biblical theologian, does relatively little here to develop the theology of passages or of the book.

Also Significant

4.35.9   Bakirtzis, Charalambos, and Helmut Koester, eds. *Philippi at the Time of Paul and after His Death.* Harrisburg, Pa.: Trinity Press International, 1998. 87pp.

4.35.10   Barth, Karl. *Epistle to the Philippians: 40th Anniversary Edition.* Louisville: Westminster John Knox, 2002. 128pp.

4.35.11   Bloomquist, L. Gregory. *The Function of Suffering in Philippians.* Journal for the Study of the New Testament Supplement Series 78. Sheffield: JSOT, 1993. 235pp.

4.35.12   Caird, G. B. *Paul's Letters from Prison: Ephesians, Philippians, Colossians, Philemon, in the Revised Standard Version.* New Clarendon Bible. Oxford: Oxford University Press, 1976. 223pp.

4.35.13   Callahan, Allen Dwight. *Embassy of Onesimus: The Letter of Paul to Philemon.* Valley Forge, Pa.: Trinity Press International, 1997. 96pp.

4.35.14   Collange, Jean-Francois. *The Epistle of Saint Paul to the Philippians.* London: Epworth, 1979. 159pp.

4.35.15   Craddock, Fred B. *Philippians.* Interpretation: A Bible Commentary for Teaching and Preaching. Atlanta: John Knox, 1985. 84pp.

4.35.16   Knox, John. *Philemon among the Letters of Paul: A New View of Its Place and Importance.* 2d ed. New York: Abingdon, 1959. 110pp.

4.35.17   Lightfoot, J. B. *St. Paul's Epistle to the Philippians.* London: Macmillan, 1913. 350pp.

4.35.18   Martin, Ralph P. *Philippians.* 2d ed. New Century Bible Commentary. Grand Rapids: Eerdmans, 1987. 187pp.

4.35.19   Reed, Jeffrey T. *A Discourse Analysis of Philippians: Method and Rhetoric in the Debate over Literary Integrity.* Journal for the Society of New Testament Studies Supplemental Series, no. 136. Sheffield: Sheffield Academic Press, 1997. 525pp.

4.35.20   Silva, Moisés. *Philippians.* 2d. ed. Baker Exegetical Commentary on the New Testament. Grand Rapids: Baker, 2005. 248pp.

4.35.21   Vincent, Marvin R. *A Critical and Exegetical Commentary on the Epistles to the Philippians and to Philemon.* International Critical Commentary. Edinburgh: T&T Clark, 1897. 201pp.

4.35.22   Witherington, Ben, III. *Paul's Letter to the Philippians: A Socio-Rhetorical Commentary.* Grand Rapids: Eerdmans, 2011. 312pp.

4.36   Thessalonian Epistles

Highly Recommended

4.36.1   Bruce, F. F. *1 and 2 Thessalonians.* Word Biblical Commentary. Waco, Tex.: Word, 1982. 228pp.

Careful, detailed exegesis, with special attention given to most problematic and difficult areas. Accepts unity and Pauline authorship of both letters. Emphasizes text-critical issues, linguistic analysis of the Greek, ideological background of Paul's thought as ascertained through his other letters, and historical background, especially Paul's relationship with the Thessalonians as this can be reconstructed from the letter itself and from Acts (which Bruce employs uncritically). Focuses on identifying and tracing the development of problems among the Thessalonians and Paul's response to these problems. Explores the contributions of theological claims in these letters to an understanding of Paul's thought and practice of pastoral care in general. Especially helpful are background articles treating Christianity in Macedonia, early Christian experience at Thessalonica, eschatology at Thessalonica, and the antichrist.

4.36.2   Donfried, Karl P., and Johannes Beutler, eds. *The Thessalonians Debate: Methodological Discord or Methodological Synthesis?* Grand Rapids: Eerdmans, 2000. 384pp.

Contains revised and, in some cases, translated seminar papers or responses to papers by some of the foremost authorities on Thessalonians, presented at the Seminar on Thessalonian Correspondence of the Studiorum Novi Testamentum Societas (SNTS). Focuses entirely on 1 Thessalonians. Especially helpful is Donfried's introductory article on the scope and nature of the debate. Each essay represents a major issue in contemporary discussion of the letter and interacts with the work of other prominent scholars. Greatest attention is given to rhetorical analysis and epistolography (study of ancient letters). Somewhat technical, but still accessible to nonspecialists.

4.36.3   Fee, Gordon D. *The First and Second Letters to the Thessalonians.* New International Commentary on the New Testament. Grand Rapids: Eerdmans, 2009. 366pp.

Like Bruce, accepts the Pauline authorship of both letters. Commentary is directed especially to ministers and students and is thus written in a clear, lively style. Especially helpful is Fee's explicit attention to the setting of each passage within the argument of the whole and his discussion of the structure of each passage as a basis for the detailed exegesis of individual verses. Fee concludes each passage with discussion of the theological and applicatory implications arising from his exegesis, a welcome feature in a commentary on books that emphasize the historical particularity of Paul's personal relationship with the members of this church. While most commentaries on the Thessalonian epistles give the lion's share of attention to 1 Thessalonians, Fee devotes approximately the same amount of space (relative to their respective lengths) to each of these epistles.

4.36.4   Jewett, Robert. *The Thessalonian Correspondence: Pauline Rhetoric and Millenarian Piety.* Foundations and Facets: New Testament. Philadelphia: Fortress, 1986. 240pp.

Not a traditional commentary, but a careful exegetical study that attempts a comprehensive synthesis of historical-critical method with rhetorical and social-scientific critical approaches. Carefully analyzes significant issues in the interpretation of Thessalonians, including authorship, sequence, and

literary integrity. Includes a rhetorical analysis of the letters that illuminates how Paul conceived the Thessalonian situation, the selection and
evaluation of sociological models for the Thessalonian congregation, concluding that the millenarian model best explains the evidence. Suggests
that Paul confronted a radical millenarianism unique in early Christianity,
promoted by a group that grossly misunderstood Paul's apocalyptic gospel
and proclaimed the "actual arrival of the millennium and proceeded to act
on that assumption." Contains solid discussion of introductory matters
and original insights, but volume becomes increasingly speculative and
"experimental" as it proceeds.

4.36.5   Malherbe, Abraham J. *The Letters to the Thessalonians*. Anchor Bible. New
         York: Doubleday, 2000. 508pp.

Argues for unity and Pauline authorship of both letters, and maintains
that 1 Thessalonians preceded 2 Thessalonians by a few months. Makes
discriminating use of Acts for background pertaining to the Thessalonian
situation. Employs linguistic analysis, historical background (especially
Paul's ministry among the Thessalonians, Pauline thought as derived from
his other letters, and Jewish and Greco-Roman writings, with particular
emphasis on Greek and Roman philosophical tradition, which Malherbe
thinks had significant affinities with Thessalonians), and history of interpretation, both ancient and modern. Focuses on the theological meaning
of the text, Paul as a model of pastoral care, and Paul's concern to address
the moral, spiritual, and emotional needs of his converts.

4.36.6   Marshall, I. Howard. *1 and 2 Thessalonians*. New Century Bible Com-
         mentary. Grand Rapids: Eerdmans, 1983. 240pp.

Careful, solid exegesis by a leading evangelical British scholar. Lucid commentary, concise, straightforward, and accessible to the nonspecialist.
Concerned throughout to present exposition relevant for those who read
these letters as Christian Scripture, emphasizing ways in which the theological claims encountered here relate to NT faith as a whole. Gives some
consideration to contemporary application.

4.36.7   Wanamaker, Charles A. *Commentary on 1 and 2 Thessalonians*. New
         International Greek Testament Commentary. Grand Rapids: Eerdmans,
         1990. 316pp.

Only major commentary to conclude that 2 Thessalonians preceded 1
Thessalonians, a position for which the author argues extensively. Recognizing that this is a minority view, Wanamaker presents his commentary
in such a way that it is useful to those who accept the traditional sequence.

Emphasizes linguistic analysis of the Greek, but is the first commentary on Thessalonians to integrate historical-critical methods with social-scientific and rhetorical-critical approaches. Employs sociological models both for Christianity in Thessalonica and for the "social character and functioning of Paul's letters within this context." Employment of sociological models generally leads interpreters to force a particular model on data of the text, but Wanamaker generally avoids this danger by cautious and restrained application of these models, and by beginning always with careful linguistic, historical, and literary analysis. Focus is on theological message, with occasional attention to contemporary significance.

Also Significant

4.36.8   Best, Ernest. *The First and Second Epistles to the Thessalonians*. Black's New Testament Commentary. Peabody, Mass.: Hendrickson, 1972. 391pp.

4.36.9   Collins, Raymond F., ed. *The Thessalonian Correspondence*. Bibliotheca Ephemeridum Theologicarum Louvaniensium 87. Leuven: Leuven University Press, 1990. 546pp.

4.36.10   Donfried, Karl Paul. *Paul, Thessalonica, and Early Christianity*. Grand Rapids: Eerdmans, 2002. 347pp.

4.36.11   Frame, James Everett. *A Critical and Exegetical Commentary on the Epistles of St. Paul to the Thessalonians*. International Critical Commentary. Edinburgh: T&T Clark, 1912. 326pp.

4.36.12   Gaventa, Beverly Roberts. *First and Second Thessalonians*. Interpretation: A Bible Commentary for Teaching and Preaching. Louisville: Westminster John Knox, 1998. 138pp.

4.36.13   Malherbe, Abraham J. *Paul and the Thessalonians: The Philosophic Tradition of Pastoral Care*. Philadelphia: Fortress, 1987. 120pp.

4.36.14   Milligan, George. *St. Paul's Epistles to the Thessalonians*. London: Macmillan, 1908. 195pp.

4.36.15   Morris, Leon. *The First and Second Epistles to the Thessalonians*. Rev. ed. New International Commentary on the New Testament. Grand Rapids: Eerdmans, 1991. 278pp.

4.36.16   Richard, Earl J. *First and Second Thessalonians*. Sacra Pagina. Collegeville, Minn.: Liturgical Press, 1995. 409pp.

4.36.17   Smith, Abraham. *Comfort One Another: Reconstructing the Rhetoric and Audience of 1 Thessalonians*. Literary Currents in Biblical Interpretation. Louisville: Westminster John Knox, 1995. 160pp.

4.36.18   Weima, Jeffrey A. D., and Stanley E. Porter. *An Annotated Bibliography of First and Second Thessalonians*. New Testament Tools and Studies 26. Leiden: Brill, 1998. 292pp.

4.36.19   Witherington, Ben, III. *1 and 2 Thessalonians: A Socio-Rhetorical Commentary*. Grand Rapids: Eerdmans, 2006. 286pp.

4.37   Pastoral Epistles

Highly Recommended

4.37.1   Collins, Raymond F. *I and II Timothy and Titus: A Commentary*. New Testament Library. Louisville: Westminster John Knox, 2002. 408pp.

Erudite and authoritative, yet readable, commentary from prominent Roman Catholic scholar. Agrees with the general critical consensus that these epistles were composed by a single post-Pauline hand around the end of the first century. Analyzes ways in which this author attempted to make relevant for his own generation the teaching of Paul. Collins attends especially to texts from Hellenism and rabbinic Judaism to shed light on the meaning of the Pastorals. Very helpful in providing background information, but gives little attention in the commentary proper to the history of interpretation or to theological reflection. Addresses select theological issues in excurses (extended discussions), e.g., Christians in the world, perspectives on women, and faith.

4.37.2   Johnson, Luke Timothy. *The First and Second Letters to Timothy*. Anchor Bible. New York: Doubleday, 2001. 494pp.

Insightful and original commentary in which this Roman Catholic scholar takes the position, unusual for contemporary critical scholars outside the evangelical tradition, that both letters were written by Paul. Consequently, Johnson reads 1 and 2 Timothy as real rather than fictional letters, to be understood within the framework of Paul's ministry and his relationship with Timothy. Attends seriously to the situation the letters purport to address, and interprets them in light of the Pauline corpus. Introduction contains extensive discussion of history of interpretation, from the Fathers to the present. Commentary consistently interacts with history of scholarship. Also makes use of linguistic analysis and Greco-Roman rhetoric and moral philosophy, which Johnson takes to be significant for the interpretation of Paul's letters. Concerned with the theological meaning of the final text, and offers some suggestions regarding contemporary appropriation.

4.37.3   Knight, George W., III. *Commentary on the Pastoral Epistles*. New International Greek Testament Commentary. Grand Rapids: Eerdmans, 1992. 514pp.

This evangelical scholar argues that Paul authored all three Pastorals just prior to his death, possibly using Luke as an amanuensis. Gives some attention to the history of interpretation, but primarily presents Knight's own construal of the Greek text, paying particular regard to lexical and syntactical analysis of the Greek and to the flow of the argument. Notable for exploration of subtle nuances of meaning. Interpretive possibilities are clearly set out with arguments for and against each, followed by Knight's own cogent conclusions. Gives little explicit attention to contemporary application, and says virtually nothing regarding potential application of even the most difficult passages (e.g., 1 Tim. 2:8-15).

4.37.4   Marshall, I. Howard. *A Critical and Exegetical Commentary on the Pastoral Epistles*. In collaboration with Philip H. Towner. International Critical Commentary. Edinburgh: T&T Clark, 1999. 869pp.

Takes an unusual position for an evangelical by arguing against Pauline authorship, asserting that these letters were produced by close associates of Paul (perhaps Titus and Timothy) shortly after Paul's death. The letters were not intended to deceive, but were manifestly known to the audience as fictionalized expansions by Paul's associates of authentic Pauline tradition. Commentary thus is concerned to interpret them both according to their fictional framework as letters of Paul to his delegates and according to their actual intention of instructing the post-Pauline church and its leaders. Approaches these letters as literary wholes, interpreting passages as they relate to the form and structure of each letter and to the whole corpus of the Pastoral Epistles. Chiefly concerned to understand the theology of

each passage on basis of detailed linguistic analysis of the Greek, historical background, and flow of argument. Gives little attention to history of
interpretation or to contemporary application.

4.37.5   Mounce, William D. *Pastoral Epistles.* Word Biblical Commentary. Nashville: Thomas Nelson, 2000. 641pp.

Argues extensively for the Pauline authorship of all three letters, and gives
great care to reconstruct the specific context of each letter within the life
setting of Paul, Titus, Timothy, and the churches in Ephesus and Crete,
showing how each letter responds specifically to particular problems or
challenges. Derives this reconstruction from the Pastorals, Acts, and early
Christian tradition. Emphasizes the uniquely Christian character and perspective of the letters, citing parallels with other canonical writings (especially Pauline) and contrasting them with Greco-Roman literary and
philosophical works. Provides immense bibliographies on individual passages. Focuses on the theological meaning of the text. This theological
interpretation implicitly reflects contemporary concerns, but gives little
explicit attention to application.

4.37.6   Quinn, Jerome D. *The Letter to Titus.* Anchor Bible. New York: Doubleday, 1990. 334pp.

This Roman Catholic scholar considers Titus to be post-Pauline, written
around 82. Probably sent from Rome to all the churches in the central
Mediterranean as a means of spanning the generation between the apostolic and post-apostolic periods. Introduction pertains to all three Pastoral Epistles, and offers a reconstructed historical setting that serves in
the commentary as the definitive framework for interpretation. "Notes"
contain citation of technical evidence (particularly linguistic analysis); parallels with canonical and extra-canonical literature (especially early church
fathers); and historical background. "Comments" build upon the notes
to reconstruct the theological meaning and pastoral significance for the
original audience.

4.37.7   Quinn, Jerome D., and William C. Wacker. *The First and Second Letters
to Timothy.* Anchor Bible. New York: Doubleday, 2000. 918pp.

Quinn had completed the manuscript through 1 Timothy 4:5 at the
time of his death in 1988, leaving voluminous unedited notes on the
rest. Wacker edited his teacher's material, adding very little of his own research. Consequently, this commentary, though published in 2000, dates
essentially to 1988. As a companion to Quinn's commentary on Titus
(§4.37.6), it shares the same format and character. Like that volume, it

is notable for its originality, erudition, depth, and comprehensiveness. It is the most detailed commentary on these letters available in English. Includes the introduction to the Pastoral Epistles found in that commentary.

4.37.8   Towner, Philip H. *The Letters of Timothy and Titus.* New International Commentary on the New Testament. Grand Rapids: Eerdmans, 2006. 886pp.

Although Towner collaborated with Marshall on the International Critical Commentary volume (§4.37.4), this is an entirely distinct work, and quite different. Massive, detailed, and erudite commentary by an evangelical NT scholar who has devoted a lifetime of study to these books. Carefully analyzes the modern arguments for and against Pauline authorship, and concludes that the arguments against Pauline authorship are not finally persuasive. Insists also that the category of "Pastoral Epistles" is unfounded and unhelpful, and argues instead that although some commonalities exist these letters must be construed according to their individual character and message. Is intentional to interpret these letters according to the cultural and religious setting of Ephesus and Crete, and thus his interpretation is to some extent dependent upon his (admittedly) hypothetical reconstruction. An extremely original, careful, informed, and insightful volume.

Also Significant

4.37.9   Aageson, James W. *Paul, the Pastoral Epistles, and the Early Church.* Peabody, Mass.: Hendrickson, 2008. 235pp.

4.37.10   Barrett, C. K. *The Pastoral Epistles in the New English Bible.* New Clarendon Bible. Oxford: Clarendon, 1963. 151pp.

4.37.11   Dibelius, Martin, and Conzelmann, Hans. *The Pastoral Epistles.* Hermeneia: A Critical and Historical Commentary on the Bible. Philadelphia: Fortress, 1972. 175pp.

4.37.12   Guthrie, Donald. *The Pastoral Epistles.* 2d ed. Tyndale New Testament Commentaries. Downers Grove, Ill.: InterVarsity, 1990. 240pp.

4.37.13   Hanson, A. T. *The Pastoral Epistles.* New Century Bible Commentary. Grand Rapids: Eerdmans, 1982. 206pp.

4.37.14 Harding, Mark. *Tradition and Rhetoric in the Pastoral Epistles.* Studies in Biblical Literature 3. New York: Peter Lang, 1998. 253pp.

4.37.15 ———. *What Are They Saying about the Pastoral Epistles?* New York: Paulist, 2000. 176pp.

4.37.16 Houlden, J. L. *The Pastoral Epistles: I and II Timothy, Titus.* New Testament Commentaries. Philadelphia: Trinity, 1989. 166pp.

4.37.17 Kelly, J. N. D. *The Pastoral Epistles.* Black's New Testament Commentary. Peabody, Mass.: Hendrickson, 1960. 263pp.

4.37.18 Lock, Walter. *A Critical and Exegetical Commentary on the Pastoral Epistles.* International Critical Commentary. Edinburgh: T&T Clark, 1924. 163pp.

4.37.19 Oden, Thomas C. *First and Second Timothy and Titus.* Interpretation: A Bible Commentary for Teaching and Preaching. Atlanta: John Knox, 1989. 190pp.

4.37.20 Prior, Michael. *Paul the Letter-Writer and the Second Letter to Timothy.* Journal for the Study of the New Testament Supplement Series 23. Sheffield: JSOT, 1989. 300pp.

4.37.21 Verner, David C. *The Household of God: The Social World of the Pastoral Epistles.* Society of Biblical Literature Dissertation Series 71. Chico, Calif.: Scholars, 1983. 207pp.

4.37.22 Witherington, Ben, III. *Letters and Homilies for Hellenized Christians, Volume 1: A Socio-Rhetorical Commentary on Titus, 1–2 Timothy and 1–3 John.* Downers Grove, Ill.: InterVarsity, 2006. 623pp.

4.37.23 Young, Frances. *The Theology of the Pastoral Epistles.* New Testament Theology. Cambridge: Cambridge University Press, 1994. 170pp.

4.38 Hebrews

Highly Recommended

4.38.1   Attridge, Harold W. *Hebrews*. Hermeneia: A Critical and Historical
Commentary on the Bible. Minneapolis: Fortress, 1989. 437pp.

Careful, judicious, balanced, and lucid. Recognizing the limits of evidence
pertaining to many disputed matters of background, the author refuses to
accept positions that must, in his judgment, be speculative. Thus he dates
the book between 60 and 100, and refuses to decide between a Jewish-
Christian or Gentile-Christian audience. Insists that the book was a sermon or homily, and develops the significance of this conclusion for both
the book's structure and its message. Exposition contains "analyses," presenting passages' form, structure, major themes, and function within entire book, while "comments" offers careful linguistic examination of the
Greek and discussion of Jewish and Hellenistic background. Excurses deal
helpfully with significant theological and literary issues. Meticulous, but
accessible to the nonspecialist.

4.38.2   Bruce, F. F. *The Epistle to the Hebrews*. Rev. ed. New International Commentary on the New Testament. Grand Rapids: Eerdmans, 1990. 426pp.

The best of Bruce's many commentaries. Makes use of his background
in classical Greek, his intimate familiarity with the thought of the OT,
and his encyclopedic knowledge of Jewish and early Christian background
to explore the homiletical intention of the book for its original readers.
Gives little explicit attention to contemporary application. Regularly cites
background material, but focuses on the theology of the text. Consistently
relates the teaching of Hebrews to other biblical passages, at times uncritically reading passages in Hebrews in the light of other NT passages,
thereby running the risk of obscuring the unique perspective of Hebrews.

4.38.3   Cockerill, Gareth Lee. *The Epistle to the Hebrews*. New International
Commentary on the New Testament. Grand Rapids: Eerdmans, 2012.
742pp.

A worthy successor to the classic volume by F. F. Bruce (§4.38.2) in that it
provides a reliable and straightforward exposition of Hebrews readily accessible to pastor and teacher. Is careful to interpret individual passages in
light of the structure and flow of argument of the whole book and analyzes
more specifically and consistently than do most commentaries the writer's
use of the OT. Believes that it is impossible to conclude with any real

confidence the specific authorship or setting of the book, and thus refuses to base interpretation upon speculative reconstructions.

4.38.4   Ellingworth, Paul. *Commentary on Hebrews*. New International Greek Testament Commentary. Grand Rapids: Eerdmans, 1993. 764pp.

No commentary on Hebrews gives more attention to lexical, syntactical, and text-critical concerns. But the supreme value of this volume is its balance between meticulous attention to detail and its relating individual passages to the broad context of the book, other early Christian writings, and the OT. Concern for sound methodology is expressed in regular discussion of methodological issues and explicit articulation of the methodological bases of the interpretive processes used. Commentary assumes knowledge of Greek. Gives little attention to contemporary application.

4.38.5   Johnson, Luke Timothy. *Hebrews: A Commentary*. New Testament Library. Louisville: Westminster John Knox, 2006. 402pp.

This Roman Catholic scholar is a quintessential commentator. All his commentaries are characterized by lucidity and elegance, and this is no exception. Believes that the conceptual world of Hebrews is primarily shaped by OT Scripture interpreted through a modified popular Platonism. Interprets passages so as to develop their deeper signficiance for human, and particularly Christian, existence, suggesting ways in which Hebrews challenges accepted ways of construing the world. Commentary is addressed more to the church than to the academy. His language is straightforward and understandable; his footnotes are few. He moves easily from discussions of ancient rhetoric, syntax, lexicography, and Greco-Roman culture to contemporary Christian appropriation.

4.38.6   Koester, Craig R. *Hebrews*. Anchor Bible. New York: Doubleday, 2001. 512pp.

Current and original. Argues that the book was written between 60 and 90, and insists that the social setting of the community is more significant for the book's interpretation than a precise decision regarding date. Introduction offers a comprehensive survey of interpretation from the Fathers to the present, a thorough investigation into the social and religious circumstances of the community, and a helpful discussion of the book's theology, which Koester understands to center around God's intentions for humanity. Commentary is accessible to students and pastors, but contains a wealth of technical information valuable to scholars. Employs historical background, history of interpretation, and linguistic analysis (primarily lexical, with less emphasis on syntax) to produce a rich theological exposition. Emphasizes sociological insights and ancient rhetoric, at times in ways that seem to superimpose these categories on the text.

4.38.7   Lane, William L. *Hebrews*. 2 vols. Word Biblical Commentary. Dallas: Word, 1991. 617pp.

Written primarily for scholars, but large portions are accessible to pastors and teachers, who will find it eminently useful. Offers comprehensive treatment of every phrase. Attends to the broad argument of Hebrews in an introduction to each of the book's five main units. Employs insights from emerging disciplines of genre criticism, sociological studies, and discourse analysis, but refuses to be bound to a rigid application of any of these methods. Emphasizes the book's sermonic character and pastoral purpose, but gives little explicit attention to contemporary application; for helpful suggestions in this area one should consult Lane's *Hebrews: A Call to Commitment* (§4.38.22).

4.38.8   Lindars, Barnabas. *The Theology of the Letter to the Hebrews*. New Testament Theology. Cambridge: Cambridge University Press, 1991. 155pp.

Remarkably clear and satisfying study of the difficult and (to modern readers) arcane theology of Hebrews. Discerns the book's theology through careful tracing of its argument, examination of its rhetoric, and consideration of its pastoral purpose. Addresses several theological issues, but gives primary attention to Christ's priesthood and sacrifice. Discusses Hebrews' contribution to NT theology and considers its contemporary significance.

4.38.9   Westcott, Brooke Foss. *The Epistle to the Hebrews: The Greek Text with Notes and Essays*. London: Macmillan, 1892. 504pp.

A classic work from one of the greatest NT commentators of the modern period. Concludes the book was written to Jewish Christians in Palestine about the time of the destruction of Jerusalem in order to address their overwhelming disappointment and despair, and to use this occasion as an opportunity to present to them "a larger hope through a new revelation of the glory of Christ." As such, Hebrews has relevance for all succeeding generations, especially as they experience severe upheavals in their corporate or personal lives. Gives minute attention to every detail of the Greek text, demonstrates how the structure of passages informs their meaning, presents relevant quotations from patristic and medieval interpreters in original Greek and Latin, relates the teachings of Hebrews to other biblical writings, and reflects on the theology of the text. Numerous excurses discuss in depth the most significant theological issues.

375

Also Significant

4.38.10   Bauckham, Richard, Daniel R. Driver, Trevor A. Hart, and Nathan Mac-Donald, eds. *The Epistle to the Hebrews and Christian Theology.* Grand Rapids: Eerdmans, 2009. 456pp.

4.38.11   Delitzsch, Franz. *Commentary on the Epistle to the Hebrews.* 2 vols. Edinburgh: T&T Clark, 1871. 401/499pp.

4.38.12   deSilva, David A. *Perseverance in Gratitude: A Socio-Rhetorical Commentary on the Epistle "to the Hebrews."* Grand Rapids: Eerdmans, 2000. 560pp.

4.38.13   Gelardini, Gabriella, ed. *Hebrews: Contemporary Methods—New Insights.* Biblical Interpretation Series, no. 75. Leiden: Brill, 2005. 304pp.

4.38.14   Guthrie, George H. *The Structure of Hebrews: A Text-Linguistic Analysis.* Grand Rapids: Baker, 1994. 161pp.

4.38.15   Hughes, Graham. *Hebrews and Hermeneutics: The Epistle to the Hebrews as a New Testament Example of Biblical Interpretation.* Society for New Testament Studies Monograph Series 36. Cambridge: Cambridge University Press, 1979. 218pp.

4.38.16   Hughes, Philip Edgcumbe. *A Commentary on the Epistle to the Hebrews.* Grand Rapids: Eerdmans, 1977. 623pp.

4.38.17   Hurst, L. D. *The Epistle to the Hebrews: Its Background of Thought.* Society for New Testament Studies Monograph Series 65. Cambridge: Cambridge University Press, 1990. 209pp.

4.38.18   Isaacs, Marie E. *Reading Hebrews and James: A Literary and Theological Commentary.* Macon, Ga.: Smyth & Helwys, 2002. 259pp.

4.38.19   Käsemann, Ernst. *The Wandering People of God: An Investigation of the Letter to the Hebrews.* Minneapolis: Augsburg, 1984. 255pp.

4.38.20   Kistemaker, Simon. *Hebrews.* Grand Rapids: Baker, 1984. 464pp.

4.38.21   Laansma, Jon C., and Daniel J. Treier, eds. *Christology, Hermeneutics, and Hebrews: Profiles from the History of Interpretation.* London: T&T Clark, 2012. 282pp.

4.38.22   Lane, William L. *Hebrews: A Call to Commitment.* Peabody, Mass.: Hendrickson, 1985. 184pp.

4.38.23   Lehne, Susanne. *The New Covenant in Hebrews.* Journal for the Study of the New Testament Supplemental Series 44. Sheffield: JSOT, 1990. 183pp.

4.38.24   Long, Thomas G. *Hebrews.* Interpretation: A Bible Commentary for Teaching and Preaching. Louisville: Westminster John Knox, 1997. 153pp.

4.38.25   Milligan, George. *The Theology of the Epistle of Hebrews.* Edinburgh: T&T Clark, 1899. 233pp.

4.38.26   Mitchell, Alan C. *Hebrews.* Sacra Pagina. Collegeville, Minn.: Michael Glazier, 2007. 357pp.

4.38.27   Moffatt, James. *A Critical and Exegetical Commentary on the Epistle to the Hebrews.* International Critical Commentary. Edinburgh: T&T Clark, 1924. 264pp.

4.38.28   Montefiore, Hugh. *The Epistle to the Hebrews.* Harper's New Testament Commentaries. New York: Harper & Row, 1964. 272pp.

4.38.29   Peterson, David. *Hebrews and Perfection: An Examination of the Concept of Perfection in the Epistle to the Hebrews.* Society for New Testament Studies Monograph Series 47. Cambridge: Cambridge University Press, 1982. 313pp.

4.38.30   Schenck, Kenneth. *Understanding the Book of Hebrews: The Story Behind the Sermon.* Louisville: Westminster John Knox, 2003. 144pp.

4.38.31   Scholer, John M. *Proleptic Priests: Priesthood in the Epistle to the Hebrews.* Journal for the Study of the New Testament Supplemental Series 49. Sheffield: JSOT, 1991. 243pp.

4.38.32   Thompson, James W. *The Beginnings of Christian Philosophy: The Epistle to the Hebrews*. Catholic Biblical Quarterly Monograph Series 13. Washington, D.C.: Catholic Biblical Association of America, 1982. 184pp.

4.38.33   Witherington, Ben, III. *Letters and Homilies for Jewish Christians: A Socio-Rhetorical Commentary on Hebrews, James and Jude*. Downers Grove, Ill.: InterVarsity, 2007. 656pp.

4.39   James

See also PETRINE EPISTLES AND JUDE (§4.40) and HEBREWS (§4.38)

Highly Recommended

4.39.1   Davids, Peter H. *The Epistle of James: A Commentary on the Greek Text.* New International Greek Testament Commentary. Grand Rapids: Eerdmans, 1982. 226pp.

Argues that the core of this book was produced by James the Just in the 40s and later edited either by him, with the assistance of others, or by his followers. In practice, Davids makes little of this two-stage development in his exposition of the text. Insists that the book is carefully structured, against many who, like Luther, consider its arrangement "chaotic." Makes significant use of his understanding of the book's structure in the commentary, along with linguistic analysis of Greek and Hellenistic, Jewish, and early Christian parallels. Introduction discusses the book's major theological issues at length.

4.39.2   Johnson, Luke Timothy. *James*. Anchor Bible. New York: Doubleday, 1995. 412pp.

Lucid, elegantly written, and theologically profound. Arguably the best commentary available on James. Argues at length that the book was written by James the Just and that it is one of the earliest NT writings. Offers the most comprehensive examination of the history of interpretation of James available in English. Commentary emphasizes linguistic analysis and the logic of the letter. Includes selective interaction with modern scholarship and fuller interaction with ancient commentators. Relates individual passages and themes to one another in an attempt to identify the dynamic structure of James' thought. Probes beneath the surface of the text to underlying theological issues that have continuing relevance for Christian thought and behavior.

4.39.3   Martin, Ralph P. *James*. Word Biblical Commentary. Waco, Tex.: Word, 1988. 240pp.

Useful for the scholar, and suggestive for those who preach and teach within the church. Characterized by thorough and current bibliographies, careful grammatical analysis employed to clarify theological meaning of the text), and extensive allusions to ancient materials. Engages in serious dialogue with other interpreters, although focuses almost entirely on modern scholars. Identifies discernible structure in the book. Argues that sayings from James the Just, originally directed to Palestinian churches, or perhaps to non-Christian Palestinian Jews, were arranged in the form of a letter by James's disciples after his death in order to address concerns of a primarily Jewish church in Antioch.

4.39.4   Mayor, Joseph B. *The Epistle of St. James: The Greek Text with Introduction, Notes, Comments and Further Studies in the Epistle of St. James*. 3d ed. London: Macmillan, 1913. 291/264/41pp.

Comprehensive and authoritative, still valuable after a century. Contains massive compilation of technical historical, linguistic, and text-critical information that is often simply adopted by later commentators. Introduction of nearly three hundred pages concludes that the book was produced by James the Just in the 40s. Meticulously examines every Greek word or phrase, with attention to flow of argument, historical setting of original readers, ancient parallels, and history of interpretation. Quotations typically appear in original Greek and Latin. Attends also to the significance of James's teaching for NT theology and, to a lesser extent, for contemporary application. Highly technical; assumes knowledge of Greek.

Also Significant

4.39.5   Adamson, James B. *James: The Man and His Message*. Grand Rapids: Eerdmans, 1989. 553pp.

4.39.6   Bauckham, Richard. *James: Wisdom of James, Disciple of Jesus the Sage*. New Testament Readings. London: Routledge, 1999. 246pp.

4.39.7   Cadoux, A. T. *The Thought of St. James*. London: James Clarke, 1944. 101pp.

4.39.8   Dibelius, Martin. *James*. Rev. by Heinrich Greeven. Hermeneia: A Critical and Historical Commentary on the Bible. Philadelphia: Fortress, 1975. 285pp.

4.39.9   Hartin, Patrick J. *James*. Sacra Pagina. Collegeville, Minn.: Michael Glazier, 2003. 319pp.

4.39.10   Hort, Fenton John Anthony. *The Epistle of St. James*. London: Macmillan, 1909. (Several sections have separate pagination.)

4.39.11   Kistemaker, Simon. *Exposition of the Epistle of James and the Epistles of John*. New Testament Commentary. Grand Rapids: Baker, 1986. 425pp.

4.39.12   Laws, Sophie. *The Epistle of James*. Black's New Testament Commentary. Peabody, Mass.: Hendrickson, 1980. 273pp.

4.39.13   McCartney, Dan G. *James*. Baker Exegetical Commentary on the New Testament. Grand Rapids: Baker Academic, 2009. 335pp.

4.39.14   Mitton, C. Leslie. *The Epistle of James*. London: Marshall, Morgan & Scott, 1974. 255pp.

4.39.15   Penner, Todd C. *The Epistle of James and Eschatology: Re-reading an Ancient Christian Letter*. Journal for the Study of the New Testament Supplement Series 191. Sheffield: Sheffield Academic Press, 1996. 331pp.

4.39.16   Ropes, James H. *A Critical and Exegetical Commentary on the Epistle of St. James*. International Critical Commentary. Edinburgh: T&T Clark, 1916. 319pp.

4.39.17   Wall, Robert W. *Community of the Wise: The Letter of James*. New Testament in Context. Valley Forge, Pa.: Trinity Press International, 1997. 354pp.

4.40 Petrine Epistles and Jude

Highly Recommended

4.40.1   Achtemeier, Paul J. *1 Peter.* Hermeneia: A Critical and Historical Commentary on the Bible. Minneapolis: Fortress, 1996. 423pp.

Cautiously concludes that the letter is pseudonymous, and offers a brief discussion of pseudonymity in the NT in an attempt to clarify the phenomenon and explain the motives behind it. Introduction includes a brief but helpful discussion of theology. Especially useful is the analysis of the coherence and structure of the thought of the letter. Focuses on linguistic analysis, parallels from Jewish and Hellenistic literature (citing many passages not known by or accessible to earlier scholars), and historical background (especially social and cultural considerations). Extensive footnotes offer interaction with history of interpretation, largely limited to modern scholars. Commentary gives more attention to theology than is typical of volumes in this series, but does not explicitly address contemporary application.

4.40.2   Bauckham, Richard J. *Jude, 2 Peter.* Word Biblical Commentary. Waco, Tex.: Word, 1983. 357pp.

The most authoritative and current commentary on these books. Although recognizing the literary dependency of 2 Peter on Jude, insists that each letter must be understood on its own terms, and that each has its own contribution to make to NT theology. Argues that Jude authored the letter bearing his name in the 50s, but insists that 2 Peter is pseudepigraphical, dating from the end of the first century. Interpretation depends largely on genre and literary structure, but also utilizes lexical and syntactical analysis, historical background, and history of interpretation, especially modern interpreters. Theologically oriented commentary is suggestive of modern significance, but does not directly address contemporary appropriation.

4.40.3   Davids, Peter H. *The First Epistle of Peter.* New International Commentary on the New Testament. Grand Rapids: Eerdmans, 1990. 266pp.

Argues that Peter was ultimately responsible for the production of this letter, though probably commissioned Silvanus to write in his name. Understands the letter to be a model for the way the early church applied the OT and Jesus' teachings to specific problems calling for pastoral response. Introduction contains relatively extensive discussion of the letter's theology, with an especially helpful excursus on suffering in 1 Peter and in the

381

NT. Interprets passages largely on the basis of literary structure and flow of argument, and in relation to other biblical passages. Gives less attention to linguistic analysis, history of interpretation, or historical background. Contains some new insights valuable to the scholar, but clearly written and understandable by the nonspecialist. Concern for theology and pastoral issues makes it useful for teaching and preaching.

4.40.4   Donelson, Lewis R. *I & II Peter and Jude: A Commentary.* New Testament Library. Louisville: Westminster John Knox, 2010. 301pp.

Insists that neither Peter nor Jude authored any of the books that bear their names, but rather that these letters were composed in the subapostolic period of the early second century. Each addresses a situation of conflict. In the case of 1 Peter the conflict is with the antagonistic social environment of the Roman world, while the conflict in 2 Peter and Jude is internal, a conflict within the church. As such, these letters use the OT and diverse early Christian traditions (especially as found in the rest of the NT) in theologically rich and original ways to instruct the church in the midst of the types of antagonisms that anticipate the church's experience throughout its history. Even those who disagree with Donelson's conclusions regarding authorship and date will benefit from his careful and theologically sensitive interpretation.

4.40.5   Elliott, John H. *I Peter.* Anchor Bible. New York: Doubleday, 2000. 956pp.

Most thorough, comprehensive, and current commentary on this letter, which Elliott takes to be pseudonymous, written between 73 and 92. Elliott builds on his earlier sociological study of 1 Peter, which pioneered sociological interpretation of NT epistles (see his *Home for the Homeless* [§4.40.15]). Although emphasizing sociological considerations in this commentary, Elliott sets the epistle in a variety of contexts, attending to literary, historical, linguistic, and theological issues, as well as the history of interpretation (both ancient and modern). Includes exhaustive bibliography comprising 150 pages. The study of each passage also concludes with a bibliography. Commentary is highly technical but written in a clear style, and thus much of it is accessible to nonspecialists.

4.40.6   Goppelt, Leonhard. *A Commentary on 1 Peter.* Grand Rapids: Eerdmans, 1993. 385pp.

This highly regarded German NT scholar completed this commentary shortly before his death in 1973. The substance of the volume is Goppelt's, but bibliographies have been updated to 1993. Introduction contains detailed and comprehensive discussions of background issues, concluding that Peter and Silvanus were responsible for the traditions behind the letter but were not its authors. Commentary is full of original exegetical insights and rich theological reflections. Attends to situation of the original community, Jewish and Hellenistic background, and history of interpretation, and to a lesser extent flow of argument and linguistic analysis. Emphasizes Peter's contribution to Christian ethics in a socially complex environment and marginalized existence.

4.40.7   Mayor, Joseph B. *The Epistle of St. Jude and the Second Epistle of St. Peter: Greek Text with Introduction, Notes, and Comments.* London: Macmillan, 1907. 239pp. + extensive introduction.

Mayor was a trained classicist and therefore gives primary attention to language, especially grammar. Attends also to text-critical issues, Jewish and Hellenistic parallels, and history of interpretation, giving citations in original Latin and Greek. All of this highly technical discussion is in the service of a theological explication of the text that at points borders on devotional. Immense introduction (two hundred pages) thoroughly presents evidence bearing on authorship, date, and the relationship between 2 Peter and Jude. Concludes that 2 Peter is a pseudonymous second-century writing, while Jude authored letter bearing his name. Contains a mass of technical information that has become foundational for all subsequent scholarship.

4.40.8   Michaels, J. Ramsey. *1 Peter.* Word Biblical Commentary. Waco, Tex.: Word, 1988. 337pp.

Michaels refutes the longstanding perception that this letter simply echoes generally held beliefs of early Christianity and makes no unique contribution to NT theology, insisting instead that 1 Peter offers a distinctive non-Pauline Christianity. Cautiously accepts Petrine authorship, and suggests that Peter might have written it as late as the 70s. Focuses on lexical and syntactical analysis and historical background (especially Jewish and Hellenistic literature, and sociocultural situation), and gives relatively little attention to history of interpretation. Emphasizes Peter's mixture of theology and ethics (i.e., ethically applied theology), but says little regarding contemporary application.

4.40.9   Neyrey, Jerome H. *2 Peter, Jude.* Anchor Bible. New York: Doubleday, 1993. 287pp.

In much the same way that Bauckham (§4.40.2) emphasizes literary aspects of genre and structure, Neyrey stresses the role of ancient rhetoric and the social, political, and economic setting of these pseudonymous letters, produced at the turn of the second century. Employs five social-scientific models as "templates" to help readers see and understand significant facets of the text. Grounds the use of these models in cultural anthropology and historical examination of ancient Greek, Roman, and Jewish literature. While providing important insights, these models at times seem to be imposed on the text and materially influence its interpretation. Tends to emphasize social and cultural phenomena rather than theological issues. Yet there are many original and illuminating interpretations, and Neyrey gives some attention to theological and pastoral concerns.

4.40.10   Selwyn, Edward Gordon. *The First Epistle of St. Peter: The Greek Text with Introduction, Notes and Essays.* 2d ed. London: Macmillan, 1947. 517pp.

For years considered the most authoritative commentary on this letter in English, it remains indispensable. Argues that letter was drafted by Silvanus at Peter's direction. Introduction contains extensive discussion of the letter's theology and ethics. Commentary focuses on the Greek text, which appears at the top of the page. Attends also to flow of argument, Jewish and Hellenistic parallels, and history of interpretation, especially the Fathers. Citations are in original Greek and Latin. Contains several "additional notes," dealing in detail with significant interpretive and theological issues. Assumes knowledge of Greek.

Also Significant

4.40.11   Bauckham, Richard. *Jude and the Relatives of Jesus in the Early Church.* Edinburgh: T&T Clark, 1990. 459pp.

4.40.12   Bigg, Charles. *A Critical and Exegetical Commentary on the Epistles of St. Peter and St. Jude.* International Critical Commentary. Edinburgh: T&T Clark, 1901. 353pp.

4.40.13   Chester, Andrew, and Ralph P. Martin. *The Theology of the Letters of James, Peter, and Jude.* New Testament Theology. Cambridge: Cambridge University Press, 1994. 189pp.

4.40.14   Earl, Richard. *Reading 1 Peter, Jude, and 2 Peter: A Literary and Theological Commentary.* Macon, Ga.: Smyth & Helwys, 2000. 394pp.

4.40.15   Elliott, John H. *A Home for the Homeless: A Sociological Exegesis of I Peter, Its Situation and Strategy.* Philadelphia: Fortress, 1981. 306pp.

4.40.16   Feldmeier, Reinhard. *The First Letter of Peter.* Waco, Tex.: Baylor University Press, 2008. 317pp.

4.40.17   Jobes, Karen H. *1 Peter.* Baker Exegetical Commentary on the New Testament. Grand Rapids: Baker Academic, 2005. 364pp.

4.40.18   Kelly, J. N. D. *The Epistles of Peter and of Jude.* Black's New Testament Commentary. Peabody, Mass.: Hendrickson, 1969. 387pp.

4.40.19   Kistemaker, Simon. *Expositions of the Epistles of Peter and the Epistle of Jude.* New Testament Commentary. Grand Rapids: Baker, 1987. 443pp.

4.40.20   Luther, Martin. *Commentary on Peter and Jude.* Grand Rapids: Kregel, 1990. (Originally published in German in 1523.) 303pp.

4.40.21   Lyle, Kenneth R., Jr. *Ethical Admonition in the Epistle of Jude.* Studies in Biblical Literature 4. New York: Peter Lang, 1998. 152pp.

4.40.22   Perkins, Pheme. *First and Second Peter, James, and Jude.* Interpretation: A Bible Commentary for Teaching and Preaching. Louisville: Westminster John Knox, 1995. 204pp.

4.40.23   Reese, Ruth Anne. *Writing Jude: The Reader, the Text, and the Author in Constructs of Power and Desire.* Biblical Interpretation Series 51. Leiden: Brill, 2000. 182pp.

4.40.24   Richard, Earl J. *Reading 1 Peter, Jude, and 2 Peter: A Literary and Theological Commentary.* Macon, Ga.: Smyth & Helwys, 2000. 394pp.

4.40.25   Senior, Donald P., and Daniel J. Harrington. *1 Peter, Jude, and 2 Peter.* Sacra Pagina. Collegeville, Minn.: Michael Glazier, 2003. 315pp.

4.40.26   Watson, Duane Frederick. *Invention, Arrangement, and Style: Rhetorical Criticism of Jude and 2 Peter.* Society of Biblical Literature Dissertation Series 104. Atlanta: Scholars, 1988. 214pp.

4.40.27 Witherington, Ben, III. *Letters and Homilies for Hellenized Christians, Volume II: A Socio-Rhetorical Commentary on 1–2 Peter.* Downers Grove, Ill.: InterVarsity, 2007. 432pp.

4.41   Johannine Epistles

See also PASTORAL EPISTLES (§4.37) and JOHN AND THE JOHANNINE SCHOOL (§4.28)

Highly Recommended

4.41.1 Brown, Raymond E. *The Epistles of John.* Anchor Bible. Garden City, N.Y.: Doubleday, 1982. 812pp.

Argues that these letters must be understood in relation to John's Gospel. They demonstrate division within the Johannine community over the meaning of the Gospel of John. The portion of the community responsible for these letters is attempting to force its construal of John's Gospel on the community as a whole. Commentary is based on this reconstruction of the history of the Johannine community and of the adversaries described in these letters. Although this reconstruction is arguably as plausible as any, there is no consensus on these matters, and Brown's interpretation is thus rendered speculative. Nevertheless, careful explication of every interpretive problem, exhaustive linguistic analysis, and thorough interaction with history of interpretation (ancient and modern) makes this volume invaluable.

4.41.2 Lieu, Judith M. *I, II, & III John: A Commentary.* New Testament Library. Louisville: Westminster John Knox, 2008. 300pp.

Written by a seasoned scholar whose academic career has focused upon the Johannine Epistles. Insists not only that the Johannine epistles were probably written by someone other than the author of the Gospel of John, but also that they should be interpreted on their own terms and not on the basis of speculation regarding their relationship to one another or to the Gospel of John. This perspective stands at the opposite extreme to that adopted by Brown, described immediately above. Rejecting an easy separation of Jewish from Gentile (or Hellenistic) Christianity, argues that these epistles, which never quote the OT, are nonetheless beholden to the OT and Jewish tradition and should be interpreted in light of these influences. Offers a fresh, theologically insightful, and generally compelling reading of these letters.

4.41.3   Marshall, I. Howard. *The Epistles of John*. New International Commen-
         tary on the New Testament. Grand Rapids: Eerdmans, 1978. 274pp.

         Maintains that these letters come from the author of the Fourth Gospel,
         probably either John the apostle or a follower of the apostle known as "the
         elder." They were written to urge members of the Johannine community
         to avoid the appeals of a heretical group that had recently seceded from
         the community. Commentary characterized by careful argumentation,
         balanced judgment, and clear and understandable presentation of current
         scholarly discussions and of complex exegetical issues. Relegates technical
         discussion to extensive footnotes. Addresses contemporary significance.

4.41.4   Schnackenburg, Rudolf. *The Johannine Epistles: Introduction and Com-
         mentary*. New York: Crossroad, 1992. 320pp.

         Against Brown (§4.41.1), insists that the relationship between these let-
         ters and John's Gospel remains unanswerable; it is impossible to determine
         which came first. Consequently, Schnackenburg interprets these letters on
         their own terms, using John's Gospel as evidence, but not relying on a
         specific reconstruction of the Johannine community. Attends to linguis-
         tic analysis of the Greek, though less rigorously than Brown. Emphasizes
         the literary structure of the letters, the theological structure of John's
         thought, historical background, Jewish and Hellenistic parallels, and his-
         tory of interpretation (ancient and modern). Excurses offer full discussion
         of theological issues. Provides richer theological reflection than any other
         commentary on these letters.

4.41.5   Smalley, Stephen S. *1, 2, 3 John*. Word Biblical Commentary. Waco,
         Tex.: Word, 1984. 386pp.

         Understands emphasis of these letters to be Christology and its implica-
         tions for Christian behavior. Smalley detects a balanced understanding
         of Jesus' person, presenting him as both fully human and fully divine.
         Concludes that the letters were written later than John's Gospel, and by a
         different author. Introduction is very brief, but commentary offers meticu-
         lous lexical and syntactical analysis of every phrase, and gives thorough at-
         tention to the flow of argument, relationship of passages within Johannine
         corpus, and historical background, especially the situation of the original
         audience. Focuses on theological meaning, and is particularly concerned
         to resolve apparent theological contradictions and tensions within the let-
         ters. Gives little explicit attention to contemporary application.

4.41.6   Strecker, Georg. *The Johannine Letters*. Hermeneia: A Critical and His-
         torical Commentary on the Bible. Minneapolis: Fortress, 1996. 319pp.

387

Insists that 2 and 3 John shared a common author and were produced first, followed by 1 John and the Gospel, which were written by different authors. Argues against any literary dependence between these writings. Insists rather that various members of the "Johannine school" shared a common (mostly oral) tradition and each employed this tradition in his own way in the process of addressing complex theological struggles within the Johannine community. Consequently, the commentary is especially concerned to explore ways in which writers of these letters edited the Johannine tradition so as to deal with the theological and pastoral challenges they faced. This approach renders the commentary somewhat speculative. Attends also to linguistic analysis of the Greek and to historical background (especially Jewish and Hellenistic). Excurses deal with key terms. Consistently probes theological significance.

4.41.7   Westcott, Brooke Foss. *The Epistles of St. John: The Greek Text, with Notes and Addenda.* London: Macmillan, 1883. 245pp.

Attends to even the minutest details of the Greek. Quotes relevant sources from classical antiquity and church fathers in original Greek and Latin. Carefully analyzes structure of the entire letter and individual passages. Regularly cites other biblical passages, exploring points of continuity and discontinuity. Excurses provide detailed discussion of theological issues. Insists that these letters, along with the Fourth Gospel, were written by the Apostle John, although refuses to take a stand on the sequence of their production. In spite of its age and its tendency to overdo analysis of Greek prepositions and particles, it remains a standard work. Highly technical, assumes knowledge of Greek.

Also Significant

4.41.8   Brooke, A. E. *A Critical and Exegetical Commentary on the Johannine Epistles.* International Critical Commentary. Edinburgh: T&T Clark, 1912. 242pp.

4.41.9   Bultmann, Rudolf. *The Johannine Epistles.* Hermeneia: A Critical and Historical Commentary on the Bible. Philadelphia: Fortress, 1973. 143pp.

4.41.10   Dodd, C. H. *The Johannine Epistles.* Moffatt New Testament Commentary. London: Hodder & Stoughton, 1946. 168pp.

4.41.11 Griffith, Terry. *Keep Yourselves from Idols: A New Look at 1 John.* Journal for the Study of the New Testament Supplemental Series, no. 233. Sheffield: Sheffield Academic Press, 2002. 247pp.

4.41.12 Houlden, J. L. *A Commentary on the Johannine Epistles.* Rev. ed. Black's New Testament Commentary. London: A. & C. Black, 1994. 107pp.

4.41.13 Lieu, Judith. *The Second and Third Epistles of John.* Studies of the New Testament and Its World. Edinburgh: T&T Clark, 1986. 264pp.

4.41.14 ———. *The Theology of the Johannine Epistles.* New Testament Theology. Cambridge: Cambridge University Press, 1991. 130pp.

4.41.15 Painter, John. *1, 2, and 3 John.* Sacra Pagina. Collegeville, Minn.: Liturgical Press, 2002. 416pp.

4.41.16 Smith, D. Moody. *First, Second, and Third John.* Interpretation: A Bible Commentary for Teaching and Preaching. Louisville: Westminster John Knox, 1991. 164pp.

4.41.17 Yarbrough, Robert W. *1–3 John.* Baker Exegetical Commentary on the New Testament. Grand Rapids: Baker Academic, 2008. 434pp.

4.42 Book of Revelation

Highly Recommended

4.42.1 Aune, David E. *Revelation.* 3 vols. Word Biblical Commentary. Dallas: Word, 1997–1998. 1354pp.

Most current, authoritative, and comprehensive commentary on Revelation available in any language. Introduction of 250 pages explores especially historical matters (concluding that the book was written by an otherwise unknown "John," a Christian prophet who had no significant connection with the Johannine community), literary issues (genre and syntax), and sources (arguing for a two-stage editing process that the author pursued over a thirty-year period). Commentary emphasizes literary structure, genre, linguistic analysis, historical background, literary precursors, and text-critical issues. Gives little attention to the history of interpretation. Emphasis on literary and historical considerations leaves little room for probing theological reflection. Highly technical; encyclopedic in amount of material assembled.

4.42.2   Bauckham, Richard. *The Climax of Prophecy: Studies on the Book of Revelation*. Edinburgh: T&T Clark, 1993. 550pp.

A helpful introduction to the most significant literary, historical, and theological issues. Series of essays cohere around "a single sustained enterprise of understanding both the form and the message of the Apocalypse in its literary and historical contexts." Essays emphasize (1) the literary unity of Revelation (over against focus on earlier sources) and significance of literary techniques and structure; (2) the author's constant and disciplined allusions to the OT, employing Jewish exegetical methods in an attempt to produce a "work of prophetic scripture, the climax of prophetic revelation"; (3) the relationship between Revelation and other apocalyptic writings; and (4) the historical context in which Revelation was produced, and especially religious, political, social, and economic circumstances. Literary and historical study serves to explicate the theology of Revelation.

4.42.3   Beale, G. K. *The Book of Revelation*. New International Greek Testament Commentary. Grand Rapids: Eerdmans, 1999. 1245pp.

Comprehensive and learned commentary that emphasizes the use of the OT according to Jewish exegetical traditions as a major key to unfolding the meaning of Revelation. Attends also to historical background and careful analysis of the development of argument. Gives less attention to linguistic analysis than is typical of volumes in this series. Slightly more theologically oriented than Aune's commentary (§4.42.1). Introduction includes helpful discussion of major approaches to Revelation and of methodological issues pertaining to the interpretation of symbolism. Excurses deal in depth with significant interpretive issues. Allows that Revelation could have been written by John the apostle (author of the Fourth Gospel) or by another "John," but insists that identification of the author is unnecessary for the book's interpretation.

4.42.4   Boxall, Ian. *The Revelation of Saint John*. Black's New Testament Commentary. Peabody, Mass.: Hendrickson, 2006. 347pp.

Boxall presents a reliable, informed, and lucid explanation of Revelation, providing an excellent entrée into the book. Gives attention to the visionary experience of the Revelator, the literary structure of the book, the significance of Patmos, the situation of the original addressees, and the history of reception (i.e., various readings of the book throughout Christian history). Packs a great deal of critical information and valuable insights into this small commentary. Its brevity avoids the problem that some larger commentaries have of losing the reader in the morass of detail, but it also results in less attention than one might wish to the theological significance of the text.

4.42.5   Caird, G. B. *The Revelation of St. John*. Black's New Testament Commentary. Peabody, Mass.: Hendrickson, 1966. 316pp.

Recognizing the inherent difficulty of Revelation for modern readers, Caird offers a lucid and straightforward exposition of this book, which he takes to have been written by an otherwise unknown Christian leader around the end of the first century to address pastorally urgent challenges facing congregations under his care. Presents an extremely short introduction, preferring to give primary attention to explication of text itself. Stresses the use of the OT and historical background, gives less consideration to genre and literary structure, and says virtually nothing about linguistic analysis or history of interpretation. Its brevity, narrow focus, and lack of technical discussion belies a depth of learning that results in a rich and theologically suggestive exposition.

4.42.6   Mounce, Robert H. *The Book of Revelation*. Rev. ed. New International Commentary on the New Testament. Grand Rapids: Eerdmans, 1998. 439pp.

Lucid commentary, solid, reliable, and balanced, if not particularly original or probing. Posits that Revelation was written by John the apostle during reign of Domitian. Adopts a generally premillennial eschatological perspective, but allows that much of chs. 4–22 describe events that were contemporary to the original audience or are symbolic representations of realities pertaining to the entire period of the church. Emphasizes historical background, flow of argument, and relationship to other biblical materials, giving less attention to linguistic analysis or to history of interpretation. Focuses on the basic meaning of the text, with little development of its theological richness and few suggestions regarding contemporary application.

4.42.7   Smalley, Stephen S. *The Revelation to John: A Commentary on the Greek Text of the Apocalypse*. Downers Grove, Ill.: Hendrickson, 2005. 633pp.

This authority on the Gospel of John and the Johannine epistles insists that the book of Revelation was the first book to be written by the Apostle John, who also composed the Gospel and all three epistles. He further argues that it was produced before the Jewish War to describe the victory of Christ over all opposition and was not meant to be specific to certain experiences within the Roman Empire at the time. These views represent a minority opinion among contemporary commentators, although they were adopted by many scholars in the past. Smalley refuses to be swept along by the assumptions of present-day interpreters and gives fresh and significant evidence for his conclusions. He argues that the book presents a cosmic drama in two acts with seven scenes, along the lines of a Greek play. Those who are unpersuaded by some of these specific conclusions will still find much help in this insightful and informed commentary. Each passage contains four sections: text-critical explorations; discussion of literary setting (role within the book and literary structure of the passage itself); comments on the specific original meaning of individual verses; and a discussion of the theology of the passage.

Also Significant

4.42.8   Bauckham, Richard. *The Theology of the Book of Revelation*. New Testament Theology. Cambridge: Cambridge University Press, 1993. 169pp.

4.42.9   Beasley-Murray, George R. *The Book of Revelation*. New Century Bible Commentary. Grand Rapids: Eerdmans, 1981. 352pp.

4.42.10   Beckwith, I. T. *The Apocalypse of John*. New York: Macmillan, 1922. 794pp.

4.42.11   Blount, Brian K. *Revelation: A Commentary*. New Testament Library. Louisville: Westminster John Knox, 2009. 462pp.

4.42.12   Boring, M. Eugene. *Revelation*. Interpretation: A Bible Commentary for Teaching and Preaching. Atlanta: John Knox, 1989. 236pp.

4.42.13   Charles, R. H. *A Critical and Exegetical Commentary on the Revelation of St. John*. 2 vols. International Critical Commentary. Edinburgh: T&T Clark, 1920. 373/497pp.

4.42.14   Ellul, Jacques. *Apocalypse: The Book of Revelation*. New York: Seabury, 1977. 283pp.

4.42.15 ————. *The Meaning of the City.* Grand Rapids: Eerdmans, 1970. 209pp.

4.42.16 Fiorenza, Elisabeth Schussler. *The Book of Revelation: Justice and Judgment.* 2d ed. Minneapolis: Fortress, 1998. 243pp.

4.42.17 Harrington, Wilfrid J. *Revelation.* Sacra Pagina. Collegeville, Minn.: Michael Glazier, 1993. 271pp.

4.42.18 Hemer, Colin J. *The Letters to the Seven Churches of Asia in Their Local Setting.* Biblical Resources Series. Grand Rapids: Eerdmans, 2001. 338pp.

4.42.19 Ladd, George Eldon. *A Commentary on the Revelation of John.* Grand Rapids: Eerdmans, 1972. 308pp.

4.42.20 Malina, Bruce J. *On the Genre and Message of Revelation: Star Visions and Sky Journeys.* Peabody, Mass.: Hendrickson, 1995. 317pp.

4.42.21 Malina, Bruce J., and John L. Pilch. *Social-Science Commentary on the Book of Revelation.* Minneapolis: Fortress, 2000. 288pp.

4.42.22 Mulholland, M. Robert, Jr. *Revelation: Holy Living in an Unholy World.* Grand Rapids: Zondervan, 1990. 376pp.

4.42.23 Muse, Robert L. *The Book of Revelation: An Annotated Bibliography.* New York: Garland, 1996. 352pp.

4.42.24 Osborne, Grant R. *Revelation.* Baker Exegetical Commentary on the New Testament. Grand Rapids: Baker, 2002. 896pp.

4.42.25 Pate, C. Marvin, ed. *Four Views on the Book of Revelation.* Counterpoints Series. Grand Rapids: Zondervan, 1998. 252pp.

4.42.26 Ramsey, William M. *The Letters to the Seven Churches of Asia.* Revised and updated by Mark W. Wilson. Peabody, Mass.: Hendrickson, 1994. 317pp.

4.42.27   Resseguie, James L. *The Revelation of John: A Narrative Commentary.* Grand Rapids: Baker Academic, 2009. 288pp.

4.42.28   Rhoads, David, ed. *From Every People and Nation: The Book of Revelation in Intercultural Perspective.* Minneapolis: Fortress, 2005. 277pp.

4.42.29   Roloff, Jürgen. *Revelation.* Continental Commentaries. Minneapolis: Fortress, 1993. 275pp.

4.42.30   Smalley, Stephen S. *Thunder and Love: John's Revelation and John's Community.* Milton Keynes, UK: Word, 1994. 223pp.

4.42.31   Sweet, John. *Revelation.* London: SCM, 1990. 361pp.

4.42.32   Swete, Henry Barclay. *Commentary on Revelation: The Greek Text with Introduction, Notes and Indexes.* London: Macmillan, 1911. 338pp.

4.42.33   Wainwright, Arthur W. *Mysterious Apocalypse: Interpreting the Book of Revelation.* Nashville: Abingdon, 1993. 293pp.

4.42.34   Witherington, Ben, III. *Revelation.* New Cambridge Bible Commentary. Cambridge: Cambridge University Press, 2003. 307pp.

Index

396

400

Made in the USA
Lexington, KY
04 November 2019